IK
COMICS

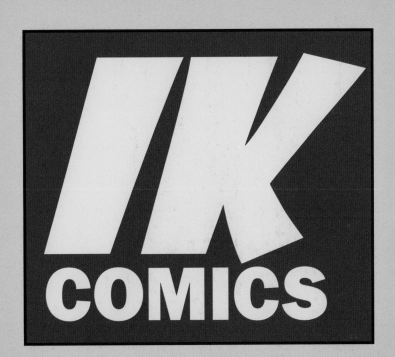

KNITSTRIPS

THE WORLD'S FIRST COMIC-STRIP KNITTING BOOK

Alice Ormsbee Beltran

Karen Kim Mar

Illustrations by
Laura Irrgang and Michele Phillips

Abrams, New York

Editor: Shawna Mullen

Designer: Shawn Dahl, dahlimama inc

Managing Editor: Lisa Silverman

Production Manager: Kathleen Gaffney

Library of Congress Control Number: 2021946848
ISBN: 978-1-4197-4066-4
eISBN: 978-1-4197-4279-8

Abrams books are available at special discounts when purchased in quantity for premiums and
promotions as well as fundraising or educational use. Special editions can also be created to
specification. For details, contact specialsales@abramsbooks.com or the address below.

Abrams® is a registered trademark of Harry N. Abrams, Inc.

ABRAMS The Art of Books
195 Broadway, New York, NY 10007
abramsbooks.com

TO OUR LOVING SPOUSES,
VINCENT & REDMOND

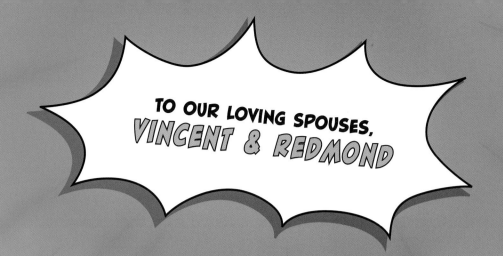

CONTENTS

Foreword......viii

Welcome to Interactive Knitting!......1

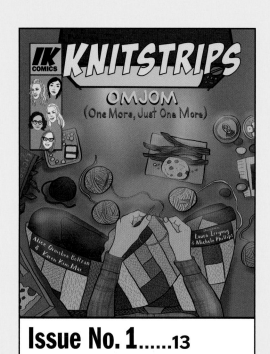

Issue No. 1......13

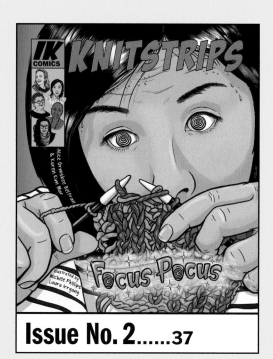

Issue No. 2......37

CHECK OUT THE STRIP "IK GAUGE" ON PAGE 7—

—AND THE "LET'S KNIT SOMETHING!" FLOWCHART ON PAGE 10.

ALL 22 PATTERNS ARE SHOWN IN THE PATTERN INDEX ON PAGE 130.

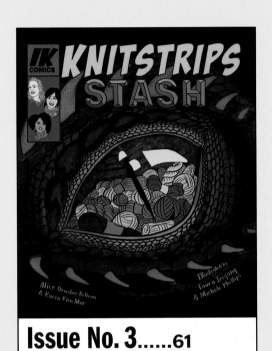

Issue No. 3......61

Issue No. 4......89

Bonus Pattern!
WELCOME TO CABLES
......115

Abbreviations......126

Technique Index......128

Pattern Index......130

Acknowledgments......138

About the Guest Designers......140

About the Illustrators......144

About the Authors......146

Epilogue......149

FOREWORD

IN 2016, WHEN ALICE TOLD US HER IDEA FOR KNITTING PATTERNS THAT USE THE FORM OF COMIC STRIPS, WE NEARLY LOST OUR MINDS. A VISUAL KNITTING PATTERN! THERE'S SOMETHING SO TIDY AND IRRESISTIBLE ABOUT IT. SO DIFFERENT. A TRADITIONAL KNITTING PATTERN REQUIRES A PROCESS THAT IS AKIN TO DECIPHERING LINES OF COMPUTER CODE WRITTEN IN A CURIOUSLY ANTIQUATED STYLE. THERE ARE NO "KAPOWS" IN AN OLD-SCHOOL KNITTING PATTERN!

LATER THAT YEAR, WE WERE THRILLED TO PUBLISH THE FIRST KNITSTRIP, A PAIR OF GARTER STITCH MITTS, AS A DIGITAL DOWNLOAD ON OUR DAILY ONLINE KNITTING MAGAZINE. THE PLAYFULNESS OF THE FORMAT, COMBINED WITH THE OPEN-ENDED, ENCOURAGING STYLE OF THE INSTRUCTIONS, CHARMED THE HANDKNIT SOCKS OFF OUR AUDIENCE OF PASSIONATE KNITTERS. OUR MOTTO AT MDK IS "KNITTING IS SUPPOSED TO BE FUN," AND WITH KNITSTRIPS, IT SUDDENLY WAS EVEN MORE FUN THAN BEFORE.

THAT FIRST PAIR OF MITTS LED TO MORE KNITSTRIPS—A WATCH CAP, A MUFFLER, EVEN A SAUCY PAIR OF LEGWARMERS, EACH ONE SPARKING AN AVALANCHE OF DOWNLOADS. NO SEASONED KNITTER WITH A LIBRARY OF BOOKS NEEDS A COMIC-BOOK-STYLE PATTERN TO MAKE A HAT OR A CHRISTMAS TREE ORNAMENT—BUT IT TURNS OUT THAT MANY KNITTERS WANT IT. IT'S LIBERATING AND MIND OPENING TO SEE KNITTING IN THIS WAY.

IT'S NO SURPRISE THAT WE LOVE KNITSTRIPS. ONE OF US CHERISHES HER CHILDHOOD COLLECTION OF ILLUSTRATED CLASSICS; THE OTHER FOUND HER WAY TO CHARLES DICKENS BY WAY OF "MR. MAGOO'S CHRISTMAS CAROL." THE BRIGHT COLORS AND IMMEDIACY OF COMIC STRIPS AND CARTOONS IMPRINTED THEMSELVES ON US AT AN EARLY AGE. EVERYTHING WE KNEW ABOUT BEING A TEENAGER WE LEARNED FROM BETTY AND VERONICA. SO IT STANDS TO REASON THAT WE FIND IT WILDLY ENTERTAINING TO KNIT PATTERNS BY OUR FAVORITE DESIGNERS, AND DESIGNERS WHO ARE NEW TO US, TRANSLATED INTO THIS ENGAGING, LIVELY STYLE.

ALTHOUGH NOTHING IS MORE IMPORTANT THAN THE JOY FACTOR, SOMETHING EQUALLY FUNDAMENTAL ATTRACTS US TO INTERACTIVE KNITTING. IN A KNITSTRIP, STITCHES AND CONSTRUCTION METHODS ARE PORTRAYED VIVIDLY, AND ASIDES AND BACKGROUND MATERIAL APPEAR AT THE MOST USEFUL MOMENT. WHEN WE SEE PICTURES THAT ZERO IN ON THE PRECISE ACTION TO PERFORM, FEW WORDS ARE NEEDED. WE SEE AT A GLANCE HOW TO PICK UP THE STITCHES FOR A LOG CABIN STRIP, OR HOW TO WORK INTARSIA IN GARTER STITCH. WITH KNITSTRIPS, ALICE AND KAREN HAVE OPENED UP THE WONDERFUL WORLD OF KNITTING TO VISUAL LEARNERS WHO MIGHT HAVE BEEN DETERRED BY THE HIDEBOUND CONVENTIONS OF WRITTEN PATTERNS.

NOW THAT WE'VE FALLEN IN LOVE WITH THIS DELIGHTFUL WAY TO KNIT, WE FIND OURSELVES WISHING FOR EVEN MORE KNITSTRIPS. WHEN IS THE NEXT BOOK COMING OUT?

Kay Gardiner and Ann Shayne
Co-founders, Modern Daily Knitting
ModernDailyKnitting.com

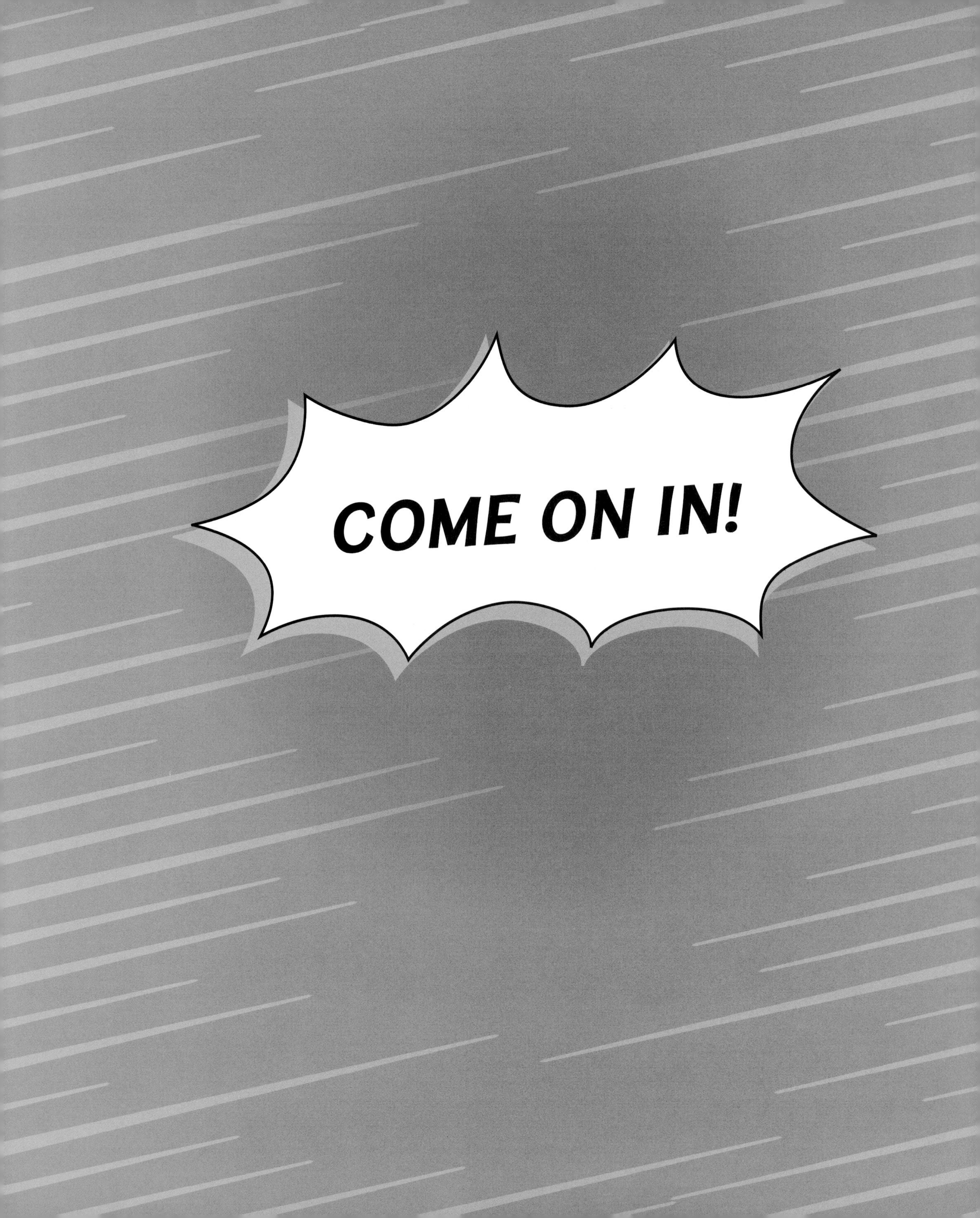
COME ON IN!

WELCOME TO INTERACTIVE KNITTING!

HI!
WE'RE ALICE AND KAREN

You hold in your hands the world's first book of comic-strip knitting patterns. We call them knitstrips. In this book you'll find four themed comics: OMJOM (One More, Just One More) explores knits that you never want to end. Focus Pocus is a celebration of clever techniques that deliver big results. In STASH (Skeins That Are Special and Here), we present a bevy of patterns designed with your yarn treasures in mind. Finally, in Bucket List, we share patterns that we want to knit before we hear that sweet music calling us home.

Interactive Knitting (IK, pronounced eye-KAY) is the philosophy at the heart of ***Knitstrips***. IK gives the knitter abundant creative control when working a pattern. Important elements of IK include:

- **Yarn-neutral patterns**, written so the knitter can choose yarn of any size, color, and texture that fulfills their vision. We celebrate the fact that yarn choices are more exciting than ever before, and a tremendous source of inspiration.

LIKE YARN? WE'VE GOT PATTERNS FOR YOU.

- **Patterns based on the wearer's body measurements**, with suggestions for ease. We guide you through the basic math, to get the fit you want.

ALL BODY TYPES AND SIZES ARE WELCOME.

- **Patterns with distinct points of view** that show the knitter how to achieve them, while leaving lots of room for personalization. The result is a deeper, stronger connection between the knitter and their final product.

LET'S CELEBRATE YOU!

Beginners, take heart: The detailed and technically accurate illustrations will help you gain skills and confidence. Experienced knitters, you'll find new depths of potential and will learn new approaches to your projects. Curious non-knitters, we hope you find a welcoming and novel entry point into the craft. All will find much to inspire and set the creative mind alight.

WHAAAT?! ANY YARN?
MY SIZE, FOR REAL?
YES!
I CAN HAVE IT JUST THE WAY I WANT IT?
I SHOULD GET MORE YARN.
I HAVE IDEAS...

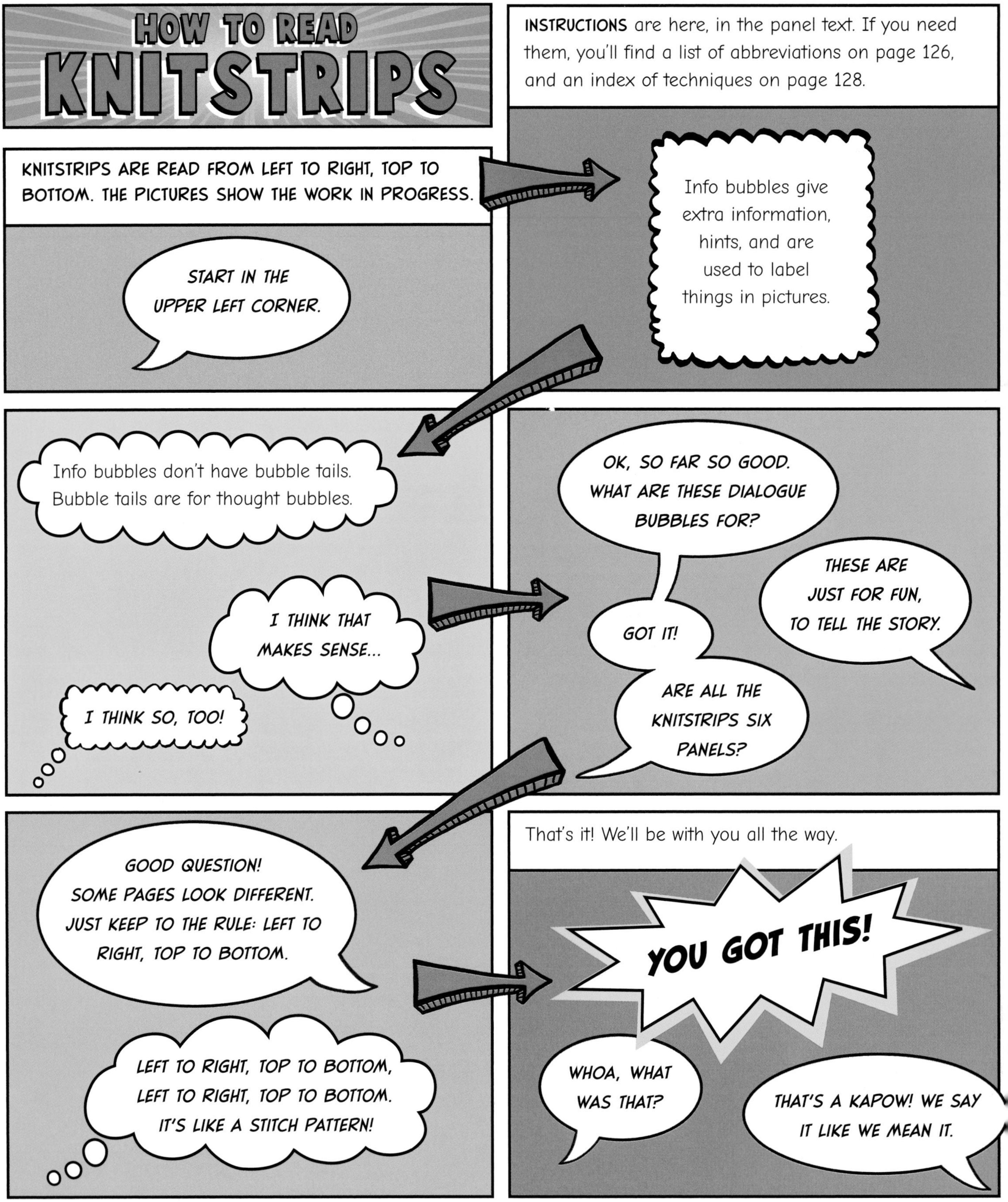
HOW TO READ KNITSTRIPS
KNITSTRIPS ARE READ FROM LEFT TO RIGHT, TOP TO BOTTOM. THE PICTURES SHOW THE WORK IN PROGRESS.
START IN THE UPPER LEFT CORNER.
INSTRUCTIONS are here, in the panel text. If you need them, you'll find a list of abbreviations on page 126, and an index of techniques on page 128.
Info bubbles give extra information, hints, and are used to label things in pictures.
Info bubbles don't have bubble tails. Bubble tails are for thought bubbles.
I THINK THAT MAKES SENSE...
I THINK SO, TOO!
OK, SO FAR SO GOOD. WHAT ARE THESE DIALOGUE BUBBLES FOR?
GOT IT!
THESE ARE JUST FOR FUN, TO TELL THE STORY.
ARE ALL THE KNITSTRIPS SIX PANELS?
GOOD QUESTION! SOME PAGES LOOK DIFFERENT. JUST KEEP TO THE RULE: LEFT TO RIGHT, TOP TO BOTTOM.
LEFT TO RIGHT, TOP TO BOTTOM, LEFT TO RIGHT, TOP TO BOTTOM. IT'S LIKE A STITCH PATTERN!
That's it! We'll be with you all the way.
YOU GOT THIS!
WHOA, WHAT WAS THAT?
THAT'S A KAPOW! WE SAY IT LIKE WE MEAN IT.

YARN

The world of yarn today is wide and wonderful. From well-produced commercial yarns at your favorite big-box store, to gorgeous small-batch yarn from select flocks, to everything in between, there is a lot of irresistible yarn out there to consider. So which yarn do you choose?

BUT WHICH YARN SHOULD I CHOOSE?

This question is particularly relevant in IK, because knitstrips patterns are yarn neutral, and knitters can choose any yarn they like.

Choose a yarn that works with your vision. IK invites you to identify the qualities you want in your garment and gives you the space to create it. This includes selecting the yarn. For those new to knitting, or to this way of thinking, here are some things to consider:

• **Know what you want.** For the project you have in mind, imagine the qualities of the fabric you aspire to. Is it light as a feather when you wear it, or does it have a satisfying, weighty drape? Is it fuzzy, or sleek? Bulky, or fine? Sturdy, or delicate? Can you see each stitch crisp and clear, or does the fabric have a fuzzy halo? Are the stitches blurred, or defined? Your creative vision of the final product will drive your yarn selection. Each pattern provides specific guidance on yarn qualities for your consideration.

• **Know the yarn.** The qualities of a yarn determine the kind of fabric it will make. For instance, a smooth silk and merino blend will not make a fluffy fabric, but could feel wonderful next to the skin and have gorgeous sheen and drape. A kid mohair blend won't give you fabric with polished ripples of sleek drape, but it will be marvelously warm and have an incredible halo. If you are shopping for yarn for a specific project, buy yarn that can do what you want it to do. Conversely, if you are looking at yarn in your awesome STASH (Skeins That Are Special and Here), consider its qualities when deciding what to do with it.

• **Experiment!** The only way to know is to try. Your point of view is worth it. Consider keeping a log of yarns you've tried with your preferred gauge and the fabric qualities (see IK Gauge, page 7).

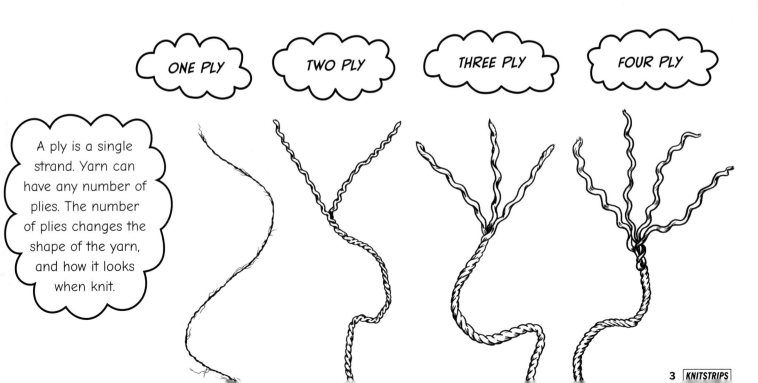

ONE PLY   TWO PLY   THREE PLY   FOUR PLY

A ply is a single strand. Yarn can have any number of plies. The number of plies changes the shape of the yarn, and how it looks when knit.

"HOW MUCH YARN DO I NEED?"

How much yarn you need depends on the size of your project, stitch type, gauge, and type of yarn. One simple way to estimate the amount you need is to use a yarn yardage calculator (they can be found online, or you can use a phone app). The calculator should take into consideration your gauge, type of garment, and finished size. Another option is to take a look at other patterns that are similar in size, shape, stitch, and yarn weight to what you want to knit; look at their recommended yarn requirements and use that information to inform your estimate. Your yarn seller is also a great resource. They are often happy to provide guidance based on their experience, to ensure that you have enough yarn.

Whatever method you choose, we strongly encourage you to err on the side of abundance. We'd rather you not experience running out of yarn before you're done with your project. Plus, having extra yarn is a terrific problem to have.

We've got lots of ideas for what to knit with leftover yarn (see STASH, page 61), and here are some no-knit options, too:

• Pom-poms are fun to make! They can embellish the wrapping of a special gift, or just look amazing adorning your house.

HURRAY!

• Gift extra yarn with a pair of needles to a non-knitting friend and teach them to knit.

I CAN'T WAIT TO LEARN!

• Swap with someone in your knitting circle, so you both have something new.

SQUEE! I LOVE IT!

ME, TOO! AWESOME TRADE.

• Donate it. Set your yarn free in the world to find its soul mate!

WOW, THANK YOU FOR YOUR SUPPORT!

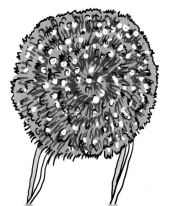

KNITTING NEEDLES

Knitting needles come in different materials, types, lengths, tip sharpnesses, and sizes. Materials include bamboo, birch, various metals, resin, and plastic. Different types include double-pointed, straight, and circular. The sizes may be expressed in either metric, UK/Canadian, or US values.

The properties of the knitted fabric you create (see IK Gauge, page 7) will depend in large part on the size of knitting needles you use. Basically, the skinnier the needle, the denser the knitted fabric. Conversely, the larger the needle, the more open the knitted fabric.

Here at Casa de IK, we like circular needles for their versatility. You can work with them like straight needles and knit back and forth to create flat fabric, or you can work in the round and knit tubes of fabric. The length of the circular needle will determine the smallest-diameter tube you can knit in the round with that needle. You will want to have several sizes of needles, so you can experiment to find the one that gives you the fabric you like the best in the yarn and stitch of your choice.

If you are just starting on your knitting journey, get needles that are likely to work with the yarn you have in mind. You can look at the recommended needle size on the yarn label as a starting point. Note that people knit differently: some tighter, some looser. The yarn label recommendation will get you in the ballpark of the gauge the manufacturer thinks is ideal for the yarn, but you may like it looser or tighter. Alice is a loose knitter, and usually goes down a few needle sizes. Karen tends to be consistent with the yarn labels. Experiment with different needle sizes to get the gauge you want for your project.

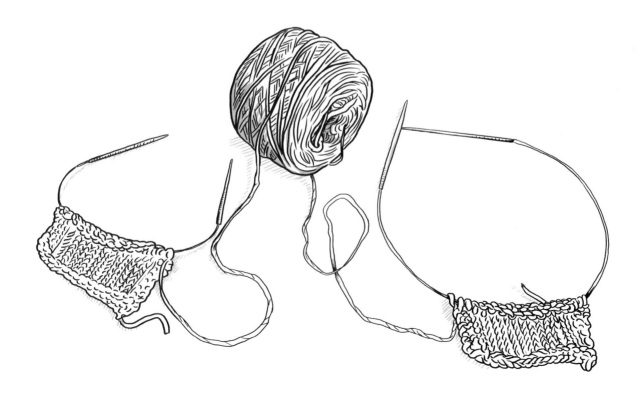

OTHER KNITTING TOOLS

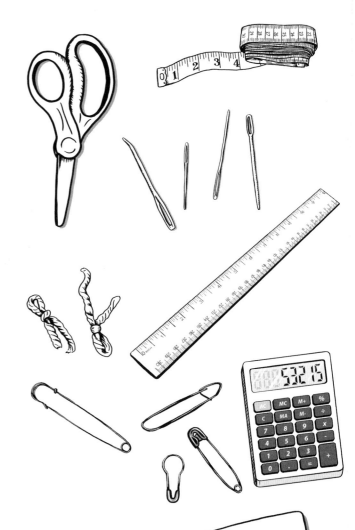

In each knitstrip, we let you know if you need any particular tools, but here are common tools we recommend you have for all patterns:

- Scissors: to trim sewn-in ends and to cut yarn
- Flexible tape measure: important for body measurements
- Ruler: for measuring gauge; works better than the tape measure
- Large, blunt darning needle: sewing in ends is part of knitting; also useful for grafting and darning
- Stitch holders or waste yarn: sometimes you need to take stitches off the needle and set them aside
- Removable stitch markers: often used to mark the beginning of a round, or identify where a particular technique needs to happen (like increasing or decreasing)
- Calculator
- Pencil and paper
- Cookies

> YES, COOKIES ARE ESSENTIAL.

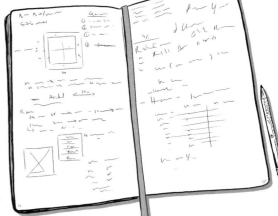

> THANKS FOR COMING TO CASA DE IK. WE'RE GLAD YOU'RE HERE!

IK GAUGE

IK patterns are yarn neutral. You can choose any yarn you like to produce each pattern. As a result, IK patterns do not have a specific target gauge; nor do they provide specific stitch counts for sizes. Instead, each pattern offers yarn and fabric qualities that, in combination with the shape and texture of the garment, achieve the design. You start an IK pattern by determining the fabric you want, and then you measure the gauge of that fabric.

This state of affairs lets you, the knitter, use your gauge, the measurements of the wearer, and the pattern to knit the garment exactly the way you want, in the yarn of your choice.

IN IK KNITTING, GAUGE FOLLOWS FABRIC; FABRIC DOES NOT FOLLOW GAUGE.

GAUGE, measured in stitches per inch, is an inherent property of every knitted fabric. It's a critical piece of information to have if you are knitting something to a specific size.

KAREN, DID I EVER SHOW YOU MY FIRST SWEATER?
I WAS ALL, "GAUGE SHMAGE!"
OH, I SEE!

Gauge swatches not your thing?

Here are patterns that don't require one: **LOG CABIN BLANKET** (p. 32), **TEAM BLANKET** (squares only) (p. 66), and **FRIENDSHIP BRACELET SCARF** (p. 63). For a lot of patterns, you can do gauge on the run: **OMNIMITTS** (p. 84), **THE DASHWOOD** (p. 39), and **DOUBLE FEATURE** (p. 21), for instance. You start the project and block it after a few inches while on a circular needle or a stitch holder. Prop the needles so they don't get wet.

SO EFFICIENT!

Gauge can be calculated for any stitch type.

TO SWATCH: Cast on ~4½ in (11.5 cm) worth of sts (you can guess based on the suggested gauge on the yarn wrap) or enough to do your lace or cable repeats. Work the way you plan to knit (flat or in the round). A speedy way to swatch in the round: Pull a long strand of your working yarn behind the work and slide your worked sts back on your circular needle, so you are always working on the RS. You might decide after only two rows that it's too loose or tight, and be ready to jump down or up in needle size. When you get what you like, work 4½ in (11.5 cm) or for the rows in your lace/cable repeats. Wet block the swatch, so you can see how it will change.

We recommend you wet block because you want to know what the fabric will be like after you launder it. You've got to wash it eventually. Make a swatch, block, evaluate. If you like the fabric, you're done! If not, adjust needle size accordingly, and repeat until you get the fabric you want.

YOU ARE THE BEST JUDGE OF YOUR GAUGE.

How to wet block your hand knits (the IK method):

Fill a container with tepid water. Swish in a squirt of whatever gentle liquid soap is handy. Shower gel or shampoo is fine. Submerge the knitting. Let it soak for at least 15 minutes. Lift it out, making sure to support it so that it doesn't draggle down under its wet weight. Squeeze out as much of the soapy water as you can. To rinse, fill your container with fresh tepid water, and submerge the item. Squeeze it out and repeat the rinse until the suds are gone. Squeeze again, loosely roll it in a towel or two, and gently step on it to press out as much water as possible.

Bath time!

LAY the piece flat on a clean, dry towel. **STRETCH** areas you want to be bigger across the grain. **PULL** areas you want to be narrower with the grain. For lace, stretch it out in all directions to show off the stitch details. Get it to lie as you'd like it to be when dry, and let it dry fully before taking your gauge or wearing it. To find gauge, measure across the middle 3 in (7.5 cm) of the swatch. Line up the edge of a ruler mark with the left side of a stitch, and count stitches across 3 in (7.5 cm), including fractions of the last stitch. Divide that number by 3 in (7.5 cm), and you have your gauge in stitches per inch/cm. If it's not a whole number, don't round it. The fraction is important.

The following scale and vocabulary will be used throughout the book to describe knitted fabric qualities. These terms attempt to capture how the fabric behaves structurally, and its visual stitch density. Much of this is informed by the type of yarn used, so a discussion of recommended yarn qualities is included in patterns where it is particularly relevant.

Remember, you are swatching to get a fabric that pleases you for your project, so consider its qualities, and what it's for.

Lacy Openwork stitches that show light, or allow a finger to poke through. Drape depends on the yarn. A fuzzy yarn will drape less than a silky yarn. There are many different lace stitches.

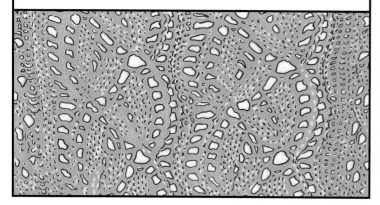

Airy Non-lace fabric with lots of negative space between stitches. It probably puddles on the ground, unless the yarn is very fuzzy. Fuzzy yarn has a lot of halo to it, allowing the yarn to stick to itself, lending structure to the fabric.

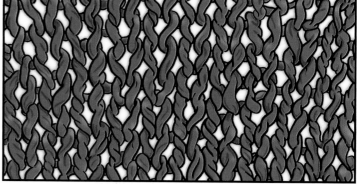

Soft Some light shows between the fabric, and it makes soft peaks when dropped.

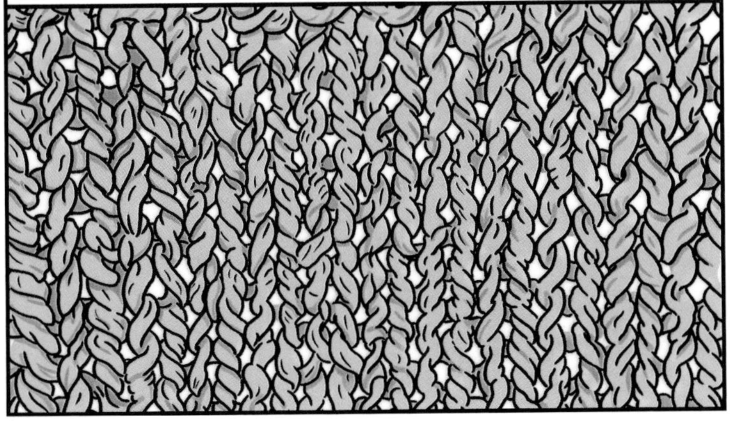

Medium Not much light shows through the fabric. It forms mounding peaks when dropped.

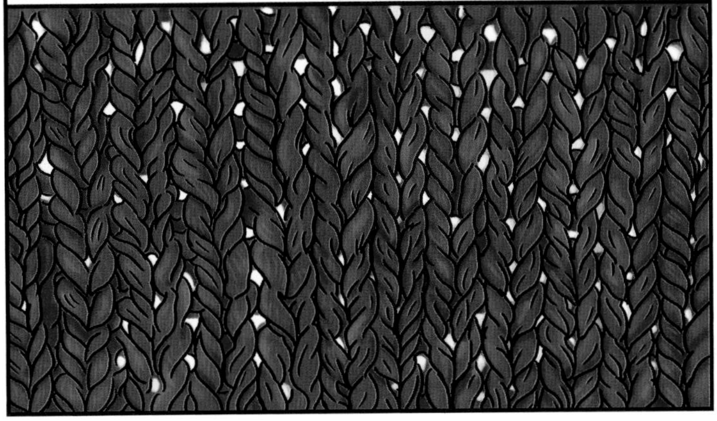

Chewy Dense, springy, and structural, but not stiff. Firm peaks when dropped. Garter stitch does well with Chewy because of its ridges. The surface depth variation makes it a squishier fabric.

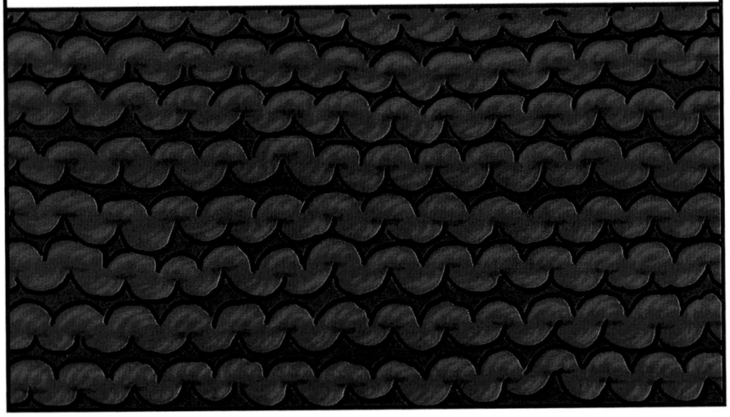

Stiff The fabric has little to no drape and is reminiscent of cardboard. No light between stitches. This is a good gauge for stuffed animals and pillows, where you don't want stuffing showing through your fabric.

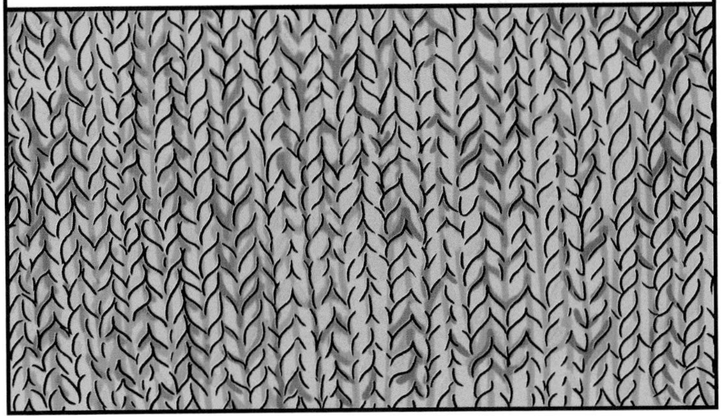

This is a book of IK. That means each pattern is yarn neutral, which means you will find the combination of yarn and needles that gives you a fabric that is exactly what you want, and you knit the project at that gauge. We do it this way because we love having that amount of creative control over a project, and think you might, too. Also, as of this writing, we are in a Golden Age of Yarn. Never before has there been such an abundance of wonderful material to choose from for hand knitters. This approach opens the door to all the yarn, for all the projects. We encourage you to knit what you love, with yarn you love, your way!

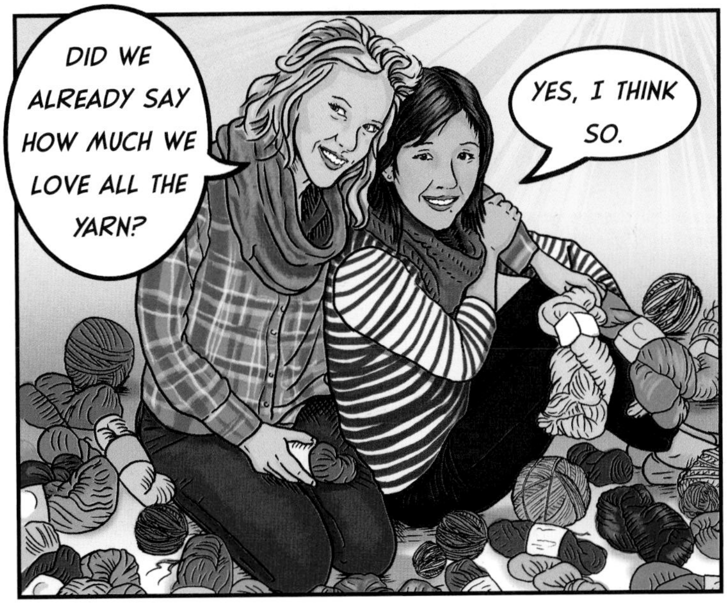
DID WE ALREADY SAY HOW MUCH WE LOVE ALL THE YARN?
YES, I THINK SO.

LET'S KNIT SOMETHING!

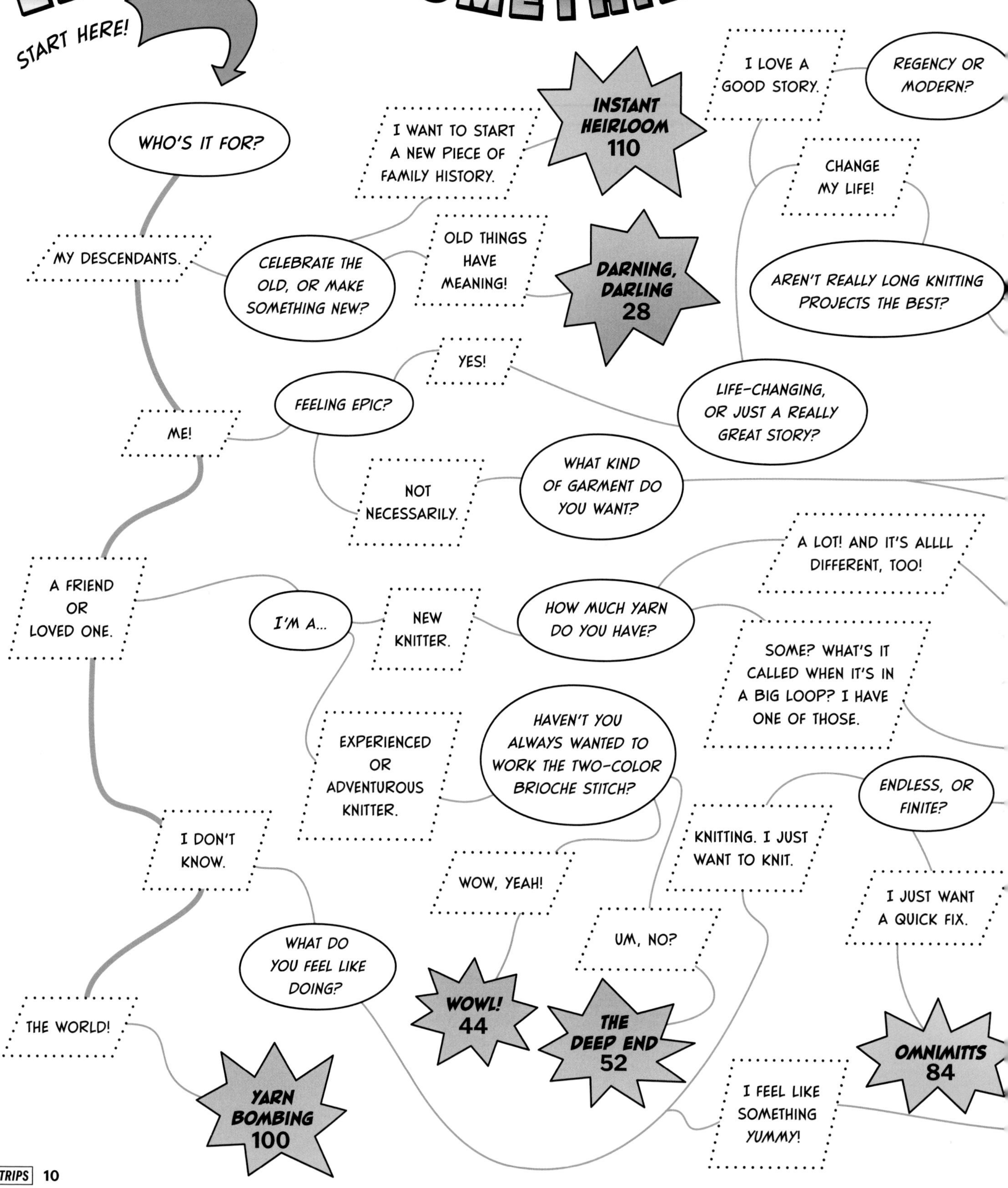
START HERE!
WHO'S IT FOR?
MY DESCENDANTS.
CELEBRATE THE OLD, OR MAKE SOMETHING NEW?
I WANT TO START A NEW PIECE OF FAMILY HISTORY.
INSTANT HEIRLOOM 110
OLD THINGS HAVE MEANING!
DARNING, DARLING 28
I LOVE A GOOD STORY.
REGENCY OR MODERN?
CHANGE MY LIFE!
AREN'T REALLY LONG KNITTING PROJECTS THE BEST?
ME!
FEELING EPIC?
YES!
LIFE-CHANGING, OR JUST A REALLY GREAT STORY?
NOT NECESSARILY.
WHAT KIND OF GARMENT DO YOU WANT?
A FRIEND OR LOVED ONE.
I'M A...
NEW KNITTER.
HOW MUCH YARN DO YOU HAVE?
A LOT! AND IT'S ALLLL DIFFERENT, TOO!
SOME? WHAT'S IT CALLED WHEN IT'S IN A BIG LOOP? I HAVE ONE OF THOSE.
EXPERIENCED OR ADVENTUROUS KNITTER.
HAVEN'T YOU ALWAYS WANTED TO WORK THE TWO-COLOR BRIOCHE STITCH?
ENDLESS, OR FINITE?
I DON'T KNOW.
WOW, YEAH!
KNITTING. I JUST WANT TO KNIT.
I JUST WANT A QUICK FIX.
UM, NO?
WHAT DO YOU FEEL LIKE DOING?
WOWL! 44
THE DEEP END 52
OMNIMITTS 84
THE WORLD!
YARN BOMBING 100
I FEEL LIKE SOMETHING YUMMY!

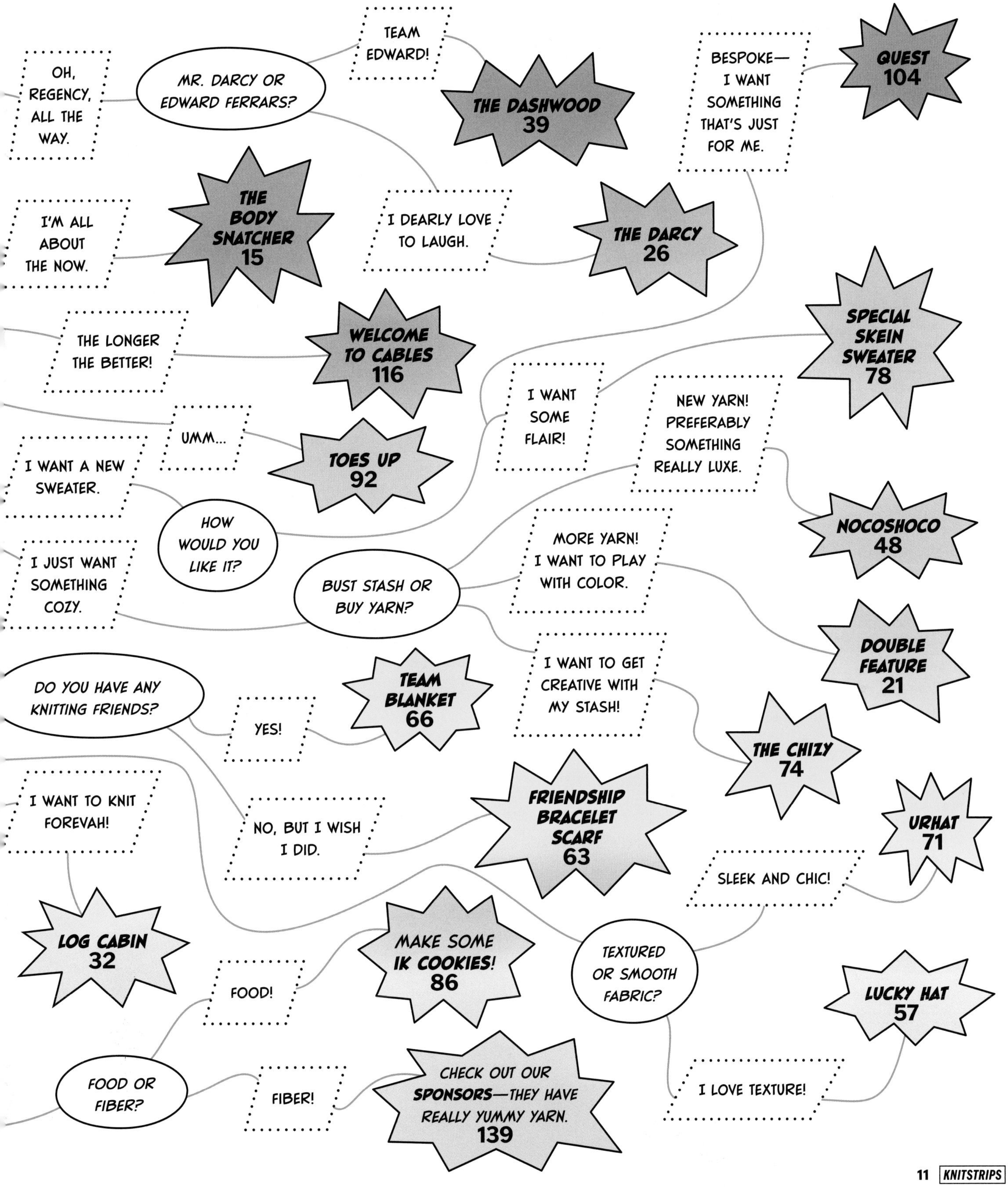
TEAM EDWARD!
BESPOKE— I WANT SOMETHING THAT'S JUST FOR ME.
QUEST 104
OH, REGENCY, ALL THE WAY.
MR. DARCY OR EDWARD FERRARS?
THE DASHWOOD 39
I'M ALL ABOUT THE NOW.
THE BODY SNATCHER 15
I DEARLY LOVE TO LAUGH.
THE DARCY 26
SPECIAL SKEIN SWEATER 78
THE LONGER THE BETTER!
WELCOME TO CABLES 116
I WANT SOME FLAIR!
NEW YARN! PREFERABLY SOMETHING REALLY LUXE.
UMM...
TOES UP 92
I WANT A NEW SWEATER.
HOW WOULD YOU LIKE IT?
NOCOSHOCO 48
MORE YARN! I WANT TO PLAY WITH COLOR.
I JUST WANT SOMETHING COZY.
BUST STASH OR BUY YARN?
DOUBLE FEATURE 21
I WANT TO GET CREATIVE WITH MY STASH!
DO YOU HAVE ANY KNITTING FRIENDS?
YES!
TEAM BLANKET 66
THE CHIZY 74
FRIENDSHIP BRACELET SCARF 63
I WANT TO KNIT FOREVAH!
NO, BUT I WISH I DID.
URHAT 71
SLEEK AND CHIC!
LOG CABIN 32
MAKE SOME IK COOKIES! 86
TEXTURED OR SMOOTH FABRIC?
FOOD!
LUCKY HAT 57
FOOD OR FIBER?
FIBER!
CHECK OUT OUR SPONSORS—THEY HAVE REALLY YUMMY YARN. 139
I LOVE TEXTURE!

READY, SET, GO!

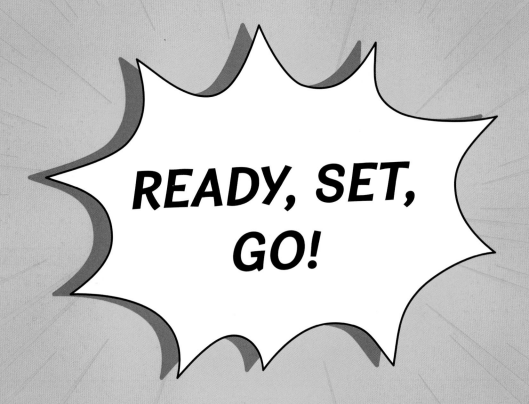

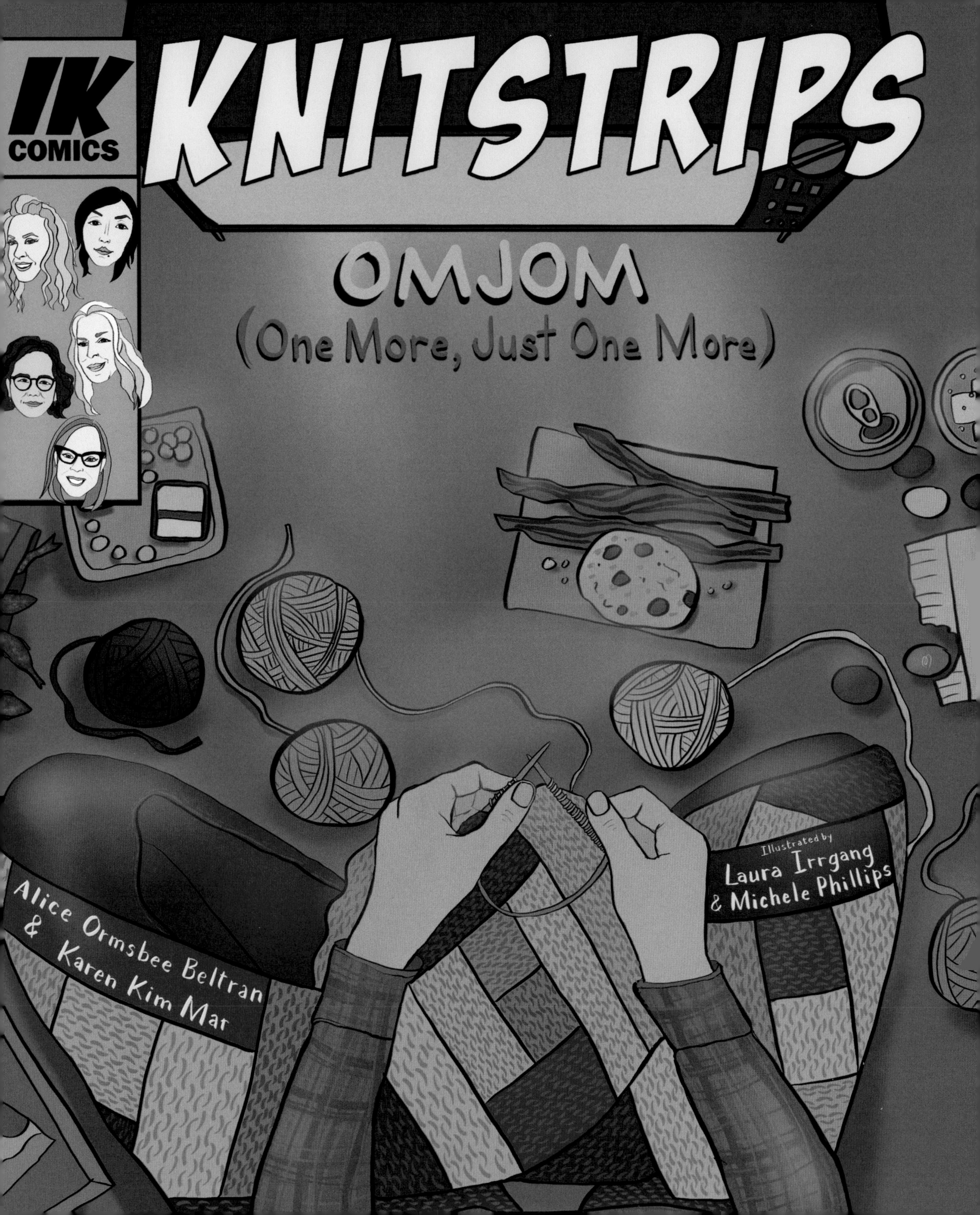
IK
COMICS
KNITSTRIPS
OMJOM
(One More, Just One More)
Alice Ormsbee Beltran
& Karen Kim Mar
Illustrated by
Laura Irrgang
& Michele Phillips

OMJOM
(One More, Just One More)

One More, Just One More (OMJOM)! Knitting does funny things with time. Small and large spans alike are transformed by its industrious productivity. Knitting speeds up waiting and slows down thinking. A finished piece is fossilized time, a monument to the creative impact of small yet steady effort.

Alice is obsessed with the idea of transforming low-value increments of time into productive time. Low-value time is unpredictable, unscheduled, unavoidable, and relatively short. It's waiting for everyone else to get their shoes on, or for the cookies to be done. Knitting is a magnificent option for those moments. I'm not waiting, I'm knitting.

Karen is blessed with a solid forty-five minutes of knitting with her train pals commuting to and from work. She saves up her end-weaving, seaming, and darning for the train, because these tasks can withstand all the socializing. A few times a year, she treats herself to an all-night knit-a-thon with the BBC's *Pride and Prejudice*, usually accompanied by a Garter stitch project. It will be done by morning.

In this issue we explore the kind of knitting we like to do in the very small and very long pieces of time we encounter. At Casa de IK, this means lots of plain knitting with minimal counting and complexity—a.k.a. mindless knitting. These are pieces you can dive in and out of for a few minutes, or set the cruise control and get comfy for a long haul of your favorite TV. After hours of their good company through thick and thin, you may be sorry to see them end. The fact that they're gorgeous takes the edge off.

ONE MORE...

...JUST ONE MORE.

THE BODY SNATCHER

BY CASEY RICH AND ALICE O. BELTRAN

A DREAMY COWL-NECK TUNIC THAT LOVES TO BE LAYERED. ENJOY SOFT CAP OR RUCHED SLEEVES. SURRENDER AND ALLOW YOURSELF TO BE ENGULFED IN SOFTNESS.

MATERIALS: This version calls for light, lofty, halo-y yarn. In this case, one strand each of lace-weight silk and lace-weight kid mohair/silk. 16 in (41 cm) and 24 in (61 cm) circular knitting needles in size to obtain desired gauge. Waste yarn for Provisional Cast-On. **GAUGE:** Airy to Soft.

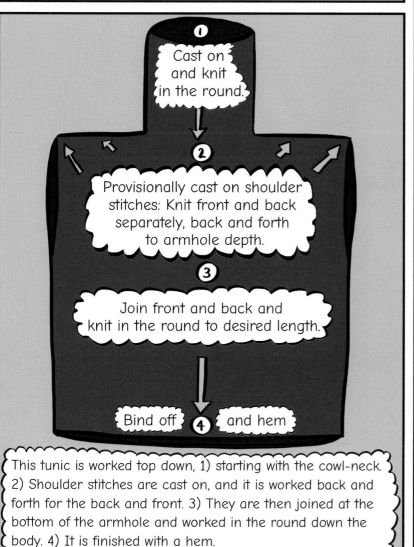

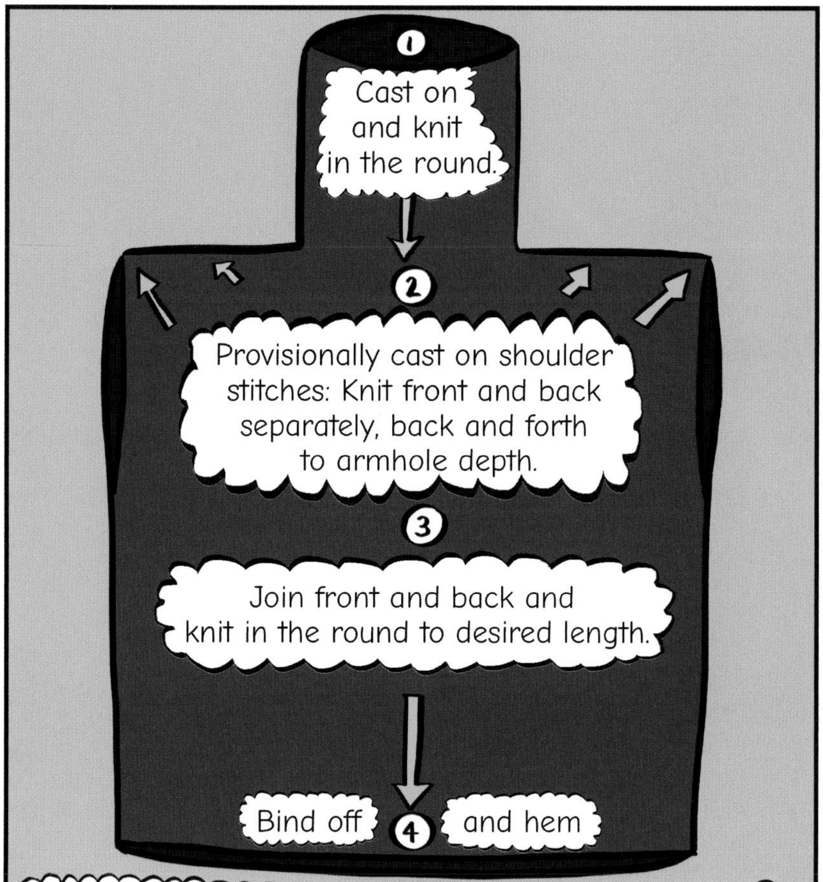
1
Cast on and knit in the round.
2
Provisionally cast on shoulder stitches: Knit front and back separately, back and forth to armhole depth.
3
Join front and back and knit in the round to desired length.
Bind off
4
and hem

This tunic is worked top down, 1) starting with the cowl-neck. 2) Shoulder stitches are cast on, and it is worked back and forth for the back and front. 3) They are then joined at the bottom of the armhole and worked in the round down the body. 4) It is finished with a hem.

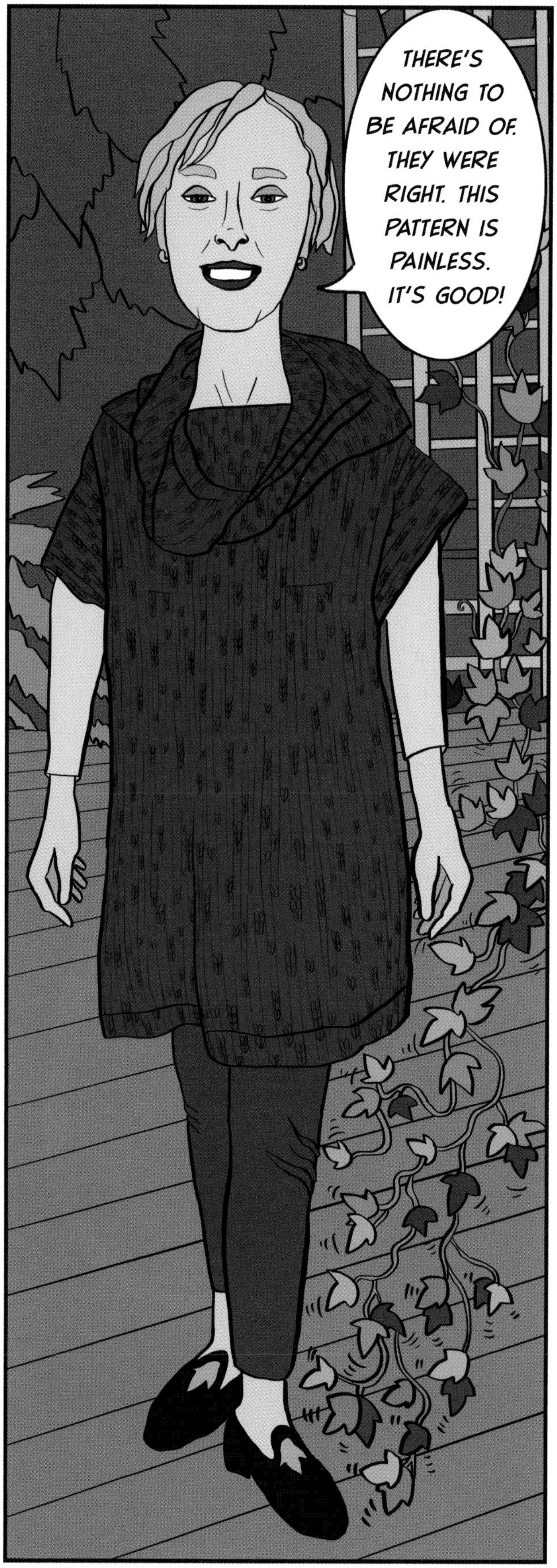
THERE'S NOTHING TO BE AFRAID OF. THEY WERE RIGHT. THIS PATTERN IS PAINLESS. IT'S GOOD!

SIZING: Measure around your neckline, where you want the cowl to fall. Make sure it won't be wider than your shoulders. Measure around your widest torso area, which could be your bust/hips/rear, then add 6–8 in (15–20 cm) for ease. Finally, measure from the top of your shoulder down to your desired armhole depth.
TECHNIQUE: Provisional Cast-On.
METHOD: Multiply your neckline by your gauge to get your cowl stitches. Long-tail cast on. Place a marker to note the beginning of the round and join your stitches in the round.

ALL TOGETHER NOW,
"BEING CAREFUL NOT TO TWIST!"

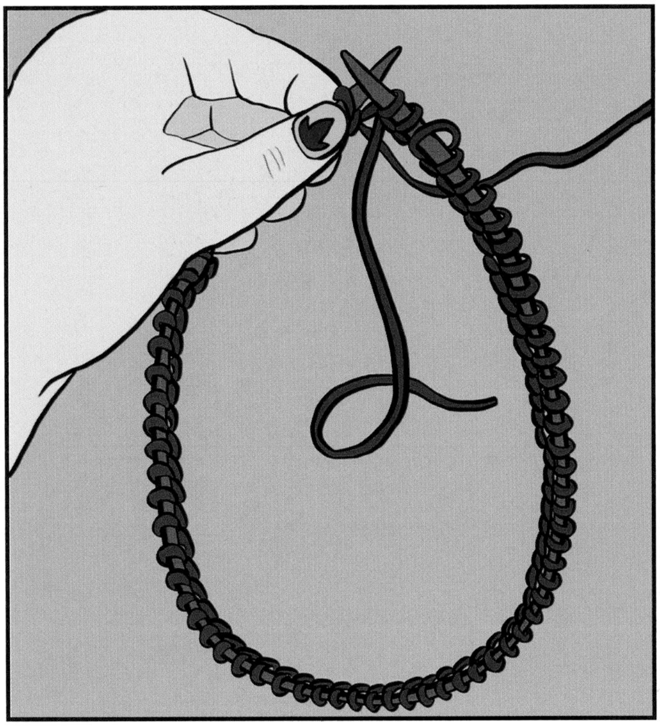

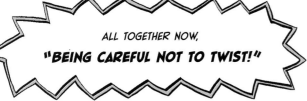

Multipy your body circumference plus ease by your gauge for your total body stitches. From this, subtract your neckline stitches, and divide by 4. That gives you your stitches to cast on for each shoulder.

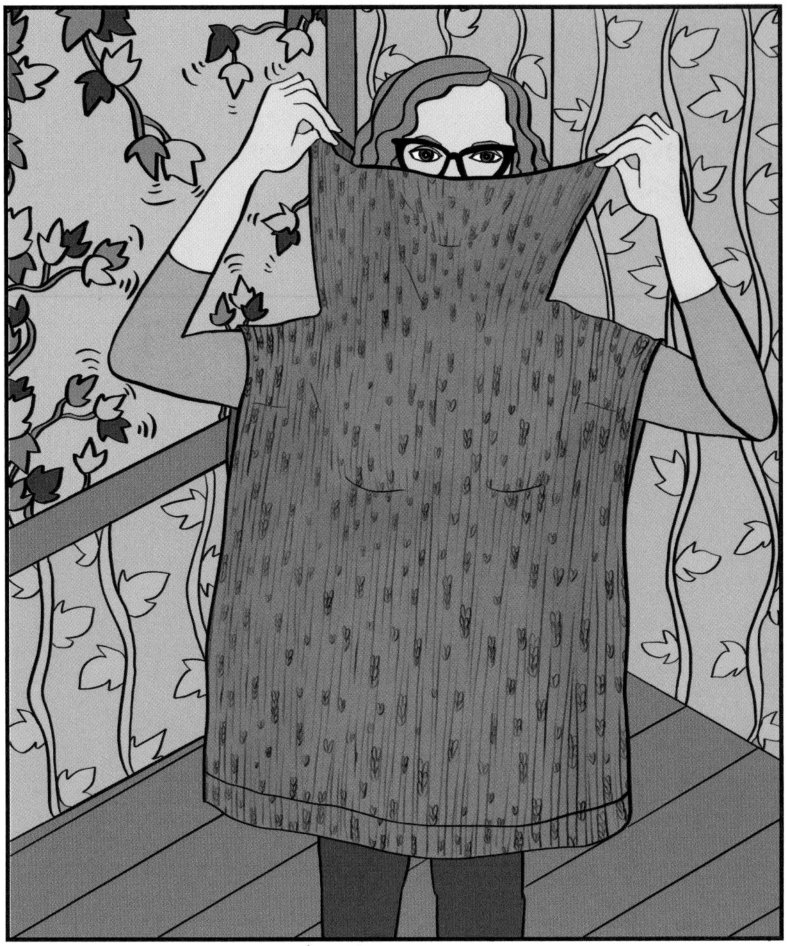

Work Stockinette stitch (St st) in the round until the cowl-neck is as long as you would like, perhaps 9 in (23 cm) or so. Put the stitches on a long stitch holder or piece of waste yarn and pop the tube over your head to try it on for size! When it's ready, divide the stitches evenly for the front and back. Place the back stitches on a holder.

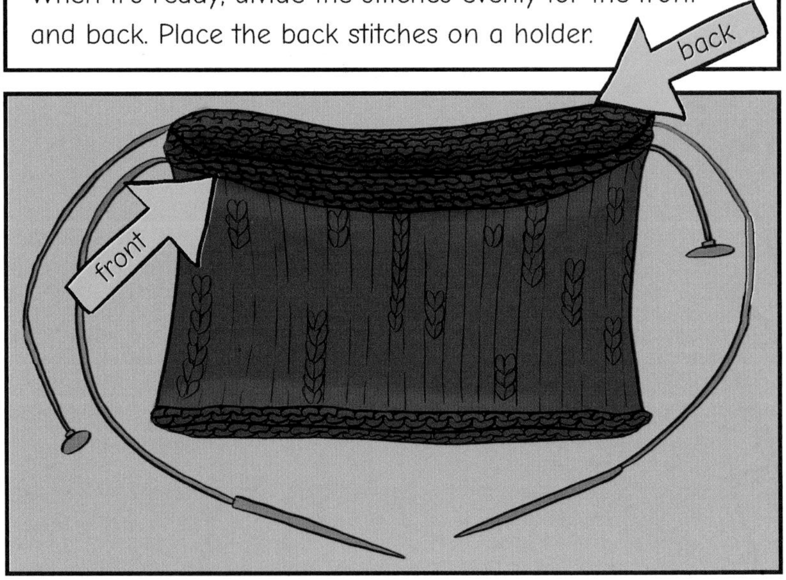
back
front

Work across the front of the cowl, and **cast on your left shoulder stitches**, using the Provisional Cast-On. These will be both front and back left shoulder stitches.

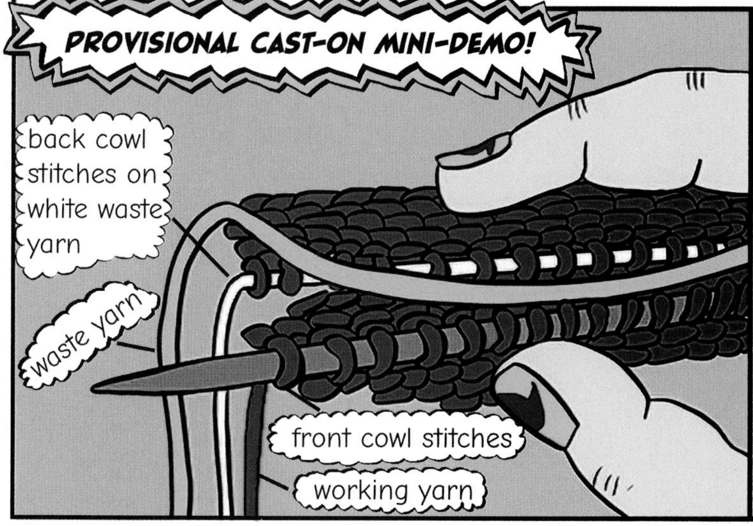
PROVISIONAL CAST-ON MINI-DEMO!
back cowl stitches on white waste yarn
waste yarn
front cowl stitches
working yarn

For the first stitch, pinch the Provisional Cast-On waste yarn against the needle, next to where the working yarn emerges. With your hands in step 1 position...
1) Catch your working yarn, scooping from the center, down, and toward you. 2) Rotate your left hand toward you, so the waste yarn is on the bottom.
3) Scoop the working yarn by going down through the center, and coming up away from you. 4) Rotate your hand back to step 1 position.
Repeat steps 1–4 until you have your left front stitch count.

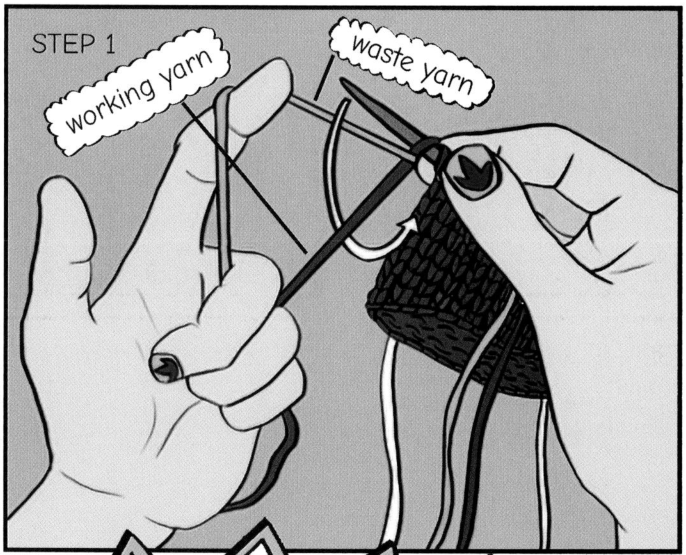
STEP 1
working yarn
waste yarn

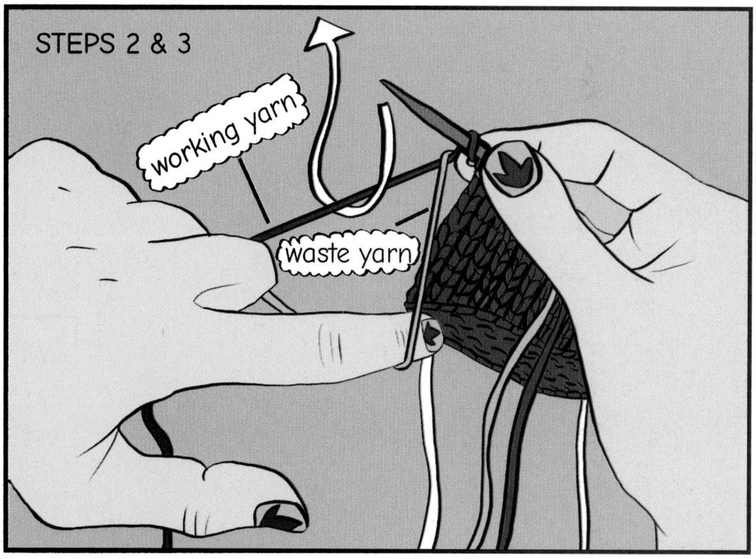
STEPS 2 & 3
working yarn
waste yarn

Note that your Provisional Cast-On stitches will have every other stitch twisted. It's like a

CONSPIRACY!

KTBL to untwist every other stitch; you'll be glad you did.

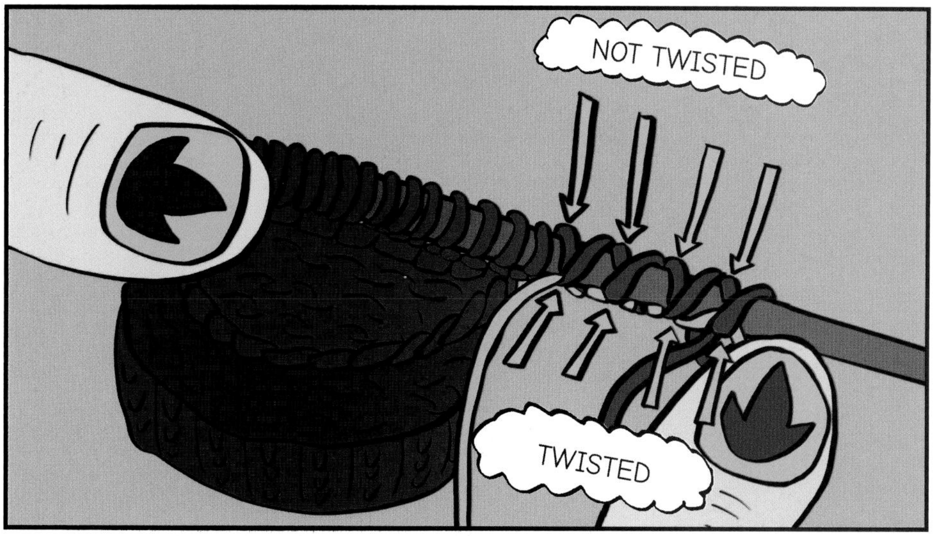
NOT TWISTED
TWISTED

After provisionally casting on your left shoulder stitches, join yarn at the back of the cowl, work across the back, and provisionally cast on your right shoulder stitches. Here's a MINI-DEMO of what it looks like, ready to be worked to armhole depth.

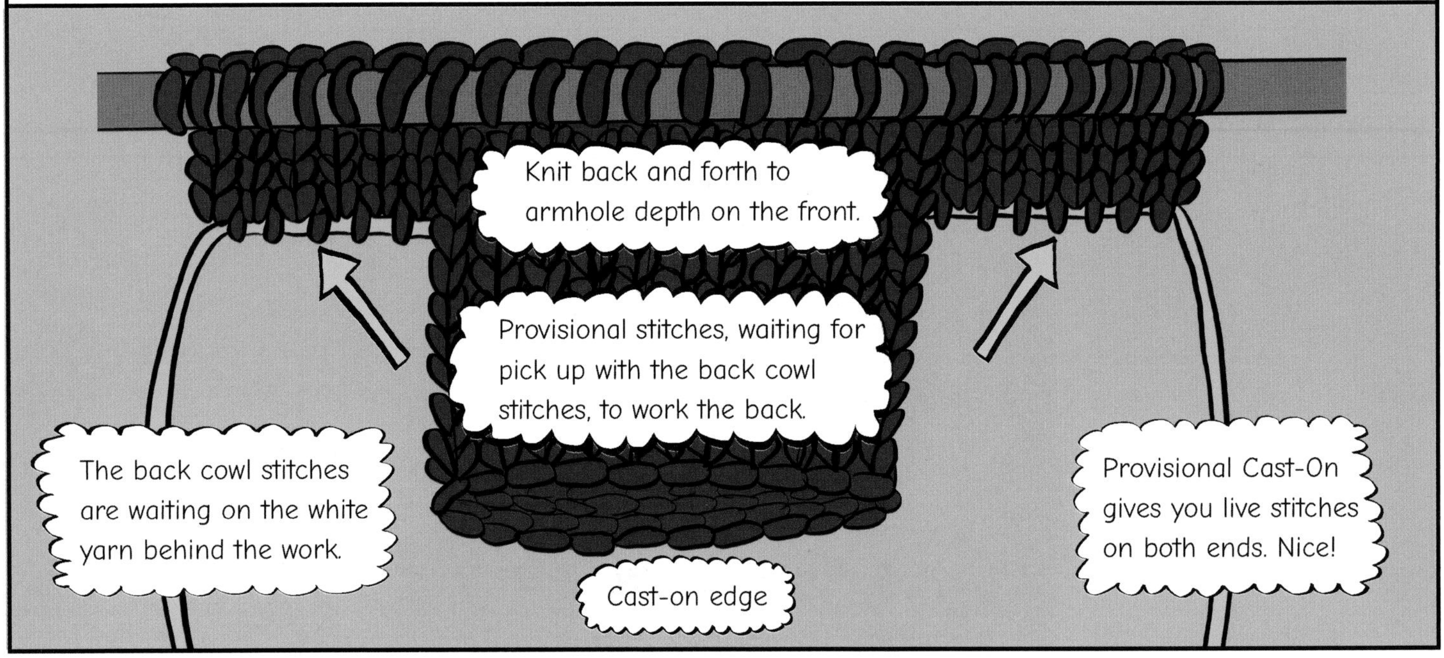

Knit back and forth to armhole depth on the front.
Provisional stitches, waiting for pick up with the back cowl stitches, to work the back.
The back cowl stitches are waiting on the white yarn behind the work.
Provisional Cast-On gives you live stitches on both ends. Nice!
Cast-on edge

Work back and forth on the front in St st until you reach your desired armhole depth. Place the front stitches on a holder. Now do the back. Put the provisional left shoulder stitches, back cowl stitches, and provisional right shoulder stitches on a needle. Join yarn and work in St st across the back stitches, untwisting the twisted stitches in the shoulder sections. Work back and forth in St st to the same depth as the front.

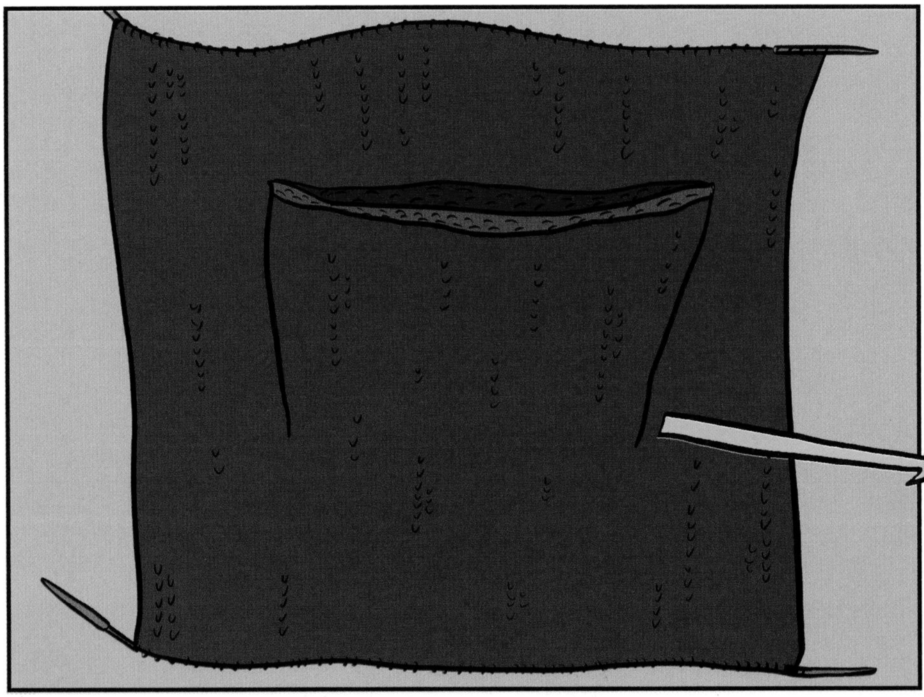

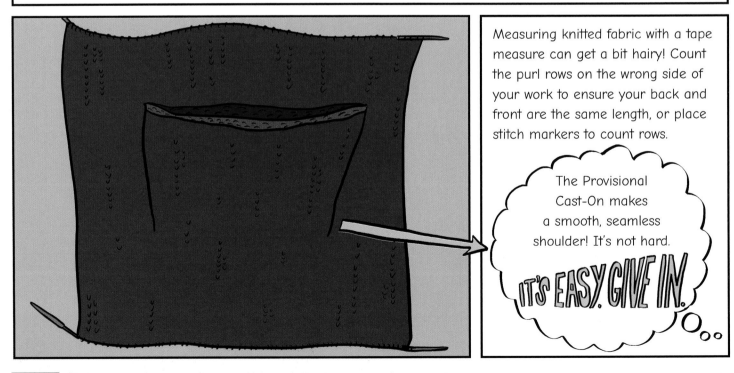

Measuring knitted fabric with a tape measure can get a bit hairy! Count the purl rows on the wrong side of your work to ensure your back and front are the same length, or place stitch markers to count rows.

The Provisional Cast-On makes a smooth, seamless shoulder! It's not hard.

IT'S EASY. GIVE IN.

Join the front and back in the round, creating the armholes. You should have your (body circumference plus ease) x gauge number of stitches. Work St st in the round until it is the length you like. For a flat, finished hem, knit to within 1½ in (4 cm) of your desired final length, and work one or two rows of purl stitch in the round. This round of purl bumps will appear as St st on the reverse and will provide you with a guide for hemming the tunic evenly. Continue in St st for another 3 in (7.5 cm) and bind off loosely.

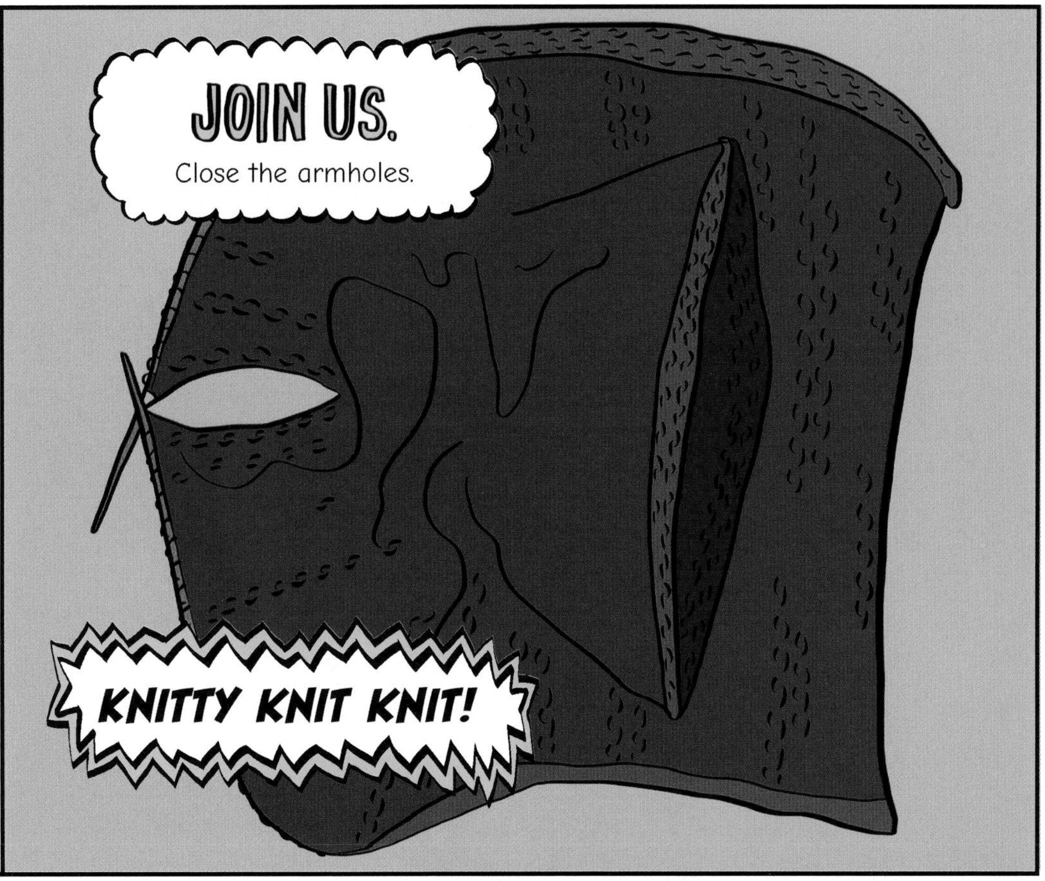
JOIN US.
Close the armholes.
KNITTY KNIT KNIT!

Fold the hem under and, using yarn and a darning needle, blind hem/whipstitch the bound-off edge to the row of purl bumps just below the row of St st on the reverse side. Be careful to line up the stitches evenly to create a nice, straight hem.

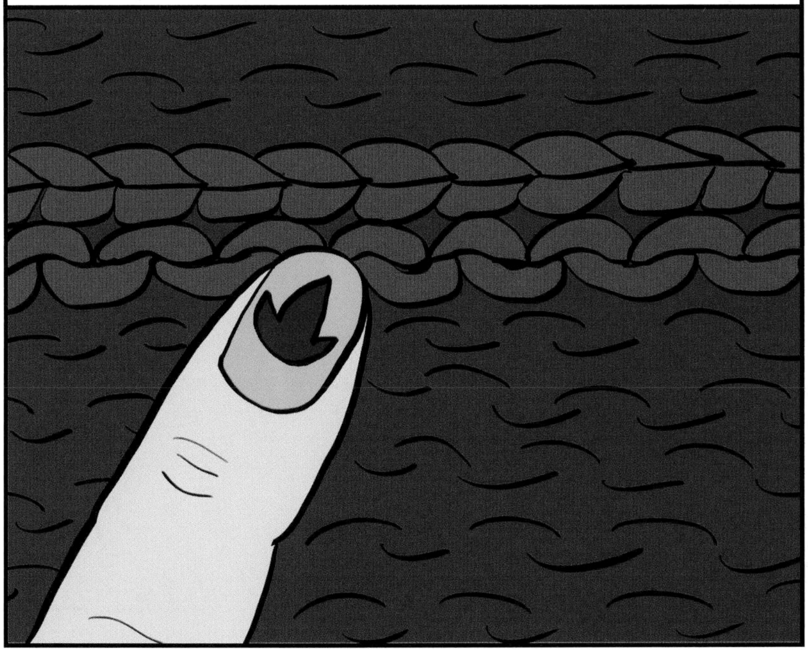

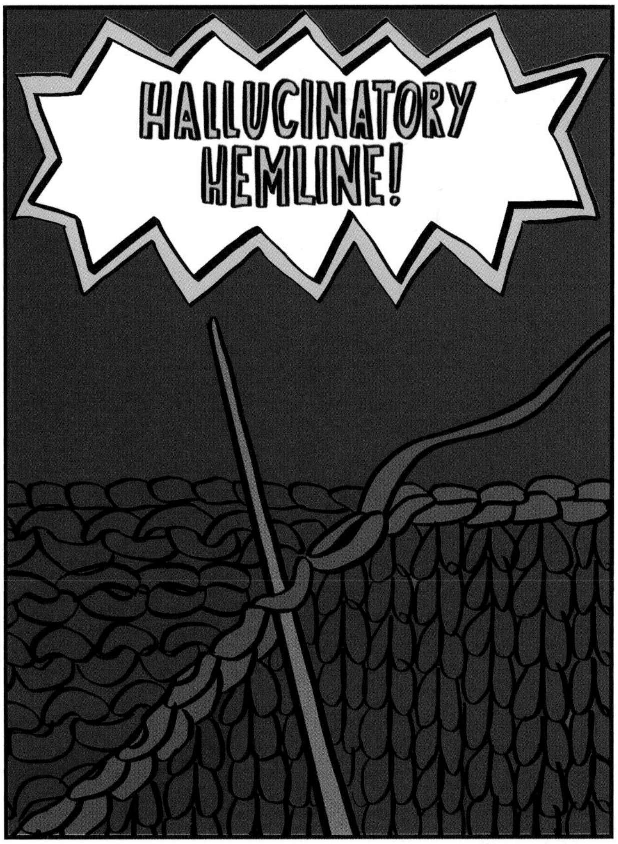
HALLUCINATORY HEMLINE!

Ruched sleeves, anyone? Use **matching yarn and a darning needle** to place a running stitch along the top of the shoulder, then gather the fabric to **ruche the sleeve. The tail of the yarn** used in the running stitch can be secured and woven in or tied off in a bow so you can easily undo it.

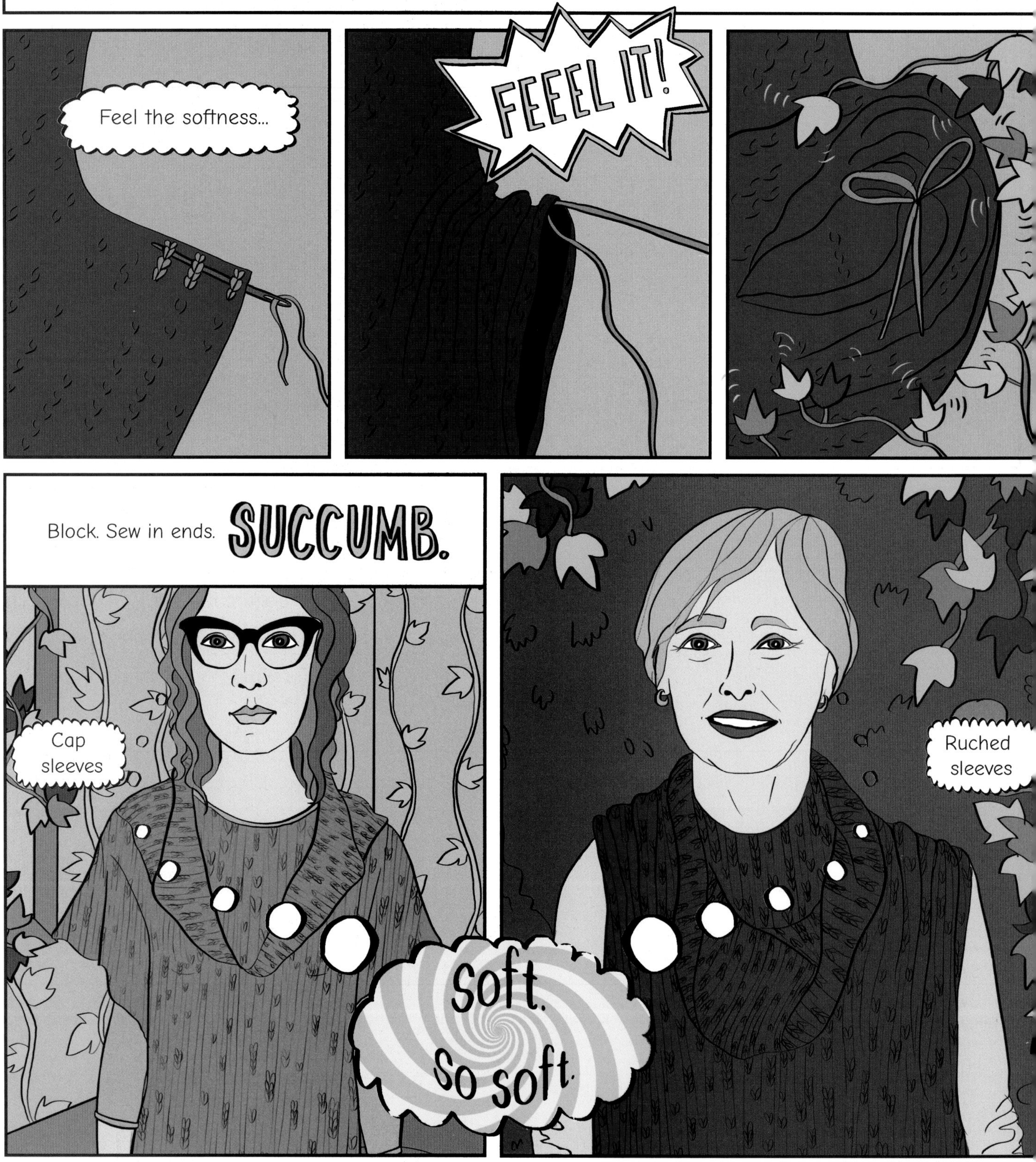

Feel the softness...
FEEEL IT!
Block. Sew in ends.
SUCCUMB.
Cap sleeves
soft.
So soft.
Ruched sleeves

DOUBLE FEATURE

BY JULIA FARWELL-CLAY

TWO ACTION-PACKED, CHEVRON-STRIPED TRIANGLES COME TOGETHER FOR DOUBLE THE FUN. HIJINKS ENSUE WITH GARTER STITCH, INTARSIA, COLOR-BLOCK STRIPES—BLACK-AND-WHITE OR FULL COLOR—EITHER WAY, IT'S AN INSTANT CLASSIC.

MATERIALS: 2 to 4 contrasting-color yarns of the same gauge. The sample is 75 in (191 cm) wingtip to wingtip, and used 1,680 y (1,540 m) sport-weight yarn. Two long circular needles. **GAUGE:** Soft, with nice drape. **SIZE:** Any. **TECHNIQUES:** Garter Tab Cast-On (GTCO) and Garter Tab Bind-Off (GTBO), Garter stitch intarsia.

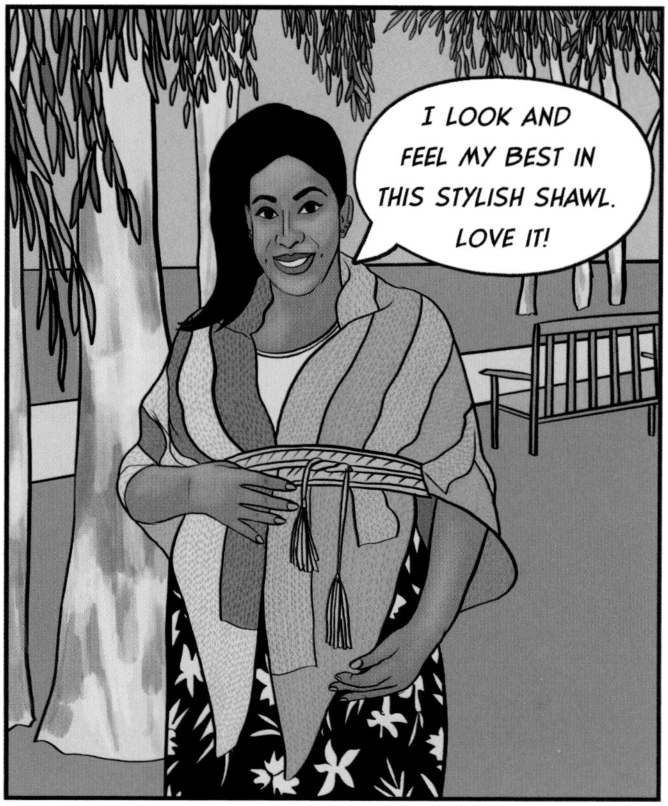

I LOOK AND FEEL MY BEST IN THIS STYLISH SHAWL. LOVE IT!

Spoiler Alert: The first half starts small and gets big. The second half starts big and gets small. Each chevron color-block stripe has two colors, Color 1 (C1) and Color 2 (C2). The colors alternate being the large or small color block in each stripe. In the small block of color in each stripe, there are the initial stitches at the beginning or bottom of the stripe, which are the ones you start with, and then there are the culminating stitches, which are what you end with at the top of the stripe.

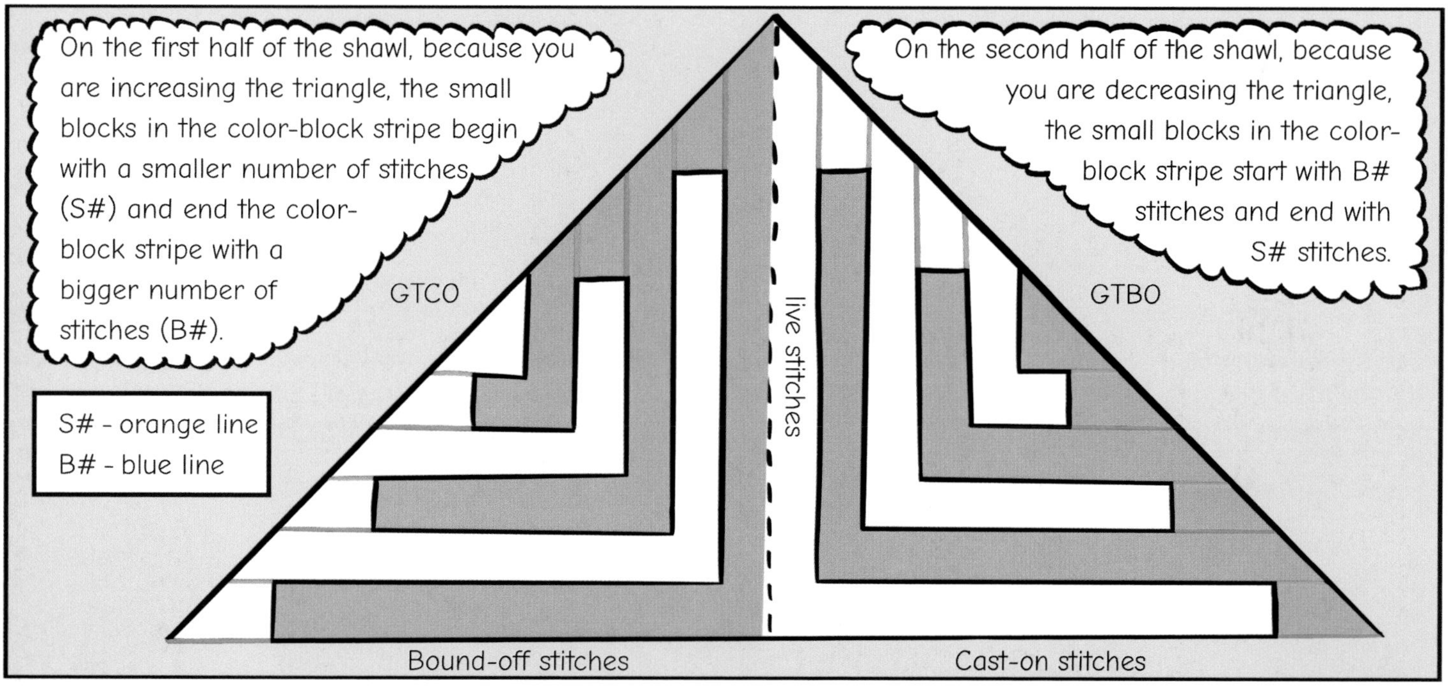

On the first half of the shawl, because you are increasing the triangle, the small blocks in the color-block stripe begin with a smaller number of stitches (S#) and end the color-block stripe with a bigger number of stitches (B#).
On the second half of the shawl, because you are decreasing the triangle, the small blocks in the color-block stripe start with B# stitches and end with S# stitches.
GTCO
live stitches
GTBO
S# - orange line
B# - blue line
Bound-off stitches
Cast-on stitches

Use a cell phone camera on the black-and-white/mono setting to help identify the yarns that have the most contrast.

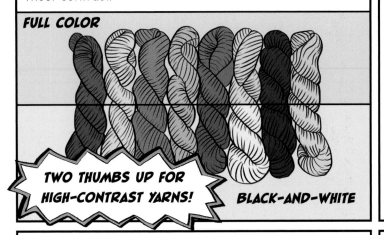

FULL COLOR

TWO THUMBS UP FOR HIGH-CONTRAST YARNS!

BLACK-AND-WHITE

METHOD: The shawl is knit in two parts. The first half starts with a GTCO and increases at four points—one at each edge and on either side of the center stitch. Once you've reached the size you want, bind off half of the stitches. The second half uses the remaining live stitches plus an equal number of new cast-on stitches, and decreases at four points—one at each edge and on either side of the center stitch. Garter intarsia color-block stripes are worked throughout, alternating the color of the large and small color blocks. When C1 is the big block, the stripe is a C1 dominant stripe. When C2 is the big block, the stripe is a C2 dominant stripe. The shawl is finished with a GTBO.

First half: Start with a GTCO. Using your first color (C1), CO 3 sts onto a circular needle. Knit 6 rows in Garter stitch. At the end of the 6th row, yarn is at the end of a RS row. Moving counterclockwise, knit up 3 sts from the Garter stitch bumps on the edge of the knitted strip. Move counterclockwise again to knit up 3 sts from CO edge.

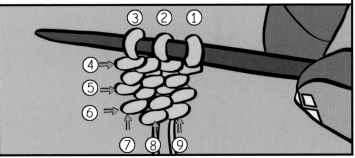

Garter Tab Cast-On is complete.

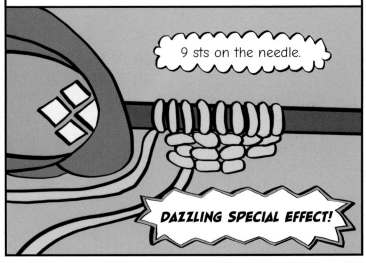

9 sts on the needle.

DAZZLING SPECIAL EFFECT!

Pm in the center st. Turn and work WS row. On the next RS row, inc 4 stitches as follows: K1, KFB, knit to your center stitch. K1P1K1 into your center stitch. Knit to the last 2 stitches. KFB, k1. Do this increase on every RS row for the first triangle. Work the WS rows plain.

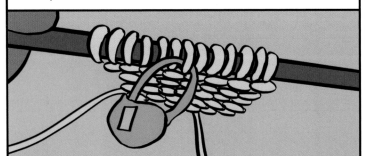

The first little triangle is a solid color with no Garter intarsia. Continue to knit, maintaining your RS increases, until you like the width and are ready to start your first two-color stripe. End with a WS row, ready to knit a RS row.

JUST ONE MORE...

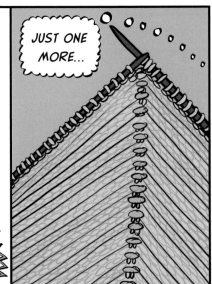

KNITTER'S CHOICE!

INTERMISSION! GET YOUR CONCESSIONS AND ENJOY THIS MINI-DEMO ON GARTER INTARSIA.

On the RS, go behind the work, lay your ending yarn down on top of your new yarn. Pick the new yarn up from underneath the ending yarn, and continue on with the new. After a couple of stitches, give the ending yarn a gentle tug to neaten the join.

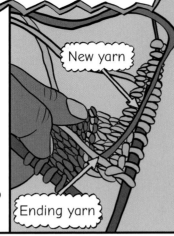

New yarn
Ending yarn

On the WS, bring the ending yarn between the needles to the front, and lay it down over the new yarn. Bring the new yarn up from under the ending yarn, take it between the needles to the back, and continue with the new. After a couple of stitches, gently tug the ended yarn to neaten the join.

Ending yarn
New yarn

Back to the shawl! You'll be working with two colors in each row from here until the last little triangle of solid color on the second half. Decide S#. In other words, choose the width you want to start with for the small block of color in your stripe, and multiply that by your gauge. The sample has S# = 3½ in (9 cm) of stitches. Work a C2 dominant stripe: On the RS row, maintaining your increases, knit C1 for S# stitches (include your increased stitch in this count). Intarsia join C2 and knit the rest of the row. Knit the WS row plain, maintaining Garter intarsia join. Continue, maintaining the intarsia join and your RS increases, until you like the width of the stripe. End so the work is ready to knit the RS. Your small color-block in C1 now has B# stitches. Write down S# and B#. They will be your guide going forward.

C1 dominant stripe: On the RS, maintaining your increases, knit C1 until there are S# stitches remaining on the left needle (including the increase you will do). Intarsia join C2, and knit the rest of the row. Knit the WS row plain, maintaining Garter intarsia join. Continue, maintaining the intarsia join and RS increases until your small color block in C2 has B# stitches. End ready to knit a RS row.

Using S# and B# gives you a consistent stripe width!

Repeat your stripes, alternating between C2 dominant and C1 dominant color-block stripes, until the first half is the size you want. Let your last stripe of the first triangle have C2 as the dominant color. End with a WS, ready to knit a RS row.

KNITTY KNIT KNIT!
READY FOR PART DEUX!
You will have an odd number of C2 dominant stripes. Your work should be ready to knit a RS row.

Second half: On the RS, bind off knitwise up to but not including your marked center stitch. Count how many stitches remain, not including the center stitch. Let's call this number X.

Spoiler Alert: You will cast on (X − 1) stitches on your second needle, using both C1 and C2. You will join these cast-on stitches to the live stitches on the first needle to make your first RS row of the second half. This row has decreases at each end, but no center decreases, so you will cast on (B# − 1) in your starting color, and then the rest of the (X − 1) stitches in your second color. The decrease on the other end of the row is worked in the live stitches.

On your second circular needle, with C2, long-tail cast on (B# − 1) stitches. Switch to C1 and cast on stitches to achieve a total in both colors of (X − 1) stitches on the needle.

You can bring in two new colors, C3 and C4!

With your first half RS facing, bring your second needle with the cast-on stitches to the marked center stitch of the first half. Using the C1 yarn from your cast-on stitches on the right needle, starting with your center stitch, knit the live stitches to the last 3 sts, k2tog, k1. Now you should have the same number of stitches on either side of the center stitch. Both sides will have (X − 1) stitches.

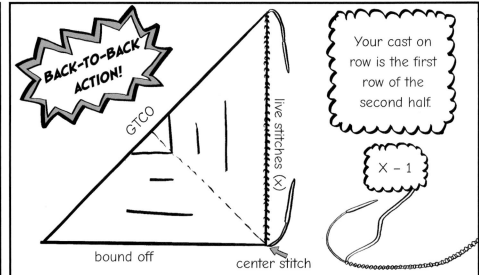

BACK-TO-BACK ACTION!

GTCO

live stitches (x)

bound off

center stitch

Your cast on row is the first row of the second half.

X − 1

Turn the work and knit the WS plain, making an intarsia join with your two colors where they meet. On the next RS and all RS rows, you will decrease as follows: K1, ssk, knit to 2 sts before center st, k2tog, k center st, ssk, knit to last 3 sts, k2tog, k1. WS rows are knit plain. Work the color-block stripe, maintaining your intarsia join and RS decreases until your minor color has S# stitches and you are ready to knit a RS row.

THIS IS GOING TO BE SO MUCH FUN TO WEAR!

Remember that for the second half, you are going big to small, so you will start your minor-color stripe with B#, and end with S#.

C2 DOMINANT STRIPE: On the next RS row, maintaining RS decreases, work C2 until there are (B# + 1) stitches remaining on the left needle (this includes the upcoming decrease—you will have B# stitches in C1 at the end of the row). Intarsia join C1 and work the rest of the row. Continue, maintaining the intarsia join and RS decreases until C1 has S# stitches and you are ready to knit a RS row. C1 dominant stripe: On the next RS row, maintaining RS decreases, work C2 for B# stitches. Intarsia join C1 and work the rest of the row. Continue, maintaining the intarsia join and RS decreases until C2 has S# stitches and you are ready to knit a RS row.

Continue with alternating color-block stripes. The second triangle will get smaller as you go. After the final color-block stripe, you'll be down to the last bit of solid C2. When you have 11–13 sts left, work a Garter Tab Bind-Off.

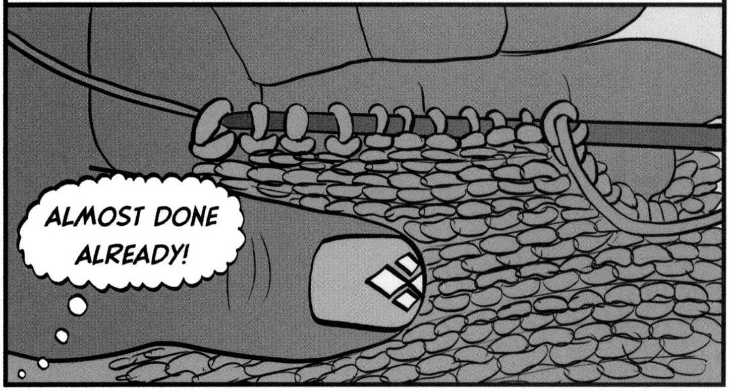
ALMOST DONE ALREADY!

To work a Garter Tab Bind-Off: *K2, ssk. Turn. WS: K3. Repeat from * until 6 total sts remain on the needle (3 on the left are unworked).

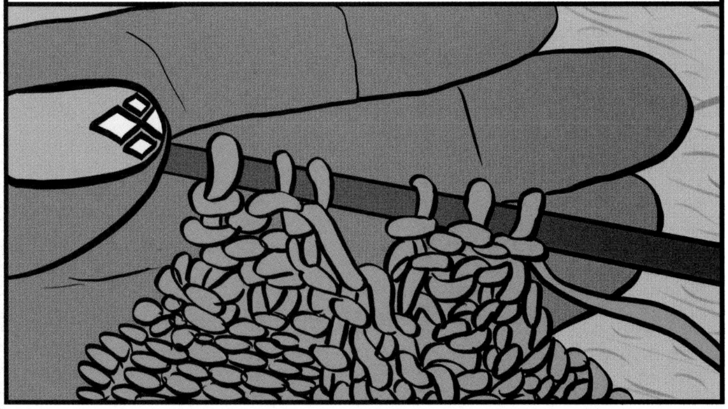

Place the first 3 sts on a different needle. Hold together to join by grafting (see page 68) or work a Three-Needle Bind-Off (see page 108).

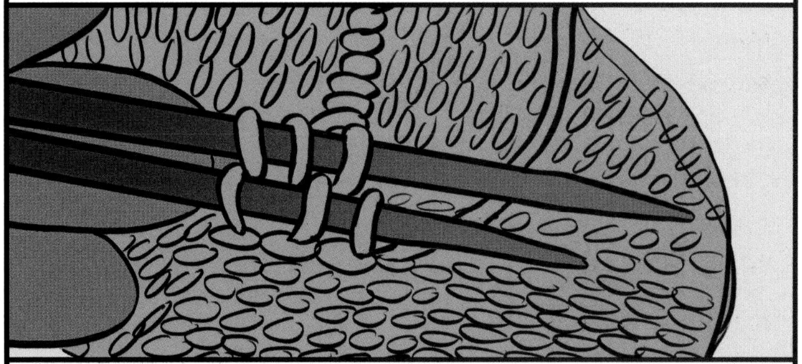

Cut yarn, weave in ends, block.

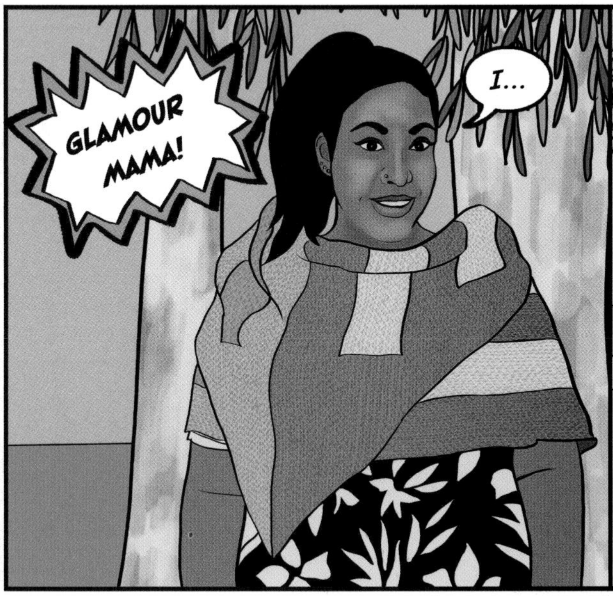
GLAMOUR MAMA!
I...

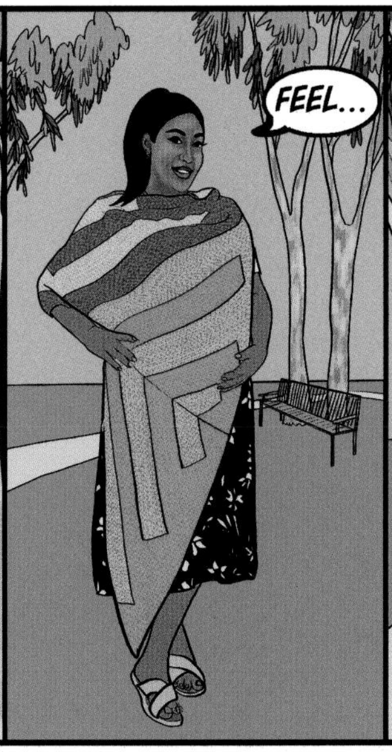
FEEL...

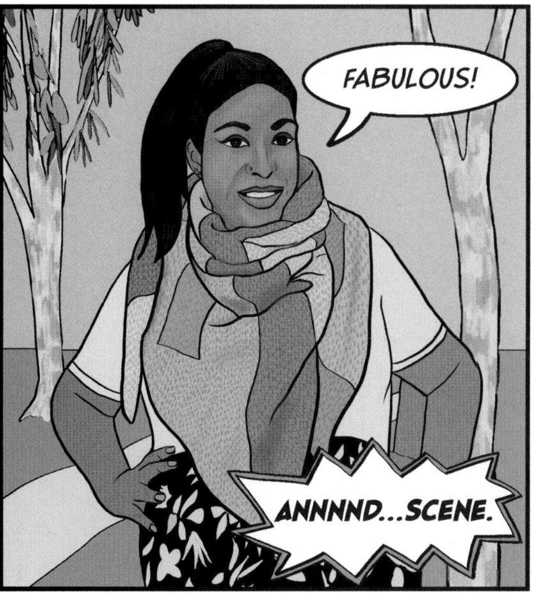
FABULOUS!
ANNNND...SCENE.

The Darcy

BY KAREN KIM MAR

DON'T LET YOUR PRIDE GET IN THE WAY OF KNITTING UP THIS ULTRA-SIMPLE GARTER STITCH PATTERN. YOU'LL DROP YOUR PREJUDICE WHEN YOU SEE THE BEGUILING RESULT.

MATERIALS: 350 y (320 m) of yarn you love to feel on your neck. 16 in (41 cm) or 24 in (61 cm) circular needles in the size that gives the fabric you like. For this version, we held a strand of laceweight kid mohair/silk and a strand of laceweight baby alpaca/merino. **GAUGE:** Soft, with nice drape. **SIZE:** Measure your head circumference and subtract 2 in (5 cm) to get your key number. To figure out the length to knit, take your key number and subtract 3 in (7.5 cm).

THIS COWL HAS BEWITCHED ME...

CAN WE GO FOR A WALK LATER?

DO HOLD STILL.

METHOD: Multiply the key number by your gauge to determine the number of stitches to cast on. Round up if it's not a whole number. Cast on and work in Garter stitch to your target length, then bind off.

Example: Your head is 21 in around, and your blocked gauge is 4 st/in. Subtract 2 in from your measurement for 19 in, your key number. Multiply the key number by gauge to get your stitch number (76). The length would be 19 in − 3 in = 16 in. Or, let's say your head is 53 cm around. Subtract 5 cm for 48 cm, your key number. Your blocked gauge is 1.6 stitches per 1 cm. Multiply key number by gauge to get your stitch number (77).

KNITTY KNIT KNIT

Now, lay your work like this.

Bind-off edge

Cast-on edge

The more the side edges meet, the smaller the neck hole will be, and vice versa.

Then fold it like this.

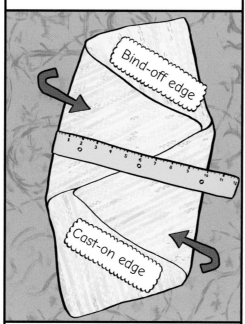

Bind-off edge

Cast-on edge

Slide the two side edges so that the folded work measures 10 in (25 cm) across the middle.

To check the fit, pin the seam and try it on before you sew.

Whipstitch the adjacent side edges, and darn in the ends.

YOU WILL ARDENTLY

LOVE...

LOVE...

LOVE...

THE VERSATILITY OF THIS PIECE!

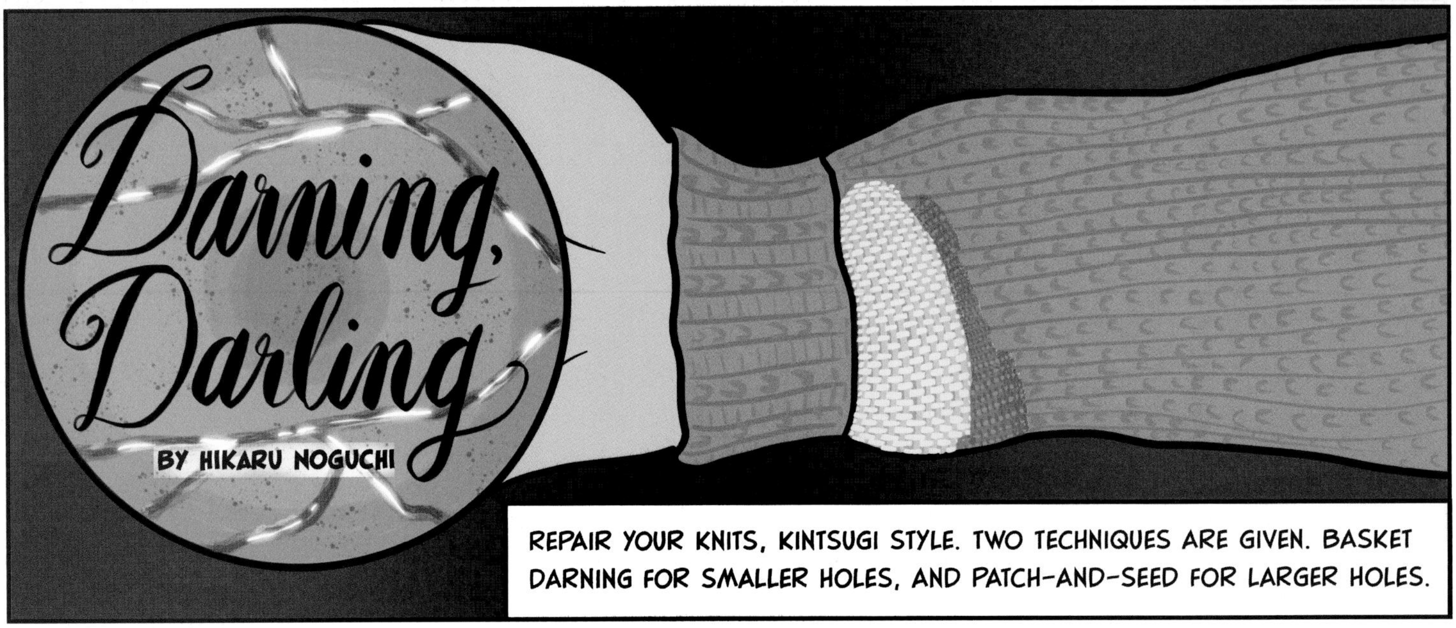
Darning, Darling
BY HIKARU NOGUCHI
REPAIR YOUR KNITS, KINTSUGI STYLE. TWO TECHNIQUES ARE GIVEN. BASKET DARNING FOR SMALLER HOLES, AND PATCH-AND-SEED FOR LARGER HOLES.

MATERIALS: Darning mushroom, elastic band, contrasting yarn, both a sharp and blunt darning needle, sewing thread, fabric, straight sewing pins, a book. **BASKET DARNING:** In this technique, you weave a patch in place by sewing on warp threads, and then weaving/sewing in weft threads.

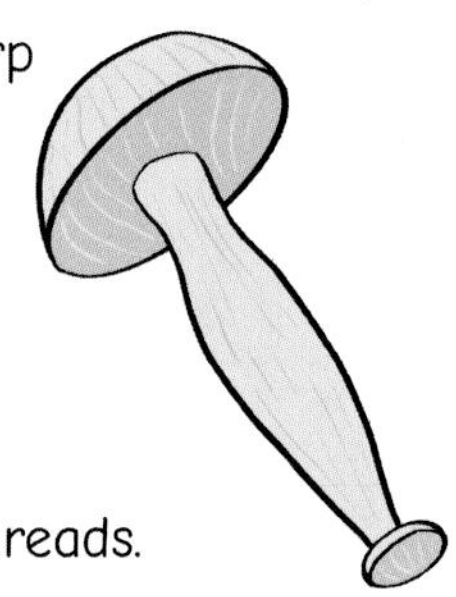

Place the darning mushroom under the hole, then secure it with an elastic hair band. You'll be working with the grain of the knitted fabric.

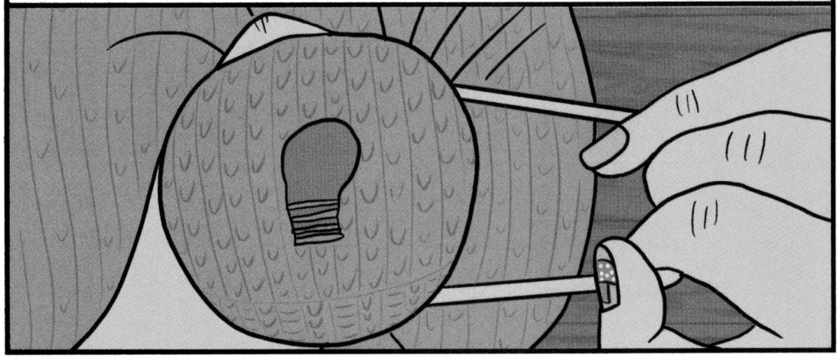

Work where the fabric is sound, ½ in (1 cm) away from the hole. To build the warp, draw your needle under both legs of a stitch from right to left at the top right corner of the hole. Leave 2½ in (10 cm) of thread for the tail.

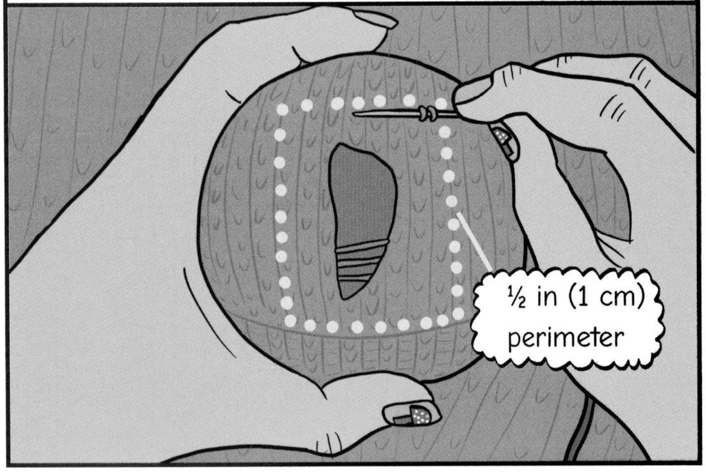
½ in (1 cm) perimeter

Draw your needle under a stitch from right to left at the bottom right corner of the hole.

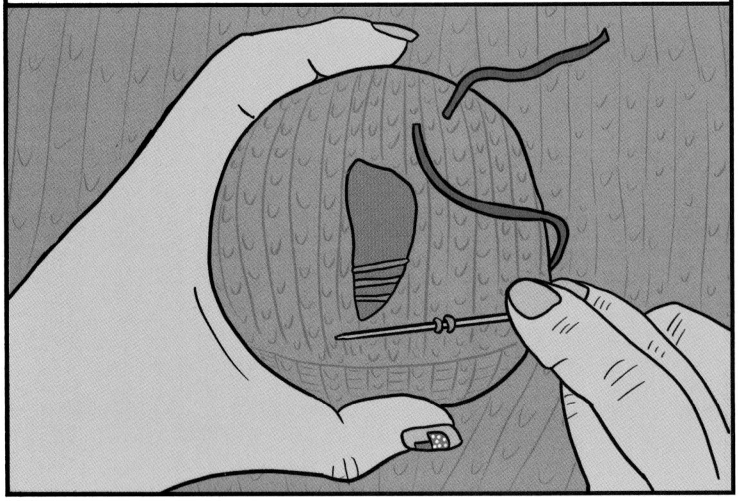

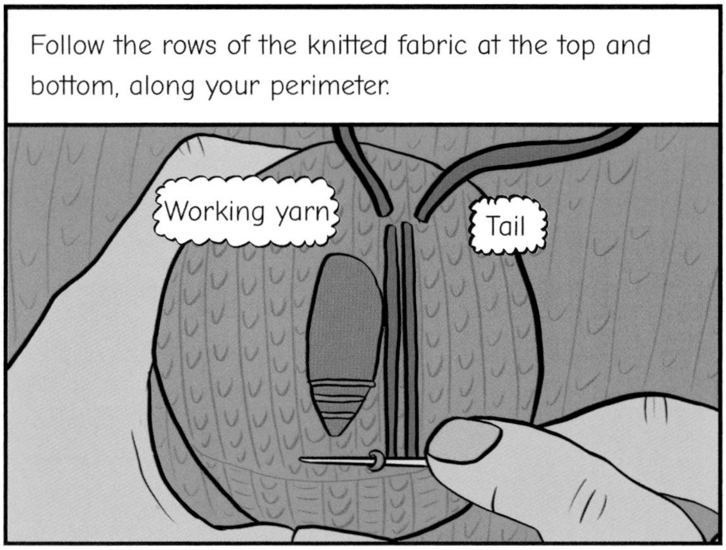
Follow the rows of the knitted fabric at the top and bottom, along your perimeter.
Working yarn
Tail

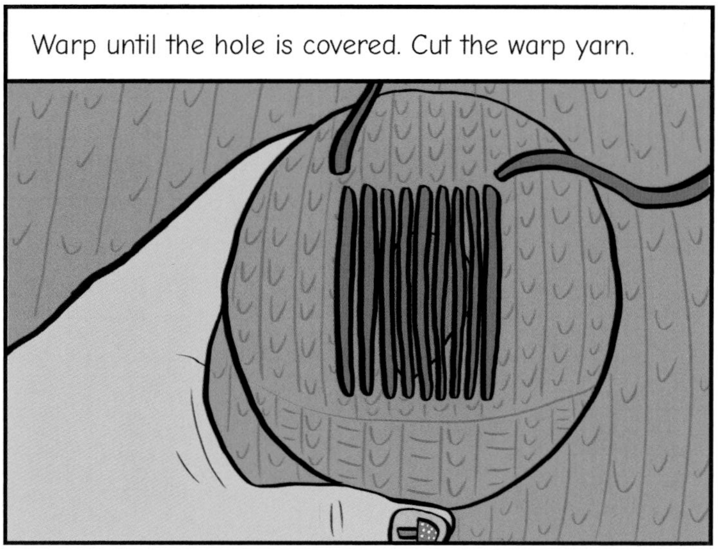
Warp until the hole is covered. Cut the warp yarn.

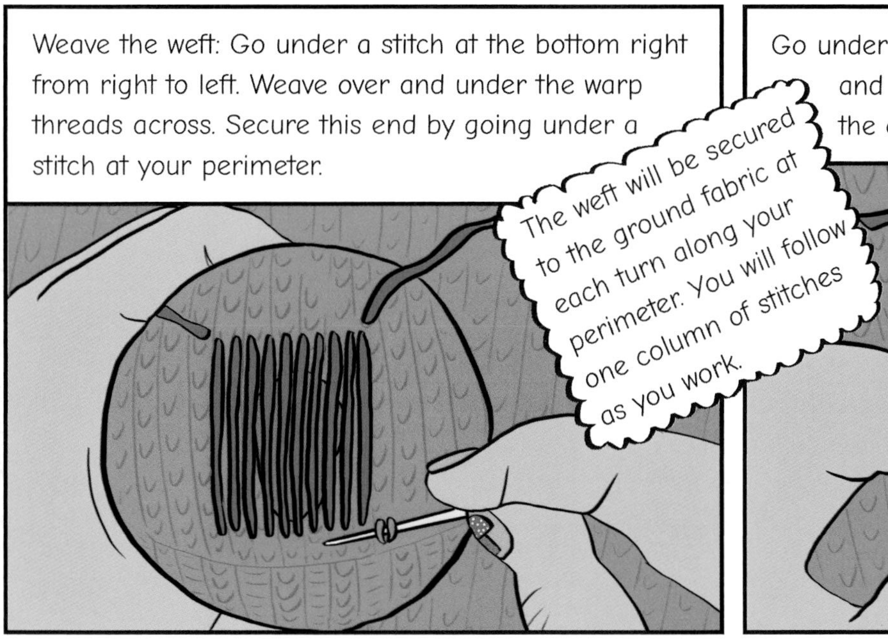
Weave the weft: Go under a stitch at the bottom right from right to left. Weave over and under the warp threads across. Secure this end by going under a stitch at your perimeter.
The weft will be secured to the ground fabric at each turn along your perimeter. You will follow one column of stitches as you work.

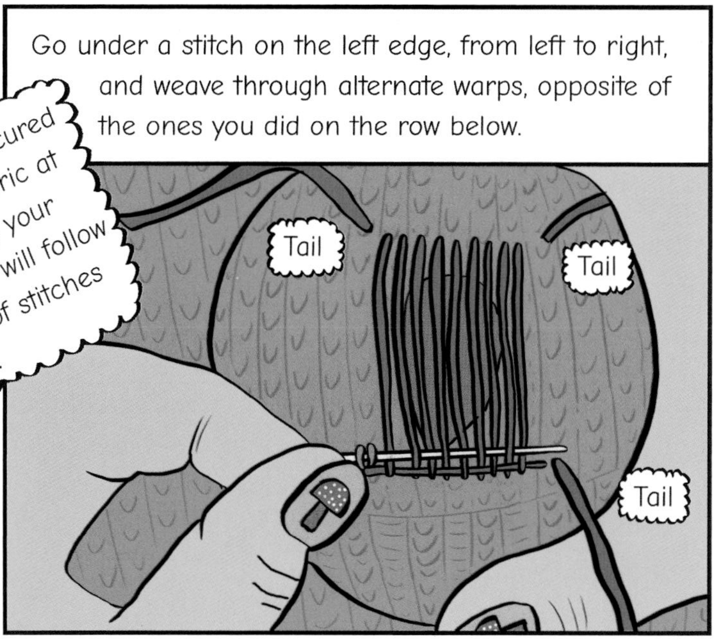
Go under a stitch on the left edge, from left to right, and weave through alternate warps, opposite of the ones you did on the row below.
Tail
Tail
Tail

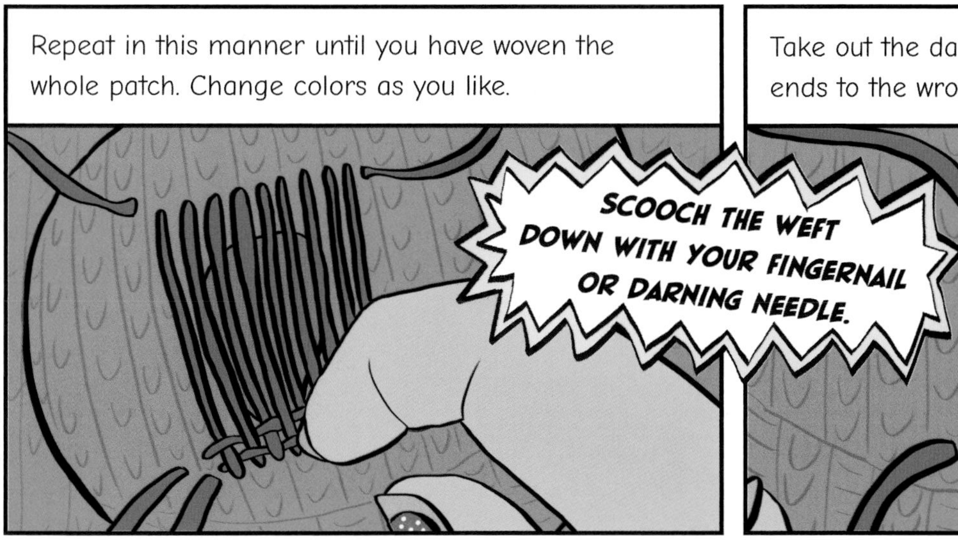
Repeat in this manner until you have woven the whole patch. Change colors as you like.
SCOOCH THE WEFT DOWN WITH YOUR FINGERNAIL OR DARNING NEEDLE.

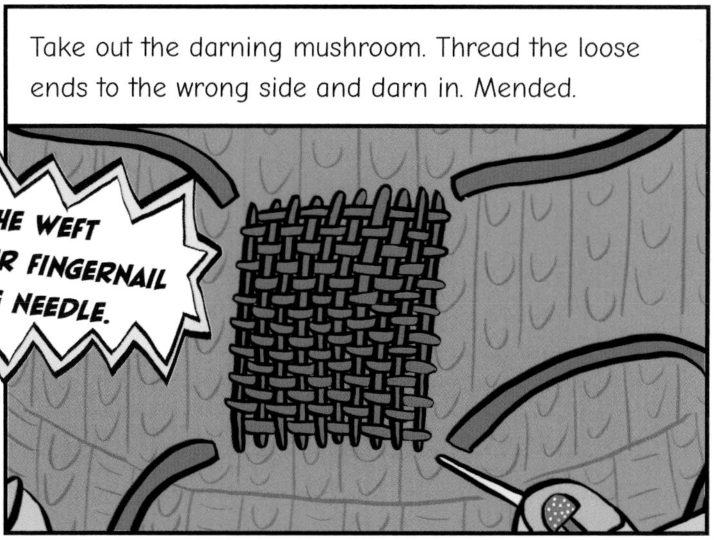
Take out the darning mushroom. Thread the loose ends to the wrong side and darn in. Mended.

PATCH-AND-SEED: This technique uses a fabric patch to bridge across large holes.

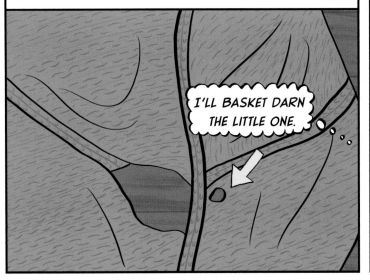

I'LL BASKET DARN THE LITTLE ONE.

With the wrong side facing out, place a book beneath the hole.

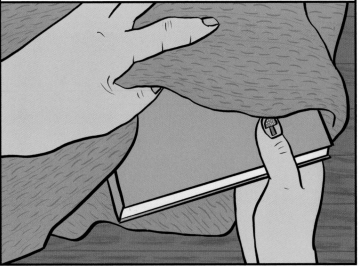

Cut a piece of fabric slightly bigger than the hole and pin it into place. Stitch it down on all sides with basting thread and your sharp darning needle.

You will remove this basting thread at the end.

Remove the pins. Turn the sweater right side out and secure the darning mushroom. With your mending yarn, make a ½ in (1 cm) stitch through all of the layers, leaving a 2½ in (10 cm) tail.

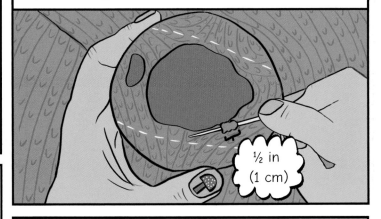

½ in (1 cm)

Now catch another ½ in (1 cm) of your layers. Let the needle go in just to the right of where the last stitch came out. This will make a small seed stitch.

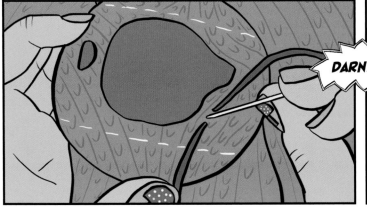

DARNY DARN DARN!

Keep on, creating small seeds and moving along in ½ in (1 cm) increments.

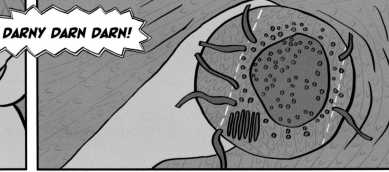

Seed stitch over the hole and basket darn any smaller adjacent holes.
Basket darn
TAILS GALORE!
Turn the sweater to the wrong side and remove the basting thread. Draw tails to the wrong side, sew them in, and trim.
On the wrong side, using your yarn, tack down the patch of fabric with very small stitches.
DARN! THIS LOOKS GREAT!

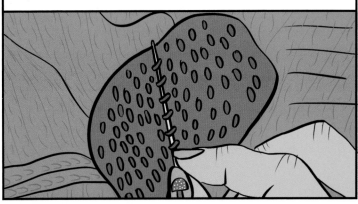

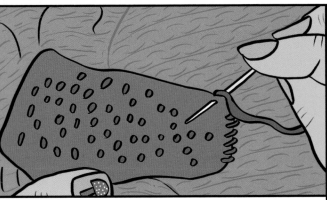

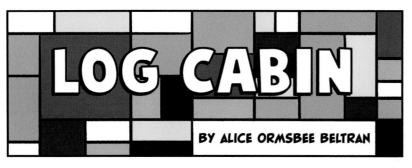

LOG CABIN

BY ALICE ORMSBEE BELTRAN

LOG CABIN! THE TECHNIQUE DREAMS ARE MADE OF, AND PRETTY MUCH ANYTHING ELSE THAT COMES TO MIND. BLANKETS ARE AN OBVIOUS AND TERRIFIC CHOICE, BUT WHY STOP THERE? THE VINTAGE/MODERN LOOK PLAYS WELL WITH OTHERS AND IS A PORTABLE, FUN, ADDICTIVE PIECE OF KNITTING.

WOOL HAS PROPERTIES THAT MAKE IT THE BEST THING EVER, ESPECIALLY FOR NAPPING (SEE P. 124). I LIKE TO GIVE WOOL TO BABIES RIGHT AWAY.

MATERIALS: Binder clips, circular needles to give you the gauge you like, and . . . yarn! Log cabin is a chance to play with colors, so have multiple colors in the same gauge. In this pattern each square is made of 9 strips. You can use a different color for each, or alternate between two, or anything in between. The type and size of yarn will depend on what you're going for. A strong, hard-wearing wool yarn would do well as a big, sturdy lap blanket for outdoor events. Cotton is ideal for washcloths. For baby blankets, Alice likes to go with wool that can handle a cold/delicate machine wash cycle.

SIZE: Individual blocks, and assemblies of blocks, can be any size. Drink coasters, anyone? For this project, Alice went with a 2 by 2 square blanket that is 24 in (61 cm) square, small enough to be used with a car seat. Each square is 12 in (30.5 cm) across. **GAUGE:** Log Cabin is worked in Garter stitch. You can use any gauge—let it suit the purpose. For this baby blanket, Alice went with a medium gauge in Aran-weight yarn for a sturdy fabric that would not have any holes for little fingers to catch, and that would be cushiony on the floor.

TECHNIQUES: Log Cabin, Quick Border. **METHOD:** The modular pattern gives instructions for a simple baby blanket of four 9-part Log Cabin squares sewn together and finished with a Quick Border.

A STACK OF DRINK COASTERS WOULD BE A CHARMING HOSTESS GIFT! AND I SHOULD DO A LOG CABIN CHIZY (P. 74)! WHILE I'M AT IT, I COULD DO JUST A FEW MORE BLANKET SQUARES, AND HOW MUCH YARN DO I...

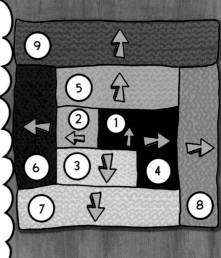

Garter ridge count is the same for each strip. St count for each strip will be a multiple of your original st count (X). Strips 1 and 2 have 1X sts. 3 and 4 have 2X. 5 and 6 have 3X. 7 and 8 have 4X, and 9 has 5X. In our sample, X = 10 sts.

To make a 12 in (30.5 cm) square with nine strips, each strip must be 2½ in (6 cm) tall. Multiply your gauge by 2½ to figure out how many stitches you need.

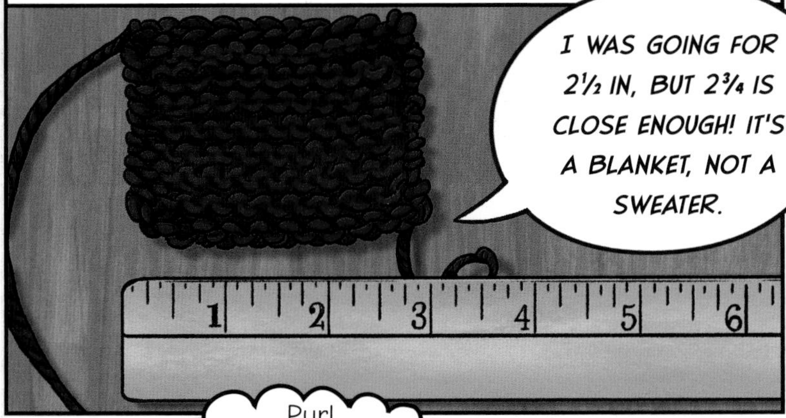
I WAS GOING FOR 2½ IN, BUT 2¾ IS CLOSE ENOUGH! IT'S A BLANKET, NOT A SWEATER.
1 2 3 4 5 6

Long-tail cast on your stitches. This will be your center strip (which is a square). Alice's secret for wall-to-wall ridges: Purl the first row. This is the RS. Knit each row after that, slipping all first stitches and knitting through the back loop (KTBL) of each last stitch, until your ridges on the RS match your number of stitches. Don't count the purled row ridge, but do count the purl bumps on the needle.

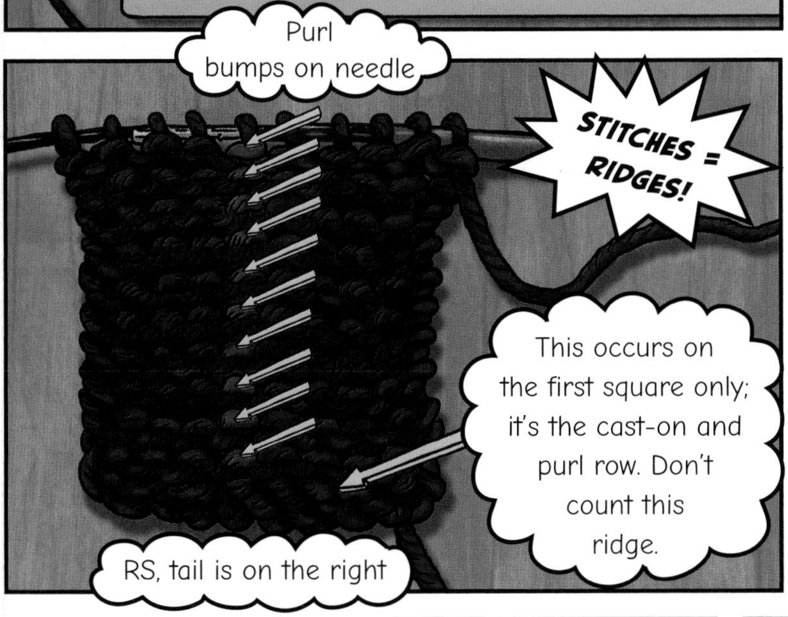
Purl bumps on needle
STITCHES = RIDGES!
This occurs on the first square only; it's the cast-on and purl row. Don't count this ridge.
RS, tail is on the right

Bind off (BO) on the right side, purlwise, leaving the last stitch on the needle. Next you will round the corner and pick up the stitches on the left side of your piece, and knit perpendicular to your previous direction.

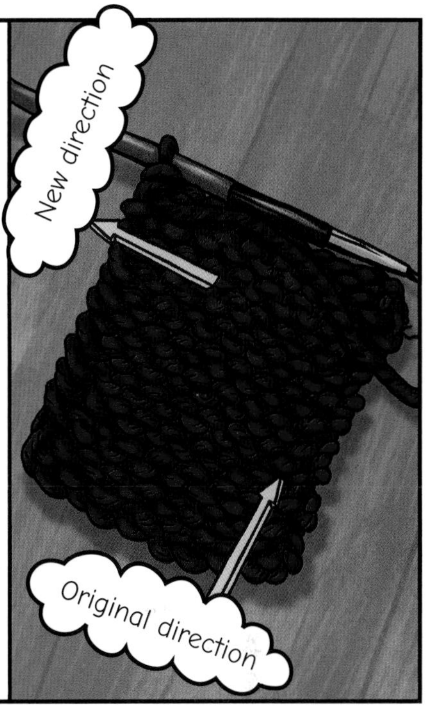
New direction
Original direction

Round the corner: Insert your left needle into the first knob along the left side. Knit into that loop with the color for strip 2, creating a stitch on your needle.

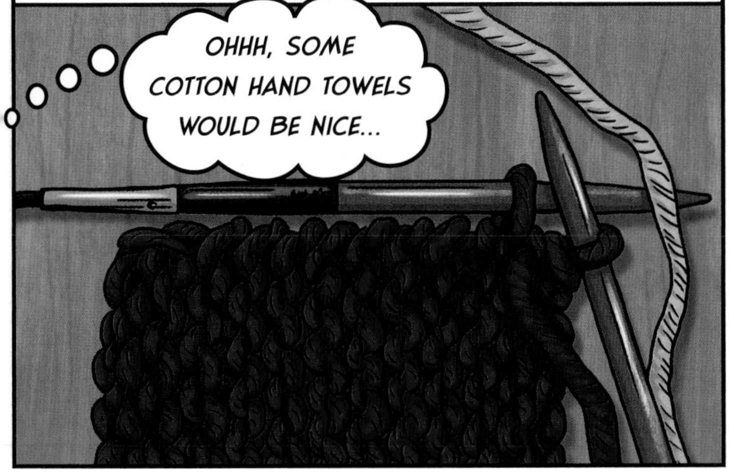
OHHH, SOME COTTON HAND TOWELS WOULD BE NICE...

BO the last stitch of the previous color. This is your first stitch in your new color. Pick up stitches with your new color at each knob until you have your original number of stitches.

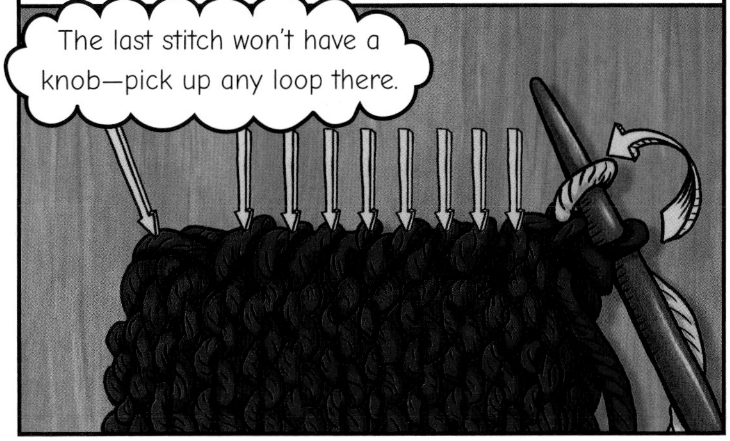
The last stitch won't have a knob—pick up any loop there.

You are on the WS. Knit the first row. Then knit every row, slipping your first st and KTBL your last st, until you have the same number of ridges as you do sts. This ridge count will be the same for all your strips. BO on the RS purlwise, leaving the last st on the needle.
* Round the corner with your next new yarn. For the rest of the square, you will be picking up a multiple of your original st count. Pick up sts along the knobs of your second square, and along the upside-down U shapes of your first square.

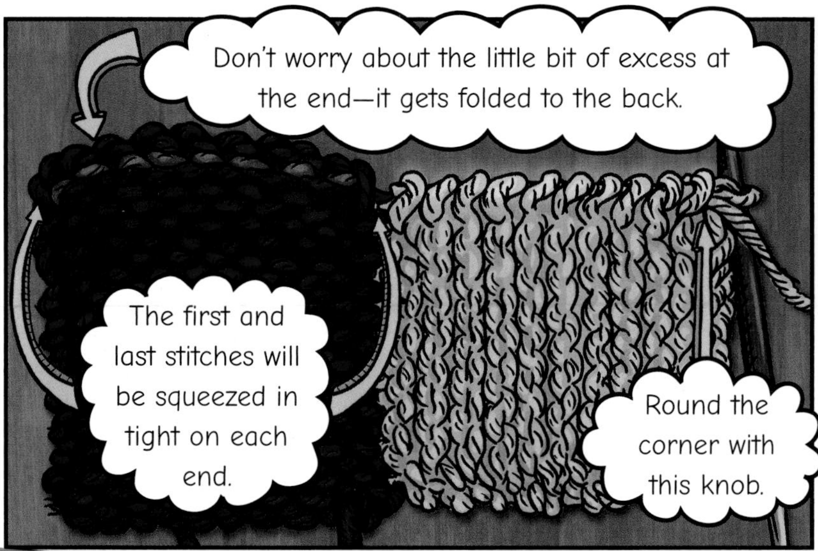
Don't worry about the little bit of excess at the end—it gets folded to the back.
The first and last stitches will be squeezed in tight on each end.
Round the corner with this knob.

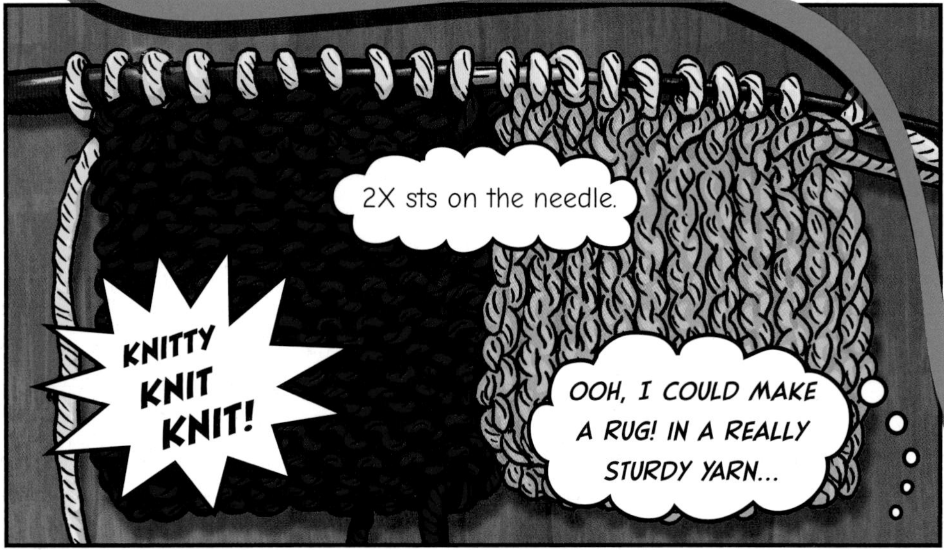
2X sts on the needle.
KNITTY KNIT KNIT!
OOH, I COULD MAKE A RUG! IN A REALLY STURDY YARN...

Knit the first WS row. Knit every row, slipping your first stitch and KTBL of your last stitch, until you have the same number of ridges as your original stitch count. BO on the RS purlwise. Repeat from *, ending with your 9th strip and a square shape. BO that last stitch and break the yarn. Pull the yarn through the last loop. One block done! Make three more blocks.

Have fun arranging the four squares. When you're ready to sew up the blanket, clip two of your squares together, RS facing and edges aligned.

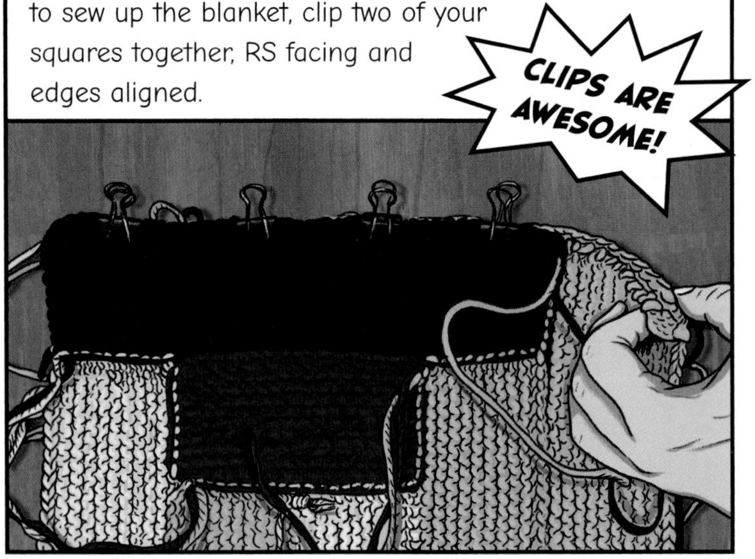
CLIPS ARE AWESOME!

There are two different kinds of selvedge—side Garter and bound-off. On the side Garter selvedge, sew through the loop that sticks out from right to left. On the bound-off selvedge, sew the outer leg from the center out.

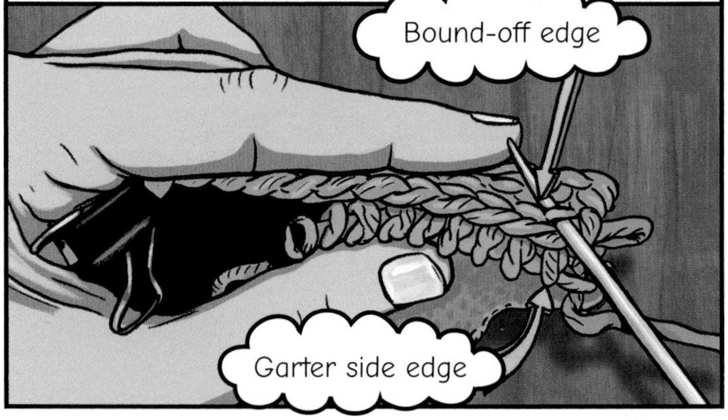
Bound-off edge
Garter side edge

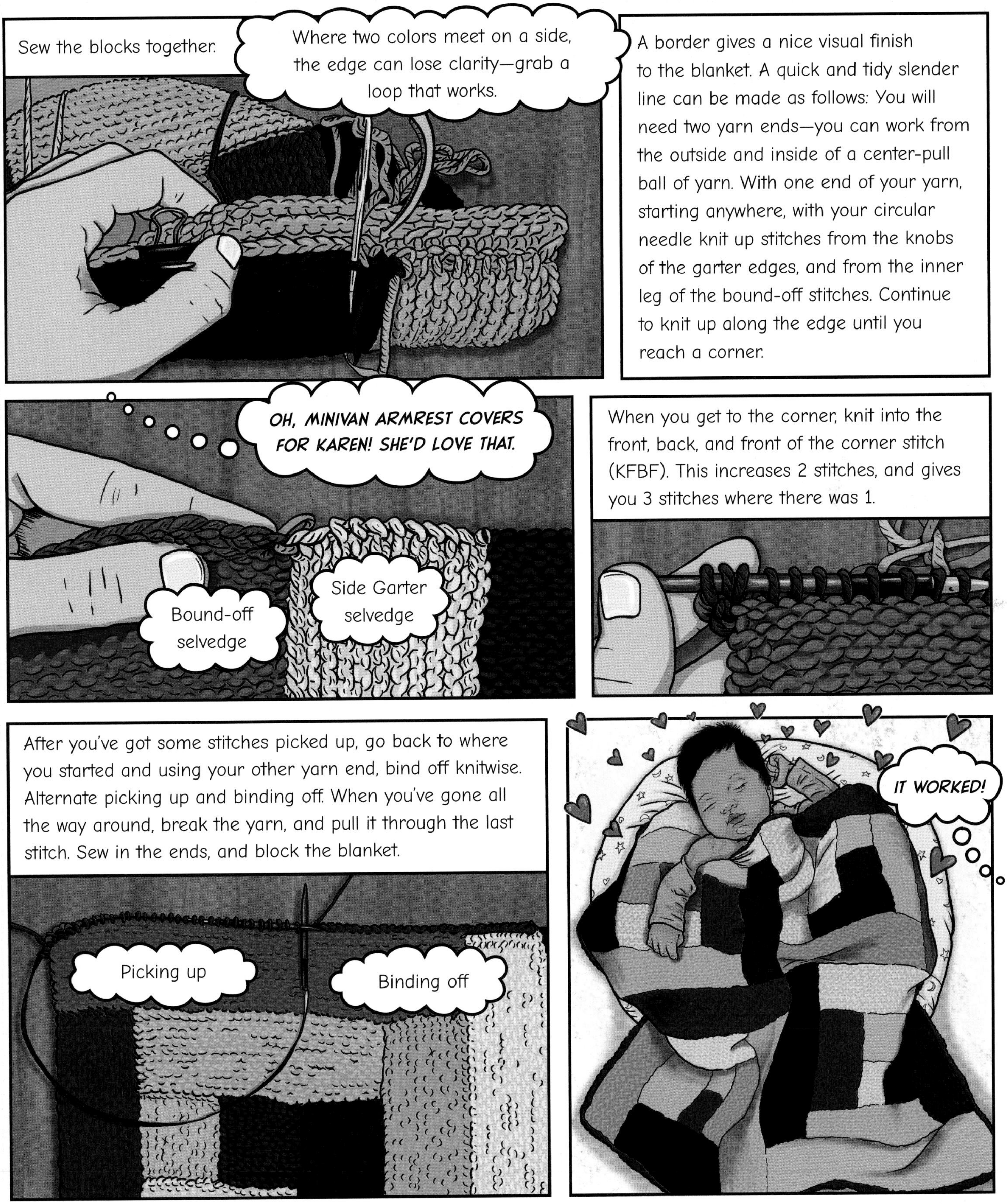
Sew the blocks together.
Where two colors meet on a side, the edge can lose clarity—grab a loop that works.
A border gives a nice visual finish to the blanket. A quick and tidy slender line can be made as follows: You will need two yarn ends—you can work from the outside and inside of a center-pull ball of yarn. With one end of your yarn, starting anywhere, with your circular needle knit up stitches from the knobs of the garter edges, and from the inner leg of the bound-off stitches. Continue to knit up along the edge until you reach a corner.
OH, MINIVAN ARMREST COVERS FOR KAREN! SHE'D LOVE THAT.
Bound-off selvedge
Side Garter selvedge
When you get to the corner, knit into the front, back, and front of the corner stitch (KFBF). This increases 2 stitches, and gives you 3 stitches where there was 1.
After you've got some stitches picked up, go back to where you started and using your other yarn end, bind off knitwise. Alternate picking up and binding off. When you've gone all the way around, break the yarn, and pull it through the last stitch. Sew in the ends, and block the blanket.
Picking up
Binding off
IT WORKED!

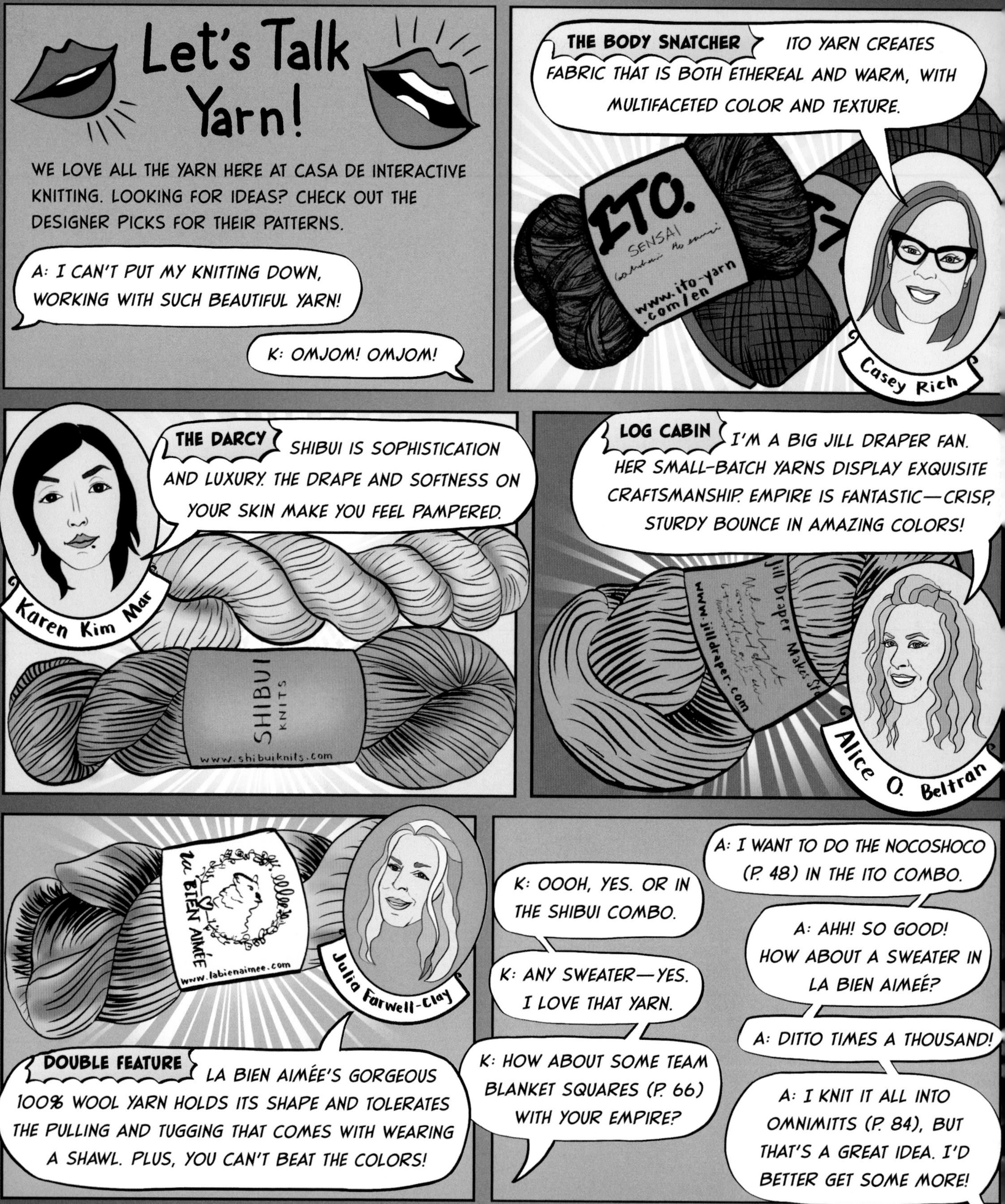
Let's Talk Yarn!
WE LOVE ALL THE YARN HERE AT CASA DE INTERACTIVE KNITTING. LOOKING FOR IDEAS? CHECK OUT THE DESIGNER PICKS FOR THEIR PATTERNS.
A: I CAN'T PUT MY KNITTING DOWN, WORKING WITH SUCH BEAUTIFUL YARN!
K: OMJOM! OMJOM!
THE BODY SNATCHER ITO YARN CREATES FABRIC THAT IS BOTH ETHEREAL AND WARM, WITH MULTIFACETED COLOR AND TEXTURE.
ITO.
SENSAI
www.ito-yarn.com/en
Casey Rich
THE DARCY SHIBUI IS SOPHISTICATION AND LUXURY. THE DRAPE AND SOFTNESS ON YOUR SKIN MAKE YOU FEEL PAMPERED.
Karen Kim Mar
SHIBUI KNITS
www.shibuiknits.com
LOG CABIN I'M A BIG JILL DRAPER FAN. HER SMALL-BATCH YARNS DISPLAY EXQUISITE CRAFTSMANSHIP. EMPIRE IS FANTASTIC—CRISP, STURDY BOUNCE IN AMAZING COLORS!
Jill Draper Makes Stuff
www.jilldraper.com
Alice O. Beltran
La BIEN AIMÉE
www.labienaimee.com
Julia Farwell-Clay
DOUBLE FEATURE LA BIEN AIMÉE'S GORGEOUS 100% WOOL YARN HOLDS ITS SHAPE AND TOLERATES THE PULLING AND TUGGING THAT COMES WITH WEARING A SHAWL. PLUS, YOU CAN'T BEAT THE COLORS!
A: I WANT TO DO THE NOCOSHOCO (P. 48) IN THE ITO COMBO.
K: OOOH, YES. OR IN THE SHIBUI COMBO.
A: AHH! SO GOOD! HOW ABOUT A SWEATER IN LA BIEN AIMÉE?
K: ANY SWEATER—YES. I LOVE THAT YARN.
A: DITTO TIMES A THOUSAND!
K: HOW ABOUT SOME TEAM BLANKET SQUARES (P. 66) WITH YOUR EMPIRE?
A: I KNIT IT ALL INTO OMNIMITTS (P. 84), BUT THAT'S A GREAT IDEA. I'D BETTER GET SOME MORE!

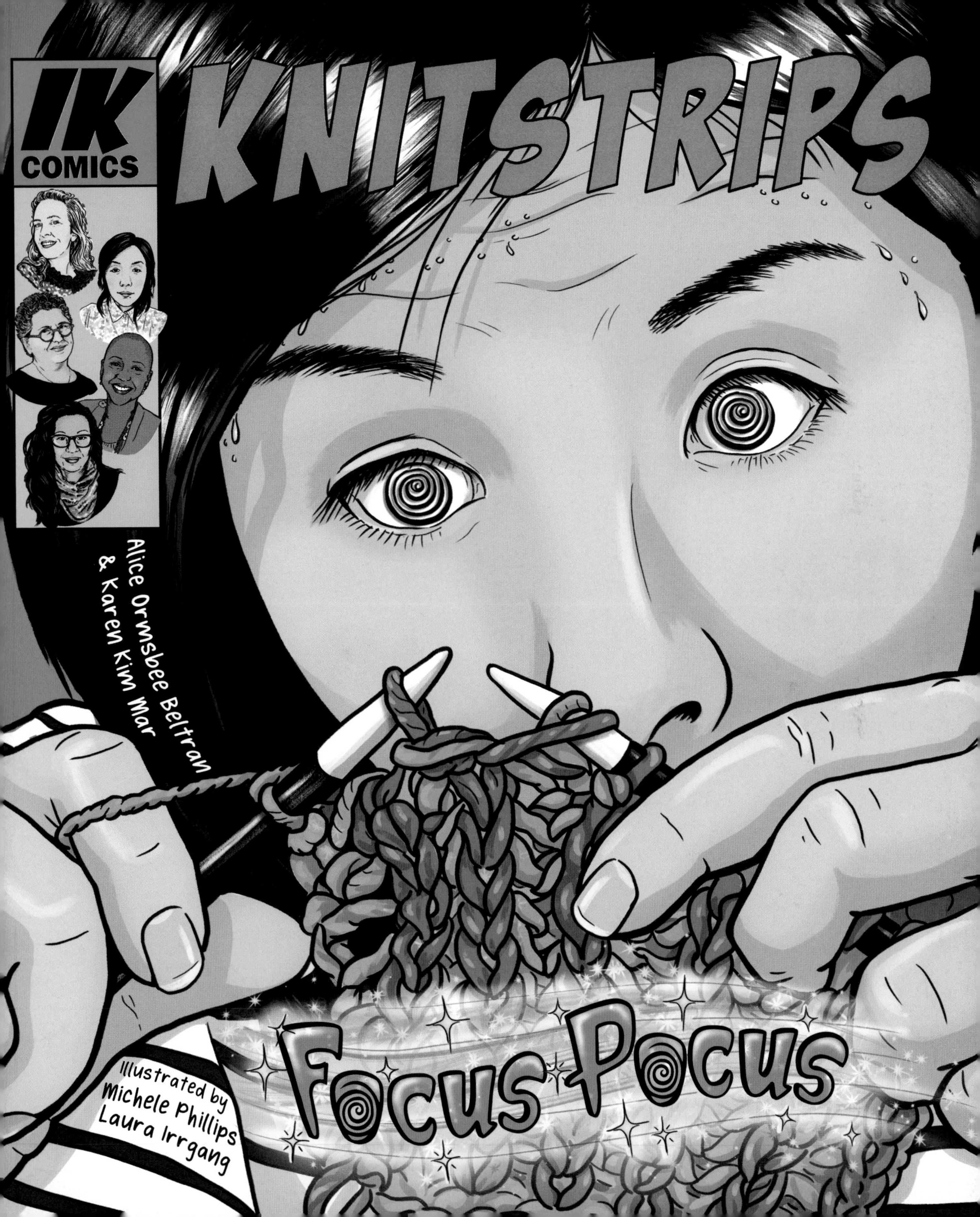
IK
COMICS
KNITSTRIPS
Alice Ormsbee Beltran
& Karen Kim Mar
Focus Pocus
Illustrated by
Michele Phillips
Laura Irrgang

Focus Pocus

We love mindless knitting at Casa de IK. But there are times when we revel in the mental exercise of plotting, counting, charting, and above all, exerting focus. The brain waves are at full tilt, and we're willing to turn the TV off and pay attention, by golly.

Karen thought laser-focus was only for quilters and scrapbookers, until she went down the rabbit hole of two-color brioche knitting. Karen's idea of colorwork is using a single strand of variegated yarn, so navigating two different strands while working each side twice meant she had to CON-CEN-TRATE! After a good night's sleep, with her careful notes, and her snacks put away for later, Karen thought-fully knit her two strands while whispering the stitch pattern. Focus was rewarded, as two-color brioche appeared before her eyes.

Alice loves Stockinette in the round and Garter stitch. So restful. But every so often, an idea like intentional color pooling comes along and mesmerizes her. Her languor falls away, replaced by wild-eyed attention. Her sole purpose is to get the rabbit out of the hat, and she will do Whatever It Takes. Alice feverishly knit a 2-inch strip for 20 feet, diced it into pieces, and seamed them up. Et voilà! Beautiful bits of color.

This issue explores techniques that require a little extra effort but have terrific payoff. Use them in the projects presented, or take them and run with them, IK-style. Embrace your focus pocus and make some magic!

I'M DOIN' IT.

The Dashwood

BY ALICE ORMSBEE BELTRAN

A SOFT AND LUXE CIRCULAR PIECE, KNIT FROM THE CENTER OUT. THE SENSIBLE WILL DELIGHT IN VERSATILE WEARABILITY AND A SURPRISINGLY SMALL PACKED-DOWN FOOTPRINT. THE COLOR PLAY AND LETTUCE-LEAF EDGE WILL SATISFY THE MOST EBULLIENT SENSIBILITY.

MATERIALS: A laceweight 70/30 kid mohair/silk blend. 920 y (840 m) of the main color (color 1) and 480 y (420 m) of the contrasting color (color 2). DPNs, 16 in (41 cm) and 24 in (61 cm) circular needles for gauge. **GAUGE:** Airy. Colorwork at this gauge with this type of yarn will give you a glimpse of the carried colors from the front, amidst the fuzzy halo of each color. Dreamy!* **SIZE:** Knit to fit. A minimum final diameter of 36 in (91 cm) is recommended to allow for tying around the neck. **TECHNIQUES:** Extra-loose colorwork, lettuce-leaf edge.

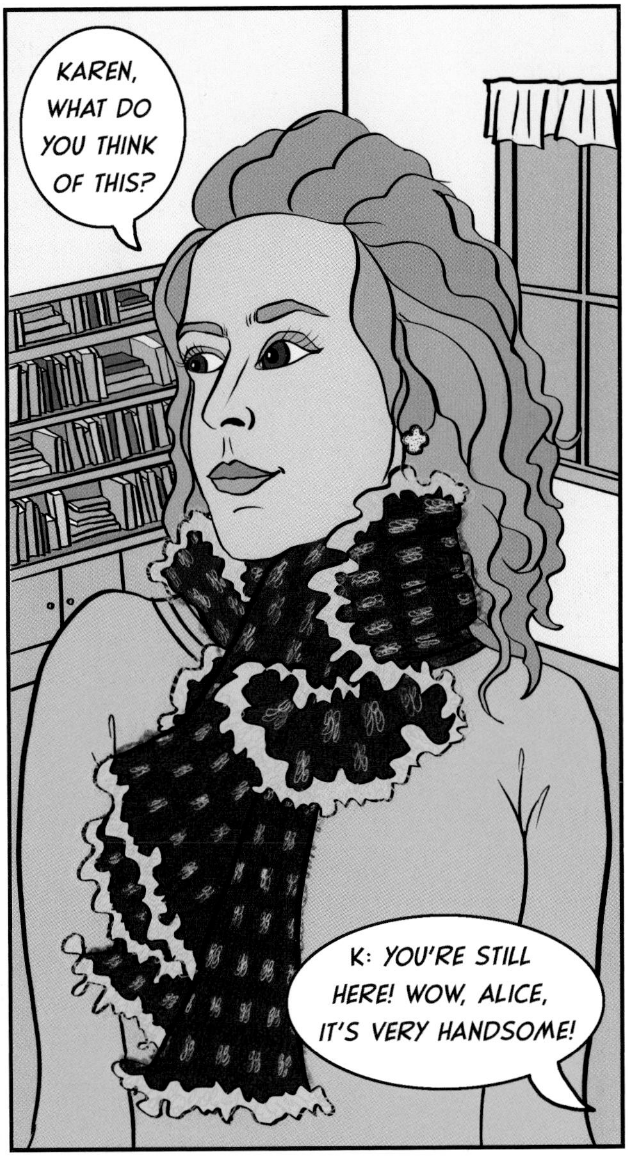
KAREN, WHAT DO YOU THINK OF THIS?
K: YOU'RE STILL HERE! WOW, ALICE, IT'S VERY HANDSOME!

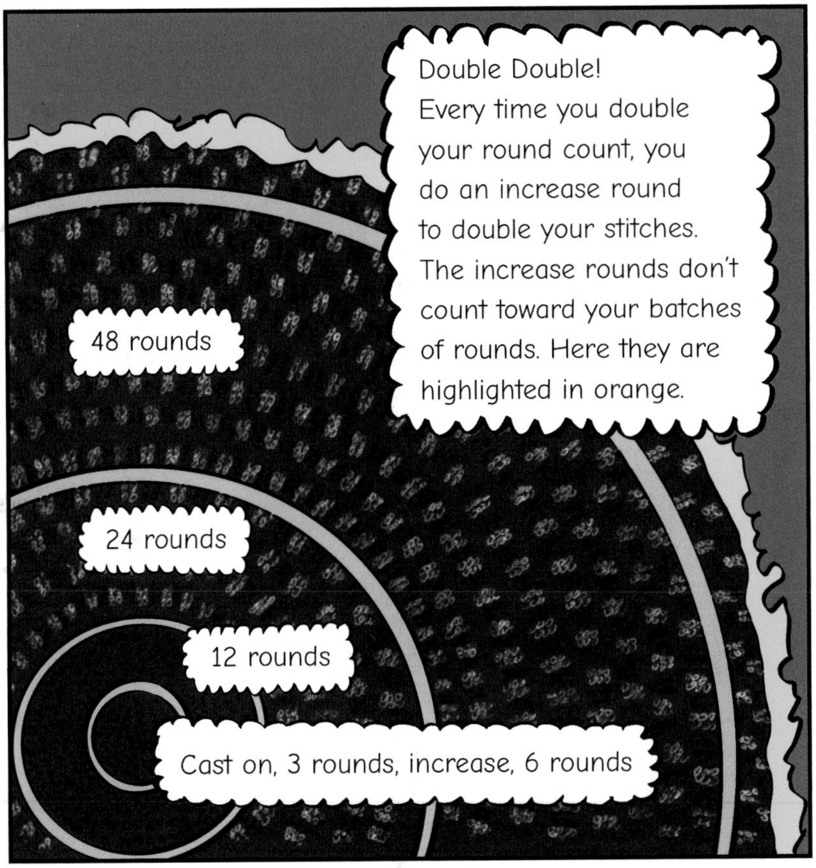
Double Double! Every time you double your round count, you do an increase round to double your stitches. The increase rounds don't count toward your batches of rounds. Here they are highlighted in orange.
48 rounds
24 rounds
12 rounds
Cast on, 3 rounds, increase, 6 rounds

METHOD: Starting at the center, you work in the round and double the stitches with each doubling of the rounds. You may knit it in a solid color or add colorwork with the chart.

Colorwork must be VERY loose! Heed our advice to avert heartbreak.

* "The Mind of a Designer: When Mohair Met Intarsia," by Julia Farwell-Clay. www.moderndailyknitting.com

Here's how: You will be knitting ever-doubling sets of rounds (3, 6, 12, 24, etc.) with a stitch-doubling increase round between them. With your main color (1), cast on 9 stitches with any method you like. KFB across (18 sts). This is your first increase round.

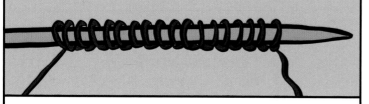

The first bit is worked back and forth, to make joining the round easier. So: turn and purl a row. Turn and knit a row. Turn and purl a row. This completes three rows on 18 sts.

Join and knit in the round for 6 rounds. KFB across (72 sts). You've doubled your stitches again! Knit around for 12 rounds. You may move onto your 16" circulars somewhere in these rounds. Place a marker at the beginning of your round. Your work will look like a dream catcher.

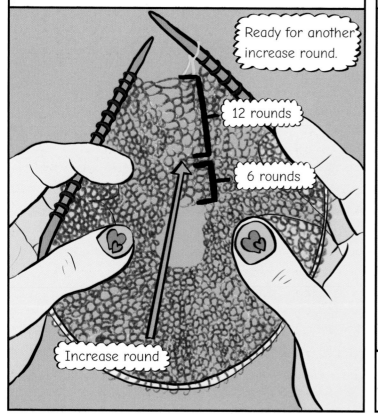

Ready for another increase round.

12 rounds

6 rounds

Increase round

KFB across (36 sts), divide work onto 3 DPNs. This was your second increase round; you've doubled your stitches.

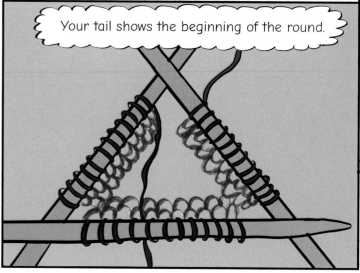

Your tail shows the beginning of the round.

KFB across (144 sts). This next set of 24 rounds is where you will start your colorwork. Start with your contrasting color (2) and in the lower right corner of the chart. Work the chart twice, for a total of 24 rounds. If monochromatic is your fancy, then knit with the main yarn for the 24 rounds.

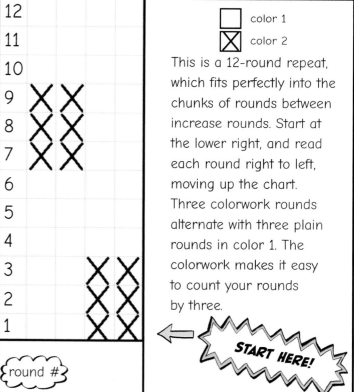

☐	color 1
☒	color 2

This is a 12-round repeat, which fits perfectly into the chunks of rounds between increase rounds. Start at the lower right, and read each round right to left, moving up the chart. Three colorwork rounds alternate with three plain rounds in color 1. The colorwork makes it easy to count your rounds by three.

START HERE!

round #

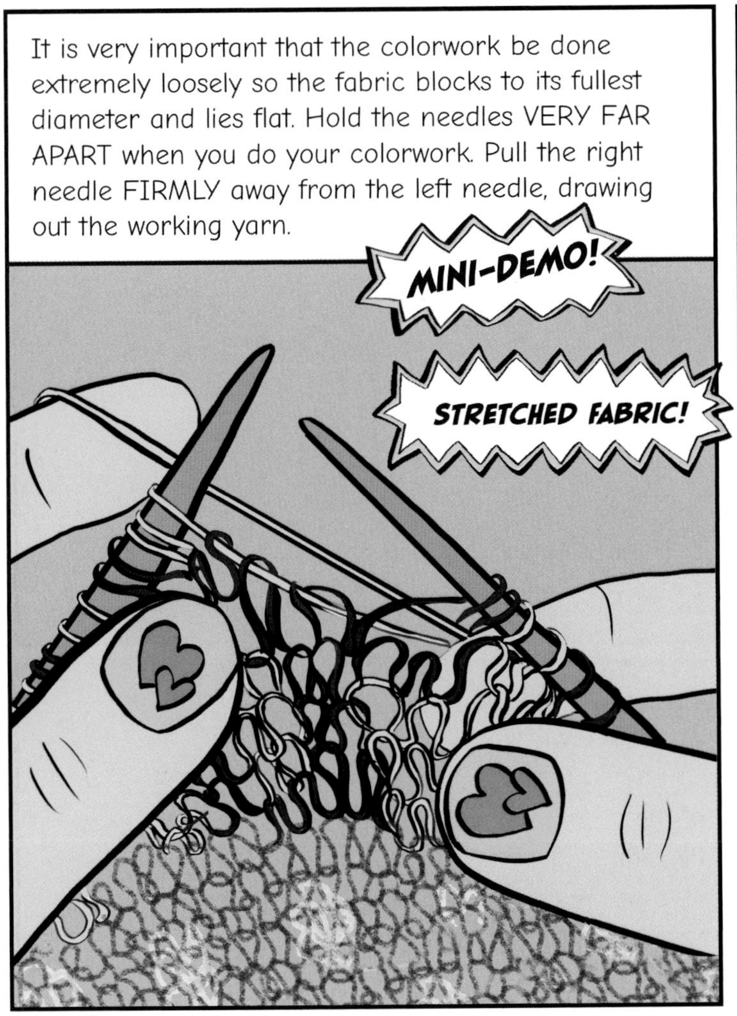
It is very important that the colorwork be done extremely loosely so the fabric blocks to its fullest diameter and lies flat. Hold the needles VERY FAR APART when you do your colorwork. Pull the right needle FIRMLY away from the left needle, drawing out the working yarn.
MINI-DEMO!
STRETCHED FABRIC!

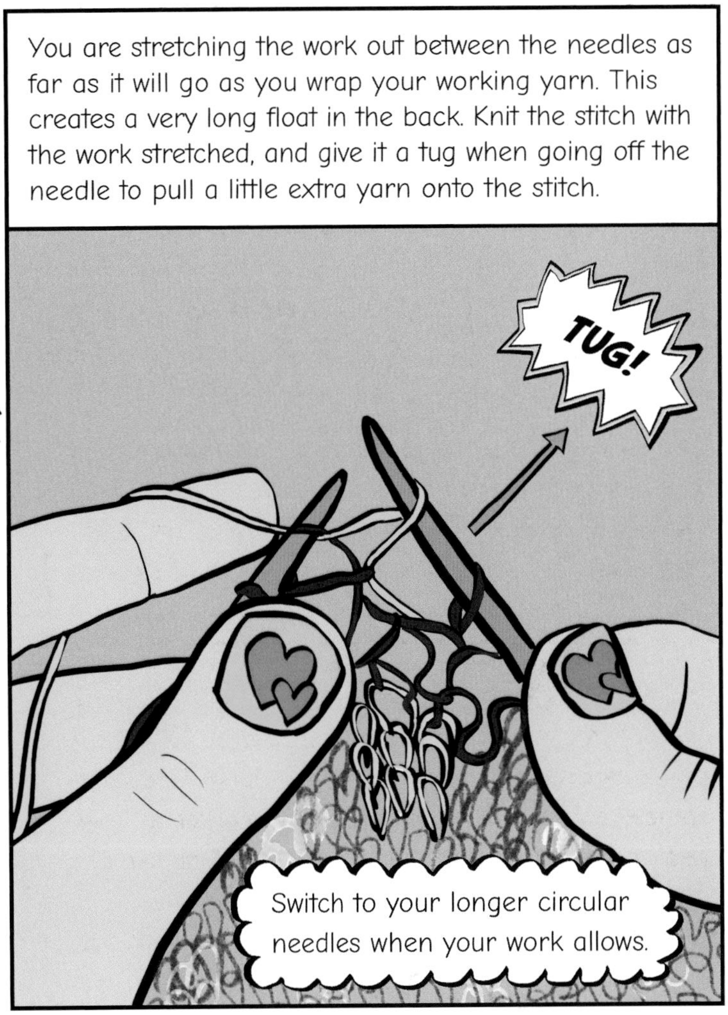
You are stretching the work out between the needles as far as it will go as you wrap your working yarn. This creates a very long float in the back. Knit the stitch with the work stretched, and give it a tug when going off the needle to pull a little extra yarn onto the stitch.
TUG!
Switch to your longer circular needles when your work allows.

Test your floats often by stretching your work. If it stretches easily, your floats are loose enough. If it tugs and puckers, they are too tight. Unravel them and try again, with hands farther apart and bigger tugs.

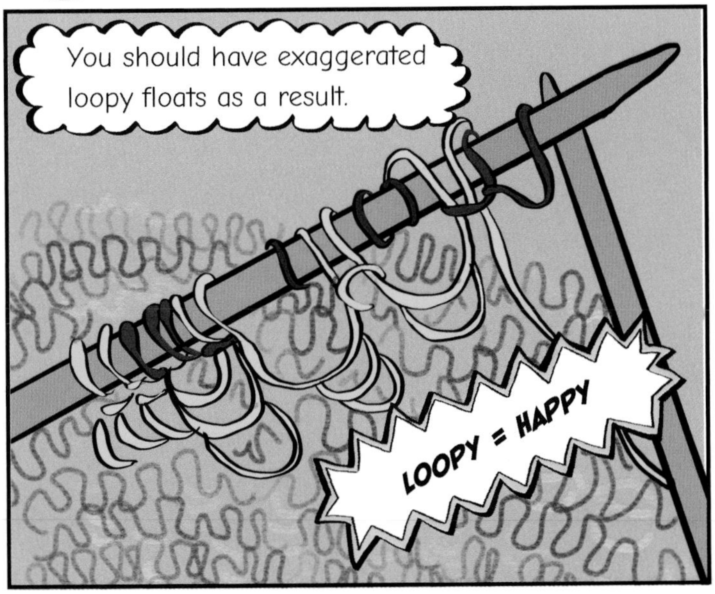
You should have exaggerated loopy floats as a result.
LOOPY = HAPPY

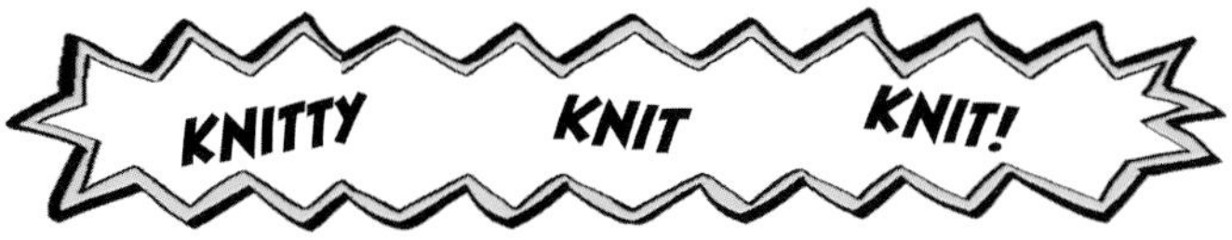
KNITTY KNIT KNIT!

KFB across (288 sts). Work 48 rounds with or without colorwork. KFB across (576 sts). Continue to your desired finished diameter. 36 in to 48 in (91 cm to 122 cm) is recommended, so it will be long enough to tie around your neck and have the ends pouf nicely. You may use your round gauge from your blocked swatch to determine your total round count (very sensible), or just hold the cast-on center at the back of your neck, and bunch up and draw the rest over a shoulder, to see half of the diameter.

Now, "lettuce" edge and seam! When you've reached your desired diameter, at the beginning of the next round, and in the contrasting color, (KFB, k1) across. Knit one round plain. (KFB, k1) across again. Now bind off loosely. You have one small seam to sew up at the back-and-forth start. Thread your darning needle with the tail of yarn there to close up the seam. Fasten off. Weave in ends.

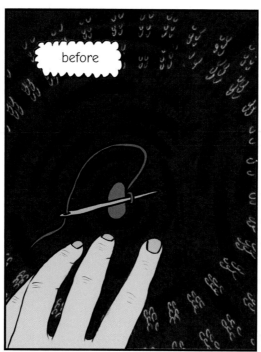

before

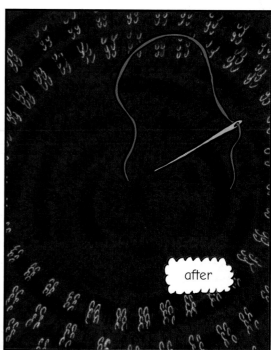

after

It will look lumpy. Don't fret! Wet block it as you did your swatch, and feel deep satisfaction when your loose floats obligingly stretch with the fabric into a nice flat circle.

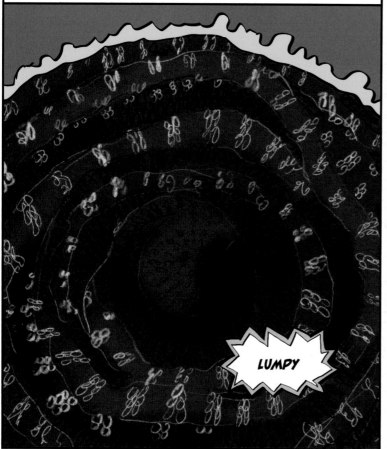

LUMPY

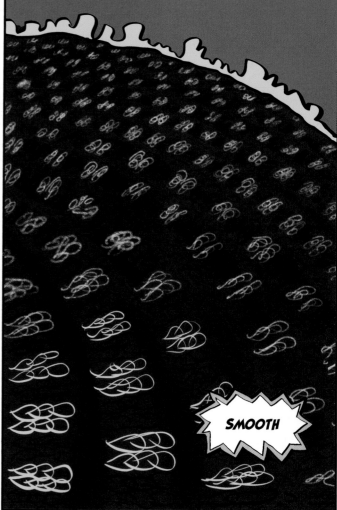

SMOOTH

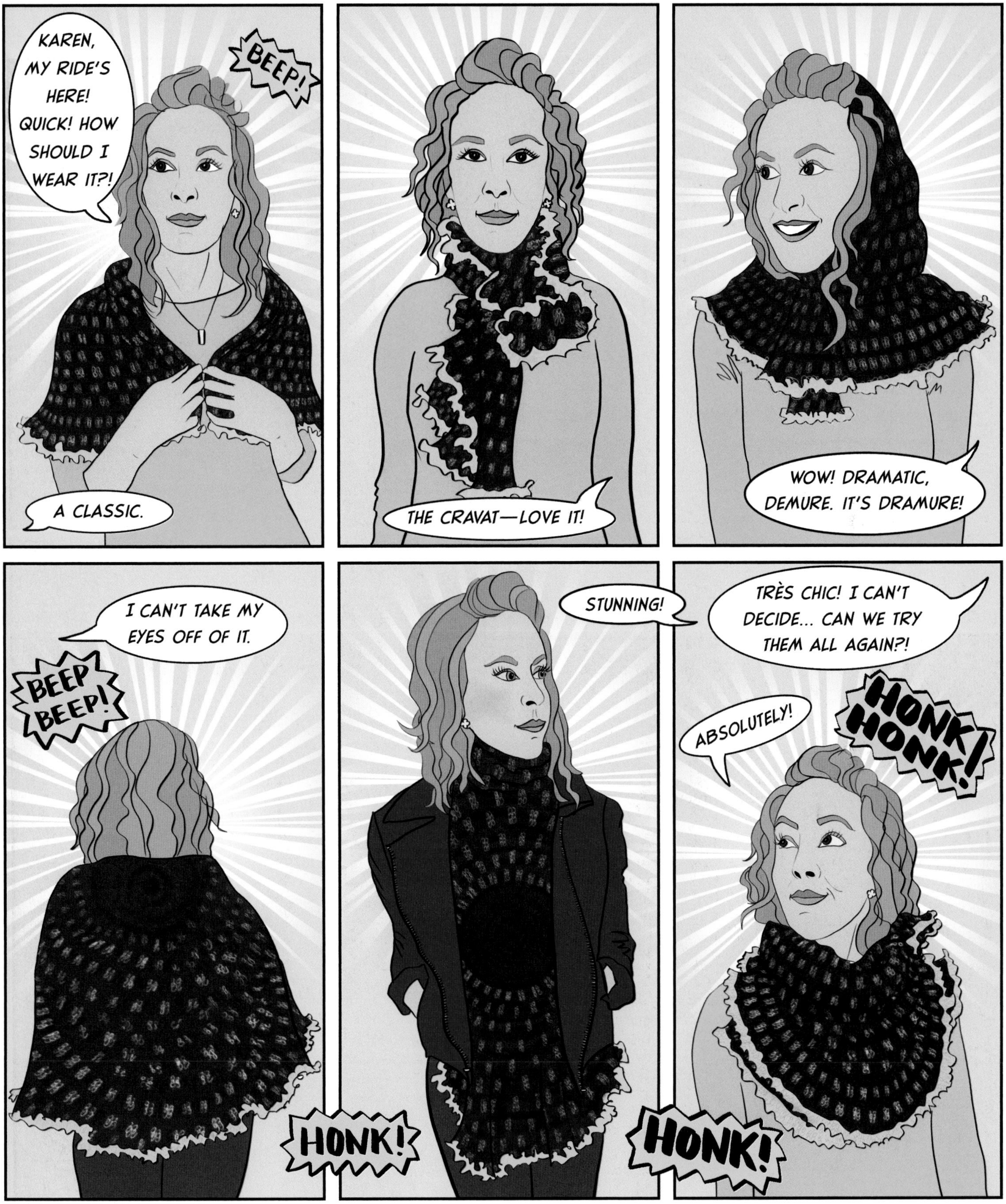
KAREN, MY RIDE'S HERE! QUICK! HOW SHOULD I WEAR IT?!
BEEP!
A CLASSIC.
THE CRAVAT—LOVE IT!
WOW! DRAMATIC, DEMURE. IT'S DRAMURE!
I CAN'T TAKE MY EYES OFF OF IT.
BEEP BEEP!
HONK!
STUNNING!
HONK!
TRÈS CHIC! I CAN'T DECIDE... CAN WE TRY THEM ALL AGAIN?!
HONK! HONK!
ABSOLUTELY!

WOWL!

BY JEANETTE SLOAN

SNUGGLY MEETS STATEMENT IN THIS REVERSIBLE TWO-COLOR BRIOCHE COWL WITH TONS OF SQUISH AND VOLUME. PULL IT UP TO YOUR EARS OR WEAR IT WITH A BIT MORE SLOUCH. WHETHER YOU WEAR IT OR GIFT IT, THIS COWL IS SURE TO GET A "WOW!"

MATERIALS: DK- to Aran-weight yarn in two contrasting colors (A and B). One circular needle in the size that gives the gauge you like. **TECHNIQUES:** Two-color brioche (2CB), Gauge Translation (p. 67). **GAUGE:** Medium gauge will maximize the volume and squish. Cast on an odd number of stitches and follow the steps below to work a swatch in two-color brioche. **SIZE:** Decide the size you'd like your cowl to be. Use a measuring tape to determine the circumference and height or measure an existing favorite cowl. Divide the circumference in half for the target length of each block. Divide that length in half for the width of Part 1 and the length of Part 2. The sample cowl is 28 in (71 cm) around and 10 in (25 cm) tall. Each block is 14 in (35 cm) wide. Each part is 7 in (17.5 cm) wide.

OK BOBA!
MY FRIEND JOSÉ IS GOING TO LOVE THIS HIGH-TECH COWL!

METHOD: The cowl is made of two blocks. The blocks are identical. Each block has two parts. The first part is worked in one direction, then stitches are picked up and worked from the right front edge, perpendicular to the first part. For added contrast, the yarns are reversed in the alternate parts. Using your blocked gauge, calculate how many stitches you'll need for the first part of your block.

Seam
Block 1
Part 1
Part 2
10 in/25 cm
14 in/35 cm
Block 2
Part 1
Part 2
10 in/25 cm
14 in/35 cm
28 in/71 cm

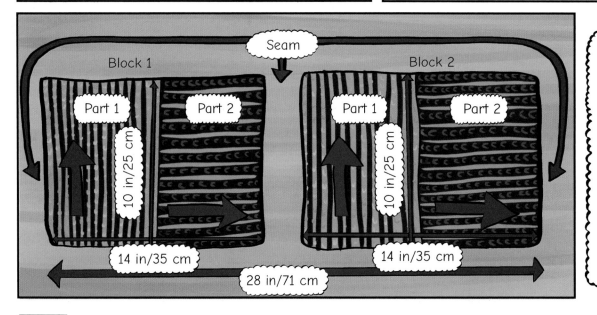

The right side (RS) is where the cast-on or picked-up yarn color forms the knitted columns. To change colors for the second part of the block, switch your yarns A and B!

ABBREVIATIONS

sl1: Slip one purlwise. **yf:** Bring the yarn from the back to the front, between the needles. **yo:** Yarn goes diagonally over the right needle from front to back, created by brk. **RS:** Right Side. The front side. Cast-on color (A) forms the knitted columns. **WS:** Wrong Side. The back. Your cast-on color is in the background, and your other color (B) forms the knitted columns. **yoATN:** Yarn over around the needle. Yarn is in the front of the work, move it over the right needle to the back and counterclockwise around the needle to bring it back to front. **brk:** Brioche knit. Yarn will be in the front. With yarn in front, knit the next stitch together with its yarn over. brk creates a yo. **brp:** Brioche purl. It is preceded by a yoATN. Yarn will be in the front. With yarn in front, purl together stitch with yarn over.

2CB is worked back and forth, on a circular needle. You knit two strands across the needle one at a time, over two passes. In other words, you work each side twice, thus making two rows before turning the work. That's why you need a circular needle—to slide the work back and work the row a second time!

I'M GOING TO PICK HIS FAVORITE COLORS!

With color A, long-tail cast on an odd number of stitches based on your size calculations for the first part of the first block. Do the two set-up rows, then work your 4-row repeats as follows.

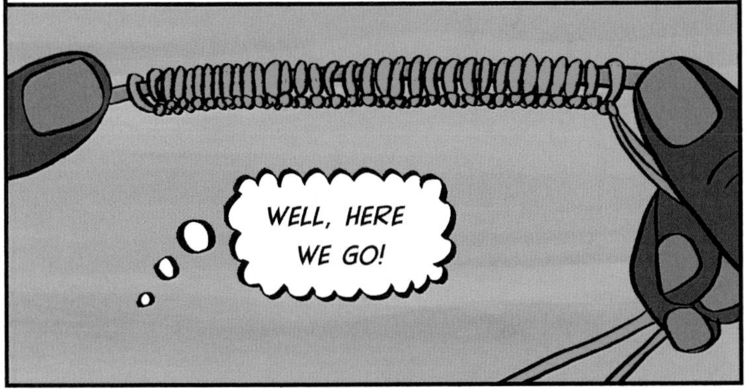
WELL, HERE WE GO!

Set-Up Row 1: (Color A) p1, *sl1, yoATN, p1. Repeat from * to end. Do not turn the work.

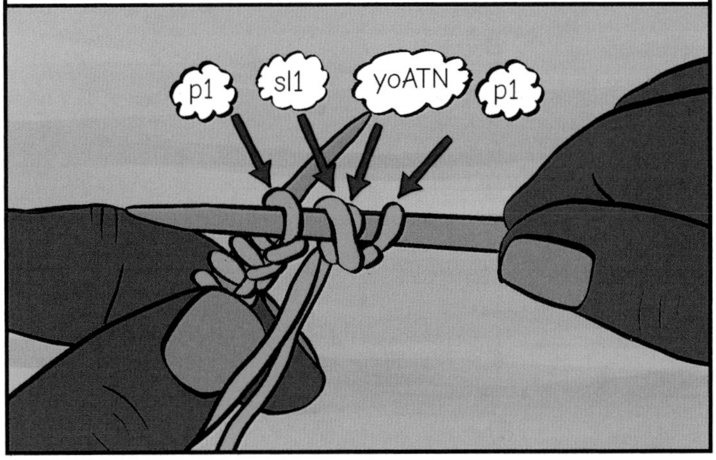
p1
sl1
yoATN
p1

Set-Up Row 2: Slide work back to work the same side again. (Color B) Sl1, knit the next st with its yo. *yf, sl1, brk. Repeat from * to last st, drop color B so yarn stays in the back, sl1. Turn work to begin the 4-row repeats.

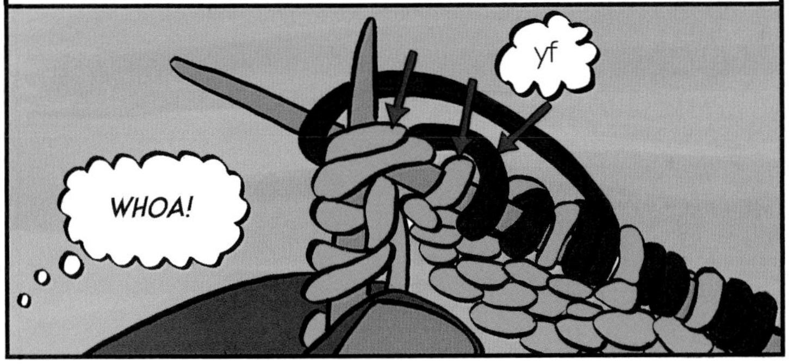
yf
WHOA!

Row 1: (RS, color A) K1, *yf, sl1, brk. Repeat from * to last 2 sts, yf, sl1, k1. Do not turn the work.

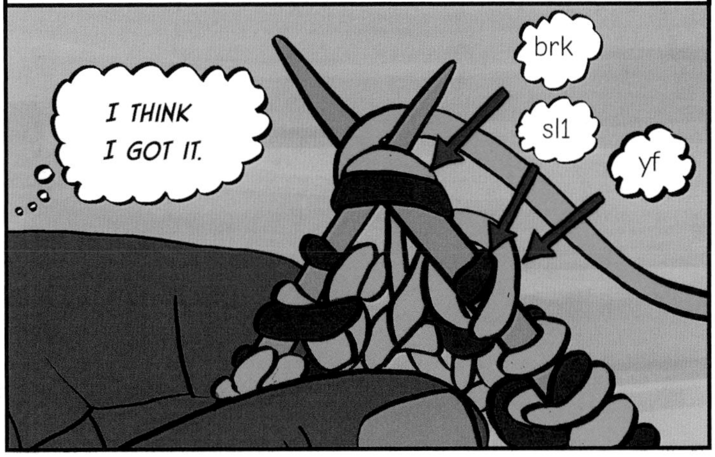
I THINK I GOT IT.
brk
sl1
yf

Row 2: Slide work back to work the same side again. (RS, color B) Sl1, purl the next stitch with its yo *sl1, yoATN, brp. Repeat from * to the last st, drop color B so it is at the front of the work, sl1. Turn the work.

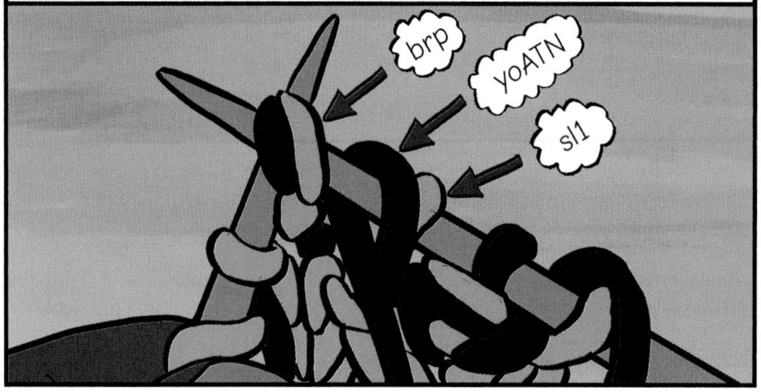
brp
yoATN
sl1

Row 3: (WS, color A) P1, *sl1, yoATN, brp. Repeat from * to last 2 sts, sl1, yo around the needle, p1. Do not turn the work.

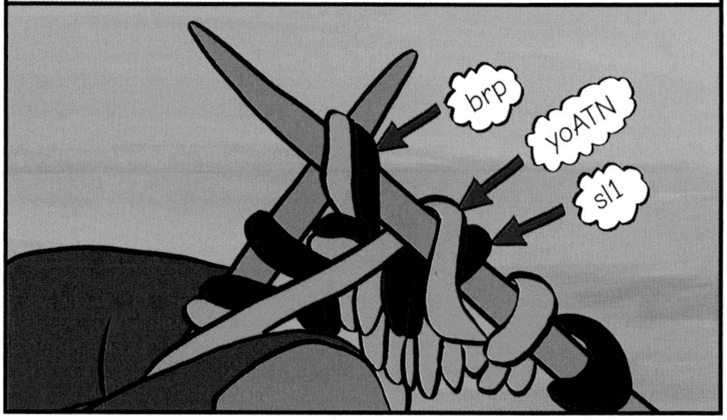
brp
yoATN
sl1

Row 4: Slide work back to work the same side again. (WS, color B) Sl1, knit the stitch with its yo, *yf, sl1, brk. Repeat from * to last st, drop color B so the yarn is in back, sl1. Turn the work.

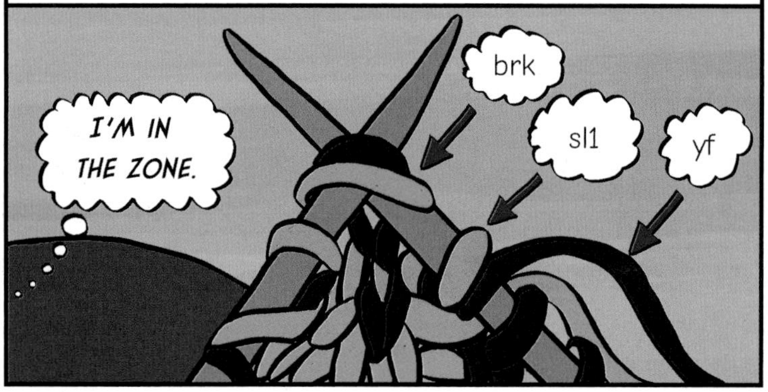
I'M IN THE ZONE.
brk
sl1
yf

Repeat the last 4 rows until you reach your desired length. Make sure you end Part 1 by working the last row of the 4-row repeat.

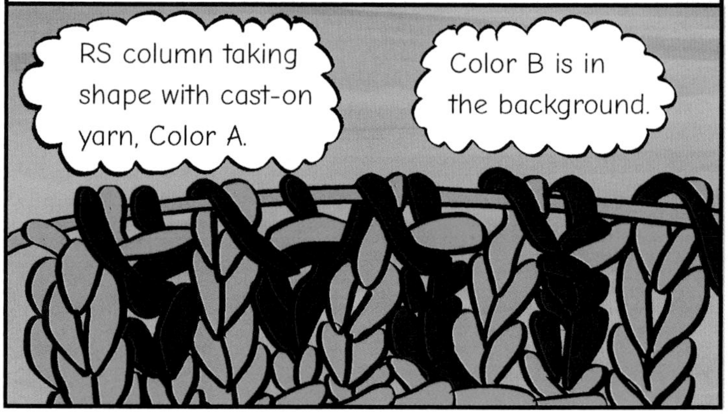
RS column taking shape with cast-on yarn, Color A.
Color B is in the background.

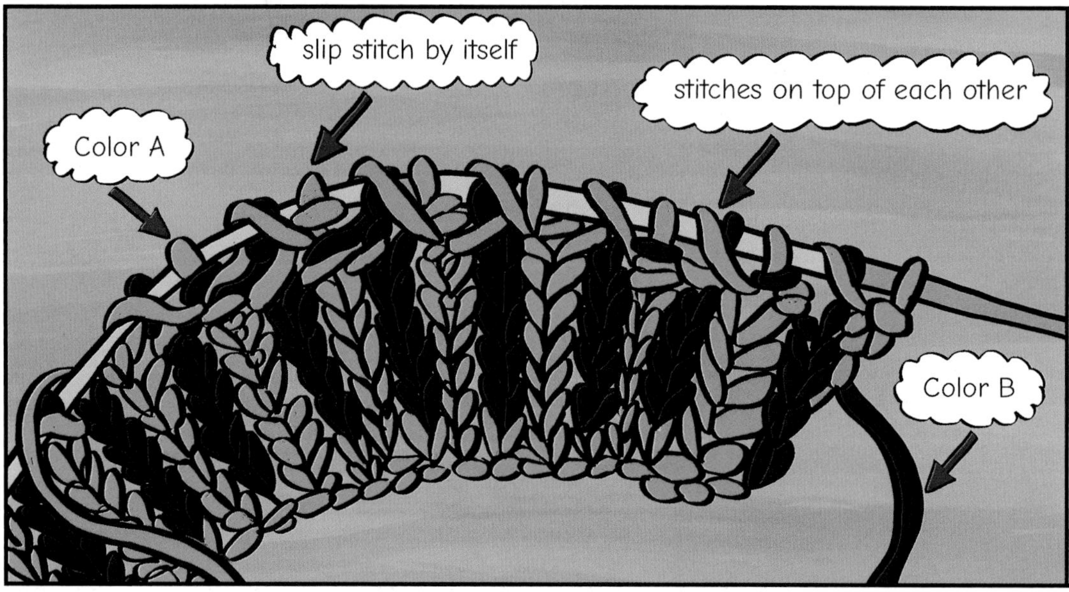
slip stitch by itself
stitches on top of each other
Color A
Color B

Forget where you are? The stitches by themselves are always slipped, and the stitch pairs on top of each other are either brk or brp depending on the row. The working yarn color is always OPPOSITE the color of the stitches by themselves.

Now to bind off: Break B. Using A, k1, p1, bind off 1, *move yarn between needles to back, then knit the stitch with its yo. Bind off 1. Bring yarn forward between needles and p1. Bind off 1. Repeat from * to last 2 stitches. Move yarn back, k1, bind off last stitch. Break off yarn and thread through last stitch.

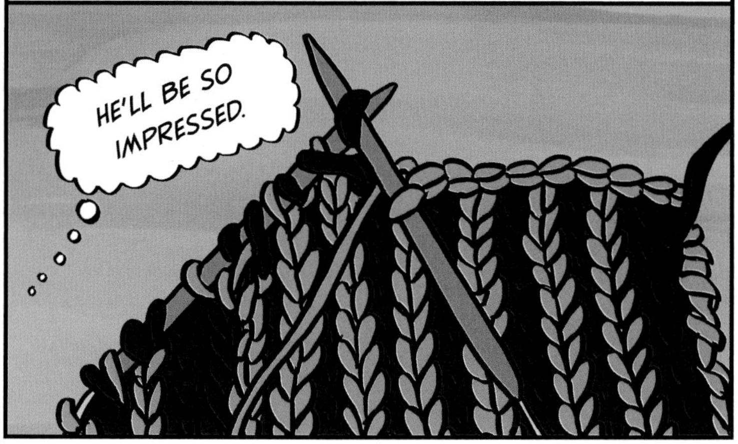
HE'LL BE SO IMPRESSED.

Now do Part 2. Use Gauge Translation to calculate your stitches by multiplying the side-edge length by your blocked gauge. Make it an odd number. With RS facing, pick up and knit the stitches from the side edge by picking up both loops of the edge stitch. This is your "cast-on" row, and the color you use will make knit columns on the RS. You can use A to match Part 1, or use B and switch the colors (swap A and B in the directions).

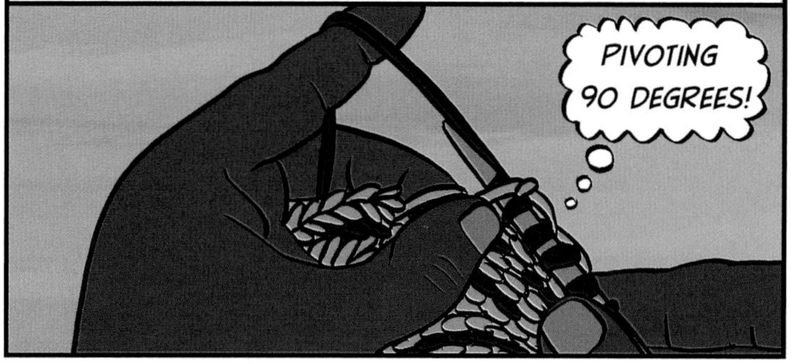
PIVOTING 90 DEGREES!

Turn work so the WS is facing and the working yarn is at the right side. Work Set-Up Rows 1 and 2. Turn work. Continue in the 4-row repeat until the length matches the width of the first half. Bind off after working the last row of the 4-row repeat. This completes Block 1. Take it from the top and make Block 2!

KNITTY KNIT KNIT!

Block the blocks. Seam together the two blocks. Sew in the ends.

The block will tend to pull in widthwise—give the bound-off edges of Part 2 of the blocks some attention while blocking to match the lengths of Part 1 of the blocks.

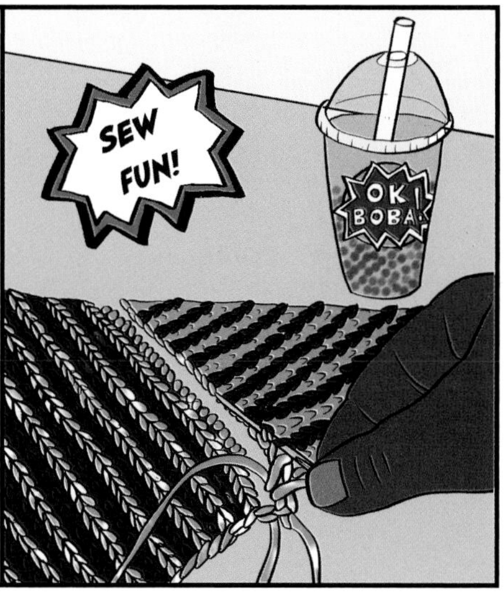
SEW FUN!
OK BOBA!

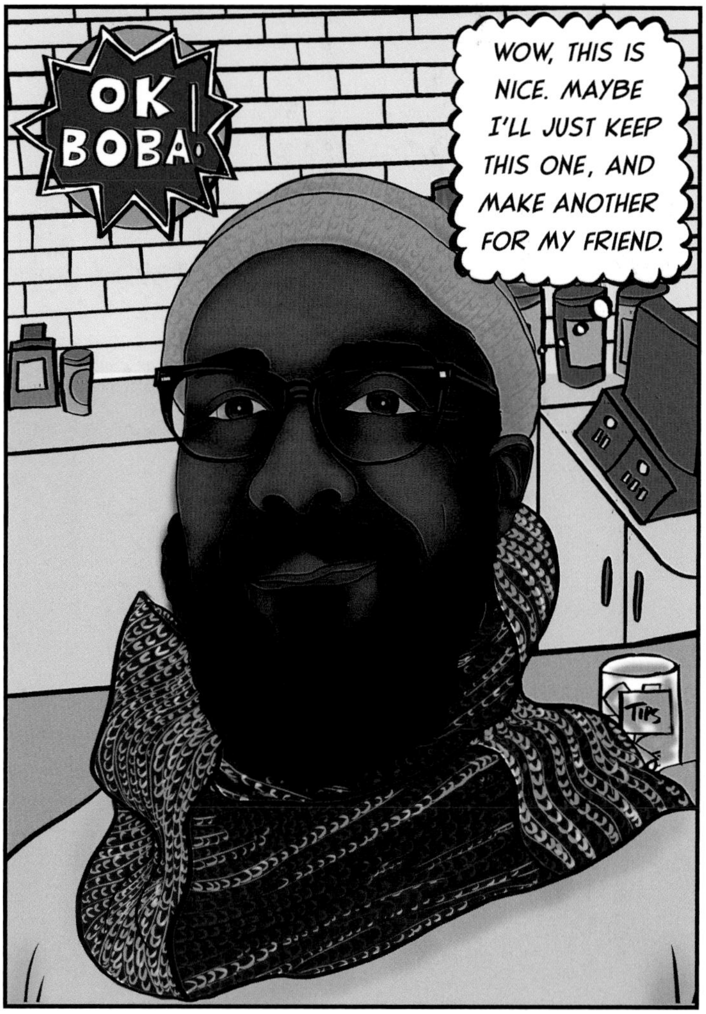
OK BOBA!
WOW, THIS IS NICE. MAYBE I'LL JUST KEEP THIS ONE, AND MAKE ANOTHER FOR MY FRIEND.
TIPS

NOCOSHOCO

(nuh-KAH-shuh-koh)

BY KAREN KIM MAR & ALICE ORMSBEE BELTRAN

THIS LOVELY NO-COLD-SHOULDERS COZY, AKA NOCOSHOCO, KEEPS YOUR SHOULDERS SNUG THROUGH THE NIGHT WITH NO UNCOMFORTABLE BUNCHING AROUND THE WAIST. THE BEAUTIFUL DETAILS ARE TOO GOOD TO KEEP UNDER THE COVERS. LAYER AND WEAR—WE WON'T TELL ANYONE YOU'RE IN YOUR PAJAMAS.

TECHNIQUE: Provisional cast-on (p. 17), M1R & M1L (p. 93), Gauge Translation (p. 67), knit 5 below bind-off (K5BBO), evenly spaced decreases (p. 59). **MATERIALS:** About two-thirds your standard sweater's worth of yarn, sock to worsted weight. Consider linen for summer and wool for winter. Stitch markers, waste yarn, stitch holder (optional), long circular needle, DPNs for sleeves.
GAUGE: Soft or Medium. Determine your stitch and row gauge in Stockinette stitch (St st) and in 1x1 ribbing.

OOH, A PAJAMA SWEATER! BRILLIANT IDEA, HARMONY!

YES, THANK YOU!

Neck

Arm

Length

Torso

SIZE: Measure the following while wearing your favorite PJs. ARM: largest arm circumference plus 3 in (7.5 cm) of ease; LENGTH: over-the-shoulder body length from empire waist front and back plus 3 in (7.5 cm) of ease; NECK: width for back of neck; TORSO: widest circumference of torso divided by 2, plus 2 in (5 cm) of ease; SHOULDER: Take your (TORSO - NECK)/2 to find the width of each side, on either side between the end of the sleeve and the edge of the neck.

SAY GOODBYE TO COLD SHOULDERS!

Marker yarn
8
7
7
4
9
1
2
5
6
9
3
Marker yarn
7
8
7

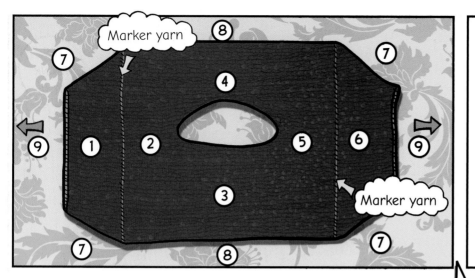

1) Cast on left sleeve, increase to full width; **2)** Work shoulder depth; **3)** Work across the back; **4)** Work the front, shaping neckline; **5)** Join front and back stitches and work shoulder depth; **6)** Decrease down to sleeve width on right sleeve; **7)** Fold the garment and seam up the sides and sleeves; **8)** Pick up stitches around, work 1x1 ribbing, then KB5BO; **9)** Work live stitches on sleeves in the round, then KB5BO.

METHOD: Nocoshoco is knit sideways, back and forth, in one piece. Multiply your St st gauge by your ARM, and **1)** provisionally cast on those stitches. Increase on every RS as follows: M1R after the first stitch, and M1L before the last stitch. Work WS rows plain. Continue, maintaining this increase, until the width of the piece equals your LENGTH measurement. That's your left sleeve. Mark this row: thread your darning needle with your marker yarn and run it through the stitches. This lets you line up with your shoulder when you try it on and also serves as a guide to measure your SHOULDER depth.

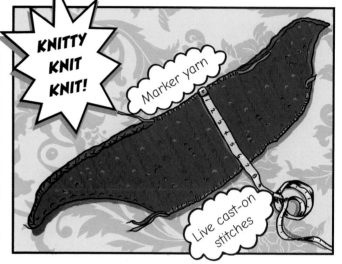

KNITTY KNIT KNIT!
Marker yarn
Live cast-on stitches

2) Work in St st for the depth of the shoulder measurement. You are at the edge of the neck and will work the back only. **3)** On the RS, knit half the stitches, and put the second half on waste yarn or a holder. Work the back sts in plain St st for the distance = NECK. Let your row count be even. Cut yarn, place the stitches on waste yarn. Count your rows.

Use a strong, smooth contrasting yarn to hold your live stitches. Cotton is ideal.

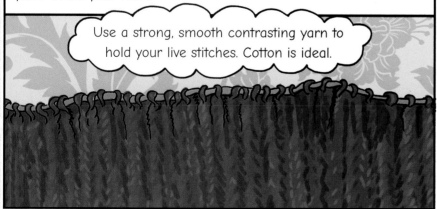

4) Next you'll work the front sts and shape the neckline over the same number of rows as for the back. For the first half shaping, knit a row, purl a row. *On the next RS row, slip the first stitch, knit the second stitch, then pull the slipped stitch over the knit stitch, knit to end. Purl a row, knit a row. Repeat from * until you run out of your first half rows. For the neck shaping on the second half of your rows, *on the next RS row slip the first stitch, then M1L through the back loop, knit to end. Purl a row. Knit a row. Repeat from * until you come to the end of your second half NECK rows. Cut yarn.

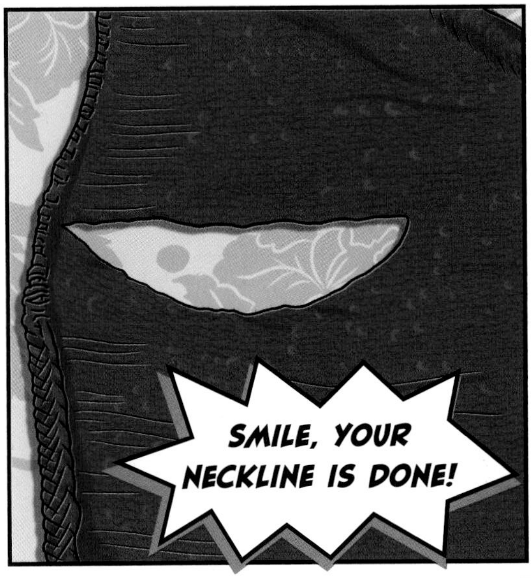
SMILE, YOUR NECKLINE IS DONE!

5) Return back stitches to the needle. Join yarn on the RS and work St st across all stitches for SHOULDER depth.

6) For the second sleeve, decrease 2 sts on every RS row by SSK after the first st then K2tog before the last st, until the original cast-on stitch count is achieved. Do not BO. Cut yarn.

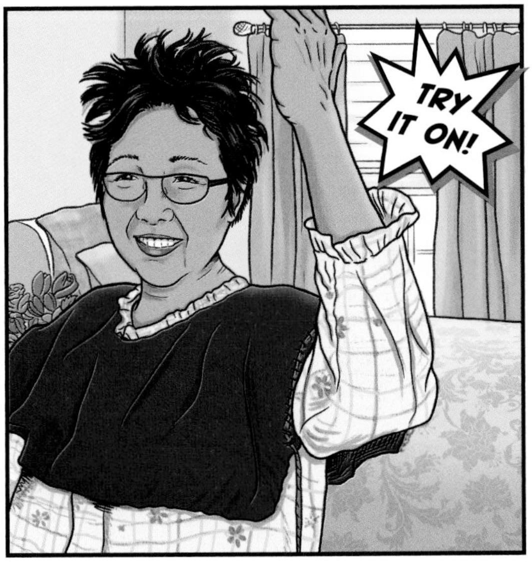
TRY IT ON!

7) Fold sweater in half, matching the edges of the body and sleeves. Your marker yarns will show the end of the sleeve seam—don't overshoot them into the bodice.

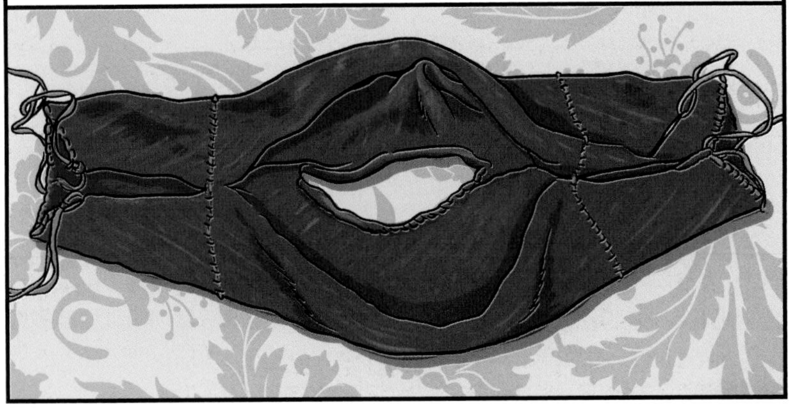

Holding the wrong sides together, sew up the side seams.

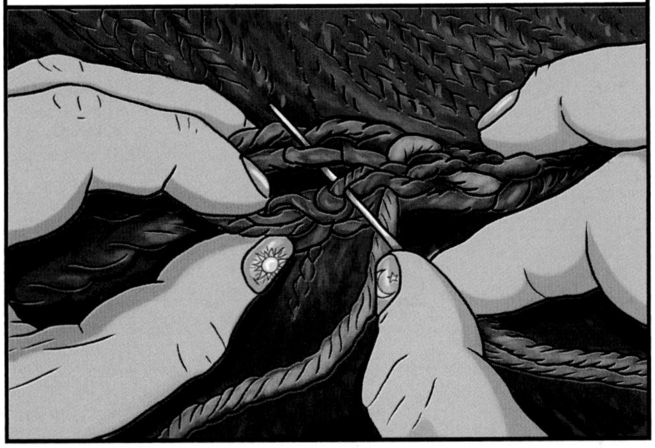

It's time for the ribbed bottom edge. **8)** Use Gauge Translation with your 1x1 rib stitch gauge to calculate how many stitches to pick up along the bottom edge. Pick up that number of stitches, and adjust to a multiple of 2. Knit 1x1 rib in the round for 3 in (7.5 cm).

For a more fitted bottom edge, use your desired measurement to calculate the number of stitches to pick up along the bottom edge. Pick them up and knit 1x1 rib in the round for 3 in (7.5 cm).

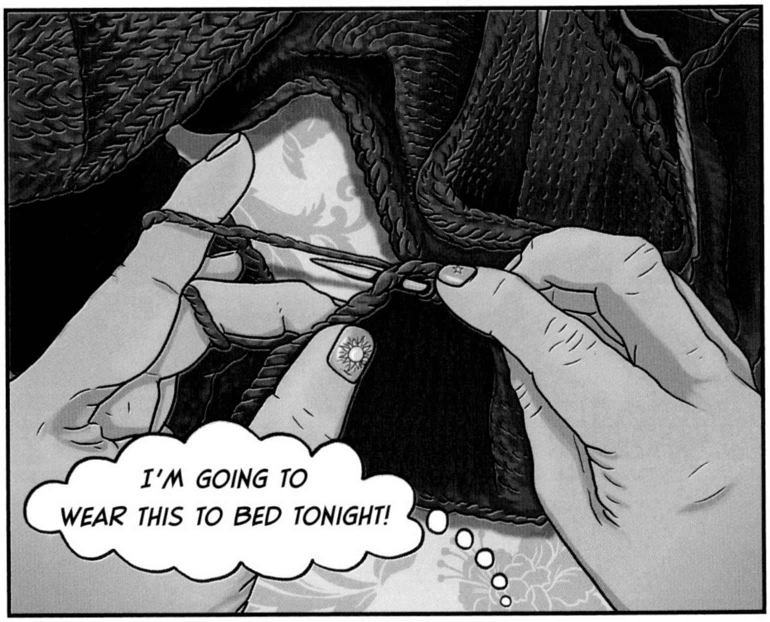
I'M GOING TO WEAR THIS TO BED TONIGHT!

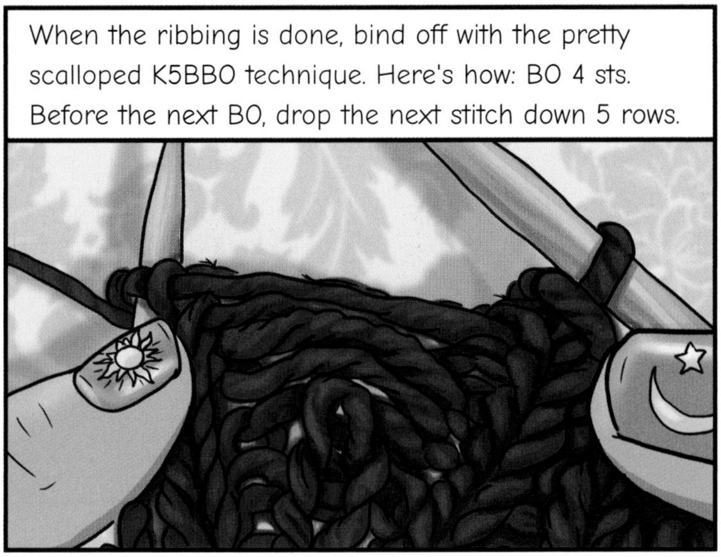
When the ribbing is done, bind off with the pretty scalloped K5BBO technique. Here's how: BO 4 sts. Before the next BO, drop the next stitch down 5 rows.

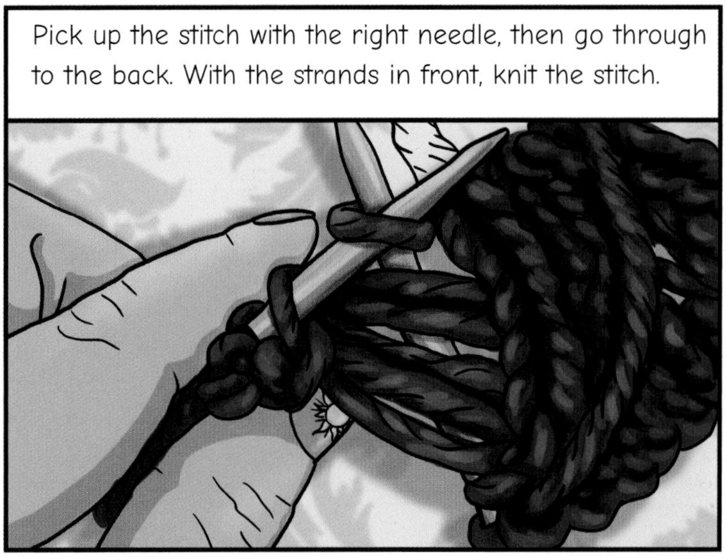
Pick up the stitch with the right needle, then go through to the back. With the strands in front, knit the stitch.

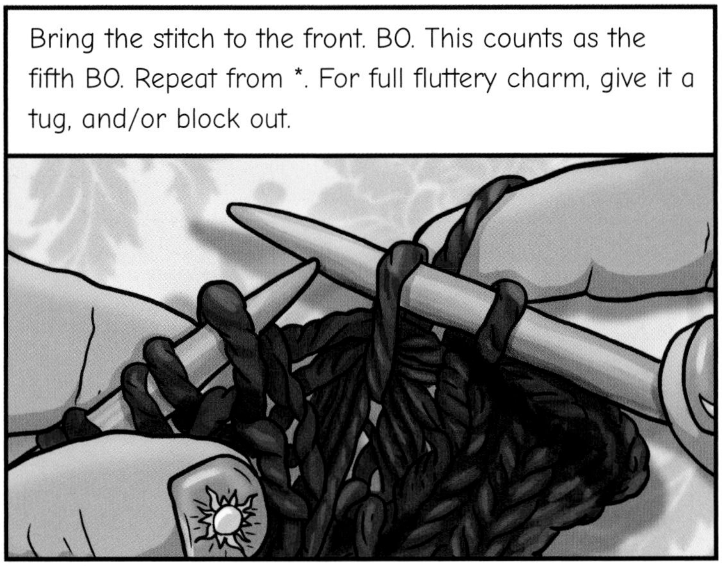
Bring the stitch to the front. BO. This counts as the fifth BO. Repeat from *. For full fluttery charm, give it a tug, and/or block out.

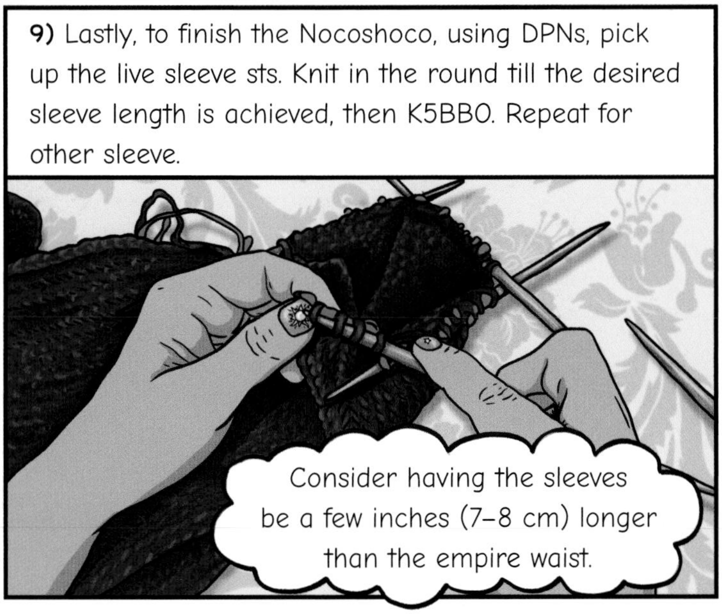
9) Lastly, to finish the Nocoshoco, using DPNs, pick up the live sleeve sts. Knit in the round till the desired sleeve length is achieved, then K5BBO. Repeat for other sleeve.
Consider having the sleeves be a few inches (7–8 cm) longer than the empire waist.

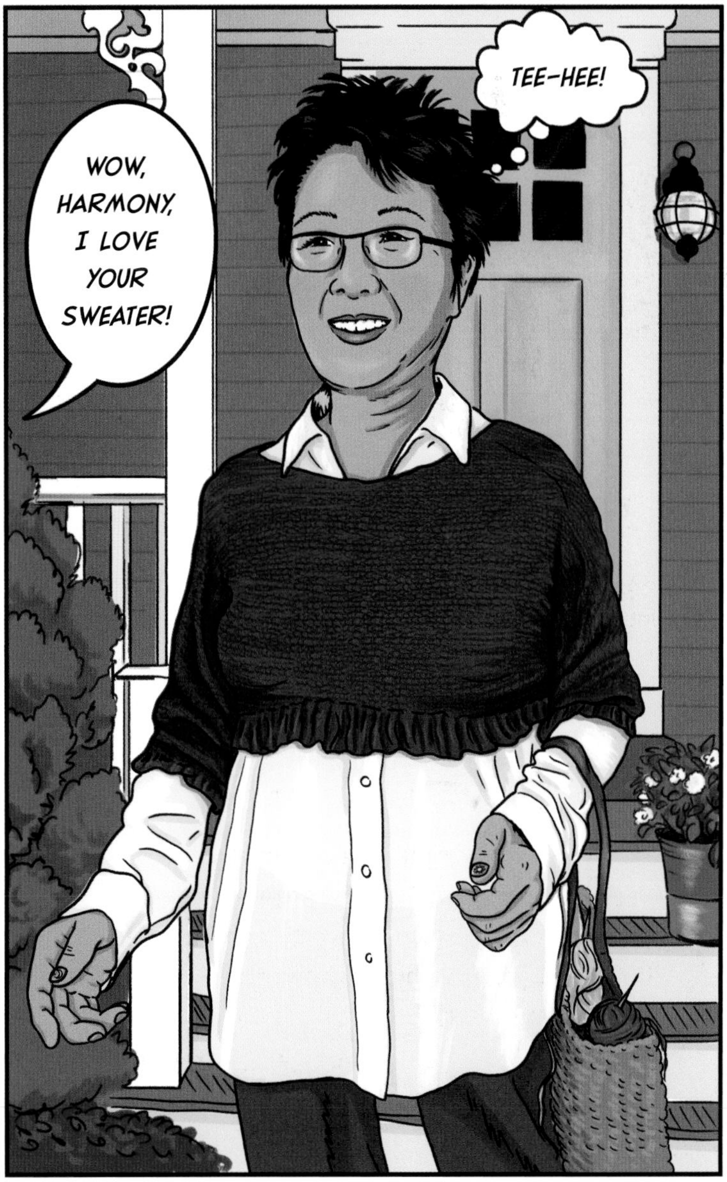
TEE-HEE!
WOW, HARMONY, I LOVE YOUR SWEATER!

THE DEEP END

BY ALICE O. BELTRAN AND SHERY COOK

INTENTIONAL POOLING IS A GREAT WAY TO SHOWCASE VARIEGATED, GRADIENT, AND OMBRÉ YARN. THIS SMART DOUBLE-SIDED COWL LETS YOU CONCENTRATE COLOR ELEMENTS AND IS THE PERFECT PROJECT FOR YARN THAT HAS A PALETTE OF COLORS YOU LOVE.

PRETTY!

SIZE: Whatever you like. Alice and Shery's preferred finished size is 23 in around and 6½ in tall (58.5 cm x 16.5 cm). **MATERIALS:** Variegated, gradient, or ombré yarn. Two long circular needles. Lots of waste yarn in two colors (A and B), optional second yarn for sewing up. Short color changes in your yarn give a pixelated effect. Long color changes give a watercolor effect. The fabric will be doubled, so consider going with finer yarn. **GAUGE:** Soft if you like it slouchy, Medium if you like it with structure. **TECHNIQUES:** Cutting your knitting apart, vertical Stockinette seaming, grafting (p. 68).

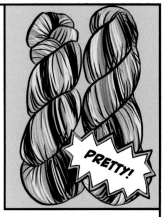

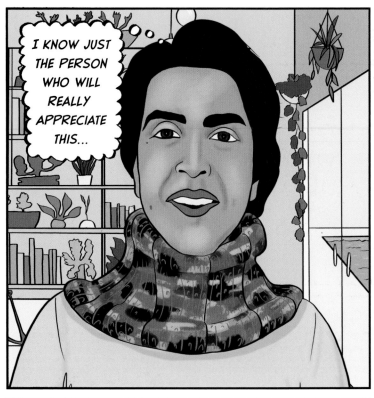

I KNOW JUST THE PERSON WHO WILL REALLY APPRECIATE THIS...

METHOD: This cowl is made of one long, skinny strip of Stockinette stitch. You will cut it into smaller strips, seam those together into a tube, and then graft the top and bottom. Choose the width of the strip to show off your colors. The narrower the strip, the thicker the pools of color will be. Consider 1–3 in (2.5–7.5 cm) for the width of the strip. The example strip is about 1¾ in (4.5 cm).

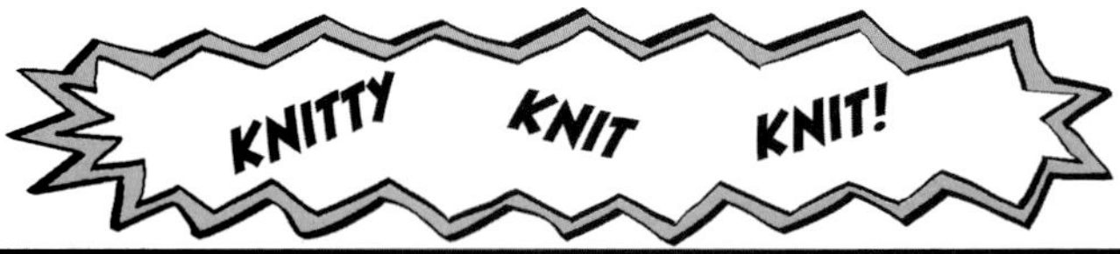

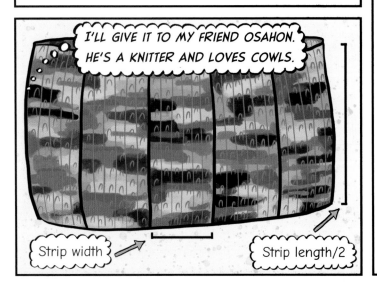

I'LL GIVE IT TO MY FRIEND OSAHON. HE'S A KNITTER AND LOVES COWLS.
Strip width
Strip length/2

Multiply your gauge by strip width for your total stitches (X). In the example, X = 10. Divide your desired cowl circumference by the width of your strip to give you the total number of strips you'll need. Add one more strip for good measure. Decide how tall you want the finished cowl, double it, and add an extra 1½ in (4 cm). This is your strip length (L). Multiply that length by your number of strips to figure out the total length you need to knit. Cast on X. To make sewing up easier, slip each first stitch, and work into the back of the last stitch on the knit rows.

KNITTY KNIT KNIT!

Knit in Stockinette stitch to length and put the top stitches on Color A waste yarn.

The sides curl relentlessly.

WOW, I JUST KNIT 18 FEET (5.5 M)!

It's time to cut it apart! For the first strip, use a ruler to measure the strip length (L), starting at the cast-on edge. Insert your darning needle in a stitch in the middle of your row at your strip length. This marks the stitch you will cut.

Cut one leg of the stitch.

SNIP!

HE'S NOT GOING TO BELIEVE I DID THIS...

AAAAH! THE POINT OF NO RETURN!

Carefully unravel to the left and right. At the top of your new short strip, unravel one full row. There will be X stitches. Place them on Color A waste yarn. Place the stitches on the bottom of your original strip on Color B waste yarn. You will have X - 1 stitches there.

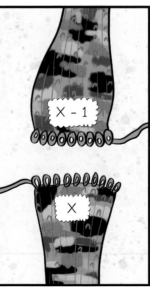

X - 1

X

To create live stitches from the cast-on edge of the first short strip, snip one leg of a stitch on the very first row, then unravel left and right. You will have X - 1 stitches. Place them on Color B waste yarn. Count the rows of your first short strip.

SNIP!

Cut the next strip from the long piece like this: *Starting on the end with X - 1 stitches, count up your row number. On the third row AFTER your target row count, place your darning needle in a stitch in the center of that row to mark for the next cut.

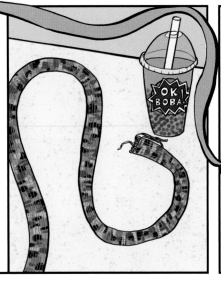

Snip a leg of this stitch. Unravel left and right, then unravel one more full row at the top of your new short strip. You will have X stitches. Place them on Color A waste yarn. Count your rows again—they should match the rows of your first strip. Place the live stitches at the bottom of your original long strip (X - 1) on Color B waste yarn. Repeat from *to create short strips from your long piece. You'll have a stack of strips, each with live stitches on waste yarn at both ends. At the bottom of each strip you'll have X - 1 stitches on Color B waste yarn. At the top you'll have X stitches on Color A waste yarn.

Now seam the strips together. Place the bottom stitches of your strips on your circular needle, and remove the waste yarn.

I SURE HOPE THIS WORKS.

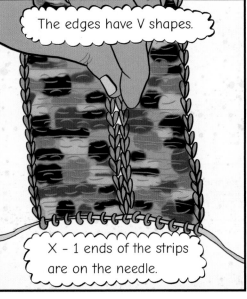

The edges have V shapes.

X - 1 ends of the strips are on the needle.

Thread your darning needle with a length of yarn 1.5 x the length of your strip. Starting at the bottom right (green): 1) Thread from left to right through the first leg, leaving a short tail. 2) Thread from right to left through the leg above it. 3) Now on the bottom left, thread from right to left through the bottom left leg. 4) Thread from left to right through the one above it. Repeat 1–4, moving up one stitch like this (purple): On the right side, 1) thread from left to right on the second leg, and 2) thread from right to left on the third leg up. On the left, 3) thread from right to left on the second leg, then 4) thread from left to right on the third leg up.

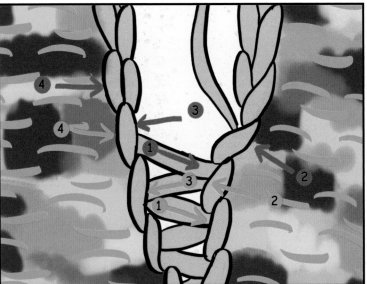

Every few stitches, pull your working yarn. The seam zips itself up in a very satisfying way. Continue, all the way up to the top.

Before

After

WATCHING THE SEAM FUSE TOGETHER NEVER GETS OLD!

Put the bottom live stitches of the next strip on your needle and remove their waste yarn. Seam the strip with the adjacent strip. Repeat seaming strips until you reach the desired circumference of your cowl. Seam it closed, so it makes a tube. The bottom live stitches are all on a needle. Slip them around the needle, untwisting as necessary, across. As you go, at the last stitch of each strip, use the little tail there to KFB that stitch. KFB the last stitch of each strip as you go around.

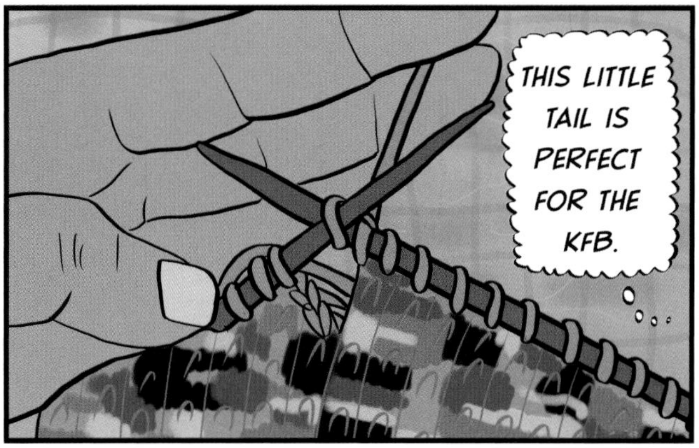
THIS LITTLE TAIL IS PERFECT FOR THE KFB.

Place all of the top live stitches on another circular needle, making sure they are not twisted, and remove the waste yarn. Trim all ends to 3 in (7.5 cm) long.

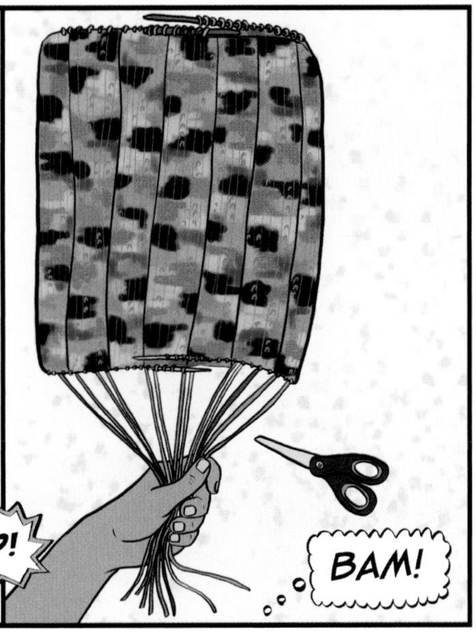
SNIP SNIP SNIP!
BAM!

Now it's time to graft your cowl shut. Bring the bottom edge of the cowl up through the center so the bottom needles are aligned with the top needles with WS facing. Tuck the tails inside. Graft the stitches together (see p. 68) all the way around.

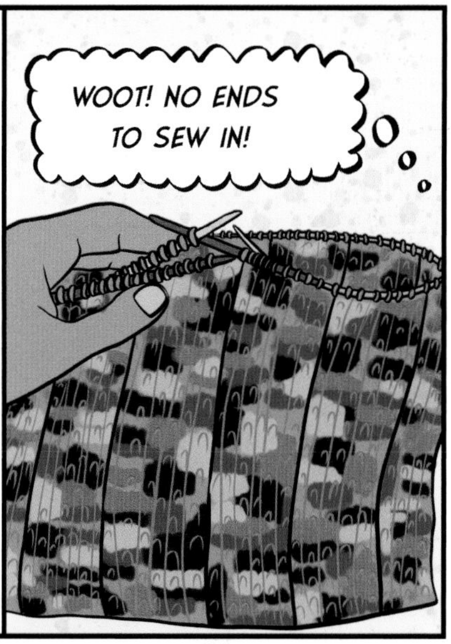
WOOT! NO ENDS TO SEW IN!

Use the tail to sew shut the small opening at the end and darn it in, pulling it through to the inside.

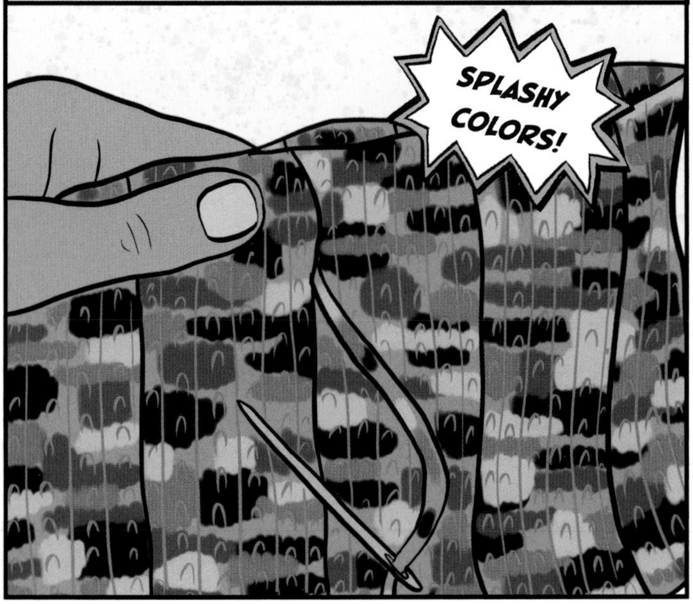
SPLASHY COLORS!

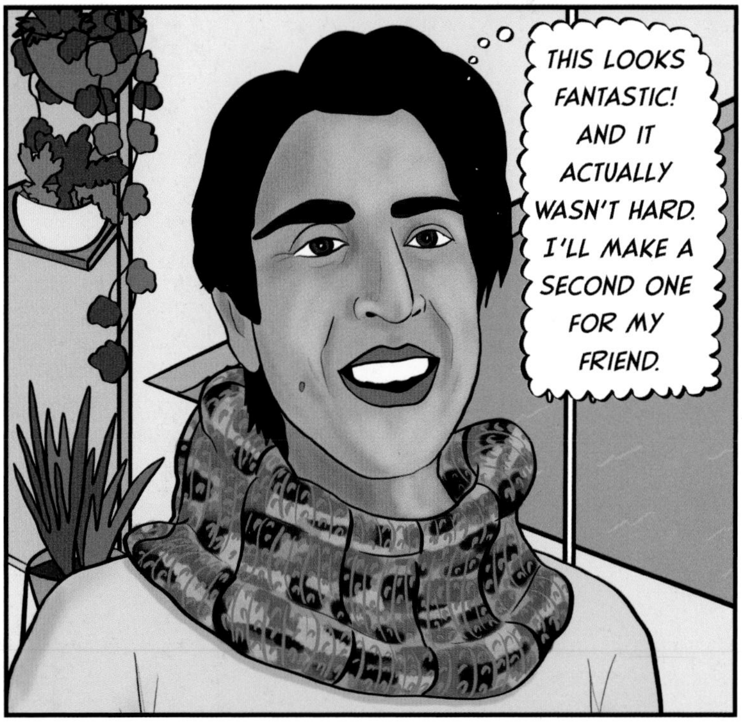
THIS LOOKS FANTASTIC! AND IT ACTUALLY WASN'T HARD. I'LL MAKE A SECOND ONE FOR MY FRIEND.

Oh BY THE Way

For perfectly identical cast-on stitches, cast on over two needles, and snug the stitches down firmly. Slide one of the needles out when you're done.

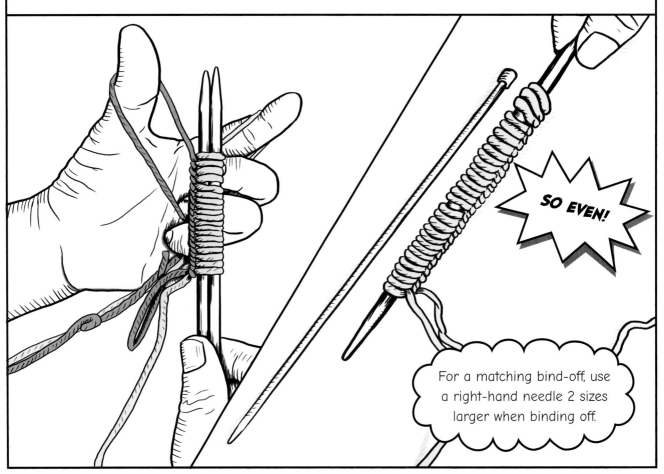

SO EVEN!

For a matching bind-off, use a right-hand needle 2 sizes larger when binding off.

Lucky Hat

BY CECELIA CAMPOCHIARO

THIS WEARABLE, SEQUENCE-KNIT CHARMER IS WORKED IN THE ROUND USING A 7-STITCH REPEAT. WHO DOESN'T NEED A LUCKY HAT?

Sequence knitting uses repeated stitch sequences to create textured fabric, like ribbing. Most sequence-knit fabrics are similar on both sides and don't curl. As the sequences get longer, the fabrics can become more interesting and varied. Sequences make different textures depending on the stitch count. Infinite variety!

MATERIALS: ~220 y (201 m) of DK to worsted-weight yarn. 16 in (41 cm) circular needles and DPNs to give your desired fabric, one size smaller 16 in (41 cm) circular needles for ribbing. 14 removable stitch markers. The yarn should be plump and smooth—merino or merino blends are ideal. A solid color will show off the texture the best.

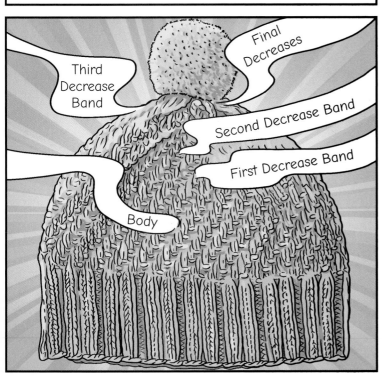

Final Decreases
Third Decrease Band
Second Decrease Band
First Decrease Band
Body

SLOUCHY STYLE

GAUGE: Chewy—this hat has structure. **SIZE:** Your head measurement minus 1–2 in (2.5–5 cm) for negative ease. **TECHNIQUES:** Even decrease distribution, reading a chart. **METHOD:** This hat uses a 7-stitch sequence: [k2, p2, k2, p1]. If the stitch count is a multiple of 7 then the knits and purls of the sequence will stack up and make ribbing. If the number of stitches is not a multiple of 7, the stitches will not stack up and will make different textures. For our hat, we will make ribbing on a multiple of 7 at the hem, and a textured pattern with a multiple of 7 + 4 for the rest.

KNIT, KNIT, PURL, PURL, KNIT, KNIT, PURL!
KNIT, KNIT, PURL, PURL, KNIT, KNIT, PURL!

Multiply gauge by your (head measurement with negative ease) to determine your stitch count. For the ribbing, adjust it to be a multiple of 7. Cast on using your smaller circular needles. Join, place a marker at the beginning, and work 3 in (7.5 cm) of ribbing with the sequence [k2, p2, k2, p1].

1
2
3

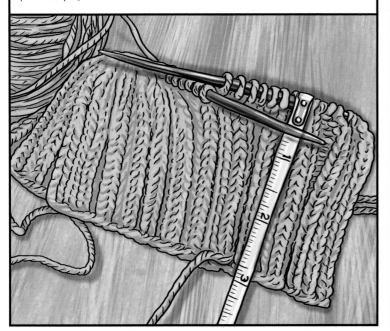

On the next round, change to the larger circular needles. Knit one round in Stockinette, and increase 4 stitches evenly across that round with M1. You will now have a multiple of 7 stitches, plus 4.

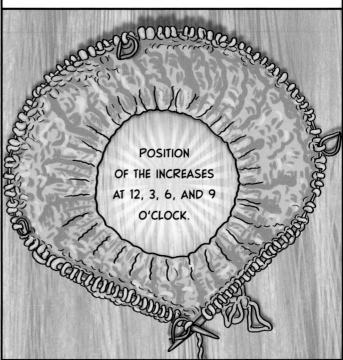

POSITION OF THE INCREASES AT 12, 3, 6, AND 9 O'CLOCK.

Work [k2, p2, k2, p1]. The sequence will only end evenly at the marker on every 7th round. Knit the sequence pattern for 3 in (7.5 cm).

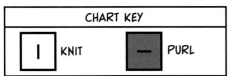

CHART KEY	
| KNIT	– PURL

HOW TO READ THE CHART:
It starts at bottom right and is read right to left for each round. Round 1 starts k2, p2, k2, p1 and ends with k2, p2. Round 2 picks up where Round 1 leaves off and begins k2, p1. A good check: The first k2 in the sequence should always be on top of a purl and a knit. The red boxes show the first two knits of the sequence on top of a purl and knit stitch. They should always line up that way!

<table>
<tr><td>–</td><td>|</td><td>|</td><td>–</td><td>–</td><td>|</td><td>|</td><td>–</td><td>|</td><td>|</td><td>–</td><td>7</td></tr>
<tr><td>–</td><td>|</td><td>|</td><td>–</td><td>|</td><td>|</td><td>–</td><td>–</td><td>|</td><td>|</td><td>–</td><td>6</td></tr>
<tr><td>|</td><td>|</td><td>–</td><td>–</td><td>|</td><td>|</td><td>–</td><td>|</td><td>|</td><td>–</td><td>–</td><td>5</td></tr>
<tr><td>|</td><td>|</td><td>–</td><td>|</td><td>|</td><td>–</td><td>–</td><td>|</td><td>|</td><td>–</td><td>|</td><td>4</td></tr>
<tr><td>|</td><td>–</td><td>–</td><td>|</td><td>|</td><td>–</td><td>|</td><td>|</td><td>–</td><td>–</td><td>|</td><td>3</td></tr>
<tr><td>|</td><td>–</td><td>|</td><td>|</td><td>–</td><td>–</td><td>|</td><td>|</td><td>–</td><td>|</td><td>|</td><td>2</td></tr>
<tr><td>–</td><td>–</td><td>|</td><td>|</td><td>–</td><td>|</td><td>|</td><td>–</td><td>–</td><td>|</td><td>|</td><td>1</td></tr>
<tr><td>4</td><td>3</td><td>2</td><td>1</td><td>7</td><td>6</td><td>5</td><td>4</td><td>3</td><td>2</td><td>1</td><td></td></tr>
</table>

Rounds

Stitches: a multiple of 7 plus 4

Start here!

Now you will knit three bands, decreasing the size of the hat in each, to make the crown. *Knit a Stockinette round with 14 evenly spaced k2tog decreases. Confirm you still have a multiple of 7 + 4 stitches and work in pattern for 1 in (2.5 cm). Repeat from * twice more to create three bands of texture with successively smaller circumferences.

TO DECREASE EVENLY OVER ONE ROUND: Place stitch markers in your decrease amount approximately evenly around the needle. No counting, just eyeballing it. Work around, decreasing on the same side of each stitch marker as you reach it. This method also works for evenly increasing.

REDUCE YOUR STITCH COUNT TO FEWER THAN 20 STITCHES: Work a round of k3tog and then a round of k2tog. You might need one more round of k2tog, depending on your gauge and size. Thread a darning needle through the remaining stitches, pull tight to close, and secure the end. If you want, add a pom-pom. Weave in ends, wash, and block.

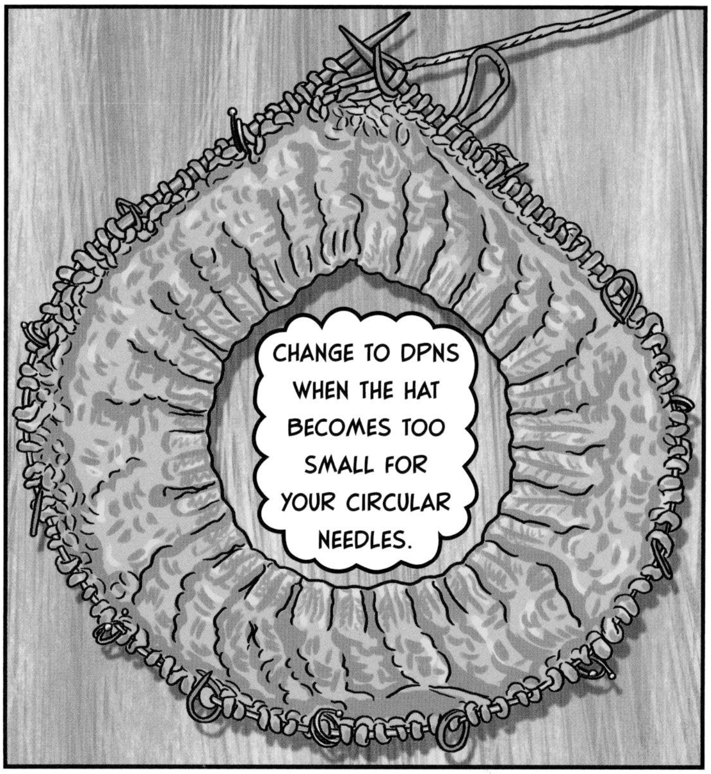
CHANGE TO DPNS WHEN THE HAT BECOMES TOO SMALL FOR YOUR CIRCULAR NEEDLES.

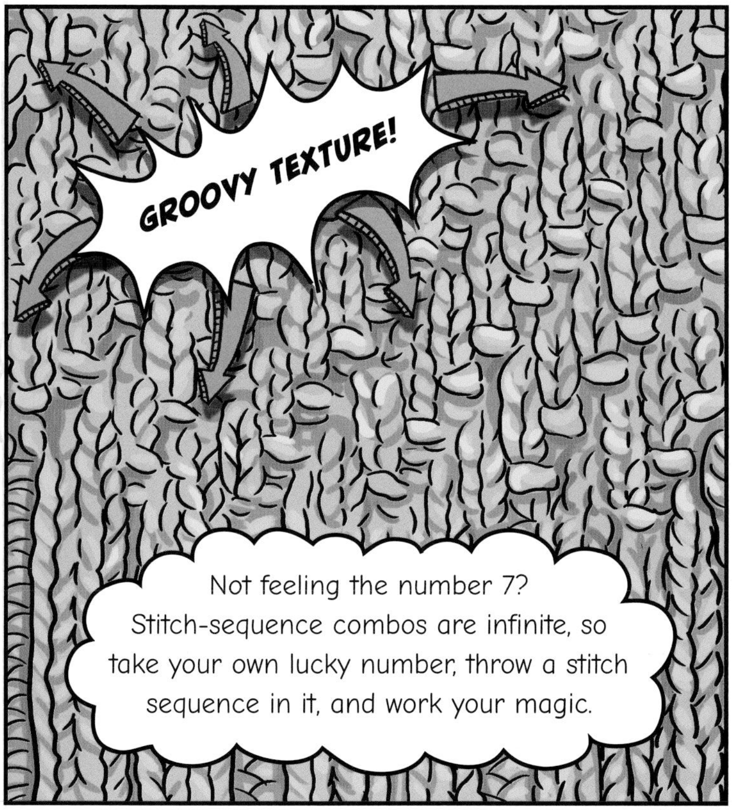
GROOVY TEXTURE!
Not feeling the number 7? Stitch-sequence combos are infinite, so take your own lucky number, throw a stitch sequence in it, and work your magic.

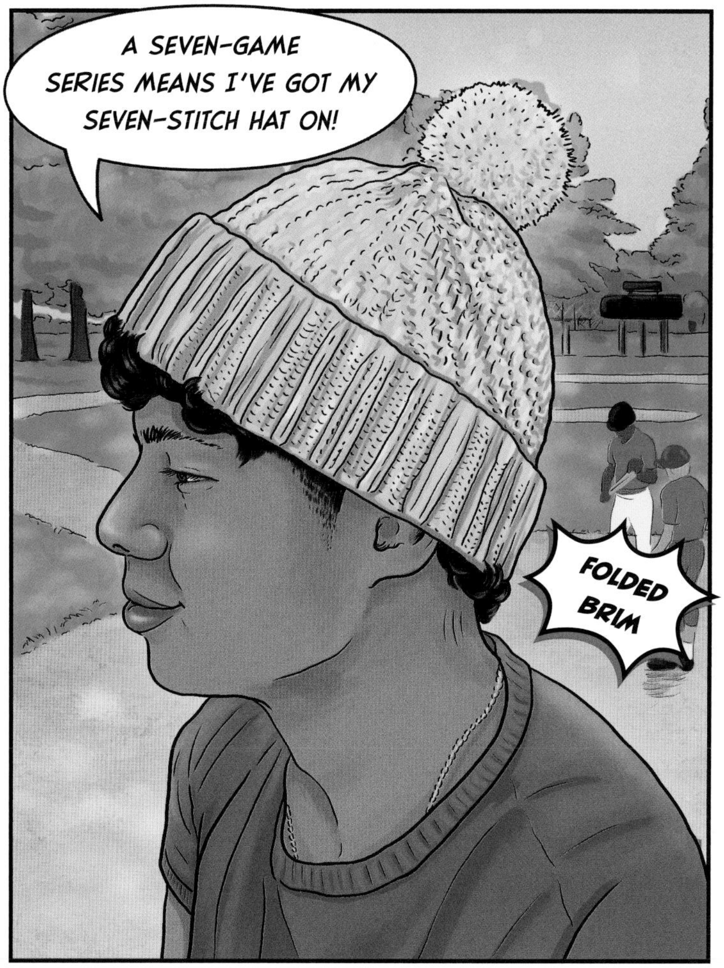
A SEVEN-GAME SERIES MEANS I'VE GOT MY SEVEN-STITCH HAT ON!
FOLDED BRIM

Let's Talk Yarn!

WE LOVE ALL THE YARN HERE AT CASA DE INTERACTIVE KNITTING. LOOKING FOR IDEAS? CHECK OUT THE DESIGNER PICKS FOR THEIR PATTERNS.

K: GREAT YARN TAKES THE EDGE OFF OF ALL THAT FOCUS.

A: TRUE! GOOD THING THERE'S LOTS OF GREAT YARN IN THE WORLD.

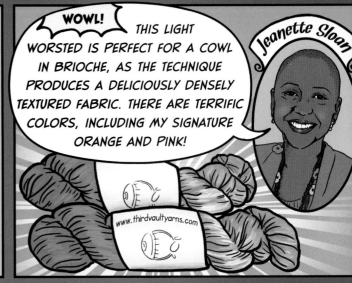

WOWL! THIS LIGHT WORSTED IS PERFECT FOR A COWL IN BRIOCHE, AS THE TECHNIQUE PRODUCES A DELICIOUSLY DENSELY TEXTURED FABRIC. THERE ARE TERRIFIC COLORS, INCLUDING MY SIGNATURE ORANGE AND PINK!

Jeanette Sloan

www.thirdvaultyarns.com

LUCKY HAT AVFKW'S DAWN IS A BEAUTIFUL ORGANIC MERINO-COTTON BLEND, LOVINGLY HANDMADE AND NATURALLY DYED IN THE USA.

Cecelia Campochiaro

www.averbforkeepingwarm.com

Shery Cook

I MADE IT!

Noir Noir www.notiyarn.com

THE DEEP END I LOVE NOTI YARN. SHERY HAS AN AMAZING, FASHION-FORWARD POINT OF VIEW. HER COLORWAYS ARE GRIPPING.

THE DASHWOOD THIS HEDGEHOG FIBRES IS DREAMY TO WORK WITH! SUPERB HALO AND FANTASTIC COLORWAYS.

shop.hedgehogfibres.com

Alice O. Beltran

JEANS JEAN VAQUEROS www.lionbrand.com

JEANS KNITS UP BEAUTIFULLY!

Karen Kim Mar

NOCOSHOCO I GREW UP KNITTING WITH LION BRAND. I APPRECIATE THE GREAT VALUE, AND THEY KEEP WOWING ME WITH THEIR YARN LINEUP. LIKE THE JEANS—FANTASTIC!

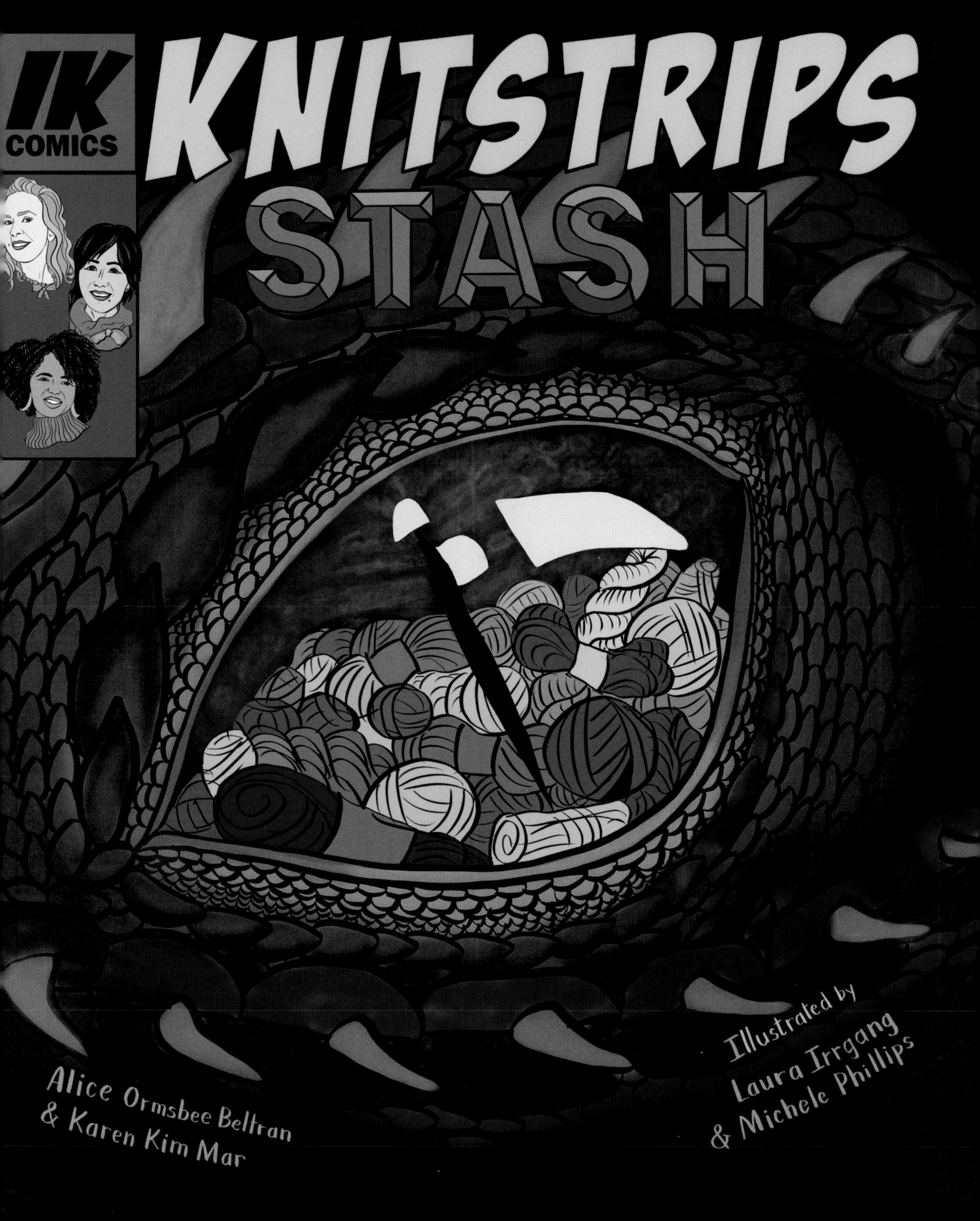
IK COMICS
KNITSTRIPS
STASH
Alice Ormsbee Beltran
& Karen Kim Mar
Illustrated by
Laura Irrgang
& Michele Phillips

STASH

Ah, the STASH. Skeins That Are Special and Here. The thumbprint of a knitter's soul. You can tell a lot about a knitter by their stash. Some people only have yarn for their current project and will wait to get more yarn until that project is done. We have only heard about doing that. Some have more yarn than can be used in their lifetime. We are a little more familiar with that.

Alice loves buying yarn and figures you may as well get a sweater-ful while you're at it, to keep your options open. She also firmly believes that there is no better souvenir than yarn. It's light, a great memento, gives you something fun to do (both on your trip and after!), and ultimately becomes a finished object with a great story built into it. (Her definition of traveling includes going across town to the local yarn store, and virtual traveling to places that sell yarn on the internet.)

Karen fears overspending, overcommitting, and overindulging. She also feels sorry for yarn that no one else wants. As a result, her stash is a mishmash of her painstakingly thought-out and finally purchased single skeins; gifted skeins; and various amounts of yarn that no longer spark joy in her friends, friends of friends, and semi-strangers, but are treasures to her.

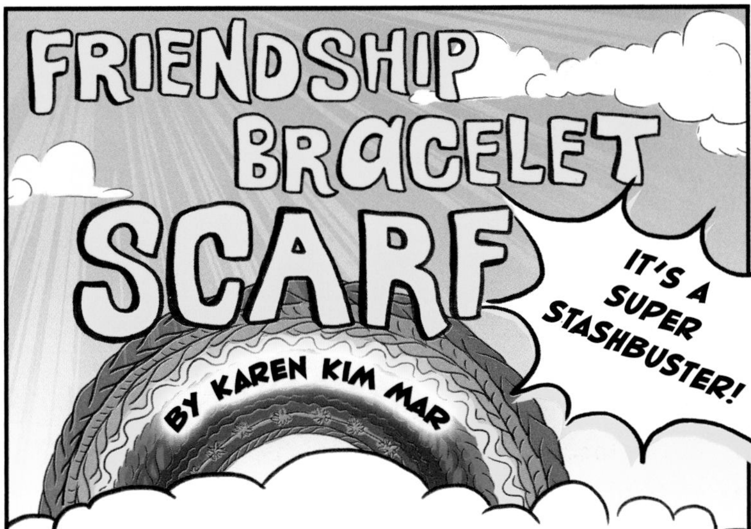
FRIENDSHIP BRACELET SCARF
BY KAREN KIM MAR
IT'S A SUPER STASHBUSTER!

FRIENDSHIP BRACELETS ARE ETERNALLY COOL. KNIT A GINORMOUS SCARF VERSION FROM YOUR STASH. IT'S SUPER FUN, EASY, AND FAST!

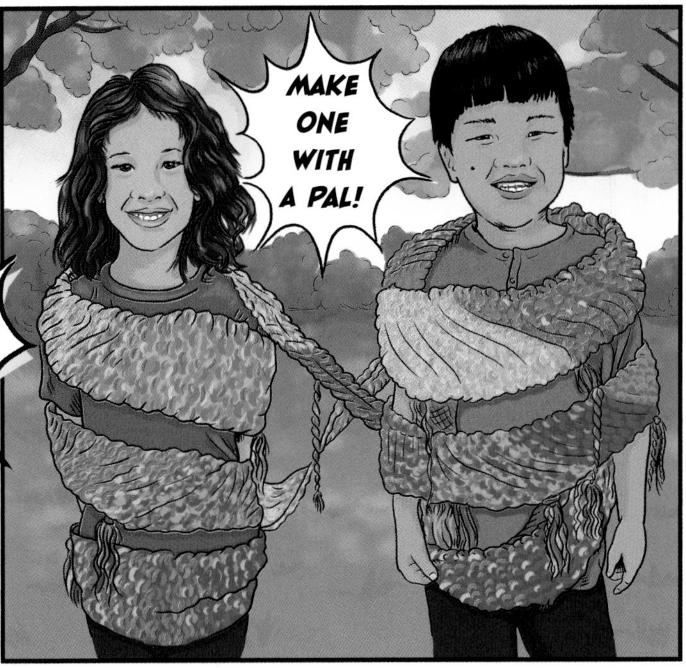
MAKE ONE WITH A PAL!

MATERIALS: Super-bulky, novelty, white elephant, impulse-buy, and "is this actually mine?" yarn. A circular needle size US 11 (8 mm) or larger. How much yarn you need depends on how long you want the scarf to be and how much stashbusting you want to do. Large crochet hook for optional fringe. **SIZE:** As long and wide as you want. Share with your friends! We made ours 5½ in x 100 in (14 cm x 254 cm).

GAUGE: This scarf is worked at ~2 stitches per 1 in (2.5 cm), so hold multiple strands together of any yarn to get this gauge. Voilà, instant bulky yarn! You will be using the same needle throughout, and changing your yarn for stripes, so there will be some variability in the fabric density and gauge from stripe to stripe (and that's OK). **TECHNIQUES:** Diagonal Garter Stitch aka Bias Knitting, adding fringe

Unexpected friendships happen with yarns, too! Introduce the plain ones to the novelties.

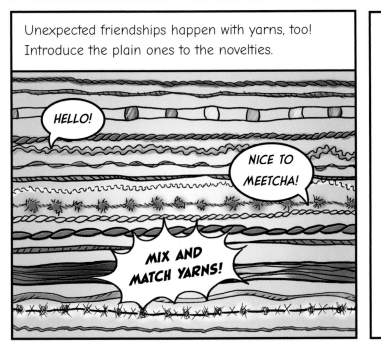

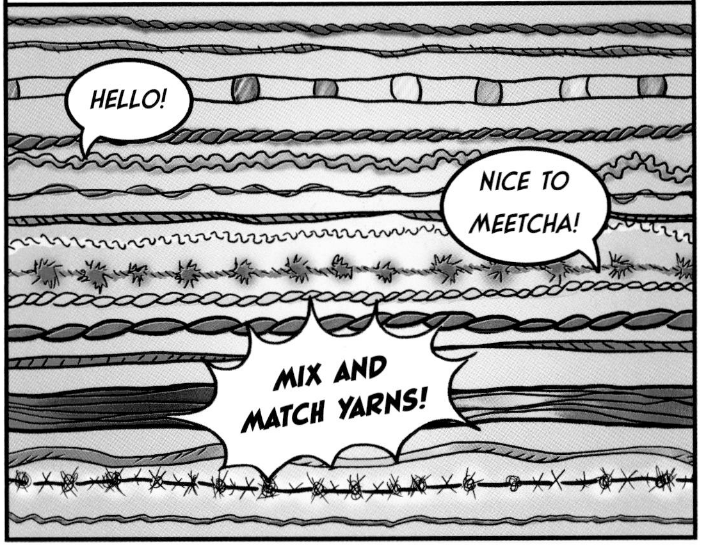
HELLO!
NICE TO MEETCHA!
MIX AND MATCH YARNS!

METHOD: Decide approximately how wide you want your scarf. The weight of the scarf will have a narrowing effect. Also, the width of the scarf will be shorter than the length of stitches on the needle because it's knit on the bias. Cast on your desired width, adding a few more inches of stitches to counteract the weight and bias.

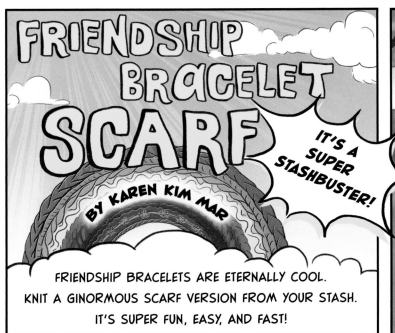

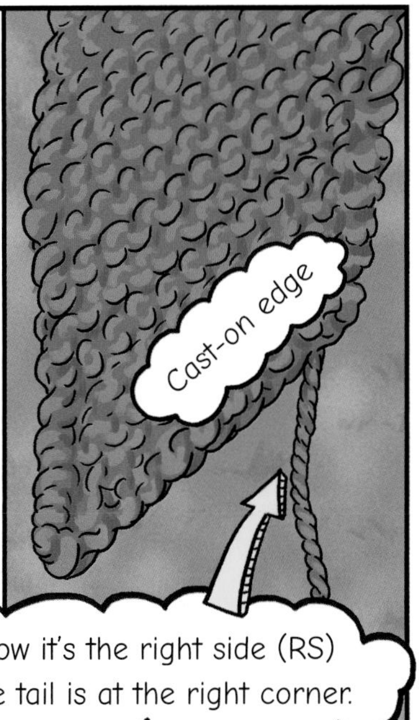
Cast-on edge

You know it's the right side (RS) when the tail is at the right corner.

To increase, you'll be using knit in the front and back (KFB). Here's how! To KFB, knit the stitch and leave it on the left needle. Swing the right needle around back and knit into the back of it, and take the stitch off. This increases 1 stitch!

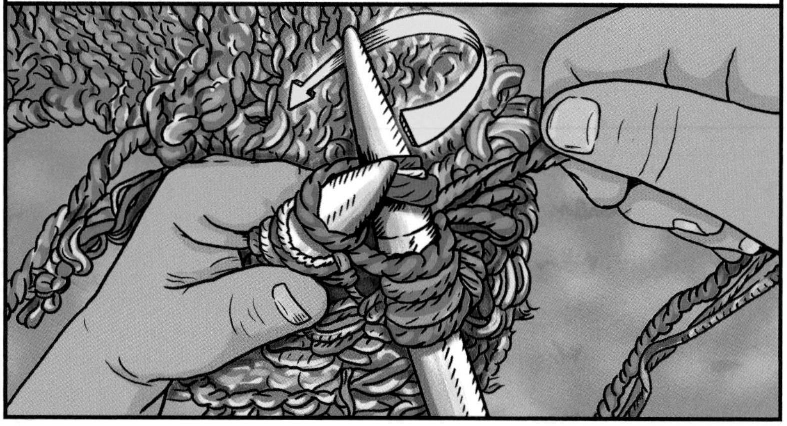

Now work Diagonal Garter Stitch: **ROW 1**: Right side (RS): Slip the first stitch knitwise. KFB the next stitch. Knit to the last three stitches then knit two together (K2tog) and k1. **ROW 2**: Wrong side (WS): Slip the first stitch knitwise. Knit to the end. Repeat Rows 1 and 2 till the desired length is achieved. To change colors: At the beginning of a RS row, knit the first stitch with your new yarn or strands of yarn. The tails are future fringe, so leave them as long as you like.

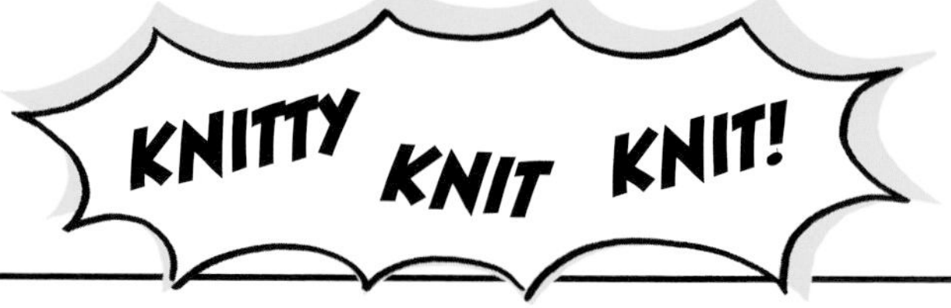
KNITTY KNIT KNIT!

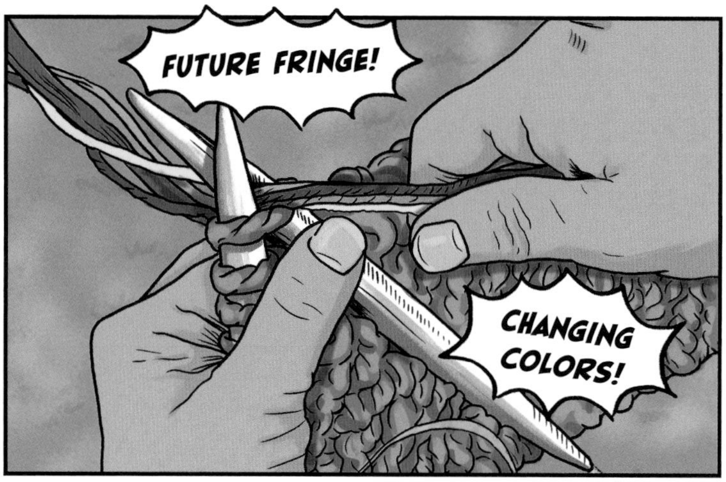
FUTURE FRINGE!
CHANGING COLORS!

When your scarf is done, bind off on the right side as follows: Work 2 stitches. *Pull the first stitch over the second and off the needle. Work another stitch. Repeat from * across. When you are down to the last stitch, break yarn and pull it through the stitch.

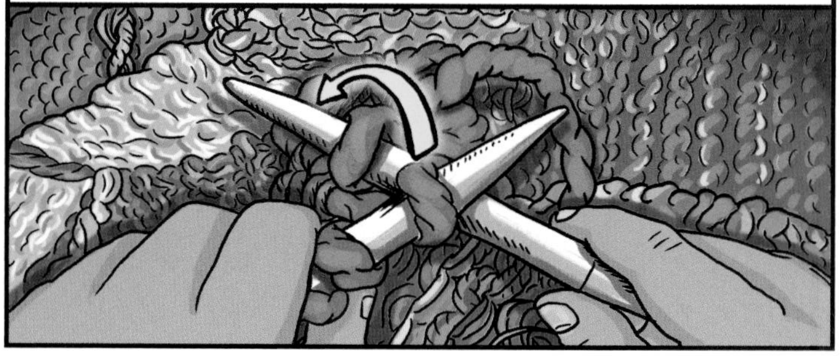

You don't have to sew in the yarn tails where you joined a new color. Wind them together, or braid them and knot them at the end, or just leave them as fringe.

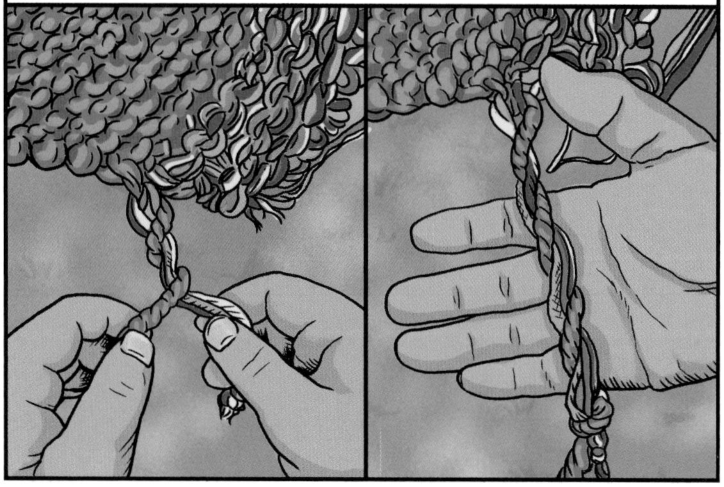

Add more fringe wherever you like, using a crochet hook. Decide how long you want your fringe, double that number, and cut it with a little extra, so you have room to trim evenly.

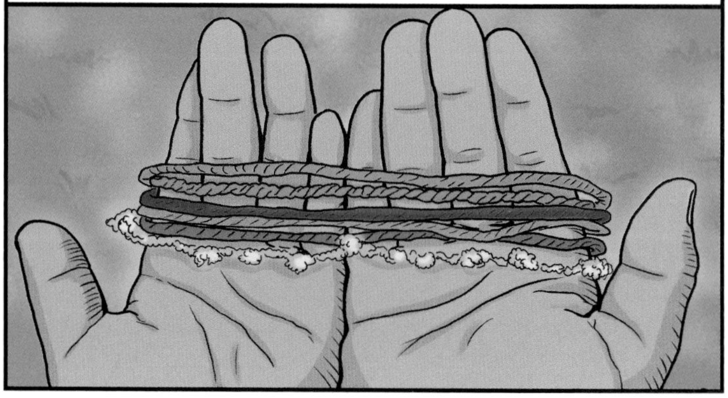

On the RS, slip the crochet hook under a stitch where you want to attach fringe.

Fold your yarn in half and use the hook to pull the loop end of the yarn through.

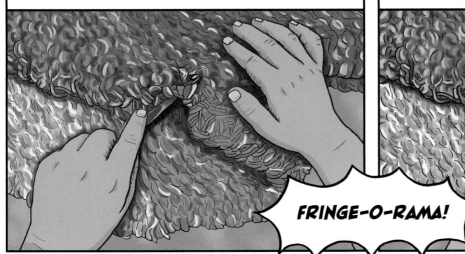

FRINGE-O-RAMA!

Use your fingers to pull the tails through the loop.

PULL

Snug them down.

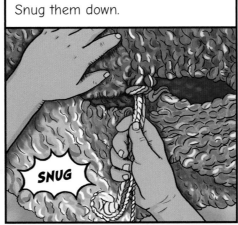

SNUG

Give the fringe a trim, and the fringe is **DONE!**

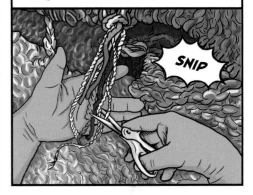

SNIP

THIS IS SO MUCH FUN! I LOVE MAKING FRINGE!

YOU'RE DOING A GREAT JOB!

LET'S MAKE IT REALLLLY LONG, OK?

OK!

WE HAVE LOTS OF YARN.

TEAM BLANKET

BY ALICE O. BELTRAN AND KAREN KIM MAR

THIS MITERED SQUARE BLANKET WITH GAUGE TRANSLATION LETS ALL THE YARNS TEAM UP AND WORK TOGETHER TO BECOME A WINNING PIECE. PLUS, IT WILL BUST SOME SERIOUS STASH. TEAM BLANKET FOR THE WIN!

K: OOH! IT'S LIKE A BOX OF TURKISH DELIGHT!
The border yarn is kind of like the binder dough in IK cookies (p. 86). It pulls all your fun stuff together!
A: THIS WOULD BE TERRIFIC AS A KING-SIZE BEDSPREAD.
K: MAGNIFICENT!

MATERIALS: Any and all yarn for the center squares. One yarn for the borders. DPNs (set of 5) and short circular needles to get the gauge you like in the various center square yarns. Two long circular needles for the center square borders and blanket border that give gauge you like in your border yarn. Waste yarn to hold stitches. Removable stitch markers. **GAUGE:** Soft or Medium for border yarn. Center square gauge can vary widely; that's part of the charm of this blanket. Play with mixing textures, weights, and colors. **SIZE:** Any. Alice and Karen like ~12 in (30.5 cm) for the final size of the blocks (center squares with borders). **TECHNIQUES:** Gauge Translation, JSSBO (p. 98), grafting, sewing up Garter stitch.

METHOD: Center squares are miter knit in Stockinette stitch (St st) from the center out. The edges are picked up with Gauge Translation in border yarn in order to work each block to a consistent finished size. Blocks are grafted together, and the border is finished.

CENTER SIZES CAN VARY!

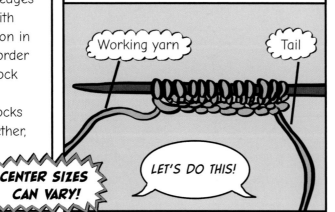

Directions for a center square: In any yarn, cast on 8 stitches, leaving an 8 in (20 cm) tail. (K1, M1 via backward loop, k1) across (12 stitches).

Working yarn
Tail
LET'S DO THIS!

Place work on 4 DPNs, with 3 stitches on each needle.

CENTER OUT!
Tail
Working yarn

Join and knit around, place marker (pm) in center stitch of each needle, in the stitch, not on the needle (12 stitches, 4 marked stitches). Your tail shows the start of the round.

IT SETTLES DOWN AFTER A FEW ROUNDS!

1) Increase round A: (Work to 1 stitch before marked st, KFB, M1, K marked stitch, KFB) around, knit remaining stitches in round (no remaining stitches on first round, 12 stitches increased). Note center stitch is off-center! That's OK. 2) Knit around. 3) Increase round B: (Work to 1 stitch before marked stitch, KFB, knit marked stitch, M1, KFB) around, knit remaining stitches in the round (12 stitches increased). 4) Knit around. Continue working these four rounds until the square is anywhere from 7 to 11 in (18 to 28 cm) across, switching to your short circular needles when you have enough stitches.

THE CENTERS CAN BE DIFFERENT SIZES, SO I'M NOT EVEN GOING TO MEASURE THEM.

THAT'S BETTER!

Bind off loosely. Use cast-on tail to sew center hole closed when darning it in. Weave in ends. Make as many squares as you need for your blanket, or as many as you are contributing to a Team Blanket. Wash and block them.

KNITTY KNIT KNIT!

When you have all your center squares done, it's time to **Gauge Translate** (GT) and give them borders! This allows your two yarns to align perfectly, with no puckers or flares.

To GT, *measure across your center square. Multiply that length by your St st gauge in your border yarn, and for this application of GT, **let your stitches be a multiple of three**. For that center square, that is how many stitches you will pick up along each edge. Divide the edge into quarters to make picking up easier.

Take the center square and fold it in half; pm at the halfway point. Fold each side in to the center halfway point, and mark the quarter points.

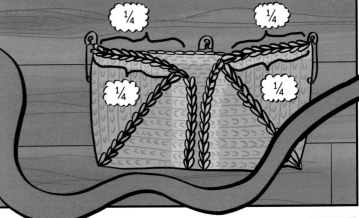

¼ ¼ ¼ ¼

Divide your number of stitches to pick up by 4. That is the number to pick up within each quarter of your edge. It may not be an even number, in which case adjust so that the sections have one more or fewer to make the total number match your target. You can skip stitches if necessary, or knit into each leg of the stitch to fit more.

Example: Border yarn gauge is 5 sts per 1 in (5 st/2.5 cm) and the side length of the center square is 10 in (24 cm), that's 5 x 10 = 50 sts per side. It must be a multiple of 3, so we rounded it to 51 sts per side. We will pick up a total of 51 stitches along each side, which is 12.75 per quarter. We will pick up 12, 13, 13, and 13 sts in each respective quarter of the side.

Pick up your stitches on all four sides, pm in each corner stitch. Work around in St st, repeating the same 4 rows as you did for your center squares. When the size of the square with the border is the size you want, count your stitches. You will have the same number on each side. That is your target stitch count for all of the following blocks for the blanket. Place each side of stitches on separate waste yarn. Let each side hold one corner stitch.

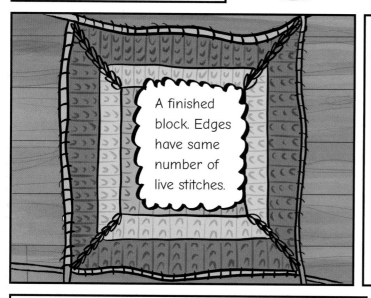

A finished block. Edges have same number of live stitches.

Repeat from * (previous page) starting with GT, for each of your center squares. Work the border miter increases until you hit your target stitch count. The block will be the same size as the first one. When you have all your blocks done, with border stitches live and on waste yarn, it's time to graft them together. Have fun laying out the blocks and deciding on the arrangement. When you're ready, take two of your adjacent blocks, place the live stitches to be grafted on separate circular needles, and align them with their WS facing each other. Thread a darning needle with a length of your border yarn 5 times longer than the seam.

To graft St st, hold the two pieces WS facing. Prepare like this: Draw your darning needle through the first stitch on the front needle as if to purl, and leave it on. Draw the needle through the first stitch on the back needle as if to knit, and leave it on.

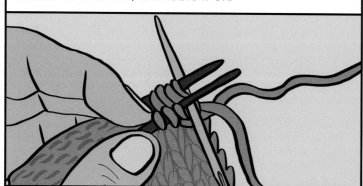

Now 1) slip the needle through the first stitch on the front needle as if to knit, and take it off. 2) Put the needle through the next stitch on the front needle as if to purl, and leave it on. Draw the working yarn through.

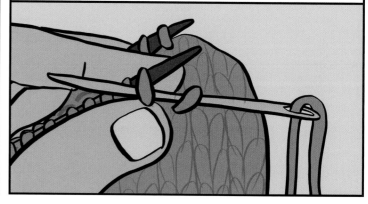

3) Slip the needle through the first stitch on the back needle as if to purl, and take it off. **4)** Put the needle through the next stitch on the back needle as if to knit, and leave it on. Draw the working yarn through.

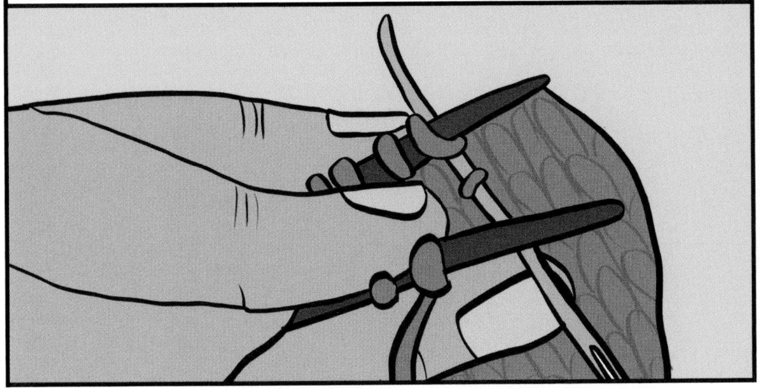

Repeat steps 1–4 until you reach the end of your stitches. You will come down to the last stitch on each needle—work steps 1 and 3. You grafted your seam!

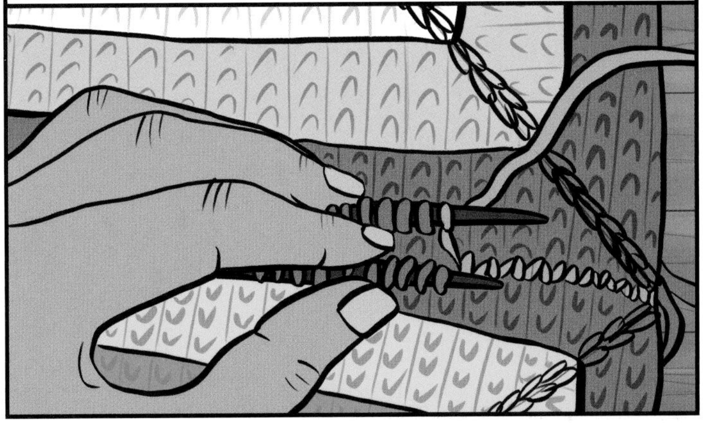

Graft all your seams together in any order to form the desired shape and size. There will be a square gap where four corners meet. Darn it with two seams.

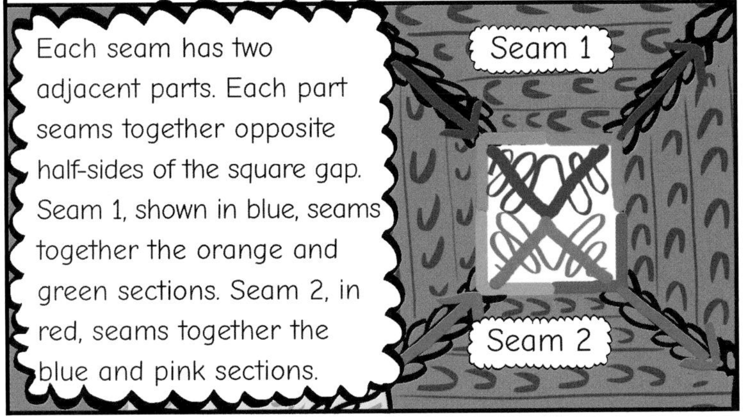
Each seam has two adjacent parts. Each part seams together opposite half-sides of the square gap. Seam 1, shown in blue, seams together the orange and green sections. Seam 2, in red, seams together the blue and pink sections.
Seam 1
Seam 2

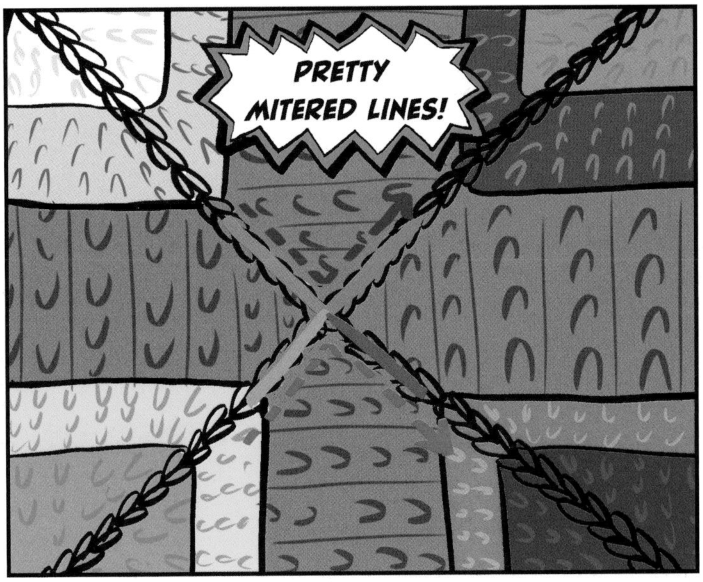
PRETTY MITERED LINES!

Work the outer Garter stitch border back and forth one side at a time. Starting at one corner, *put your live stitches on your needle. When you come to the gap between your live stitches, use the tail hanging there to pick up stitches from the edge to cross the gap. Repeat from * across. Remove all waste yarn. Join border yarn on the RS, and (k8, k2tog) across. Knit the WS. On the next and all following RS rows, slip the first stitch of the edge, M1, work to 1 stitch before the end, M1, KTBL. Knit all WS rows. Work the border for 2 in (5 cm) or more, then bind off with JSSBO. Do this on each side of your blanket.

Sew up the short seams at the corners of your border by taking a Garter knob from each side, back and forth. Wash, block, darn in ends.

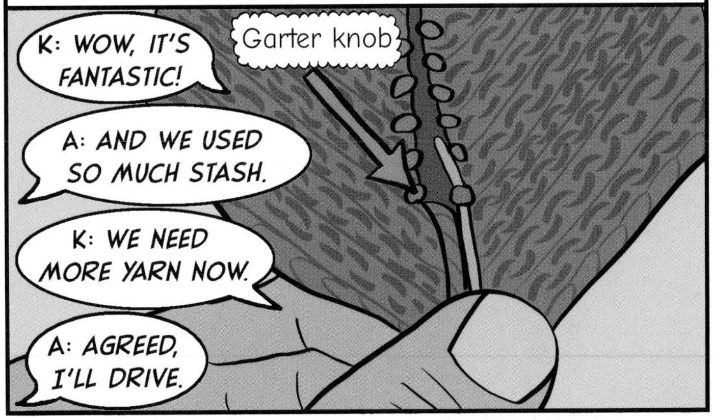
K: WOW, IT'S FANTASTIC!
Garter knob
A: AND WE USED SO MUCH STASH.
K: WE NEED MORE YARN NOW.
A: AGREED, I'LL DRIVE.

Oh by the Way

At Casa de IK, we may not always darn in our ends, but when we do, we make sure to trim the darned ends after washing and blocking. This prevents the trimmed ends from popping out. Superstition, or just good sense? We're not taking any chances.

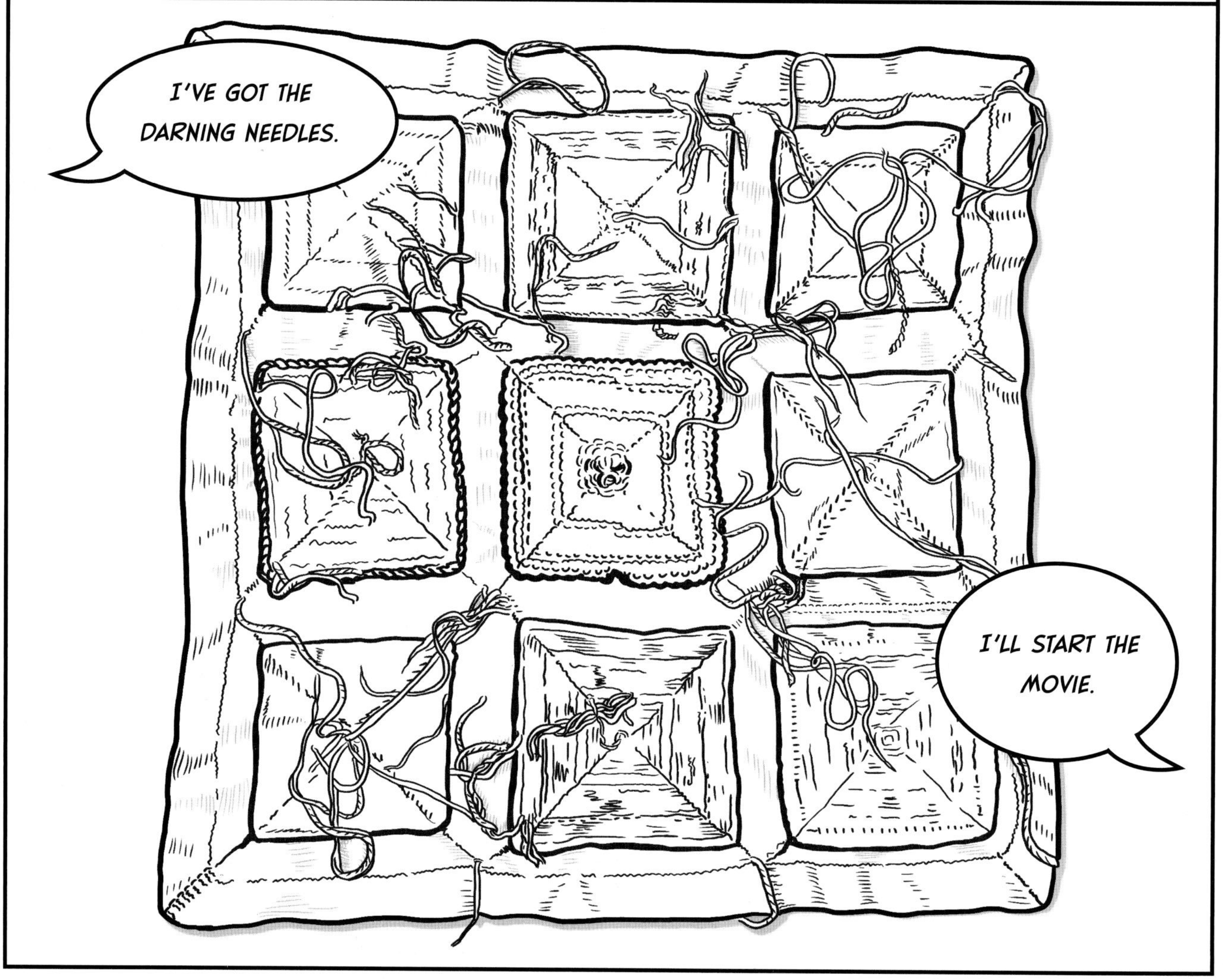
I'VE GOT THE DARNING NEEDLES.
I'LL START THE MOVIE.

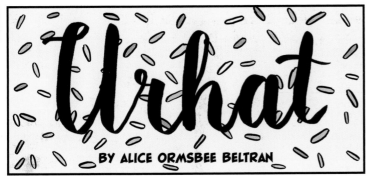

Urhat

BY ALICE ORMSBEE BELTRAN

THIS CLASSIC, FLATTERING TAM IS THE PERFECT DESTINATION FOR A SINGLE PRECIOUS SKEIN. A FAIR ISLE OPTION IS INCLUDED, IDEAL FOR THE SMALLEST BITS OF TREASURED YARN IN YOUR STASH. CHOOSE BETWEEN A CLOSE OR FULL SILHOUETTE. MAKE IT BIG, SMALL, SOLID, OR COLORFUL—MAKE IT YOURS!

MATERIALS: Sock to heavy worsted yarn. Short circular needles and DPNs in the size to give your desired gauge, stitch markers. Optional graph paper for colorwork. If you plan to do Fair Isle, let your different-color yarns be the same size, to get the same gauge. **SIZE:** Measure your head and multiply that by 0.85. This is your head measurement with negative ease (H). **GAUGE:** Stockinette stitch (St st). Soft to Medium is recommended. **TECHNIQUES:** Two-Stranded Long-Tail Cast-On (TSLTCO) (p. 84), Fair Isle charting, increase/decrease evenly (p. 59), folded hem, loose colorwork (p. 41), k3tog (p. 111), S2KPsso.

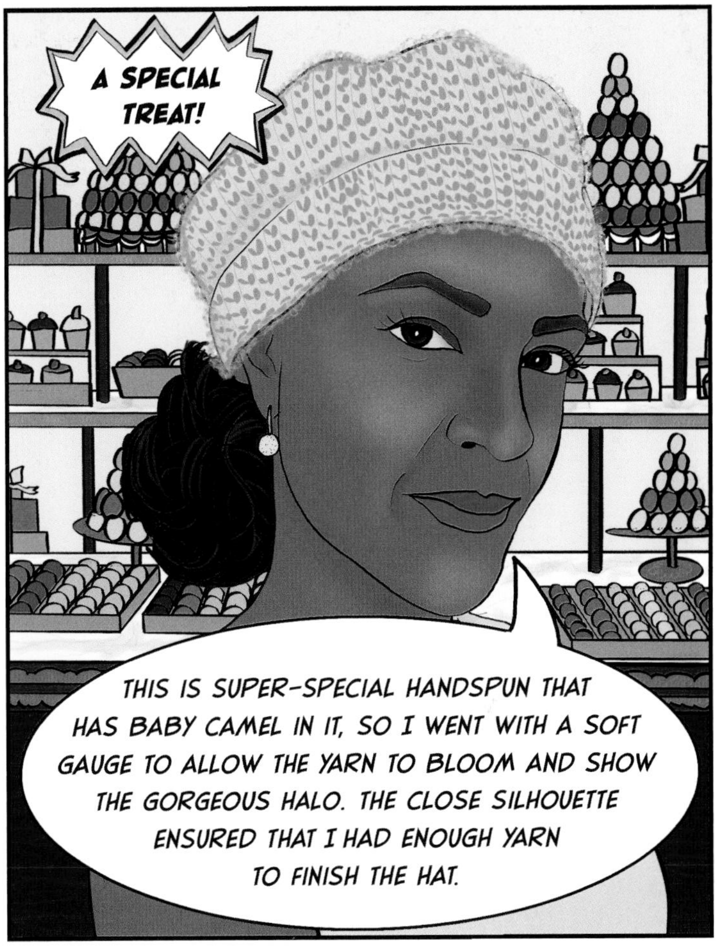

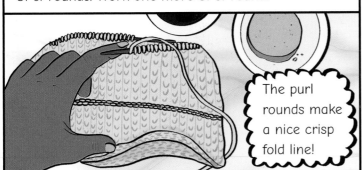

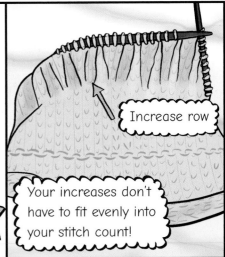

A SPECIAL TREAT!
THIS IS SUPER-SPECIAL HANDSPUN THAT HAS BABY CAMEL IN IT, SO I WENT WITH A SOFT GAUGE TO ALLOW THE YARN TO BLOOM AND SHOW THE GORGEOUS HALO. THE CLOSE SILHOUETTE ENSURED THAT I HAD ENOUGH YARN TO FINISH THE HAT.

METHOD: This hat is worked from the bottom up and starts with a folded hem. The body of the hat can be plain or include Fair Isle colorwork. The crown is decreased over 7 points, giving the hat 7 panels. It is finished with an I-cord stem.

Multiply your gauge by (H). TSLTCO your sts. Join and work in St st in the round 2 in (5 cm). Count your rounds. Purl two rounds. Work another 2 in (5 cm) of St st rounds. Work one more St st round.

The purl rounds make a nice crisp fold line!

It's time to expand your hat. For a close silhouette, *K3, M1 around (33% increase). For a fuller hat, *k2, M1 around (50% increase).

YOUR HAT, YOUR CALL!

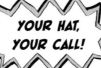

Increase row
Your increases don't have to fit evenly into your stitch count!

Do an adjustment row, increasing or decreasing evenly around as necessary to attain a multiple of 7 sts because the hat has seven panels. Divide your sts by 7 to see how many sts are in each panel.

Single color: Work St st for 3½–4½ in (9–11.5 cm) from your adjustment row. Place 7 markers evenly around, IN the last stitch of each of your seven panels. Your crown decreases will be centered on these. *Work to 1 stitch before the marked stitch, slip 2 stitches knitwise together, knit the next stitch, pass the slipped stitches over the knit stitch (S2KPsso) around. Work one knit round. Repeat these two rounds from *, switching to DPNs when necessary.

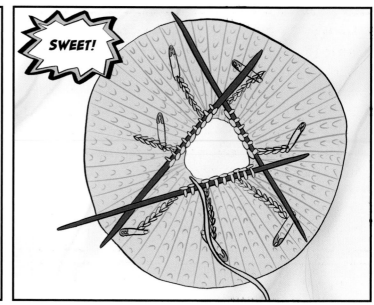

SWEET!

Fair Isle: First chart your colorwork on graph paper. Draw one of your seven panels, starting at the plain row at the top of your hem and going all the way to the top. The body of the hat will go straight up for the rows you need to get your target depth. To draw the decreases, reduce 1 st on each side every other row. When drawing your Fair Isle colors, keep to the following rules: no more than two colors per row, no more than 1 in (2.5 cm) of a single color of stitches, and carry your non-working color in the back very loosely.

Follow your chart for each of the 7 panels of your hat and knit the hat body. Place 7 markers evenly around, IN the last stitch of each of your seven panels. To decrease, *work to 1 stitch before the marked stitch, slip 2 stitches knitwise together, knit the next stitch, pass the 2 slipped stitches over the knit stitch (S2KPsso) around. Work a plain row. Repeat these 2 rows from *, switching to DPNs when necessary.

OOH, I WANT TO TRY COLORWORK, TOO!

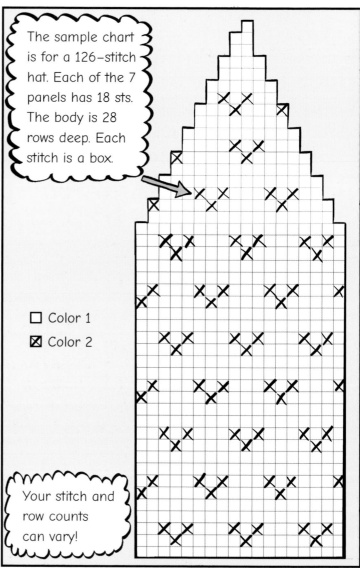

The sample chart is for a 126-stitch hat. Each of the 7 panels has 18 sts. The body is 28 rows deep. Each stitch is a box.

☐ Color 1
☒ Color 2

Your stitch and row counts can vary!

For both the solid and Fair Isle hats, finish with I-cord. When you have a total of 15 or fewer sts, k2tog across. Work one round plain. Next round, use k2tog and k3tog as needed to get 4 sts total. Put sts on one DPN and work them on the RS. Do not turn work. Slide sts to the front of the needle, pull the working yarn around behind, and work them on the RS again. Do this once more, then to bind off, k2tog twice, pull the first stitch over the second one. Break yarn and draw the tail through your last stitch and down the center of your I-cord, all the way through to the inside of the hat.

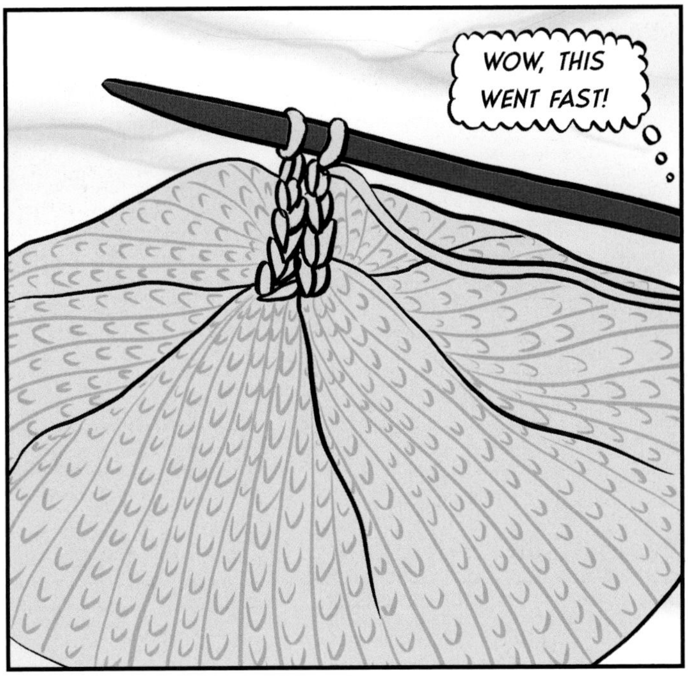
WOW, THIS WENT FAST!

Turn the hat inside out. Fold up the hem. It will turn nicely on the purl rows. In matching yarn, with small sewn stitches, tack down the bottom edge of the hem right underneath your increase row.

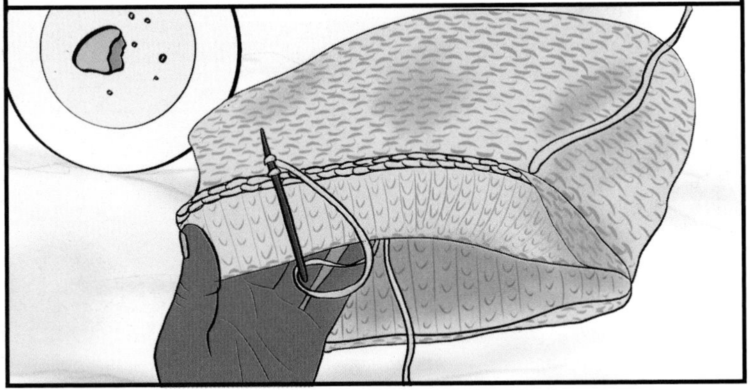

Block, inserting a plate to stretch and shape the hat as it dries. When dry, sew in ends.

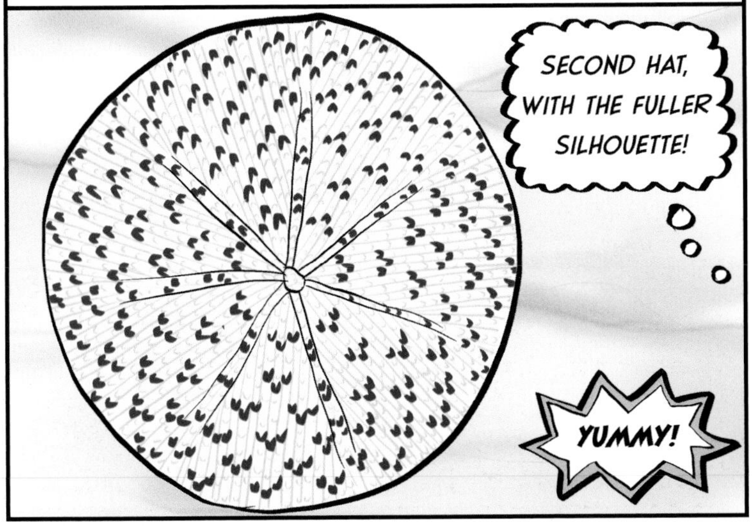
SECOND HAT, WITH THE FULLER SILHOUETTE!
YUMMY!

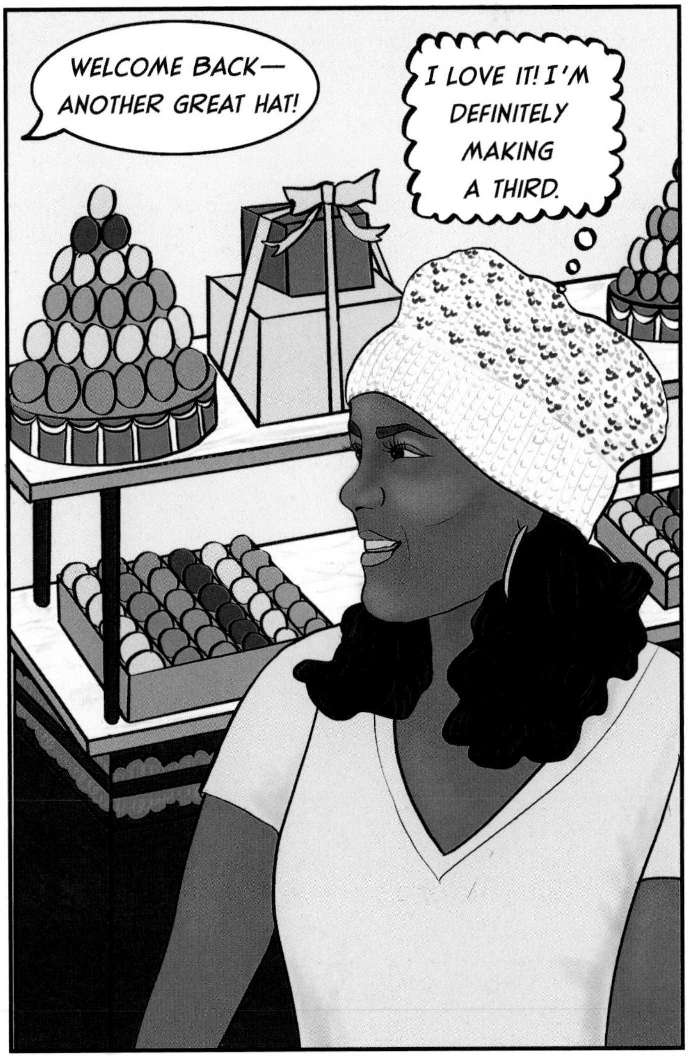
WELCOME BACK— ANOTHER GREAT HAT!
I LOVE IT! I'M DEFINITELY MAKING A THIRD.

the Chizy

(SHI - zee)

BY KAREN KIM MAR

IT'S CHIC. IT'S COZY. IT'S CHIZY, A CUSTOMIZABLE RECTANGULAR SHRUG. USE THIS CLEVER PATTERN TO QUICKLY TRANSFORM YOUR STASH INTO A STACK OF GORGEOUS, ONE-OF-A-KIND WRAPS! GOOD THING, BECAUSE ALL YOUR FRIENDS WILL WANT ONE.

MATERIALS: Yarn for center squares and the border. Center squares may have different gauges. Bust stash! The border will take about 2.5 times more yarn than the whole center. You will need DPNs and short circular needles for the center squares, a long circular needle for the borders, plenty of waste yarn, and safety pins. **GAUGE:** Soft if you like it cuddly, Medium if you want more structure. Determine your gauge in your center squares and border stitches. The sample uses 5 x 5 basket weave on the sides and bottom, and 7 x 7 basket weave on the top. **SIZE:** Measure the widest part of the torso and add 12 in (30.5 cm) to get your Total Length (TL). If the sum is a fraction or an odd number, round up to an even number. Divide TL by 4 to get the side length of each center square (S).

CHIC

COZY

SHOULD I GO OUT?

SHOULD I STAY IN?

Example: Widest part of the torso is 44 in (112 cm), the total length (TL) will be 56 in (142 cm). Divide that by 4 to get 14 in (36 cm). Each center square will be 14 in x 14 in (36 cm x 36 cm).

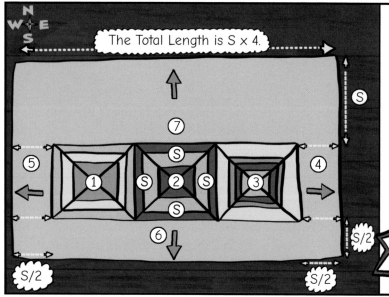

The Total Length is S x 4.

METHOD: Chizy starts with three center-out miter squares of the same size, sewn together in a row (1–3). The right border is picked up and worked to the east for S/2 (half the length of your square; 4). The left border is picked up and worked to the west for S/2 (5). The bottom is picked up and worked to the south for S/2 (6), and finally the top border is picked up and worked to the north for S (the full side of a square; 7). **TECHNIQUES:** Center-out mitered square (p. 66), Gauge Translation (GT) (p. 67).

YOUR SQUARES CAN BE LOG CABIN, LACE, CABLES, OR JUST ONE BIG RECTANGLE. IK IT!

After you calculate the size of the mitered square (S), knit three squares, and bind them off purlwise. Seam them together in a row with Horizontal Stockinette seams. Scoop a stitch from each side.

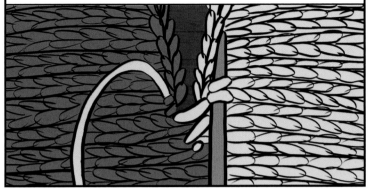

For borders, select a reversible stitch like . . .

Moss

Seed

Garter

Basket weave has alternating blocks of Stockinette and reverse Stockinette. The sample has a 7-stitch, 7-row basket weave on the top border, and 5-stitch, 5-row on the bottom and sides.

To do a basket weave border, first adjust your border stitch count to be a multiple of X. **1)** Work (X stitches of Stockinette and X stitches of reverse Stockinette) across. Work as established for a total of X rows.
2) Then reverse your St st and rev St st for the next X rows. Repeat these 2 steps to desired depth.

Calculate the border depths. Side and bottom borders are half the depth of the square (S/2, steps 4–6). The top border is the full depth of the square (S, step 7).

Example: S/2, or half of our 14 in (36 cm) square, gives us a 7 in (18 cm) border depth on the sides and bottom, and S or 14 in (36 cm) on the top.

FRET...FRET...FRET...

Use GT to calculate the number of stitches to pick up for each border stitch you use. Pick up, knit, and bind off the side, bottom, and then top borders. Break yarn.

Example: Karen's first side border has 70 bound-off stitches. Her 5 x 5 basket weave gauge times the length of the side gave her 59 stitches. She rounded up to 60 to have a multiple of 5 for her basket weave.

IN? OUT? MAYBE I'LL FLIP A COIN.

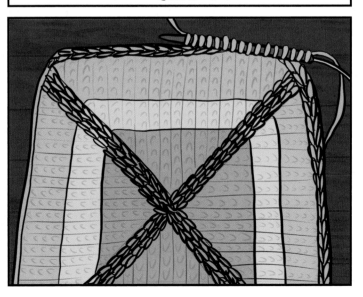

To make the armholes, lay the rectangle wrong side up. Fold the upper right and left corners of the collar to the waistband. Align the corners—there will be excess fabric around the collar. For standard armholes, place safety pins 8 in (20 cm) from the left and right outer corners.

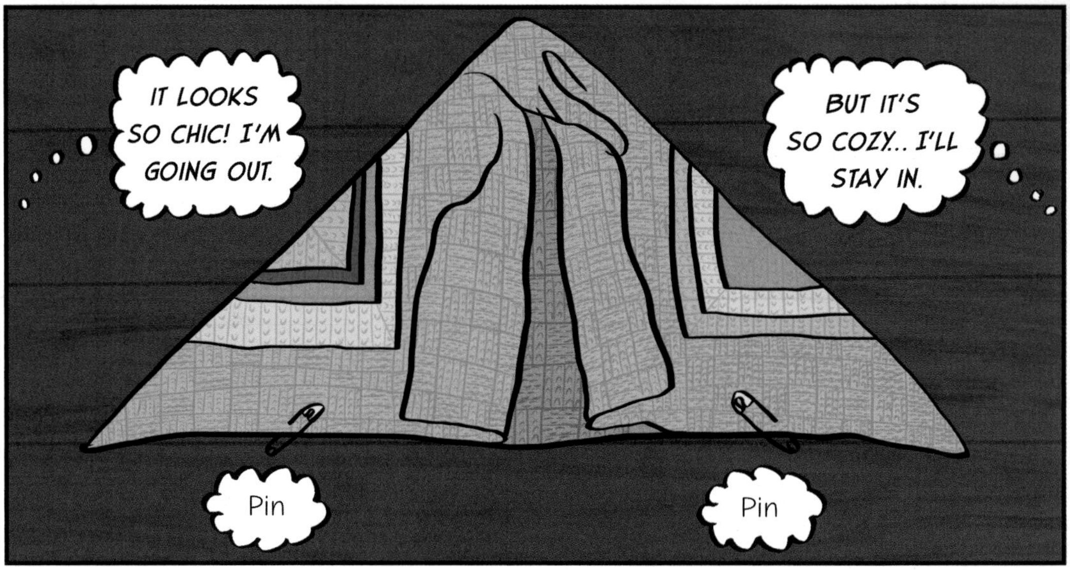
IT LOOKS SO CHIC! I'M GOING OUT.
BUT IT'S SO COZY... I'LL STAY IN.
Pin
Pin

Try it on.

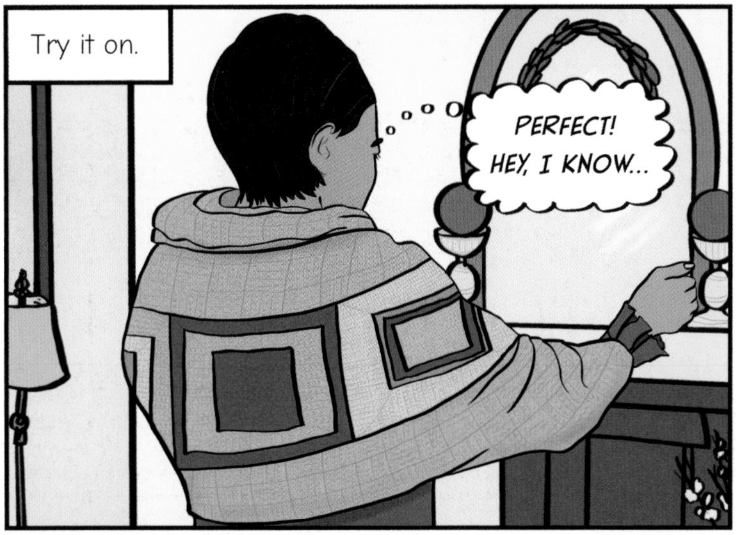
PERFECT! HEY, I KNOW...

If you'd like more ease around the torso, make the armholes smaller by adjusting the pins evenly on both sides. When it's where you like it, sew the sides together with a few stitches at each point.

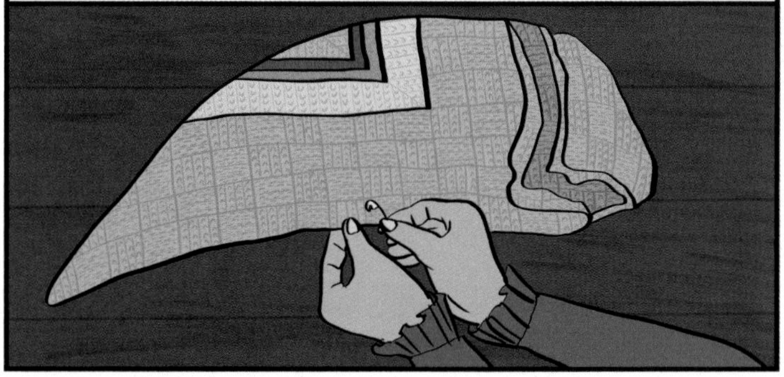

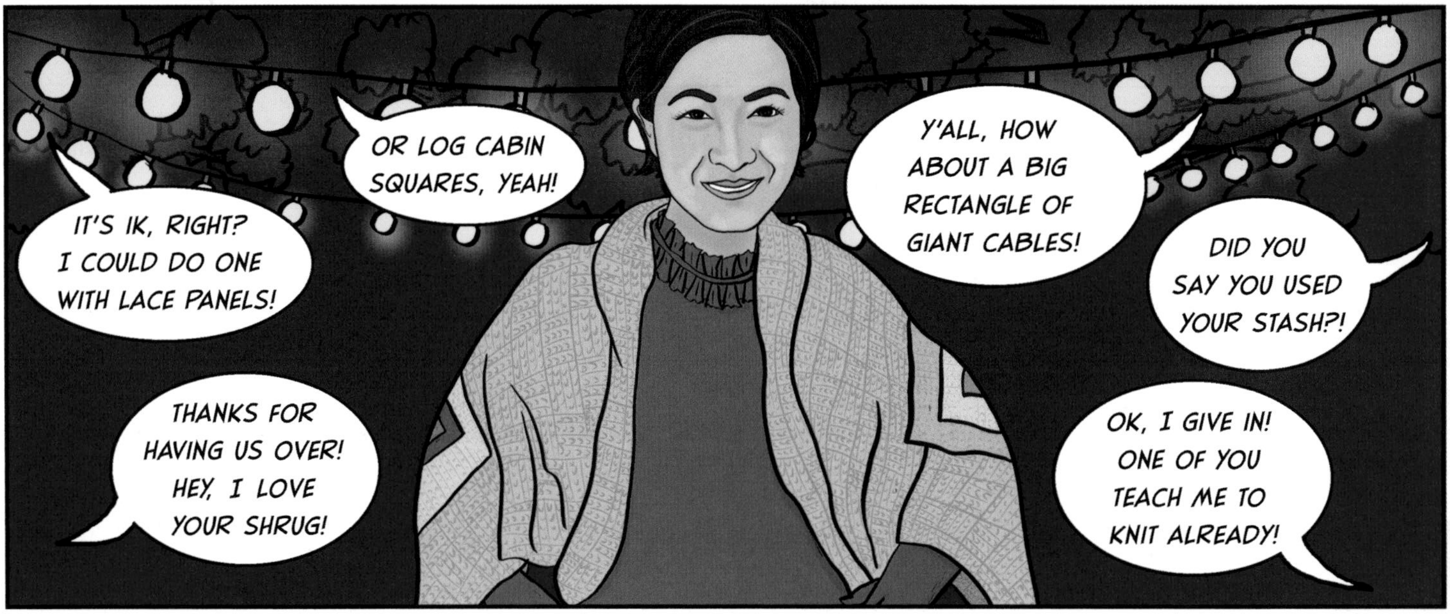
IT'S IK, RIGHT? I COULD DO ONE WITH LACE PANELS!
OR LOG CABIN SQUARES, YEAH!
Y'ALL, HOW ABOUT A BIG RECTANGLE OF GIANT CABLES!
DID YOU SAY YOU USED YOUR STASH?!
THANKS FOR HAVING US OVER! HEY, I LOVE YOUR SHRUG!
OK, I GIVE IN! ONE OF YOU TEACH ME TO KNIT ALREADY!

Oh BY THE Way

A sweater yoke is basically everything above the armpits. The yoke encompasses how the sleeves are joined to the body of a sweater. There are many ways to accomplish this. Here are four of the most common sweater yoke treatments.

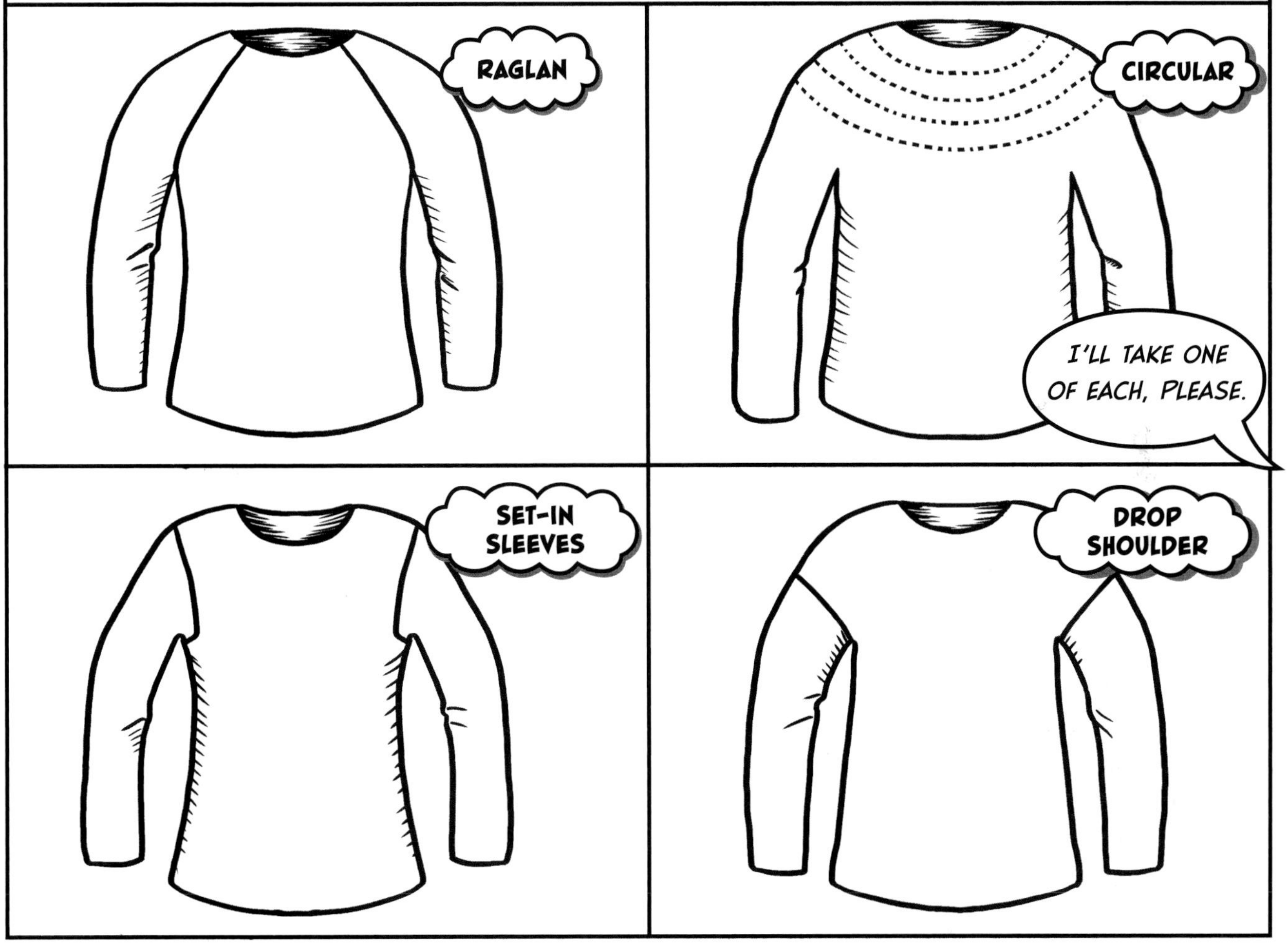
RAGLAN
CIRCULAR
I'LL TAKE ONE OF EACH, PLEASE.
SET-IN SLEEVES
DROP SHOULDER

S3 Special Skein Sweater

BY LAUREN McELROY

SHOWCASE YOUR MOST PRECIOUS HANDSPUN, SOUVENIR, OR LIMITED-EDITION YARN IN THIS ONE-OF-A-KIND SWEATER. HAVE FUN WITH LAUREN'S SADDLE-RAGLAN YOKE, OR SWAP IN THE TOP-DOWN YOKE OF YOUR CHOICE!

MATERIALS: In addition to your special skein, you will need a sweater's worth of main-color yarn. Let the yarns be close in size; you will want to achieve the same gauge with both. Long and short circular needles and DPNs to get your gauge. Make a note of what needle you need for each, if they are different. **GAUGE:** Soft to Medium.

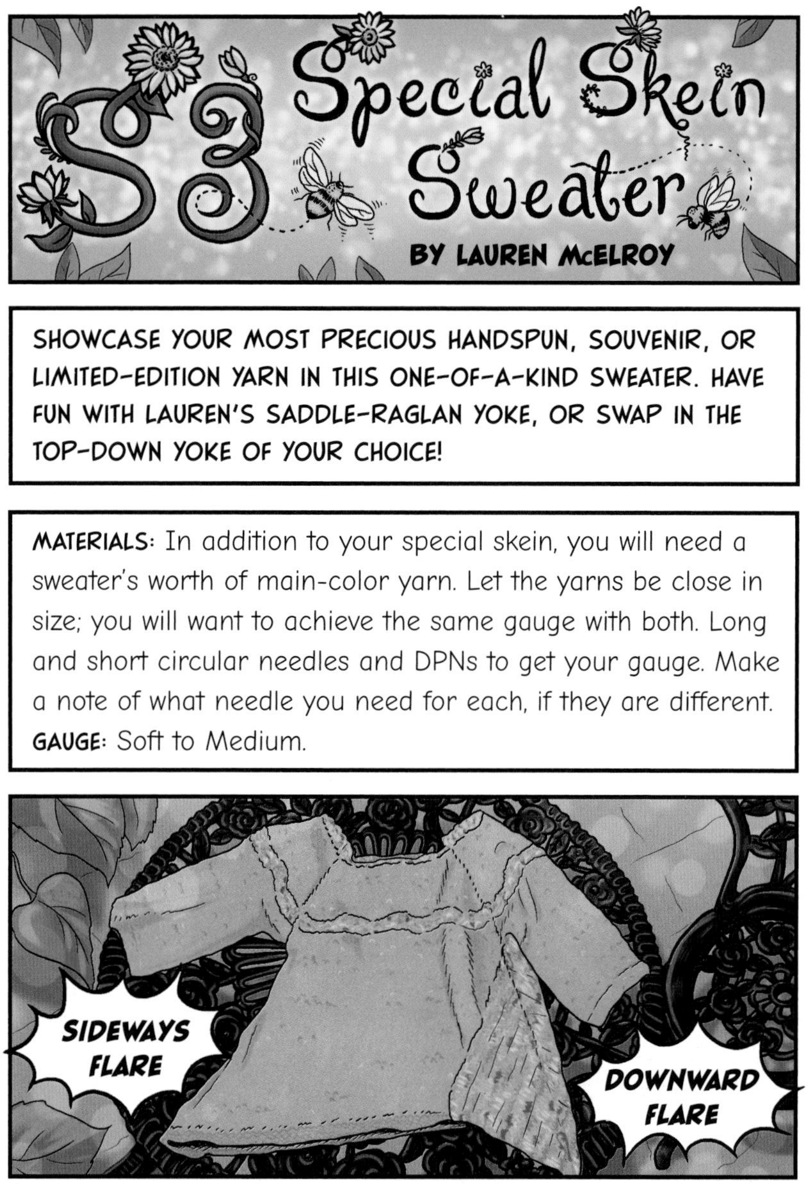
SIDEWAYS FLARE
DOWNWARD FLARE

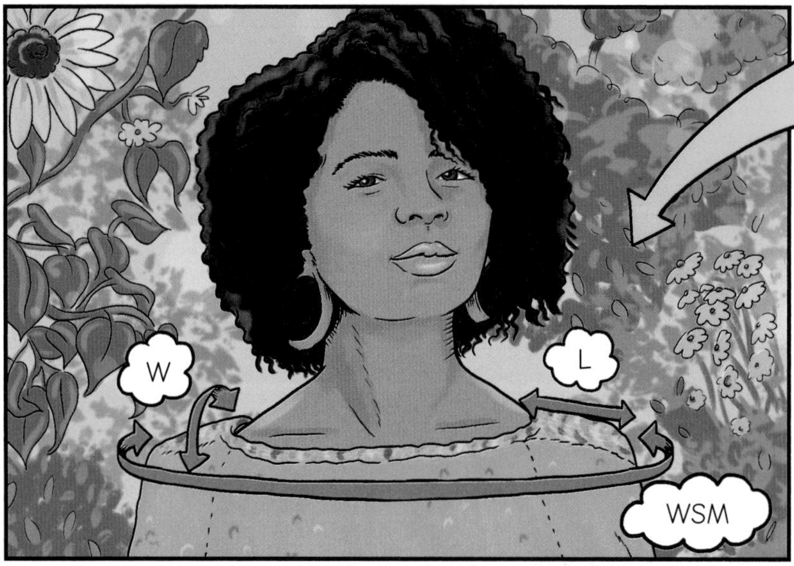
W
L
WSM

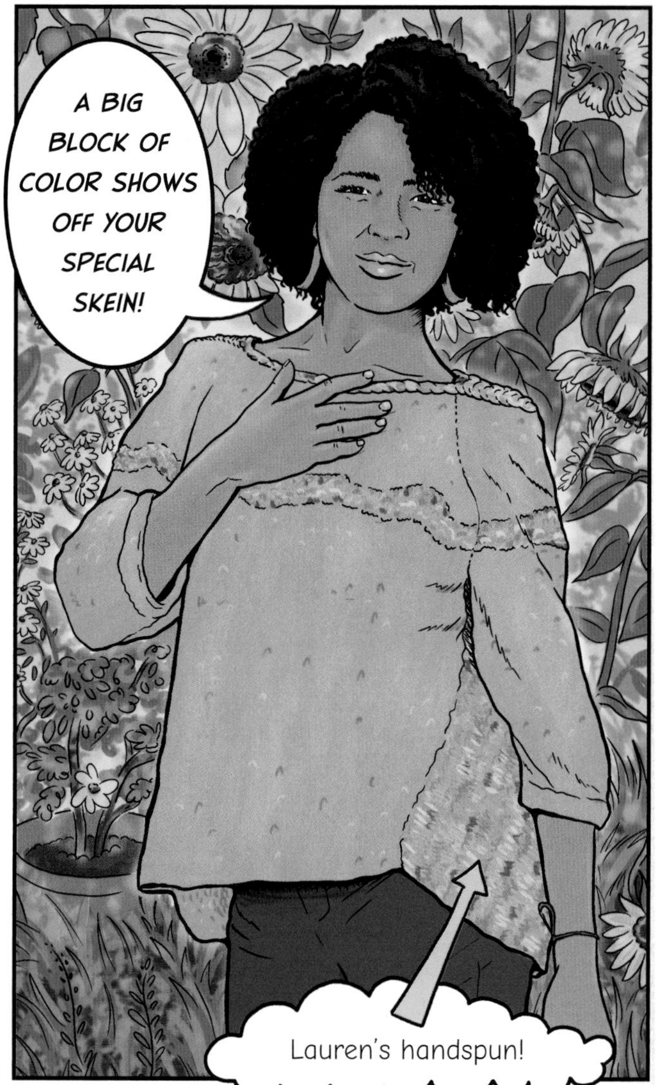
A BIG BLOCK OF COLOR SHOWS OFF YOUR SPECIAL SKEIN!
Lauren's handspun!

SIZE: Measure around your shoulders (Wide Shoulder Measurement–WSM), and measure the length (L) and width (W) you want for your shoulder saddles. **TECHNIQUES:** Short rows, grafting (p. 68), wrapping (p. 93), knitted cast-on. **METHOD:** This is top-down, so you can try it on as you go to inform the fit. Directions are given for the saddle-raglan yoke, but you can work any yoke you like down to the underarm. The two side flare panels begin at the underarms, after your yoke shaping. One side flare panel is worked in your main-color yarn. The opposite side is worked as a cutout, which you come back and fill in with your special skein yarn.

Multiply your **WSM** × gauge. This is the total number of stitches you will ultimately have on your needle (X).

> For example, **WSM** = 29 in (74 cm), and the gauge is 6 st/in (6 st/2.5 cm). Multiply gauge by measurement for X = 174 stitches.

X will have stitches you pick up from the length (L) of the saddles, all the live stitches at the ends of each saddle (W), and cast-on stitches front and back between the saddles.

Long-tail cast on the width (W) of your saddle (your gauge multiplied by W) and knit to the desired length (L) in a non-curling stitch. (1 & 2 on figure below.).

SOME OF OUR FAVORITES ARE GARTER, BROKEN RIB, AND MOSS STITCH.

Slip the first stitch of each row to make it easier to pick up stitches along the edge in the next step. Leave stitches live, break the yarn, and set aside. Work the second saddle.

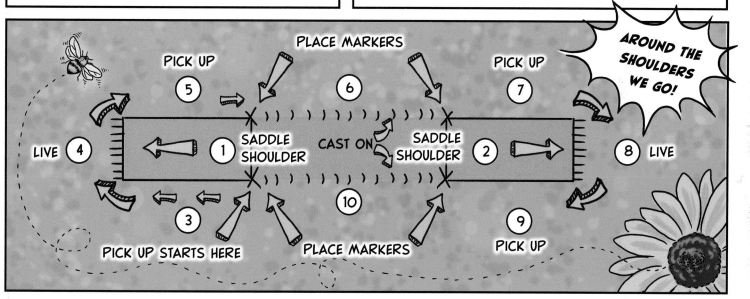

PICK UP **5** PLACE MARKERS **6** **7** PICK UP

AROUND THE SHOULDERS WE GO!

LIVE **4** **1** SADDLE SHOULDER CAST ON SADDLE SHOULDER **2** **8** LIVE

3 **10** **9**

PICK UP STARTS HERE PLACE MARKERS PICK UP

Live stitches

Long side

LEAVE THE LIVE STITCHES LOOSE (IF YOU LIVE ON THE EDGE) OR PUT THEM ON A HOLDER.

3) Place marker (pm), pick up and knit stitches along the length (L) of your first saddle. **4)** Pick up the live stitches on the end (W). **5)** Pick up and knit the stitches from the other side (same number of stitches as for 3), pm. You have picked up three sides of one shoulder saddle. **6)** Use a knitted cast-on to cast on for the neck back like this: Take X and divide it by 2. Subtract the stitches you just picked up from the three sides of the saddle. Cast on the remaining stitches, pm. **7)** Pick up and knit the length of your second saddle. **8)** Pick up the live stitches on the end. **9)** Pick up and knit stitches along the other length, pm. **10)** Cast on the same number of stitches for the front that you did for the back. Join, being careful not to twist. X stitches and 4 markers total.

The picked-up and live saddle stitches are the sleeve stitches. The markers are where your raglan increases occur. Work Stockinette stitch (St st) in the round, increasing one stitch on each side of the four raglan markers every other round. Use any increase you like.

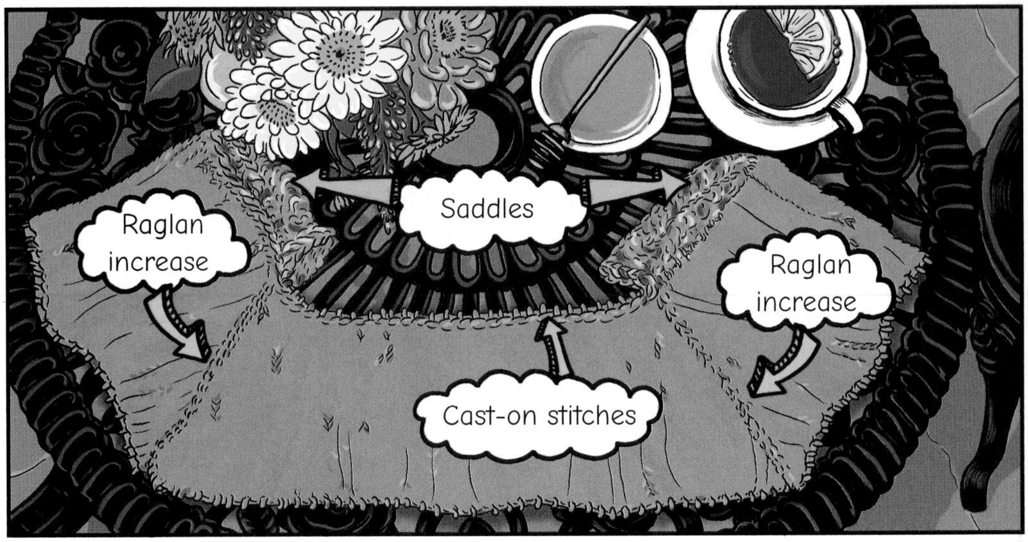
Raglan increase
Saddles
Raglan increase
Cast-on stitches

Continue with your increases, trying on frequently, until you reach your desired body width and armhole depth. If you like the width but need more armhole depth, you can stop increasing and just work straight. This is a chance to work a bit of lace in your showcase yarn.

Feather and Fan, for instance, requires a multiple of 18 stitches and takes a multiple of 4 rows.

To work Feather and Fan in the round (rnd), **RNDS 1 AND 2:** Knit. **RND 3:** [K2tog 3 times. (Yo, k1) 6 times. K2tog 3 times] around. **RND 4:** Purl. Repeat these 4 rounds as desired.

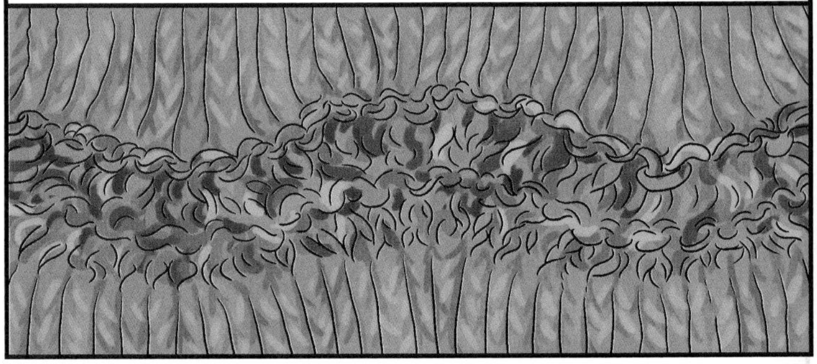

When the armhole depth is where you want it, separate your sleeve stitches from the body stitches. Starting at the back of the left sleeve, place the sleeve stitches on waste yarn, knit across the front, place the right sleeve stitches on waste yarn, knit across the back, and join the body in the round. Remove your stitch markers as you go. Place 2 new markers, each directly centered in an underarm. One will mark your main-color flare, and the other your cutout.

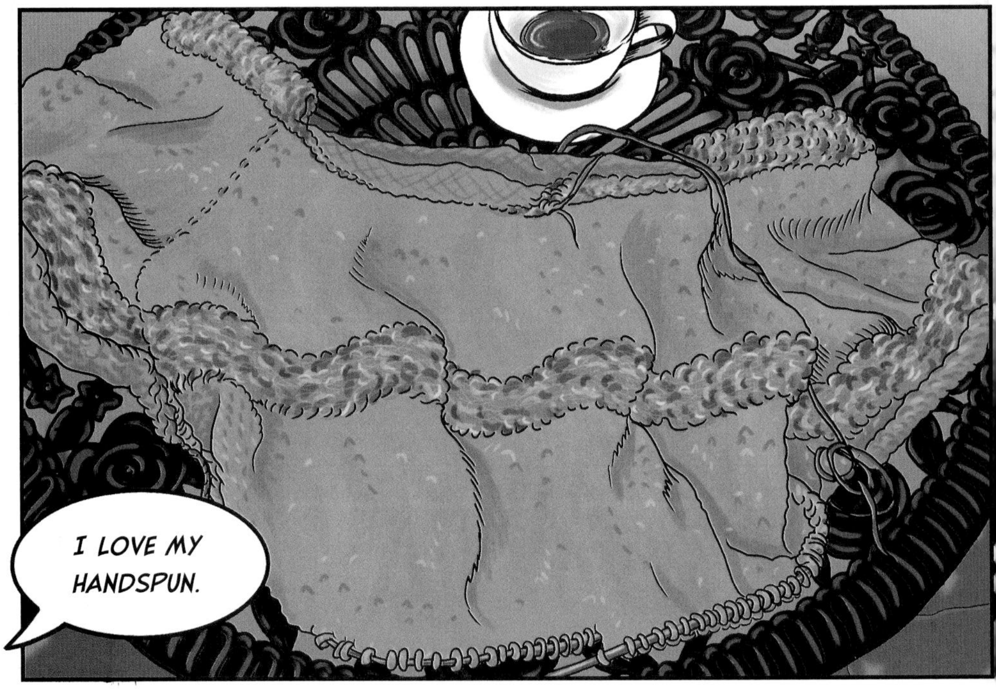
I LOVE MY HANDSPUN.

OPTIONAL: short rows and increase stitches for bust ease over the next 2–3 in (5–7 cm). Decide your bust depth. Divide this by how many short rows you want. This is the depth to work plain between your short rows. Work short rows across the front of the sweater as follows: *Knit to the last stitch of the front, M1, k1, wrap and turn, purl back across the WS of the front to the last stitch, M1, p1, wrap and turn. Work your calculated depth. Repeat from * until you have worked your bust depth. The sample sweater has 4 total short rows.

IF YOU DON'T WRAP THE YARN, YOU WILL HAVE HOLES IN THE SIDE SEAMS AT THOSE POINTS. NO MATTER, JUST SEW THEM TOGETHER WHEN YOU WEAVE IN YOUR ENDS.

YOU CAN DO ANY TOP-DOWN SWEATER YOKE UP TO THIS POINT, AND CONTINUE THE INSTRUCTIONS FROM HERE.

Decide which side you want your cutout on, and call the marker at that underarm the first marker. The marker at the other underarm is the second marker. From your first marker, on the RS, knit across and increase one stitch on each side of the second stitch marker. Work to one stitch before the first marker, wrap and turn the work. Purl back to one stitch before that same stitch marker, wrap and turn. Continue wrapping and turning one stitch before the last wrapped stitch, maintaining your RS increases around the second marker, until you have reached 1 in (2.5 cm) from your desired total length of the garment on the long side. For the last inch, continue the shaping but knit each row for Garter stitch.

Bind off the stitches between your two wrapped-stitch end points. You now have a cutout triangle shape on one side of your garment beginning at the underarm, and a fully knit sideways flare on the other side with the increases running directly from the other underarm.

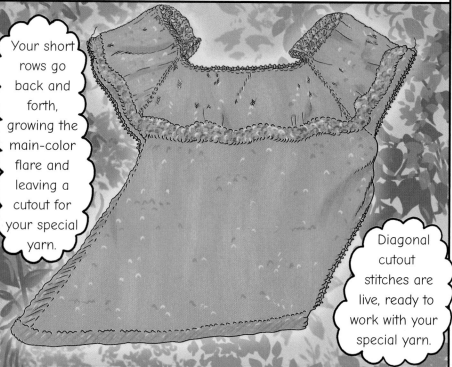

Your short rows go back and forth, growing the main-color flare and leaving a cutout for your special yarn.
Diagonal cutout stitches are live, ready to work with your special yarn.

MY HANDSPUN: INSPIRED BY BEES, HONEY, AND SUNFLOWERS.

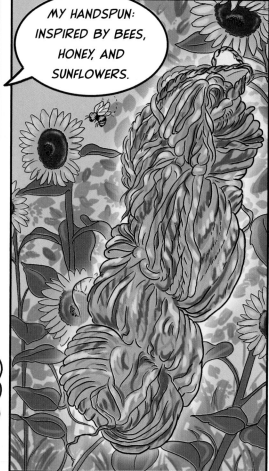

Make sure your marker is in the exact middle of the stitches, at the underarm. Leave both sides of the diagonal cutout on a long circular needle.

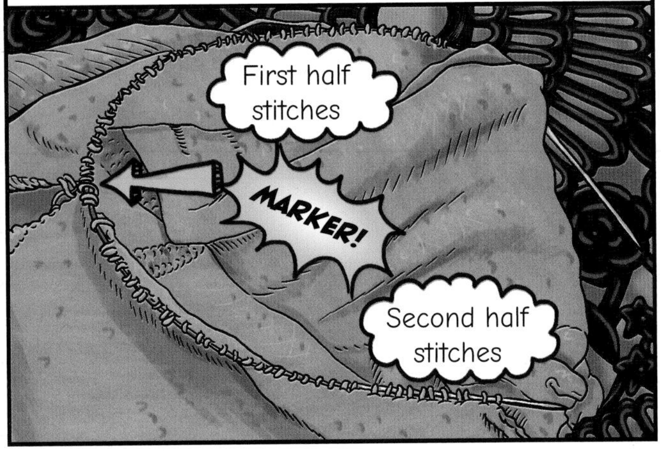
First half stitches
MARKER!
Second half stitches

Fill the cutout with your special skein. On the RS, work all the way across both sides of the triangle like this: *(knit 1 stitch, knit its wrap, knit 1) across. You are increasing every other stitch by knitting one wrap and not knitting the next wrap.

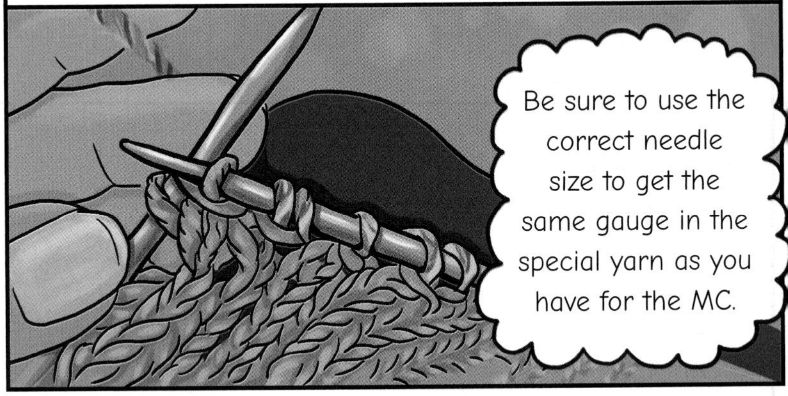
Be sure to use the correct needle size to get the same gauge in the special yarn as you have for the MC.

Now you will work one half of the triangle at a time, stopping at the stitch marker. For the first half, create a Garter-edged hem as follows: Starting at the hem edge, on the WS, knit the first inch of stitches, pm, purl to 1 stitch before the marker, wrap and turn, knit to the marker, knit the last stitches. Turn and purl to 2 stitches before your last turned stitch and wrap and turn. Knit to marker, knit the last stitches. Continue in this manner until all stitches on that side of the marker have been worked.

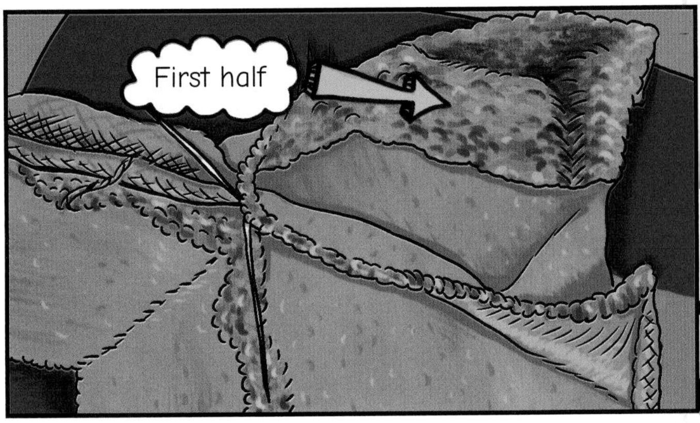
First half

Cut yarn, attach yarn on the other hem edge, RS facing, and knit the first inch of stitches, pm, knit to 1 stitch before the marker, wrap and turn, purl to the marker, knit the last stitches. Turn and knit to 2 stitches before your last turned stitch and wrap and turn. Purl to marker, knit the last stitches. Continue in this manner until all stitches on that side of the marker have been worked.

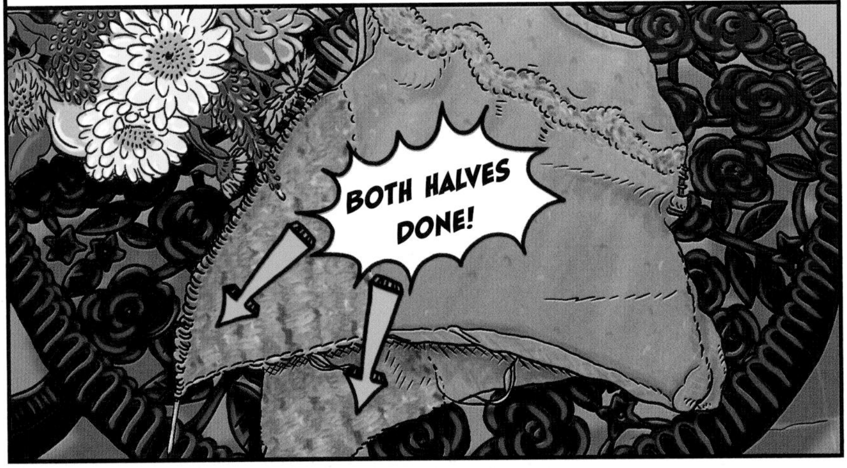
BOTH HALVES DONE!

When you have finished the second half, knit across all stitches, from hem to hem. Cut yarn, leaving 1 y (1 m). Graft the sides of the special panel together.

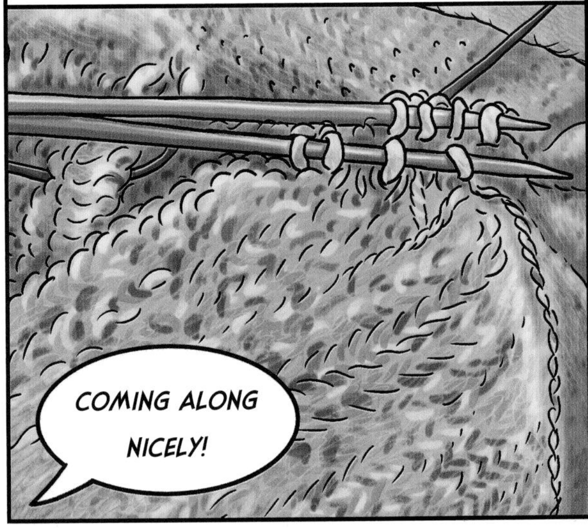
COMING ALONG NICELY!

At last, the sleeves and neckline! Put stitches from the waste yarn for one sleeve back on a circular needle or DPNs. Using your main color, begin your decrease round: ssk, knit to last 2 stitches in round, k2tog. Knit one round plain. Continue on, alternating a decrease round and plain round, until the arm width is to your liking. Knit around until you are 1 in (2.5 cm) from preferred length, then work the last 1 in (2.5 cm) in Garter and bind off. Repeat for second sleeve. Pick up the stitches around the neck with your special yarn. Bind off purlwise, or work an edge in a non-curling stitch to desired depth, then bind off.

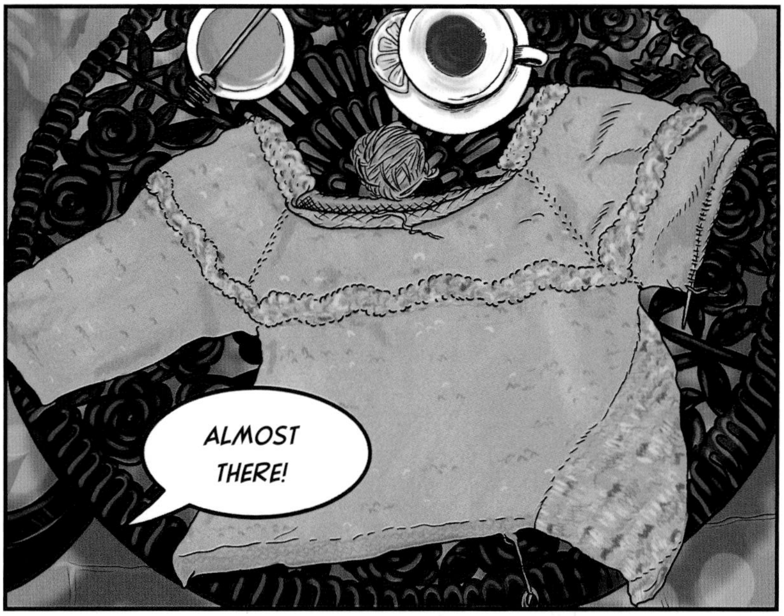
ALMOST THERE!

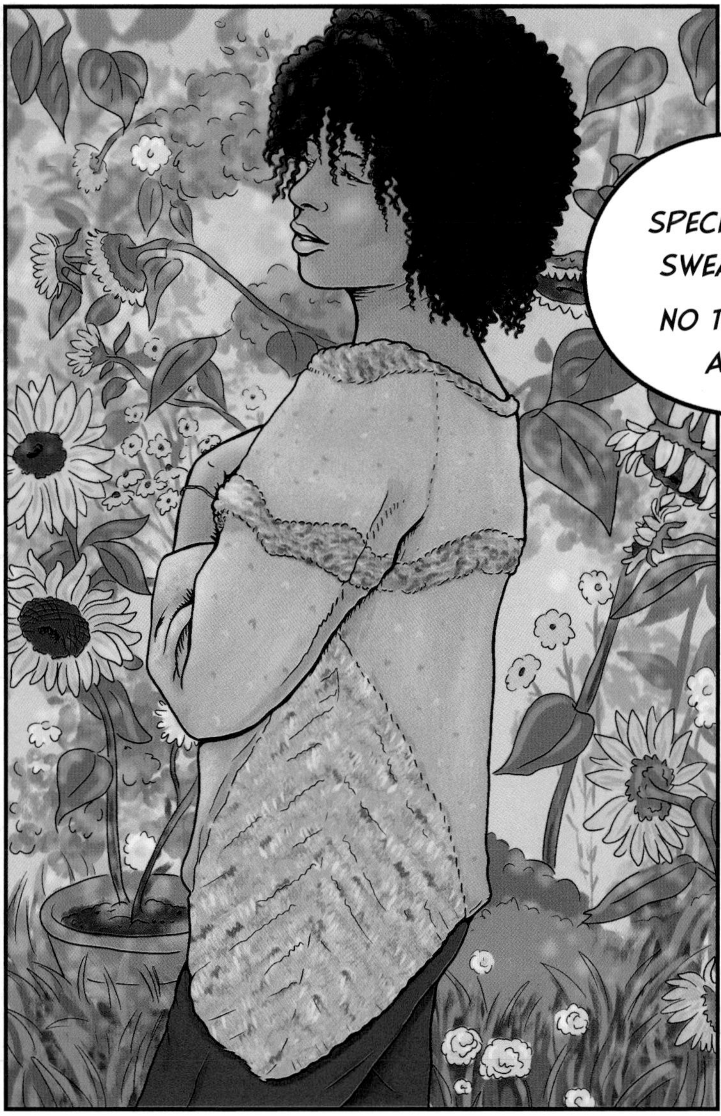

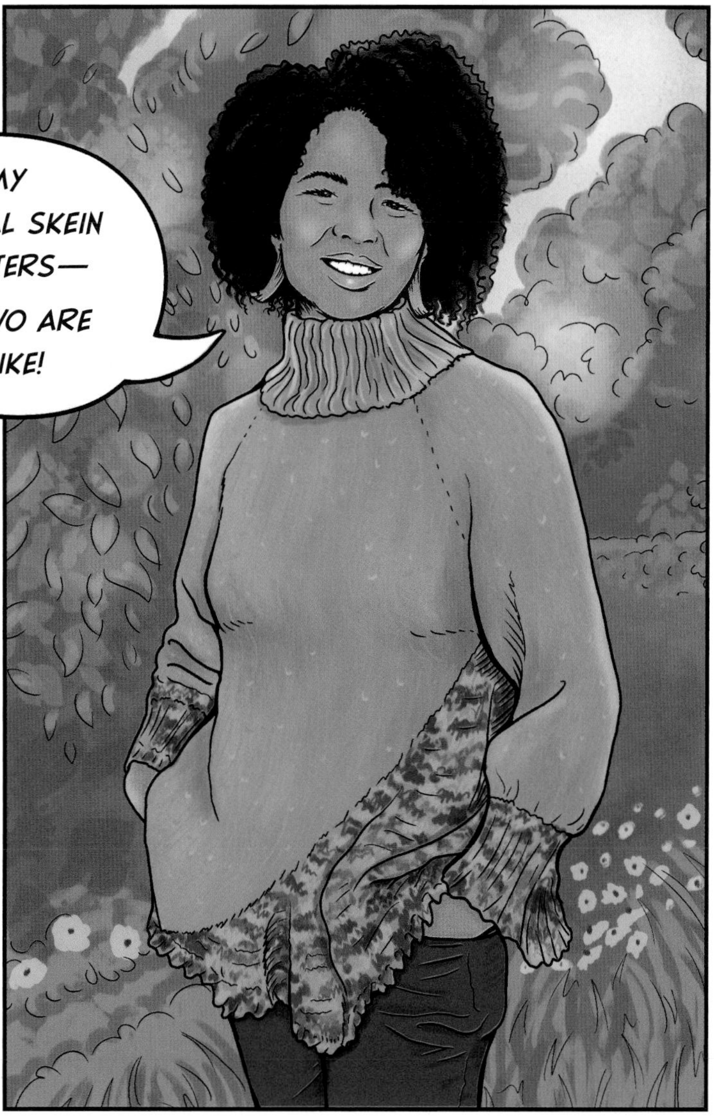
MY SPECIAL SKEIN SWEATERS— NO TWO ARE ALIKE!

OMNIMITTS

BY ALICE ORMSBEE BELTRAN

THESE BEGINNER-FRIENDLY FINGERLESS MITTS DO IT ALL FOR US. EASY TO KNIT AND EVEN EASIER TO WEAR, THEY CAN BE SOLID, OR ANY COMBINATION OF COLORS. USE THE RAREST, MOST PRECIOUS SKEIN IN YOUR STASH, OR A WORKHORSE YARN. WE DEFY ANYONE TO HOLD AN OMNIMITT WITHOUT SLIDING IT ON; THEY ARE IRRESISTIBLE.

MATERIALS: 2 colors of same size yarn, circular or straight needles. **SIZE:** Knit to fit the hand. **GAUGE:** Medium to Chewy. **TECHNIQUES:** Two-Stranded Long-Tail Cast-On (TSLTCO), sewing up. **METHOD:** The mitts are knit sideways in Garter stitch and seamed.

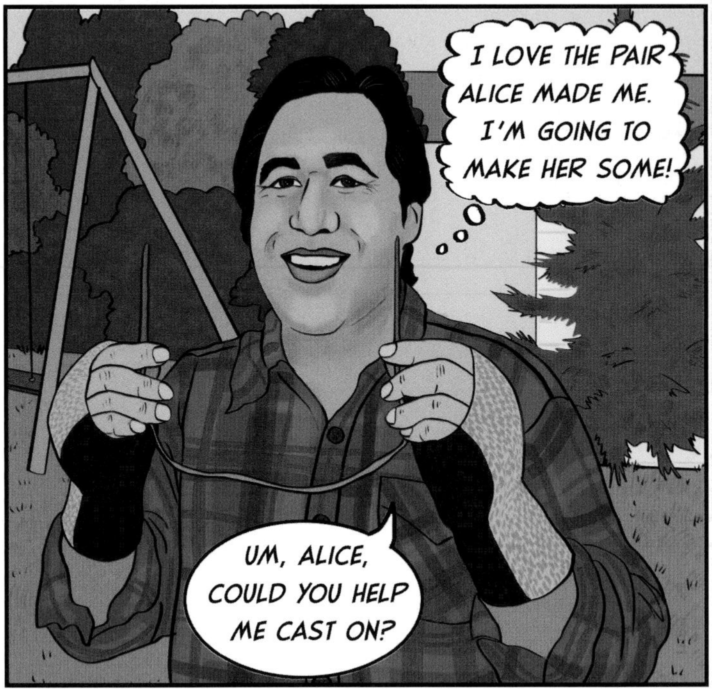
I LOVE THE PAIR ALICE MADE ME. I'M GOING TO MAKE HER SOME!
UM, ALICE, COULD YOU HELP ME CAST ON?

Measure length for a custom fit or go with a standard 8–8½ in (20–21.5 cm). Multiply length by your gauge to get your stitches (sts) to cast on.

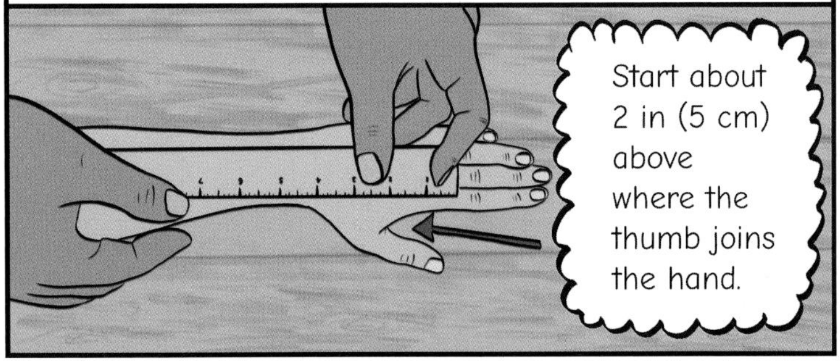
Start about 2 in (5 cm) above where the thumb joins the hand.

To **TSLTCO**, hold both needles together, and take an end from the center and from the outside of your center-pull cake of yarn. You could also use the ends from two balls. Pinch your needles and both yarns together in your right hand.

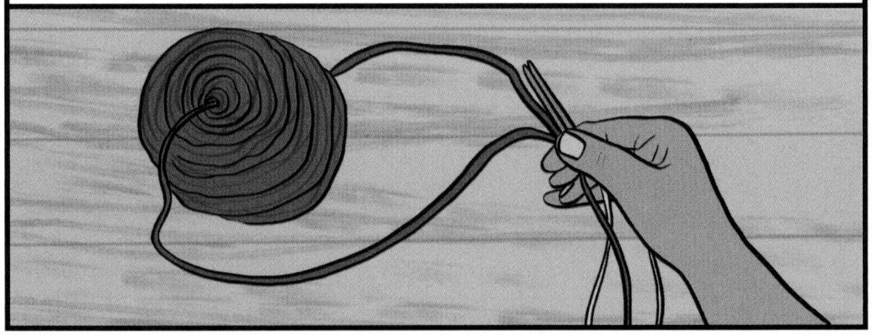

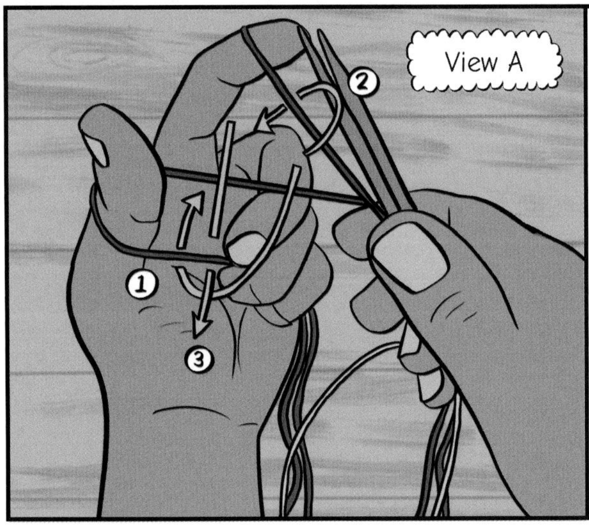
View A
1
2
3

Hold the yarn like this, and

1) Scoop the left outer side.

2) Scoop the right center side.

3) Out through the window.

4) Snug down the st and repeat.

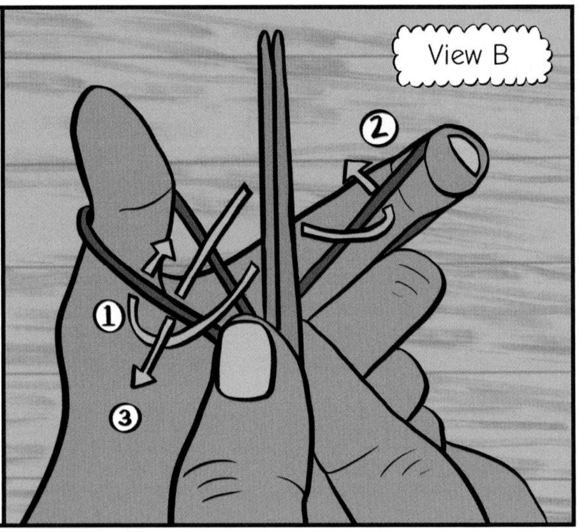
View B
1
2
3

Cast on your stitches with your first color. Knit the first row, and knit through the back loop (ktbl) of the last st.

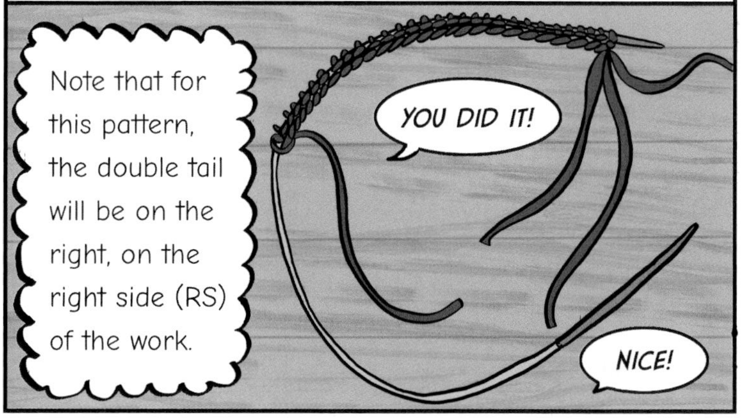

Note that for this pattern, the double tail will be on the right, on the right side (RS) of the work.
YOU DID IT!
NICE!

Knit each row. For tidy edges, slip the first st of each row and ktbl the last st of each row. Work until the piece fully covers the palm of the wearer.

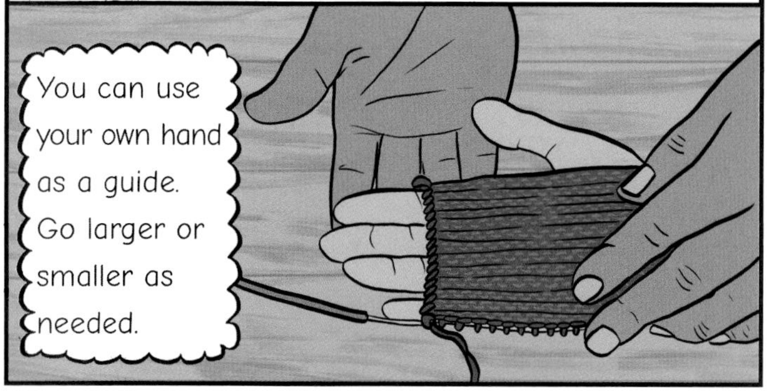

You can use your own hand as a guide. Go larger or smaller as needed.

Count the ridges on the RS. If you like, change to your second color on the next RS row. Work for the same number of ridges you counted, ending ready to work a RS row. Bind off knitwise. Work a second mitt, starting with your second color this time.

Fold your rectangles the long way. Measure 2–2½ in (5–6.5 cm) from what will be the top edge of the mitt, and 1½ in (4 cm) from there toward the bottom of the mitt for the thumbhole. Mark the thumbhole with stitch markers.

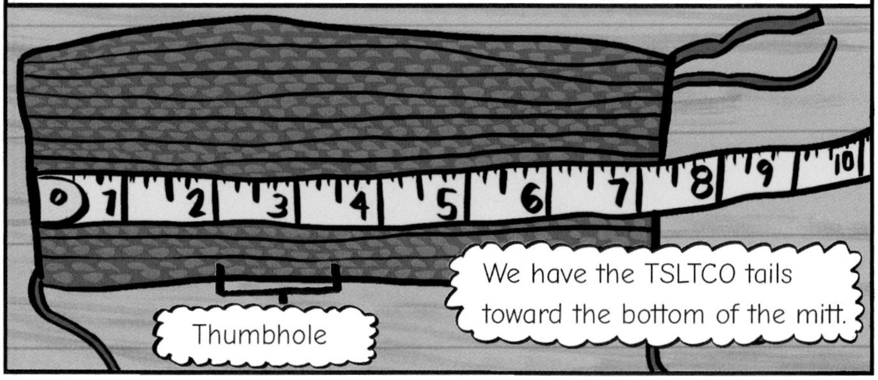

0 1 2 3 4 5 6 7 8 9 10
Thumbhole
We have the TSLTCO tails toward the bottom of the mitt.

Sew the first seam from the bottom to the base of the thumb-hole, and secure it. Skip the thumbhole, sew up the rest of the seam. Darn in ends, block, and wear!

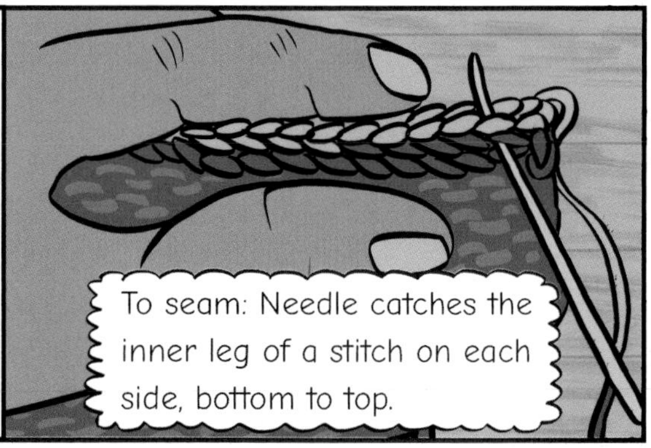

To seam: Needle catches the inner leg of a stitch on each side, bottom to top.

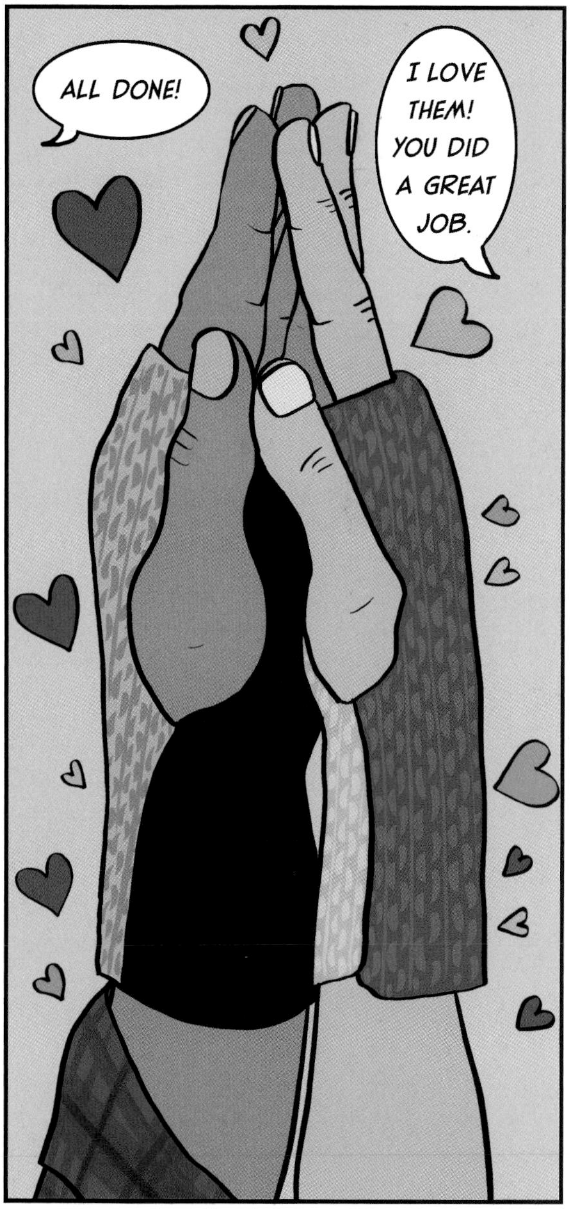

ALL DONE!
I LOVE THEM! YOU DID A GREAT JOB.

IK COOKIES

BY ALICE O. BELTRAN

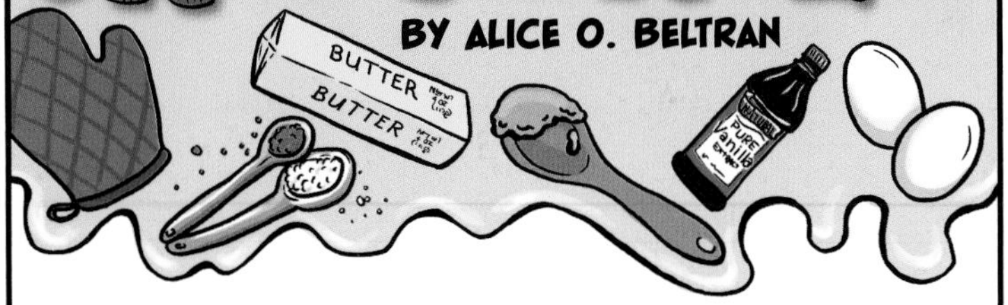
BUTTER
BUTTER
PURE Vanilla

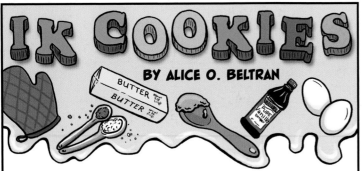

THE OFFICIAL BREAKFAST... ER, COOKIE, OF CASA DE INTERACTIVE KNITTING. THIS CUSTOMIZABLE COOKIE COMES TOGETHER IN TWO PARTS: THE BINDER DOUGH AND THE MIX-INS. NO NEED TO SIFT OR FUSS TOO MUCH; IT'LL ALL WORK OUT.

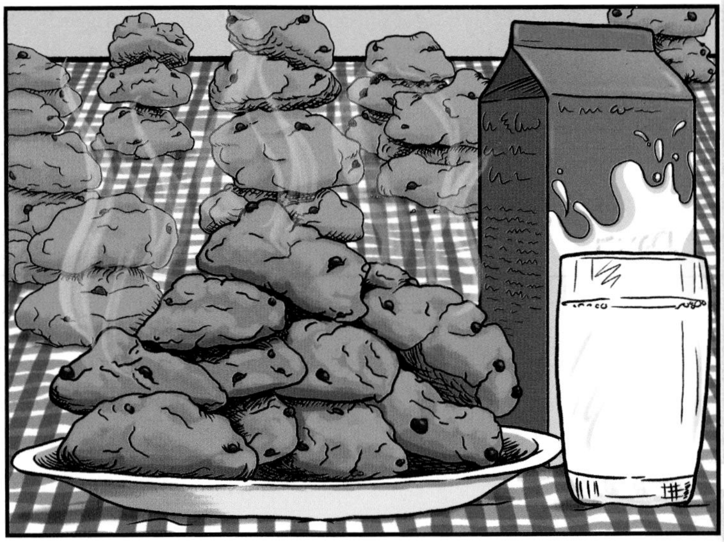

YIELD: Over 100. Alice ate them and did not count. **TOOLS:** Hand mixer, spatula, measuring cups and spoons, bowl or pot large enough to hold 2 gallons/ 4 liters of dough with room to mix. **PREP TIME:** 30 minutes to mix them up, 2 hours to chill, 20 minutes to ball them up for freezing. **BAKE TIME:** 8 to 15 minutes (frozen dough will take longer)

This recipe makes a LOT of dough. Freeze cookie-size balls in a single layer on a baking sheet, and store in gallon freezer bags. Exult in a stash of homemade cookies at your fingertips.

BINDER DOUGH: This will bind your mix-ins.

- 3 cups (720 g) unsalted butter
- 32 oz (4½ packed cups or 900 g) brown sugar
- 8 large or extra-large eggs
- 3 tablespoons (45 ml) vanilla extract
- 8 cups (960 g) whole-wheat pastry flour
- 1 heaping tablespoon (20 g) baking soda
- 1 teaspoon (6 g) salt
- One 18-oz canister (200 g) old-fashioned rolled oats
- 13½ cups (3.2 L) of your choice of mix-ins. See the next page for ideas!

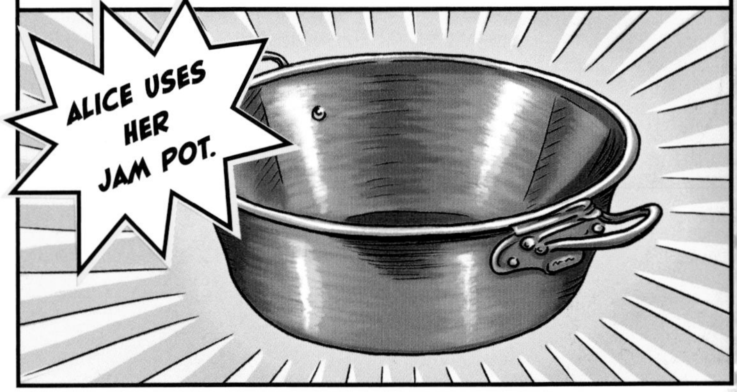
ALICE USES HER JAM POT.

Alice makes them gluten-free with a medley of the GF flours she has on hand. Be ready to scrutinize the dough and add more flour if it looks and feels too wet.

METHOD: In the largest pot you can find, cream together the butter and brown sugar until fluffy. Beat in the eggs, vanilla, baking soda, and salt. Partially mix in the flour and oats. It will get fully blended after you stir in your mix-ins. You will have approximately 13½ cups (~3 liters) of binding dough. Stir in your mix-ins. Cover and chill the dough for an hour to a couple of days.

Preheat oven to 350°F (177°C, Gas Mark 4). When you are ready for cookies, space dough balls accordingly on an ungreased cookie sheet, and bake. Like your IK knitting gauge, how long you bake your cookies is up to you. Watch the first batch closely, mark the time when you think they are perfect, and repeat for subsequent batches.

It only looks like it will take forever to ball up your 2 gallons of dough. It goes quickly. Promise. You'll be glad you did it.

ENJOY YOUR FREEZERFUL OF DOUGH. NOW THAT'S A STASH!

The **ORIGINAL RECIPE** mix-ins are 32 oz (900 g) of semisweet chocolate chips and 8 cups (960 g) pecan pieces. These amounts are designed to match whole bags, for no measuring! **MAKE THEM YOURS.** Binder dough and mix-ins have a 1:1 ratio, so measure out whatever volume of binder dough you like, and add the same volume of mix-ins. Go for your favorites, or clean out your cupboard. Half-empty bag of trail mix? Sure. Mini bag of pretzels? Why not. Crush 'em up and in they go. Cookie Party!

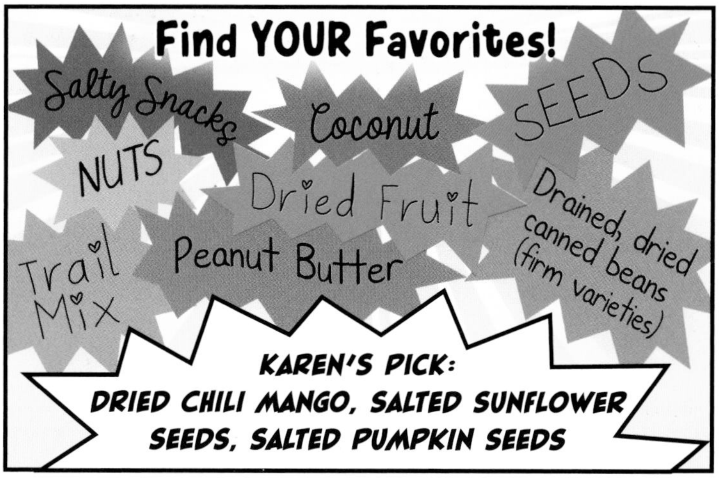
Find YOUR Favorites!
Salty Snacks
Coconut
SEEDS
NUTS
Dried Fruit
Drained, dried canned beans (firm varieties)
Trail Mix
Peanut Butter
KAREN'S PICK: DRIED CHILI MANGO, SALTED SUNFLOWER SEEDS, SALTED PUMPKIN SEEDS

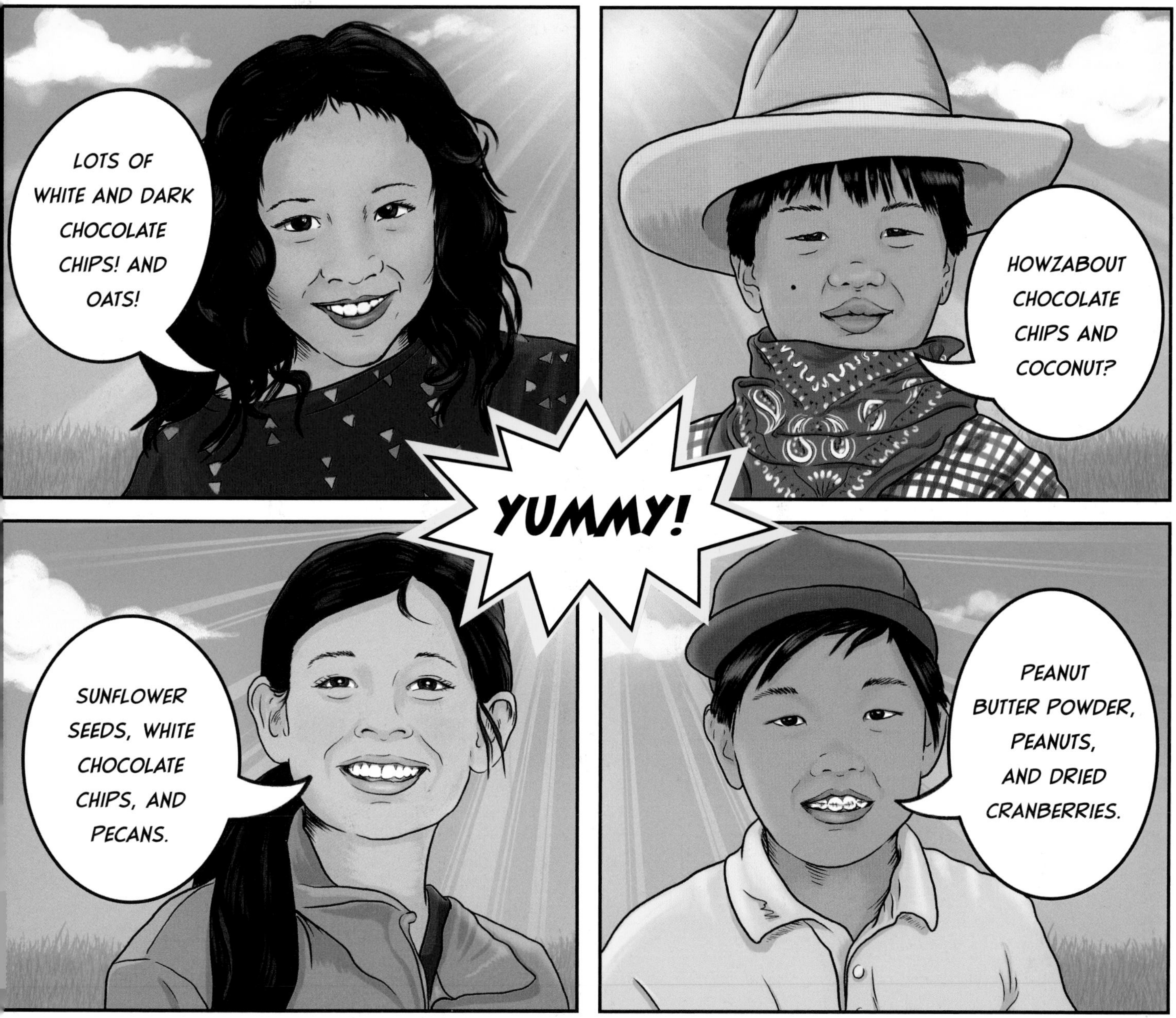
LOTS OF WHITE AND DARK CHOCOLATE CHIPS! AND OATS!
HOWZABOUT CHOCOLATE CHIPS AND COCONUT?
YUMMY!
SUNFLOWER SEEDS, WHITE CHOCOLATE CHIPS, AND PECANS.
PEANUT BUTTER POWDER, PEANUTS, AND DRIED CRANBERRIES.

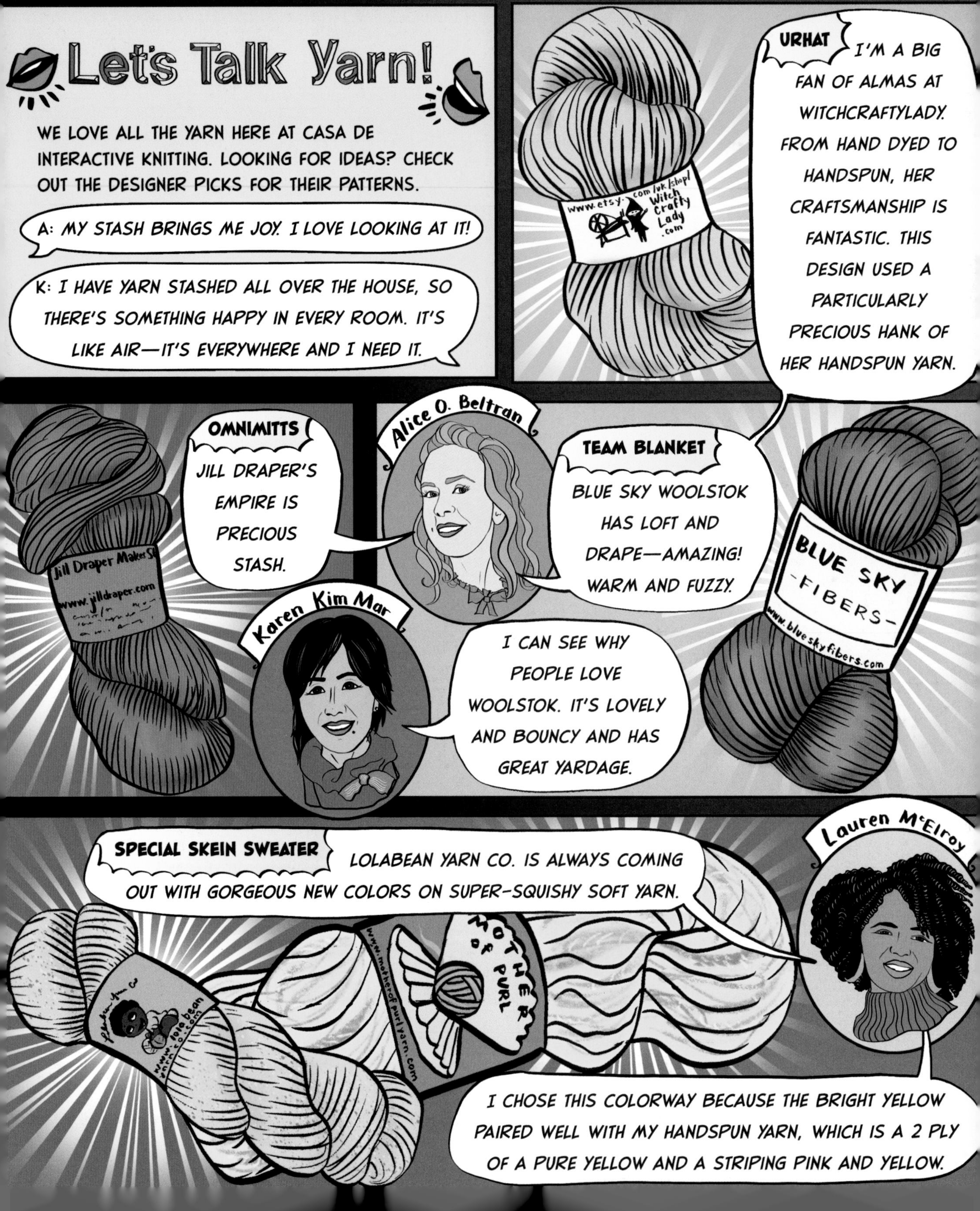
Let's Talk Yarn!
WE LOVE ALL THE YARN HERE AT CASA DE INTERACTIVE KNITTING. LOOKING FOR IDEAS? CHECK OUT THE DESIGNER PICKS FOR THEIR PATTERNS.
A: MY STASH BRINGS ME JOY. I LOVE LOOKING AT IT!
K: I HAVE YARN STASHED ALL OVER THE HOUSE, SO THERE'S SOMETHING HAPPY IN EVERY ROOM. IT'S LIKE AIR—IT'S EVERYWHERE AND I NEED IT.
www.etsy.com/uk/shop/ Witch Crafty Lady .com
URHAT
I'M A BIG FAN OF ALMAS AT WITCHCRAFTYLADY. FROM HAND DYED TO HANDSPUN, HER CRAFTSMANSHIP IS FANTASTIC. THIS DESIGN USED A PARTICULARLY PRECIOUS HANK OF HER HANDSPUN YARN.
www.jilldraper.com
OMNIMITTS
JILL DRAPER'S EMPIRE IS PRECIOUS STASH.
Alice O. Beltran
TEAM BLANKET
BLUE SKY WOOLSTOK HAS LOFT AND DRAPE—AMAZING! WARM AND FUZZY.
Karen Kim Mar
I CAN SEE WHY PEOPLE LOVE WOOLSTOK. IT'S LOVELY AND BOUNCY AND HAS GREAT YARDAGE.
BLUE SKY -FIBERS-
www.blueskyfibers.com
SPECIAL SKEIN SWEATER
LOLABEAN YARN CO. IS ALWAYS COMING OUT WITH GORGEOUS NEW COLORS ON SUPER-SQUISHY SOFT YARN.
Lauren McElroy
MOTHER of PURL
www.motherofpurlyarn.com
I CHOSE THIS COLORWAY BECAUSE THE BRIGHT YELLOW PAIRED WELL WITH MY HANDSPUN YARN, WHICH IS A 2 PLY OF A PURE YELLOW AND A STRIPING PINK AND YELLOW.

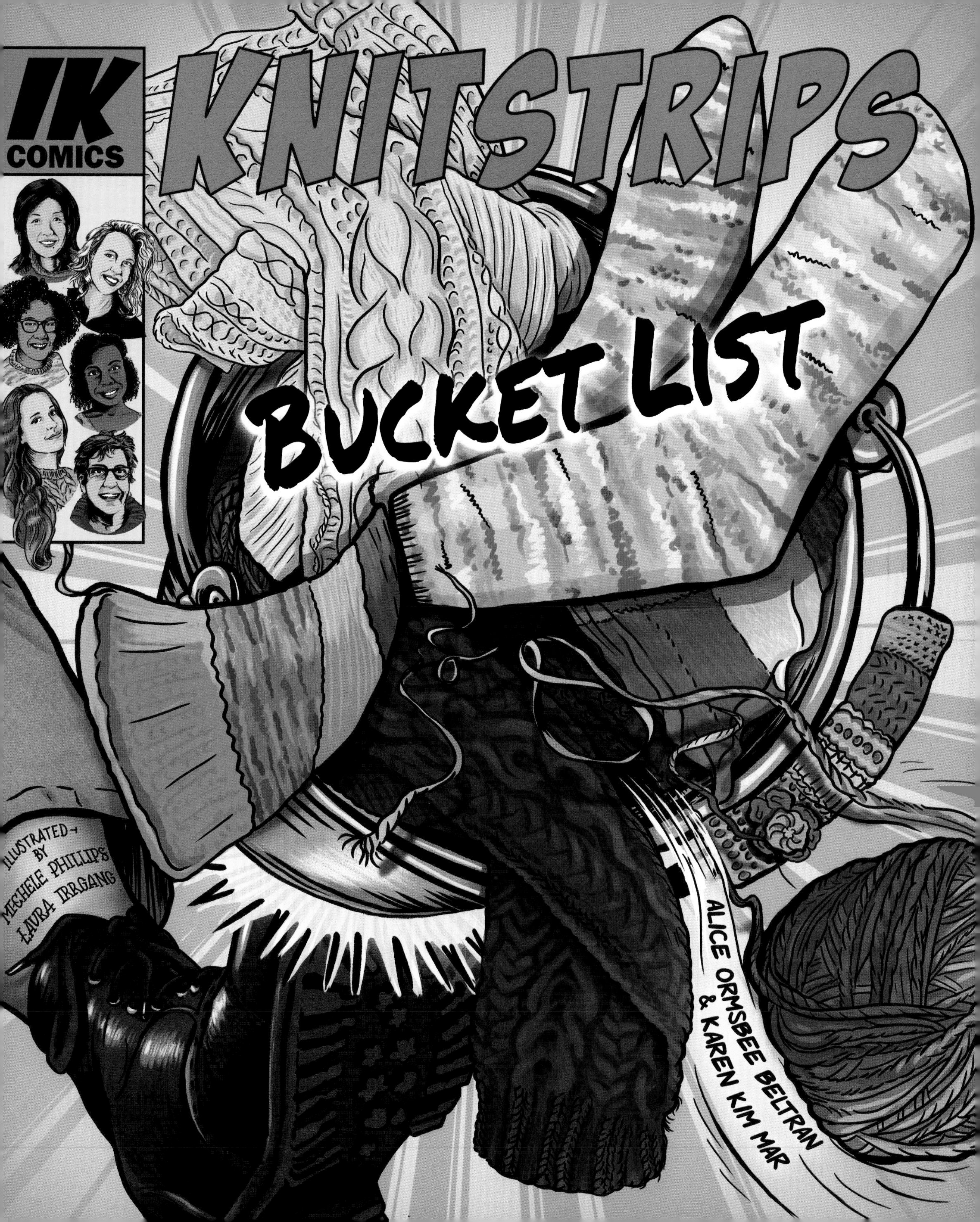
IK
COMICS
KNITSTRIPS
BUCKET LIST
ILLUSTRATED BY
MICHELE PHILLIPS
LAURA IRRGANG
ALICE ORMSBEE BELTRAN
& KAREN KIM MAR

Bucket List

What about the projects that we fantasize about and hope to knit, but are too busy living ordinary life to do? We're talking about our knitting bucket lists. There are many reasons a knitting project could remain an elusive, misty vision on a distant horizon. Perhaps the technique is daunting, and we worry that our hands can't learn new tricks. Or maybe the project is too epic. We think it's for other people, and not for us. Something puts it outside our comfort zone. Don't underestimate the strength and intensity of mental barriers. For this type of project, you need more than yarn and needles. You need to change your paradigm.

When Karen was in fifth grade, her parents took her to the annual county fair. In the arts & crafts building, there was a VW bus that had been yarn bombed down to the hubcaps. She was awestruck. It was like three-dimensional stained-glass art. The piece let her see knitted shapes differently. Blankets and shawls transformed into car sidings. Berets became hubcap covers, and scarves turned into bumper cozies.

From that moment, she wanted to yarn bomb the world. But what should she start with, and where? And is it even legal? It took thirty-something years for the urge to become stronger than her trepidation, and for her to get up the gumption to do it. See page 100 for her inspiring adventure.

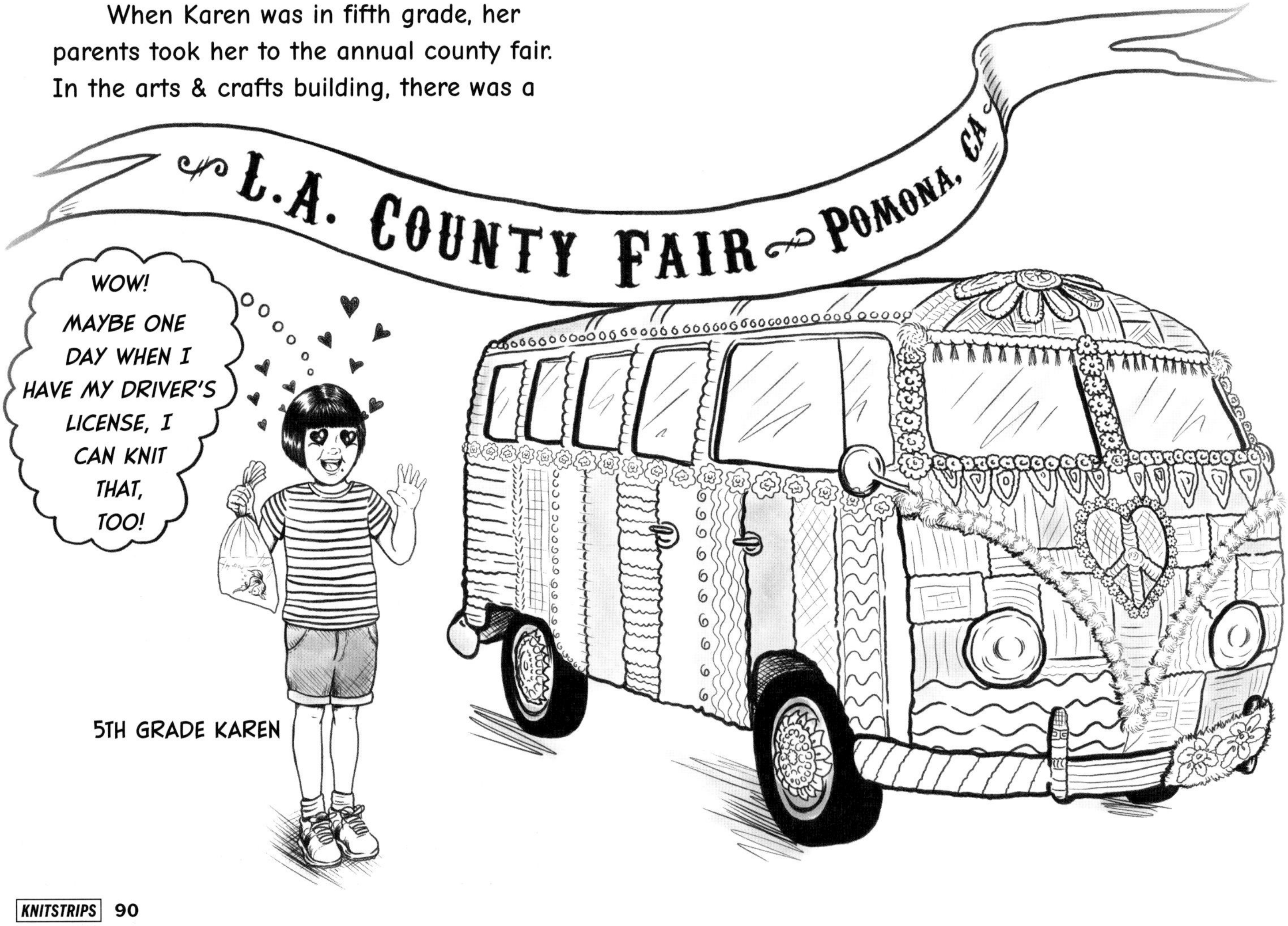
L.A. COUNTY FAIR POMONA, CA
WOW! MAYBE ONE DAY WHEN I HAVE MY DRIVER'S LICENSE, I CAN KNIT THAT, TOO!
5TH GRADE KAREN

Knitting a cable sweater had been Alice's heart's desire ever since she first read the "January" chapter in her beloved *Knitter's Almanac* by Elizabeth Zimmermann. Alice Starmore fueled the fire with her incredibly gorgeous designs. But…cables! You have to keep track of constant crisscrossing, and purl a whole bunch, and how do you even know what's going on?

After dithering over it for thirty years, it was time. In the spirit of "go big or go home," she coupled her bucket list knitting with another bucket list item—traveling to see a super-favorite art installation* with her sister. To forestall a last-minute retreat into her comfort zone of mindless knitting (OMJOM, we're looking at you), Alice took only her cable sweater project on the airplane. It worked! Sculptural cables emerged slowly and purposefully. The impossible-to-conceive cadence of crosses became entirely predictable once the work was in hand. The inevitable errors had fixes that were within her grasp—they'd been there all along!—and made her a better knitter. The things about it that had seemed impossible, weren't.

Fair warning: This is not your everyday knitting. Undertaking a bucket list project changes you. We hope you'll think about what's on your list and take the plunge, and we wish you buckets of knitting and joy.

XOXO,
Alice and *Karen*

ALICE EMBRACES THE INTENSITY OF TWO BUCKET LIST DREAMS COMING TRUE AT THE SAME TIME.

* *The Visitors* by Ragnar Kjartansson, 2012

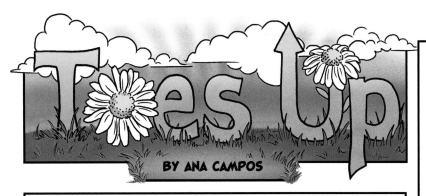

Toes Up

BY ANA CAMPOS

IT'S TIME. LET'S KNIT A PAIR OF PERFECTLY FITTING SOCKS AND CROSS THEM OFF THE BUCKET LIST. WE'LL WALK YOU THROUGH IT! THESE SOCKS ARE WORKED FROM THE TOE UP AND USE A SHORT-ROW HEEL.

SOCK 101: This sock starts with the toe box. As you work up the foot, the instep is on top of your foot, and your sole on the bottom. Why do they call it an instep? No one really knows. From there, things get more exciting because you have the heel, which turns the whole thing 90°, making it anatomical. This brings you to the leg, canvas for your imagination, so make it as long or short as you like. The cuff brings your sock to a tidy conclusion.

TECHNIQUES: Judy's Magic Cast-On (JMCO), M1L and M1R, wrapped short rows, Jeny's Surprisingly Stretchy Bind-Off (JSSBO). **MATERIALS:** Any, but sock yarn makes comfortable socks. 400 y (366 m) of sock yarn is an average amount for a pair of crew-length socks. DPNs that give you your gauge. **GAUGE:** Chewy to Stiff. Ana likes to knit her socks at 8 st/in in sock yarn. Use a gauge that will give you a fabric you feel will be comfortable to wear inside shoes and will hold up well to wear and tear.

Socks work best with a little bit of negative ease, so they will stretch over the foot. Try half an inch of negative ease. For example, if your foot is 7½ in (19.5 cm) around, you might want to knit a 7 in (18.25 cm) circumference sock.

SIZE: Measure around the ball of your foot for your total stitch count. Measure the length of your foot.

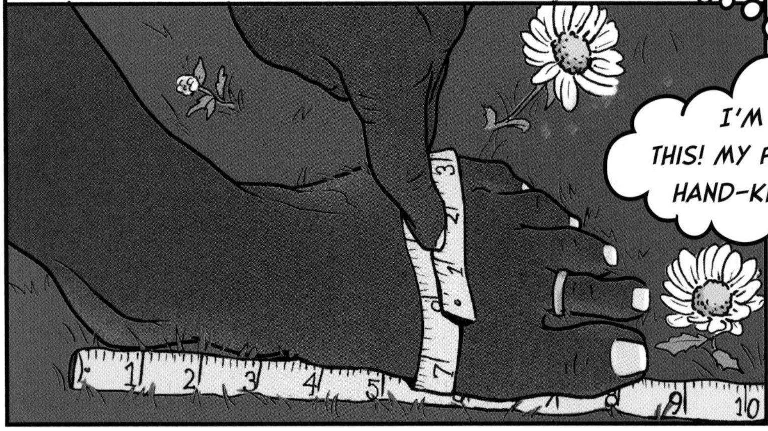
I'M DOING THIS! MY FEET DESERVE HAND-KNIT SOCKS.

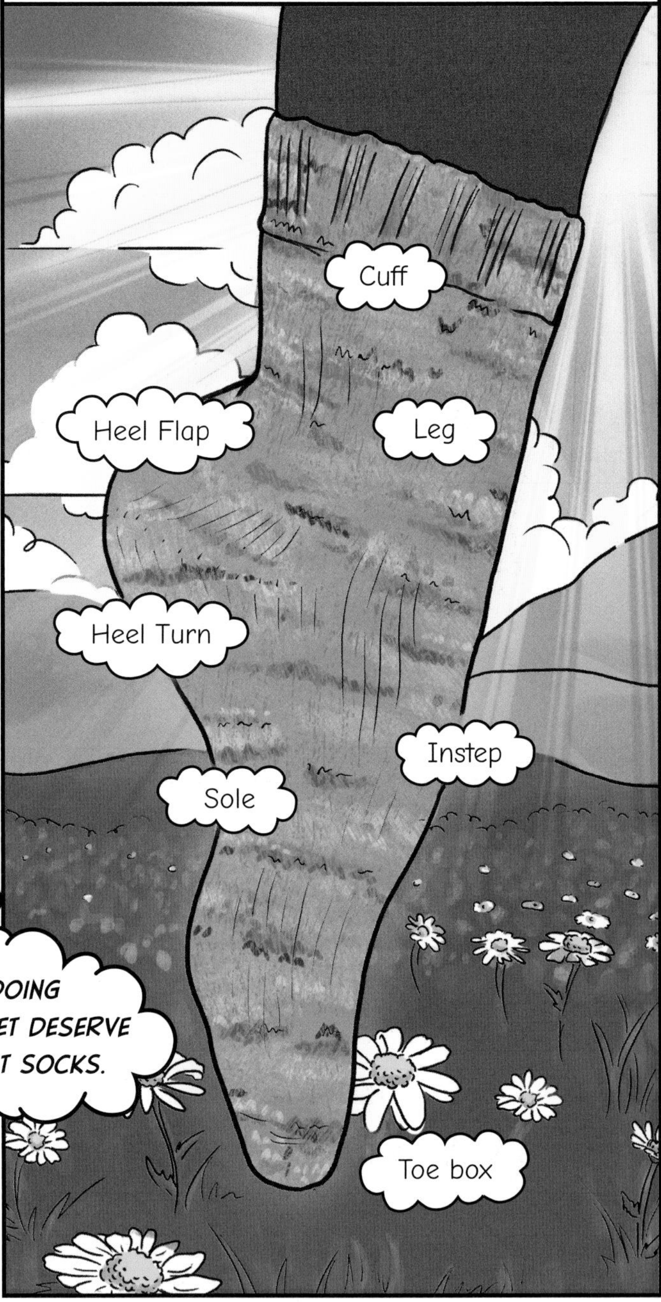
Cuff
Heel Flap
Leg
Heel Turn
Instep
Sole
Toe box

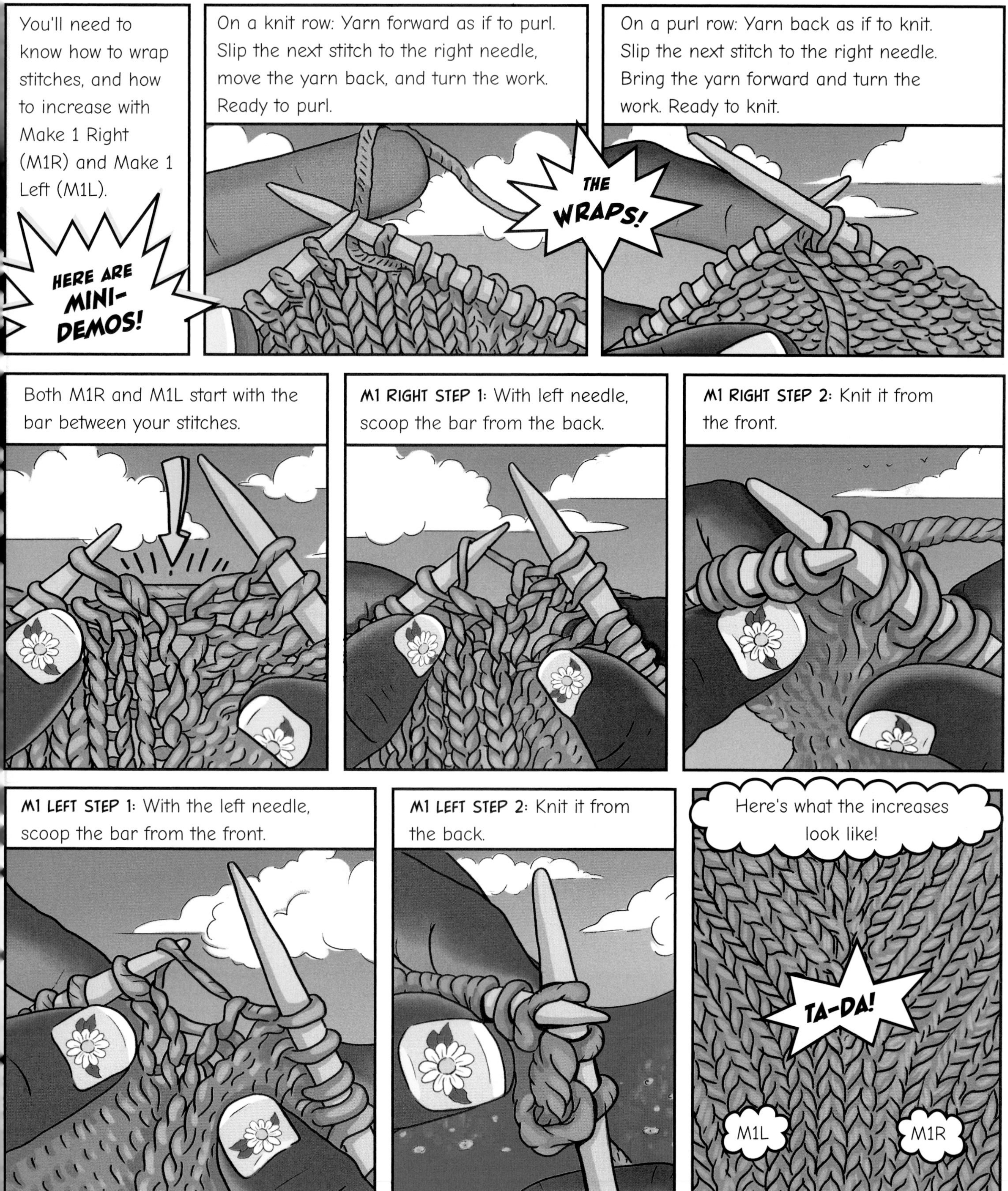

You'll need to know how to wrap stitches, and how to increase with Make 1 Right (M1R) and Make 1 Left (M1L).
HERE ARE MINI-DEMOS!
On a knit row: Yarn forward as if to purl. Slip the next stitch to the right needle, move the yarn back, and turn the work. Ready to purl.
THE WRAPS!
On a purl row: Yarn back as if to knit. Slip the next stitch to the right needle. Bring the yarn forward and turn the work. Ready to knit.
Both M1R and M1L start with the bar between your stitches.
M1 RIGHT STEP 1: With left needle, scoop the bar from the back.
M1 RIGHT STEP 2: Knit it from the front.
M1 LEFT STEP 1: With the left needle, scoop the bar from the front.
M1 LEFT STEP 2: Knit it from the back.
Here's what the increases look like!
TA-DA!
M1L
M1R

METHOD: Your total stitch count will be your gauge x desired finished circumference. Adjust so that the total number of stitches is divisible by 8. Aha, but we're going toes up! That means we will cast on fewer than our total stitch count to start with the toe box, and widen out to the full stitch count. To get your toe box cast-on number, take your total stitch count, and divide it by 2.

EXAMPLE: 8 stitches per inch x 7.25 in circumference = 58 stitches. 58 is not divisible by 8, so you would make either a slightly smaller sock with 56 stitches or a slightly larger sock with 64 stitches. This example will use 56 stitches for the total stitch count. Toe box stitches: 56/2 = 28. So we'll cast on 28 stitches.

Cast on your toe box stitches using Judy's Magic Cast-On. Here's how:

1. Make a slipknot, leaving an 18-in (45-cm) tail, and place it on the top needle. This is your first stitch on the top needle.

2. First hand position: Using your left hand, hold the tail over your index finger, and the working yarn over your thumb. Keep your palm facing down.

3. Scoop the yarn from your index finger with the bottom needle so it goes around the outside of the needle, to the center. This is your first stitch on the bottom needle.

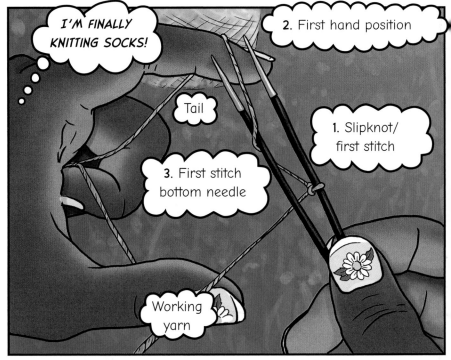

I'M FINALLY KNITTING SOCKS!
2. First hand position
Tail
1. Slipknot/ first stitch
3. First stitch bottom needle
Working yarn

4. Second hand position: Flip your left hand away from you, so now your thumb is on top.

5. Scoop the yarn from your thumb with the top needle so it goes around the outside of the needle to the center. This is your second stitch on the top needle. Flip your hand back to the first position.

6. Repeat steps 3 through 5 until you have the desired number of stitches, ending with step 3. This will ensure your stitch count will be the same on top and bottom needles.

4. Second hand position
Working yarn
5. Second stitch top needle
Tail

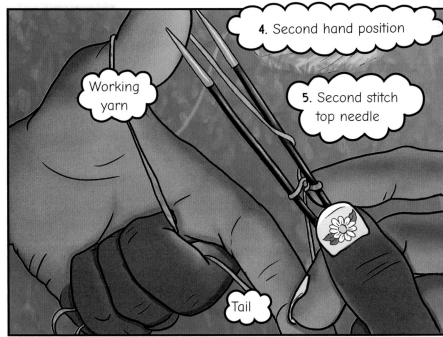

Check that you've got the correct number of toe box stitches. Rotate the work 180° so the tail and working yarn are on the right-hand side, and the needles switch places from top to bottom.

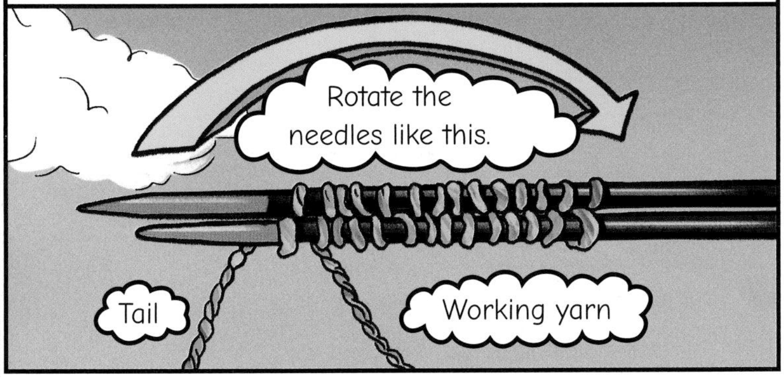

Rotate the needles like this.
Tail
Working yarn

Pull the working yarn around in front of the tail yarn and knit the top needle stitches onto a DPN.

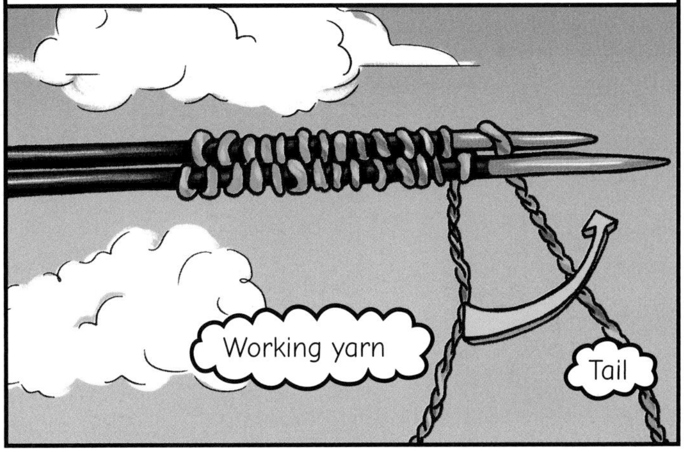

Working yarn
Tail

Continue around and knit through the back loop (KTBL) half the bottom stitches onto a second DPN. KTBL the remaining stitches onto a third DPN.

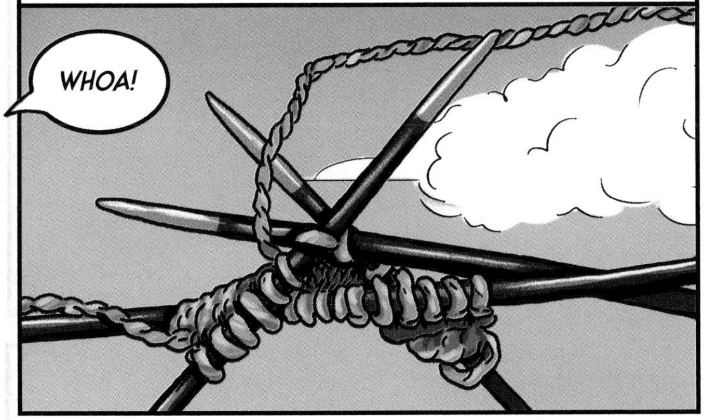

WHOA!

The needle with the larger number of stitches is your "big" needle (BN). The two other needles are your "small" needles (SN1 and SN2). Big needle = instep, small needles = sole stitches.

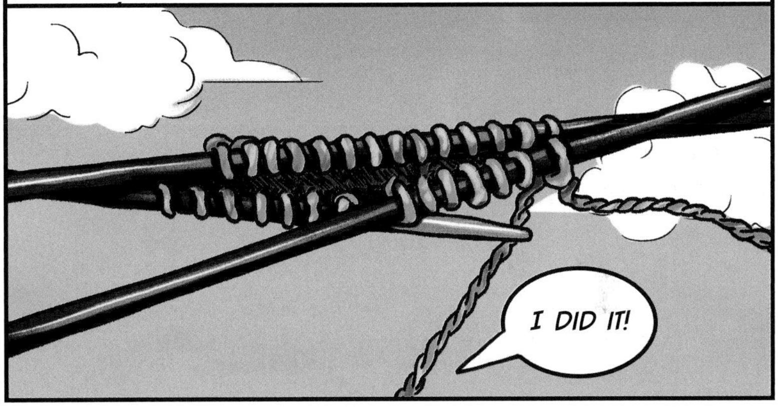

I DID IT!

Increase up to the full foot stitch count. ***ROUND 1** (BN): K1, M1R, K to 1 before end of BN, M1L, k1. SN1 and SN2: K1, M1R, K to 1 before the end of SN2, M1L, k1 (4 stitches increased). **ROUND 2:** K all. Repeat from * until total foot stitch count is reached. Then knit every round until you're approximately 1½ in (4 cm) from your total desired foot length.

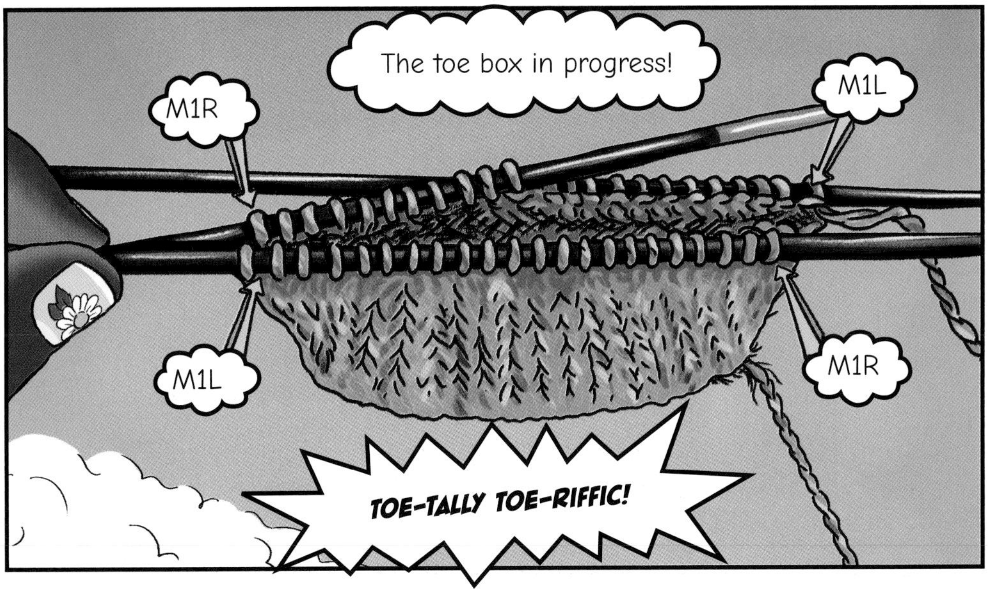

The toe box in progress!
M1R
M1L
M1L
M1R
TOE-TALLY TOE-RIFFIC!

TURNING THE HEEL (MANY PEOPLE'S ACHILLES...AHEM.)

Your stitches are still evenly divided between your BN and two SNs. Note that the BN stitches will be the top of the foot, aka the instep, and the other half make up the sole, or the bottom of the foot. So! Knit across your BN to get to the sole stitches on your SNs. You will be working flat with the sole stitches for the heel.

On sole stitches: **STEP 1 (RS):** K to last sole stitch. Wrap the last sole stitch and turn the work. **STEP 2 (WS):** Slip wrapped stitch. P to last sole stitch. Wrap the last stitch and turn the work. **STEP 3 (RS):** Slip wrapped stitch. K to one stitch before the previously wrapped stitch. Wrap it, and turn the work. **STEP 4 (WS):** Slip wrapped stitch. P to one stitch before the previously wrapped stitch. Wrap it, and turn the work.

Don't pull your wraps too tight, or you'll have a hard time picking up your wraps later!

Repeat steps 3 and 4 until your heel is in the range of 1¼–1½ in (3-4 cm) long at the tallest point. You will have a matching number of wrapped stitches on either side of unwrapped stitches. On our example, we have 9 wrapped stitches on either side of 12 stitches. Your mileage may vary, but your wrapped stitches will be the same number on each side.

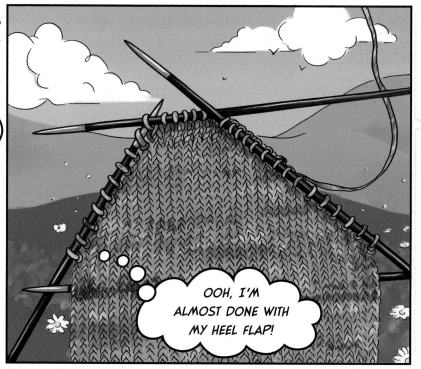

OOH, I'M ALMOST DONE WITH MY HEEL FLAP!

When your heel flap is complete, you will pick up all the wraps with their stitches, finishing the heel.

STEP 5 (RS): Slip the wrapped stitch. K all until the first wrapped stitch on the other side of the center stitches. Pick up the wrap at the base of that stitch and knit together with its stitch. Wrap the next stitch and turn the work. This stitch will now have two wraps.

STEP 6 (WS): Slip the wrapped stitch. P to the first wrapped stitch. Pick up the wrap at the base of it, and purl together through the back loop with slipped stitch. Wrap the next stitch and turn the work. This stitch will now have two wraps.

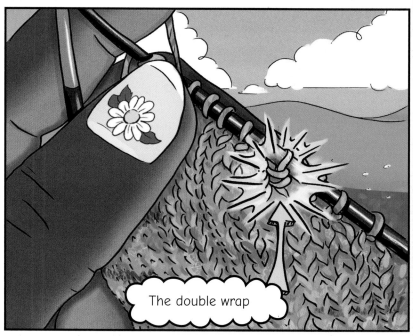

The double wrap

To pick up wraps:
Slip the wrapped stitch onto your right needle. Using the tip of your left needle, pick up the wrap, and lift it onto the right needle. At double-wrapped stitches, pick up both wraps.

STEP 7 (RS): Slip the double-wrapped stitch. K all until the first double-wrapped stitch. Pick up both wraps and knit together with slipped stitch. Wrap the next stitch and turn the work.

STEP 8 (WS): Slip the double-wrapped stitch. P all until the first double-wrapped stitch. Pick up both wraps and purl together through the back loop with slipped stitch. Wrap the next stitch and turn the work.

About halfway through the heel turn

IT'S TURNING! IT'S REALLY TURNING!

Repeat steps 7 and 8 until you have picked up all but two wraps (one on each side). Work flat for three more rows as follows: **STEP 9 (RS):** K all until the double-wrapped stitch. Pick up both wraps and knit together with slipped stitch. Wrap the next stitch, which will be the first stitch of the top of the foot. Turn the work. **STEP 10 (WS):** P all until the double-wrapped stitch. Wrap the next stitch, which will be the last stitch of the top of the foot. Turn the work. **STEP 11 (RS):** K all. You are now ready to continue working in the round. As you come to the wrapped stitches, pick up the wraps and knit together with their stitch.

BEHOLD, THE HEEL!

Your heel is turned! Knit in the round for your ankle and leg. This is a chance to have some fun, so consider stripes, lace, cables, colorwork, and ribbing. Work the leg and cuff to the length you desire. When you're ready, use a stretchy bind-off like JSSBO. It's like the standard bind-off, but you "process" each stitch before it jumps or is jumped over. This extra step gives slack that makes your BO stretchy.

READ ON FOR A MINI-DEMO!

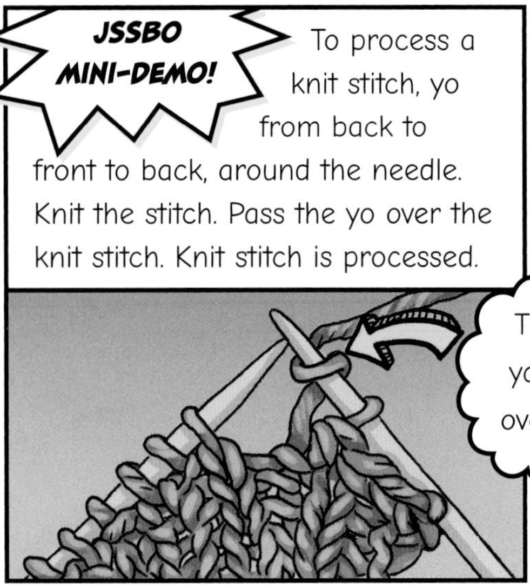
JSSBO MINI-DEMO!
To process a knit stitch, yo from back to front to back, around the needle. Knit the stitch. Pass the yo over the knit stitch. Knit stitch is processed.
The yarn overs!

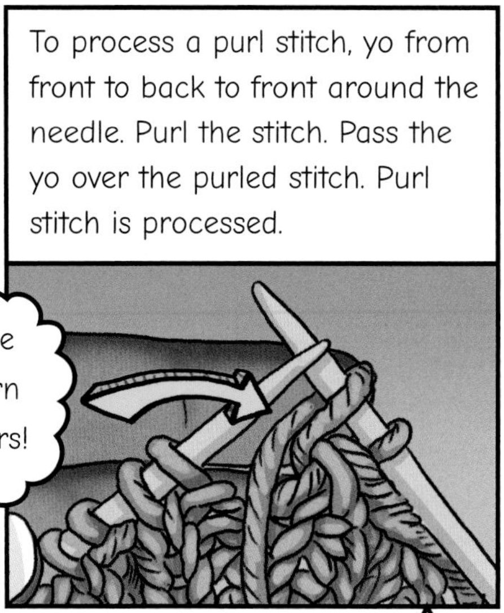
To process a purl stitch, yo from front to back to front around the needle. Purl the stitch. Pass the yo over the purled stitch. Purl stitch is processed.

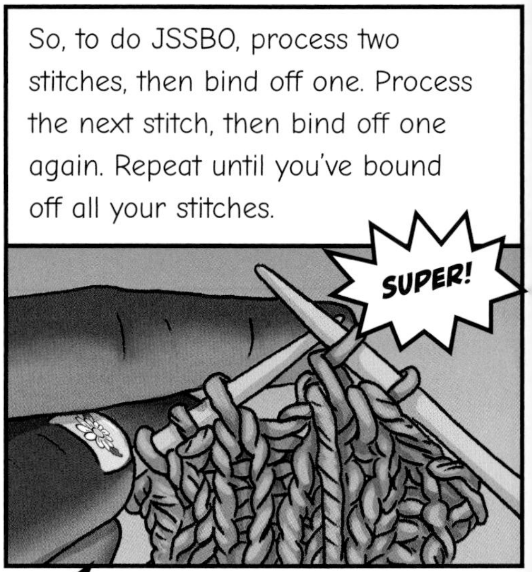
So, to do JSSBO, process two stitches, then bind off one. Process the next stitch, then bind off one again. Repeat until you've bound off all your stitches.
SUPER!

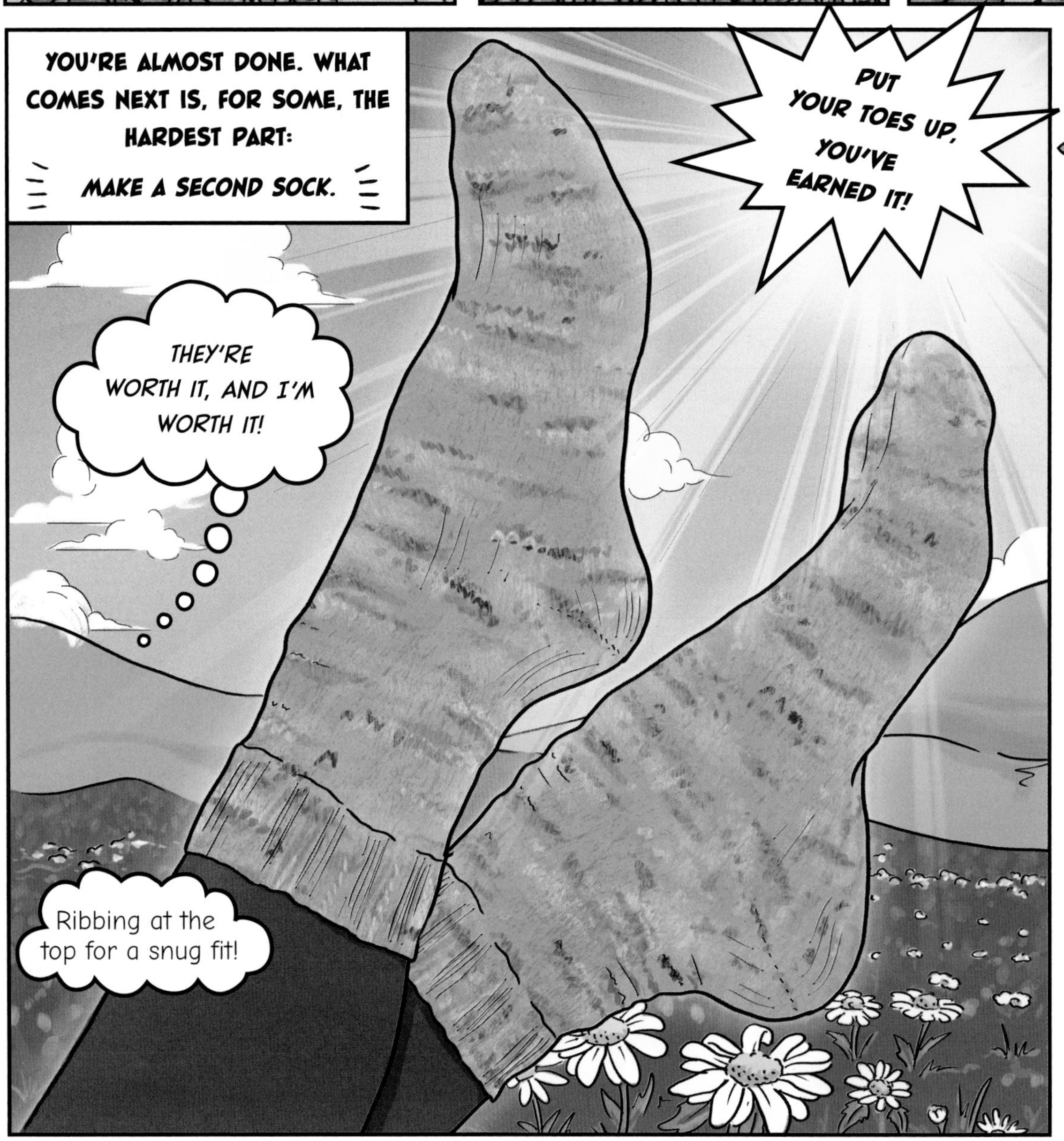
YOU'RE ALMOST DONE. WHAT COMES NEXT IS, FOR SOME, THE HARDEST PART:
MAKE A SECOND SOCK.
PUT YOUR TOES UP, YOU'VE EARNED IT!
THEY'RE WORTH IT, AND I'M WORTH IT!
Ribbing at the top for a snug fit!

Karen has never knit a pair of socks. She says: Ankle socks! That's the only way it's gonna happen.

Alice knit a single sock 20 years ago. She says: Thigh-highs or bust!

Judy's Magic Cast-On: *Knitty*, Spring 2006; Jeny's Surprisingly Stretchy Bind-Off: *Knitty*, Fall 2009

If you need to cut yarn but you don't have scissors handy, you may be able to break it with your hands. Hold the yarn with your hands at least 6 in (15 cm) apart, and give it a strong, steady pull. Widen your grip if it resists. This works best with wool.

SNAP!

Warning: Some yarns are too strong to break with your hands. Think twice before trying this with cotton and silk. Alice and Karen learned the painful way.

YARN BOMBING

BY
KAREN KIM MAR
AND
JULIE KORNBLUM

Calle Olvera

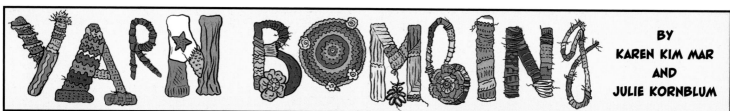

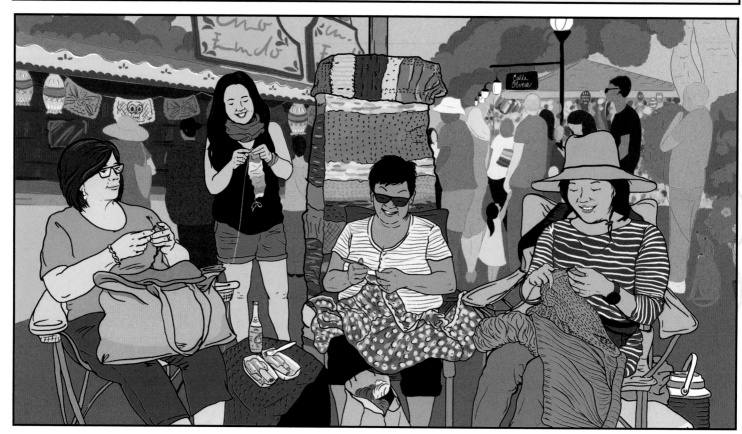

Dear Bullet Journal,

Tonight's entry is special. I finally did it. Today, I yarn bombed and it was glorious. I did it with my Eat-n-Stitch *hermanas* on this beautiful, warm Sunday in the heart of L.A.—Olvera Street. I've been wanting to YB for—oh gosh—30 years?! I ♡ everything about it! It's expressive, quirky, methodical, unexpected, a bit naughty, fun, communal—it's me! Here's what I found: YB is a powerful visual message. YB is union with friends and comrades. It makes me feel as if I'm waving my hands in the air. Why did it take me so long?

– YB the world? I've been contemplating for years just what to YB. Ideas included: our grand piano, staircase, city bench, historic bell, minivan, spinning wheel. None were exactly it.

– Trouble with the law? Some cities and jurisdictions consider YB vandalism and/or littering and you can be fined. My stomach turns at the thought of jaywalking and overdue library books.

– What do you mean it's gone? The biggest hurdle for me about YB is the fact that you don't get to keep it forever. You work hard to knit and cover the object, only to see it grow weathered and frayed, or gone... I get attached to things, OK?

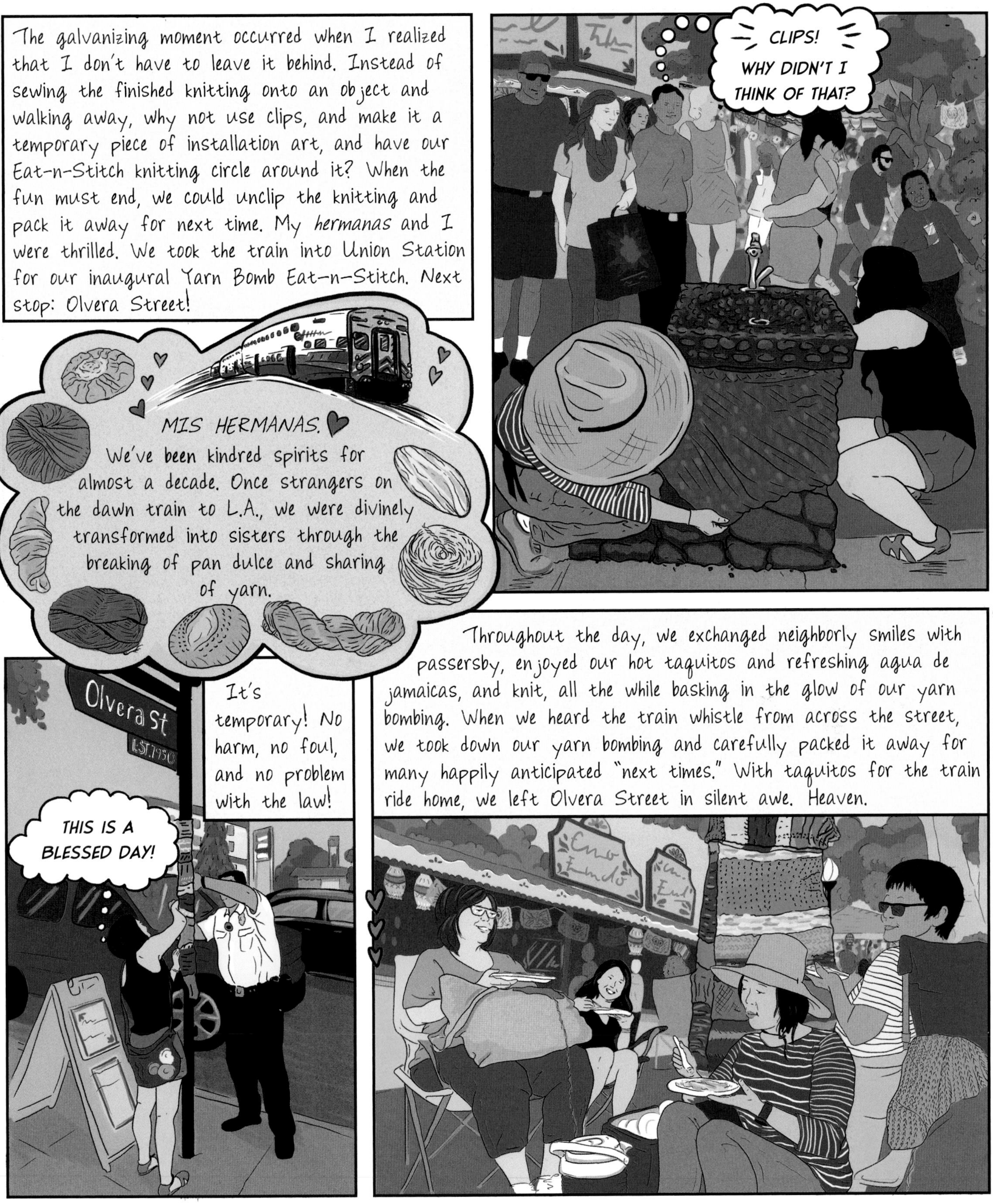
The galvanizing moment occurred when I realized that I don't have to leave it behind. Instead of sewing the finished knitting onto an object and walking away, why not use clips, and make it a temporary piece of installation art, and have our Eat-n-Stitch knitting circle around it? When the fun must end, we could unclip the knitting and pack it away for next time. My *hermanas* and I were thrilled. We took the train into Union Station for our inaugural Yarn Bomb Eat-n-Stitch. Next stop: Olvera Street!
MIS HERMANAS.
We've been kindred spirits for almost a decade. Once strangers on the dawn train to L.A., we were divinely transformed into sisters through the breaking of pan dulce and sharing of yarn.
CLIPS! WHY DIDN'T I THINK OF THAT?
Olvera St
It's temporary! No harm, no foul, and no problem with the law!
THIS IS A BLESSED DAY!
Throughout the day, we exchanged neighborly smiles with passersby, enjoyed our hot taquitos and refreshing agua de jamaicas, and knit, all the while basking in the glow of our yarn bombing. When we heard the train whistle from across the street, we took down our yarn bombing and carefully packed it away for many happily anticipated "next times." With taquitos for the train ride home, we left Olvera Street in silent awe. Heaven.

READY TO TRY IT? HERE'S HOW!

MATERIALS: Lots of yarn! For outdoors: Acrylic yarn is best. It's economical and holds up the longest outdoors. For eye-catching, go bold and bright. For indoors: You can use any type of fiber content. Emergency crochet hooks, **PLENTY OF STRONG BINDER CLIPS**, and a lucky spare ball of yarn. **GAUGE:** Any! Woot! **SIZE:** If you have a specific object in mind to YB, take pics for reference, measure the object, and knit away. If you're not sure what to YB, or want your pieces to be flexible for years to come, knit 4-sided fabric in various shapes and sizes: long, skinny rectangles for poles; large, wide rectangles for benches; or just about anything (YB is a great way to repurpose UFOs). **METHOD:** Knit all your pieces in advance. Wrap objects with the knitted fabric, hold in place with strong binder clips, and enjoy. When the party's over, take it down and save it for next time!

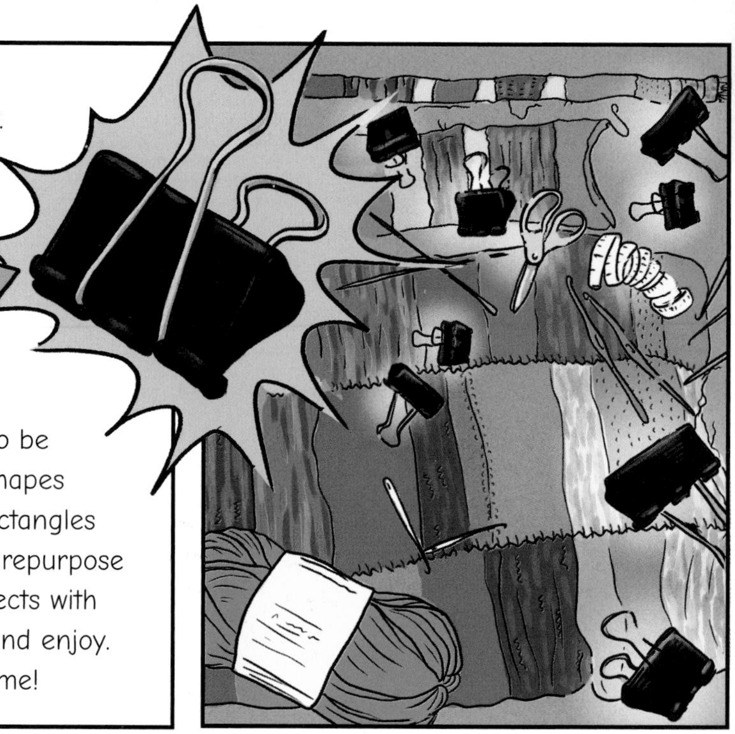

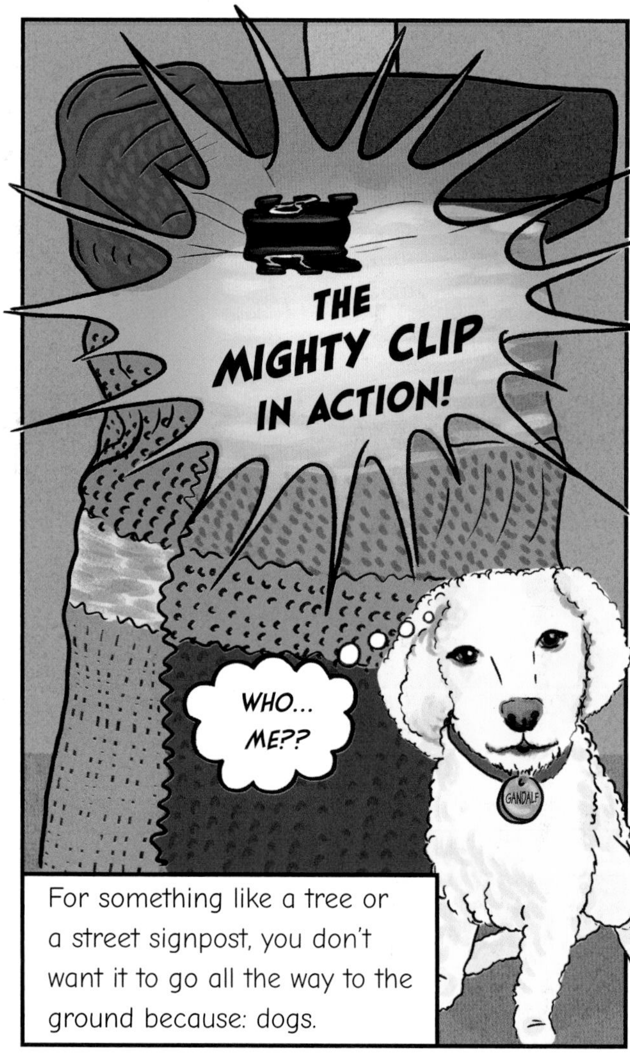
THE MIGHTY CLIP IN ACTION!
WHO... ME??
GANDALF
For something like a tree or a street signpost, you don't want it to go all the way to the ground because: dogs.

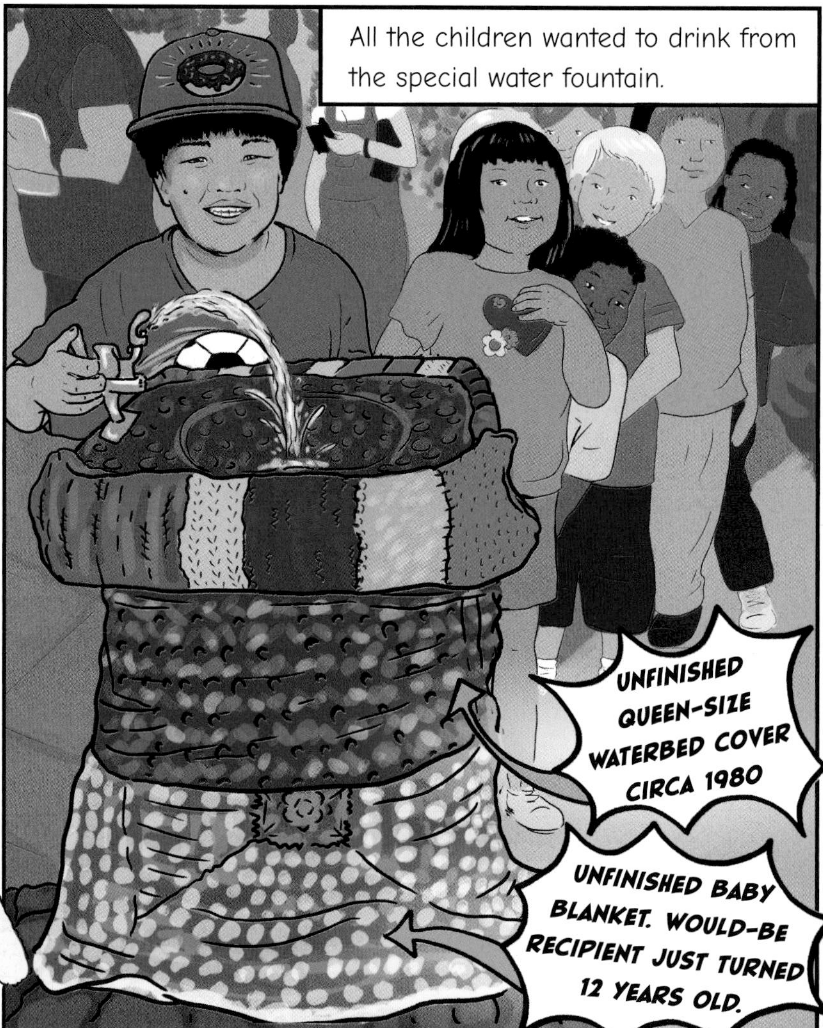
All the children wanted to drink from the special water fountain.
UNFINISHED QUEEN-SIZE WATERBED COVER CIRCA 1980
UNFINISHED BABY BLANKET. WOULD-BE RECIPIENT JUST TURNED 12 YEARS OLD.

Oh BY THE *Way*

Consider a felted join when you need to join a new ball of yarn. It is ideal for any feltable fiber, such as wool, mohair, or alpaca. It will not work with unfeltable fibers such as cotton, silk, or acrylic. Lick your palm.* Overlap the two ends by 2–3 in (5–7.5 cm) in the palm of your hand. Rub and roll the yarns together vigorously between your palms, creating heat and friction, until the two are felted together.

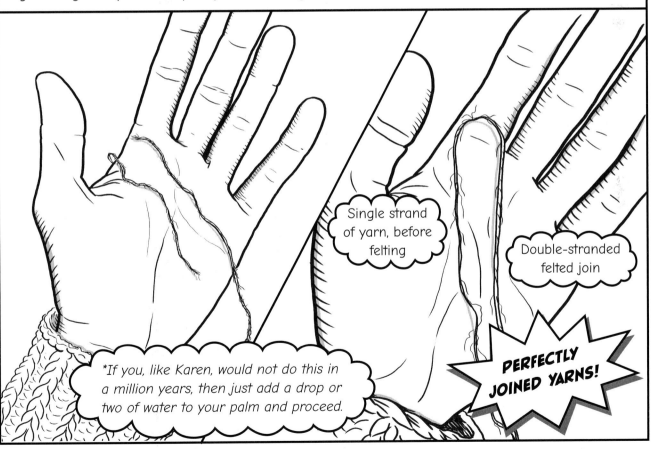

Single strand of yarn, before felting

Double-stranded felted join

*If you, like Karen, would not do this in a million years, then just add a drop or two of water to your palm and proceed.

PERFECTLY JOINED YARNS!

QUEST

REBECCA McKENZIE

JOIN US ON A QUEST FOR A PERFECT FIT! CUSTOMIZED BUST SHAPING, NECKLINE, AND CHARMING STITCH DETAILS MAKE THIS DROP-SLEEVE SWEATER A FLATTERING AND WEARABLE FAVORITE. PERFECT FIT ACHIEVEMENT: UNLOCKED.

MAKE IT YOURS!

MATERIALS: Fingering or DK yarn. Thicker yarn will give a boxier look and may create bulk near the drop-shoulder armholes. DPNs and circular needles for stitch and row gauges, and both two sizes smaller for ribbing. **GAUGE:** Soft, for nice drape.

TECHNIQUES: Bust shaping, neckline shaping, knot stitch pattern, Three-Needle Bind-Off (3NBO), Gauge Translation (GT) (p. 67), Jeny's Surprisingly Stretchy Bind-Off (JSSBO) (p. 98). **SIZE:** Using a measuring tape, measure the wearer and add ease to the body measurements. If you measure the wearer's favorite fitted sweater that has the ease built in, you don't have to add any more ease. Here's what you need.

THIS DESIGN IS ABOUT TAKING THE LEAP INTO BECOMING YOUR OWN PERSONAL KNITWEAR TAILOR.

Neck width (NW) = _____
Over bust to waist (OBTW) = _____
Bicep (Bicep) = bicep circumference + ease = _____
Bust (B) = bust circumference + ease = _____
Wrist (Wrist) = wrist circumference + ease = _____
Waist (W) = waist circumference + ease = _____

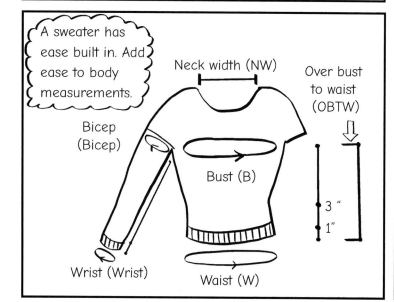

A sweater has ease built in. Add ease to body measurements.

Neck width (NW)

Over bust to waist (OBTW)

Bicep (Bicep)

Bust (B)

3"

1"

Wrist (Wrist)

Waist (W)

Positive ease means the garment is bigger than the body measurement, and negative ease means the garment is smaller than the body measurement. For a close-fit bust, Rebecca recommends 1 in (2.5 cm) positive ease. For a defined but roomy waist and an hourglass look, let W be less than your bust circumference, but more than your waist circumference. Rebecca reduced 3 inches from her bust measurement, which gave her 4 inches of positive ease at her waist. She used 1–3 in (2.5–7.5 cm) positive ease for bicep, and 1–2 in (2.5–5 cm) positive ease for the wrist.

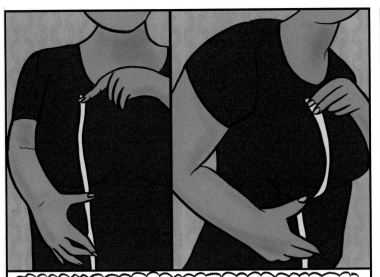

OBTW gives the total length from the underarm line to the waist, going over your bust.

YOU'VE GOT THIS CUSTOM SHAPING!

METHOD: This sweater is knit in the round from the bottom up to the underarm. Front and back are then worked separately, back and forth, to the shoulder. Shoulders are joined with a 3NBO, and sleeves are picked up and worked down, in the round.

Let's embark on your sweater! Multiply W x gauge. For K2P2 ribbing, adjust the number to a multiple of 4. If you plan to do the knot stitch pattern, then make sure your sts are a multiple of 8. With the smaller needle, long-tail cast on your stitches. Join in the round, and place a marker (pm). Work K2P2 ribbing for 1–2 in (2.5–5 cm). Subtract the length of the ribbing from the OBTW length, so you know how much more length to work to the armholes. Switch to the larger needles. The marker indicates the first side seam. Pm at the halfway point to mark the second side seam. **Shaping will be worked along these side seams.** Before you begin your shaping, work 2 in (5 cm). This can be in plain Stockinette stitch (St st). Alternatively, you can add single knot sts to your St st, or work the full knot stitch pattern.

SINGLE KNOT STITCH: P3tog, leaving sts on left-hand needle. Bring yarn to back and K3tog, leaving them on the left needle. Move yarn to front and P3tog again. Slip the stitches from the left needle over to the right. The knot stitch does not change the stitch count of your work. **KNOT STITCH PATTERN:** Rounds 1 & 2: Knit. Round 3: *K5, make a knot stitch; rep from * to end. Rounds 4 & 5: Knit. Round 6: *K1, make a knot stitch, k4; rep from * to end. Rep Rounds 1–6 once more (2 times total). Rep Rounds 1–3 one more time.

PUT THESE PRETTY KNOTS ANYWHERE YOU WANT!

Let's start the bust shaping. The shaping rows will increase one st on either side of each side seam for a total of 4 sts. To calculate the number of your shaping rows, first subtract the W sts from the B sts to know how many sts to increase. Adjust it to a multiple of 4. Divide that by 4 to determine the total number of shaping rounds needed.

Subtract the length you have already knit from your OBTW. Multiply the remaining OBTW length with your row gauge to figure out how many rounds to knit to reach OBTW. To determine the number of rounds between increase rounds, take the leftover OBTW length in rounds, then divide by the total number of increase rounds you need.

Sts to increase __ /4 = # inc rounds __

Remaining OBTW rnds __ /# inc rnds __
= Frequency of inc spacing __

In the sample, Rebecca's B x gauge is 46 in x 5¼ st/inch = 241½. She rounded this to 242. Her B stitches (242) minus W stitches (224) is 18 stitches to increase. She rounded this to 20, for 20/4 = 5 increase rounds. She had 68 rounds remaining in her OBTW length, so 68/5 increase rounds = 13.6, which she rounded to 13. She increased 4 stitches on every 13th round 5 times.

Work your shaping, then knit St st to your full OBTW length. Try it on to see if you like the fit.

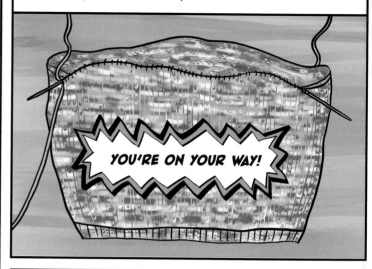

YOU'RE ON YOUR WAY!

Now it's time to work the front and back separately. Divide your Bicep in half. This number is your armhole depth for the front and back. Knit from your beginning marker to your halfway marker. This will be the front of your garment. Slip the remaining sts onto scrap yarn for the back. Turn your work. Continue the front in St st until 2 in (5 cm) from your armhole depth. Time to design your custom neckline! Let's start with the front.

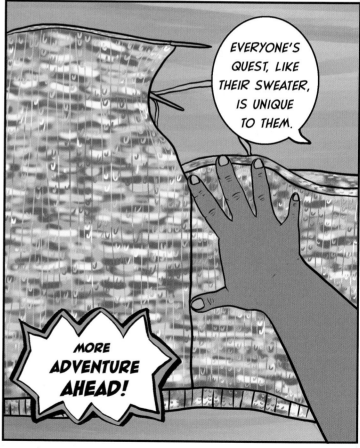

EVERYONE'S QUEST, LIKE THEIR SWEATER, IS UNIQUE TO THEM.
MORE ADVENTURE AHEAD!

You will bind off half your NW sts in the center of your neckline, then chart the evenly spaced bind-off steps on each side of the neckline. Multiply your neckline width by your gauge, and divide by 2 to get the number of sts to bind off to begin at the center for the start of your neckline shaping.

½NW x gauge = front neck bind-off sts

For the shoulder stitch count, take your total stitch count for the front, subtract your neckline bind-off stitches, then divide it by 2.

(Front st count – front neck bind-off sts)/2
= starting front shoulder sts

The total number of stitches to bind off to reach your desired neck width will be the same as the number you bound off for the neckline. Each side of the neck will bind off half of them.

Calculate the number of rows between decreases by multiplying 2 in (10 cm) by your row gauge. You will bind off on the right side (RS) for the right shoulder and the wrong side (WS) for the left shoulder. Sketch out your neckline and draw the bind-off steps so they make a nice curve. Here's what Rebecca's looked like:

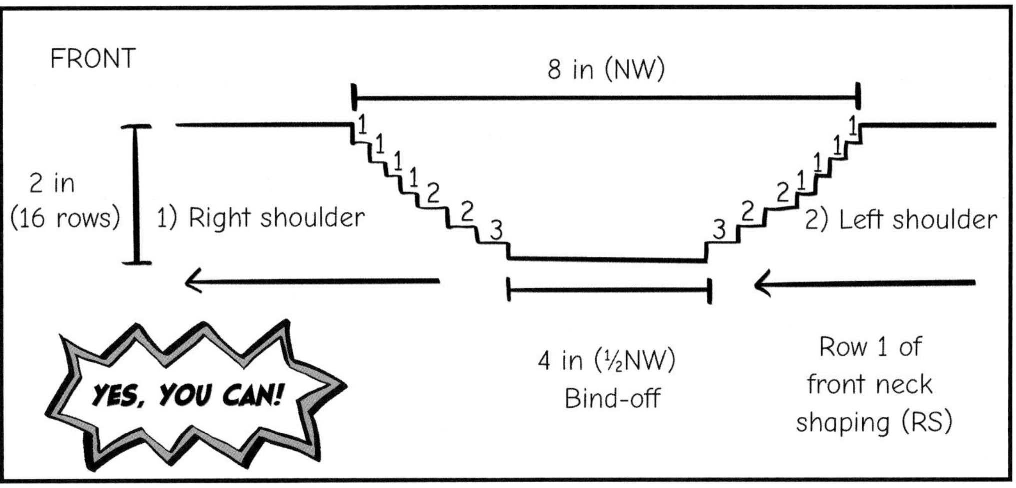
FRONT
8 in (NW)
2 in
(16 rows)
1) Right shoulder
1
1
1
1
2
2
3
3
2
2
1
1
1
1
2) Left shoulder
4 in (½NW)
Bind-off
Row 1 of
front neck
shaping (RS)
YES, YOU CAN!

Now knit what you drew! 1) Front Right Shoulder: Starting on the RS, knit across the sts for the left shoulder, bind off your center neckline stitches, and knit the sts for the right shoulder. Keep the left shoulder sts on your needles as you work the right shoulder only, purling every WS row and binding off your calculated neckline decreases every RS. End with a WS row, and slip the shoulder stitches onto scrap yarn (for 3NBO) or bind off to be seamed later. 2) Front Left Shoulder: Join yarn at neck edge on the WS of the left shoulder, bind off your sts at the beginning of every WS row, and knit the RS rows plain. End with a WS row, slip the shoulder sts onto scrap yarn (for 3NBO) or bind off to be seamed later.

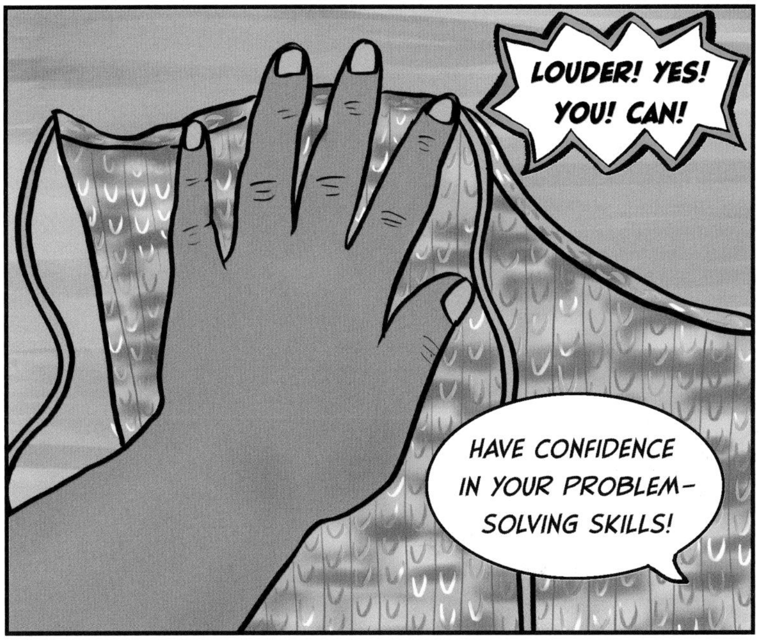
LOUDER! YES! YOU! CAN!
HAVE CONFIDENCE IN YOUR PROBLEM-SOLVING SKILLS!

Now the back! Slip stitches for the back onto your needles. Join yarn on the RS. Work in St st until the back measures 1 in (2.5 cm) from armhole depth. Draw a sketch of your back neckline, as you did for the front. You only have 1 in (2.5 cm) to do the shaping. Multiply ¾NW by your gauge to get the number of stitches to bind off at the center of your back neckline shaping.

¾NW x gauge = center back neck bind-off sts
(Back st count – center back neck bind-off sts)/2 = starting back shoulder sts
Here's what Rebecca's looked like:

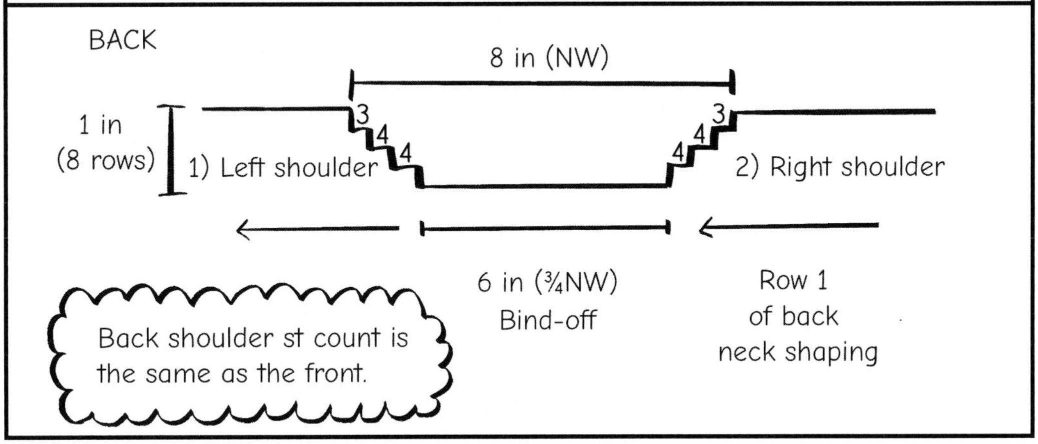
BACK
8 in (NW)
1 in
(8 rows)
1) Left shoulder
3
4
4
4
4
3
2) Right shoulder
6 in (¾NW)
Bind-off
Row 1
of back
neck shaping
Back shoulder st count is the same as the front.

1) Back Left Shoulder: Starting on the RS, knit across the sts for the right shoulder, bind off the center neck sts, and knit the sts for the left shoulder. Keep the right shoulder sts on the needles as you work the left shoulder only, purling every WS and binding off your calculated decreases every RS. End with a WS row, slip the shoulder sts onto scrap yarn (for 3NBO) or bind off to be seamed later. 2) Back Right Shoulder: Join yarn at neck edge on the WS of the right shoulder, bind off your calculated decreases at the beginning of every WS row, and knit RS rows plain. End with a WS row, slip the shoulder sts onto scrap yarn (for 3NBO) or bind off to be seamed later.

Here's a Mini-Demo of **3NBO**! Turn the garment inside out, then match up the shoulder seams.

MINI-DEMO TIME!

Knit the first stitch on both needles at the same time.

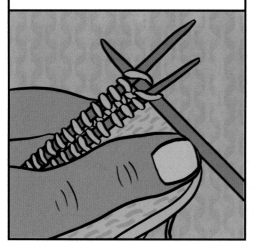

Knit the second stitch on both needles at the same time, and bind off the first stitch.

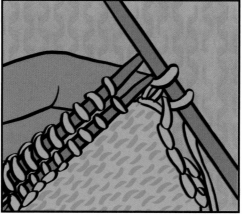

Work another stitch with the front and back needle stitches together, and continue binding off.

SEAMS EASY, RIGHT?

Time to connect the shoulders. For 3NBO, you can slip the front and back shoulder stitches on opposite sides of one circular needle, or they can be on separate needles. Right-side front and back shoulder stitches are on needles and have the same number of stitches. Position them RS together and use a third needle to do 3NBO. Repeat 3NBO for the left shoulder seam. If you bound off the stitches instead, seam them together.

Now for the sleeves! Use GT to pick up your sleeve sts. Multiply your Bicep by your gauge to see how many sts you need to pick up. Starting at the underarm, evenly pick up the desired number of sts, pm, and join in the round.

If you don't get the correct number of sts while picking up, increase or decrease as necessary in the first round to get the correct number.

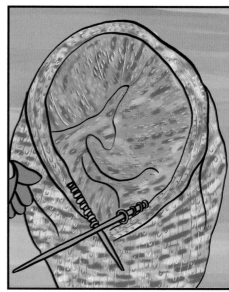

TO TAPER THE SLEEVE: With the garment on, measure from the end of the drop shoulder to the desired sleeve length. Multiply this by your row gauge to get the total rounds of the sleeve. To get the number of total sts to decrease, multiply Wrist by gauge, and subtract that from the number of stitches you picked up at the armhole. You will decrease 2 sts at a time, so divide your decrease sts by 2 to calculate how many times to work the decrease round. To determine the number of rounds for decrease, divide your total sleeve rounds by how many times to work the double decrease round. End with a multiple of 4 sts for K2P2 ribbing. Work your sleeve, and repeat for the second sleeve. Consider adding knot details at the cuff!

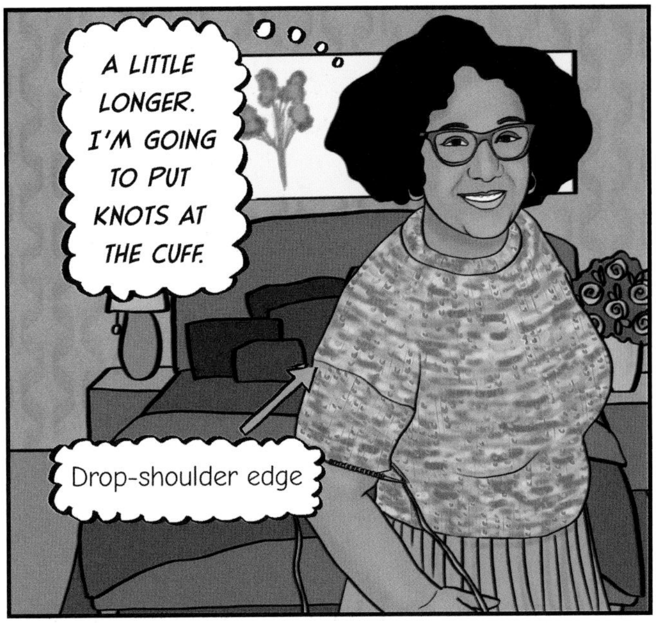
A LITTLE LONGER. I'M GOING TO PUT KNOTS AT THE CUFF.
Drop-shoulder edge

Example: Rebecca wanted to decrease 42 sts total to get to Wrist. She had 128 total sleeve rounds / 21 double decrease rounds = frequency of 6 rounds. She did a double decrease every 6th round, 21 times.

Neck: On smaller needles, starting at the back right shoulder, pick up 3 sts for every 4 sts where straight, and 3 sts for every 4 rows along the sides. Pm, join in the round, and increase or decrease as necessary evenly around to achieve a multiple of 4. Work K2P2 ribbing for 1 in (2.5 cm) or until desired length. Bind off with Jeny's Surprisingly Stretchy Bind-Off. Darn in ends, block, and wear.

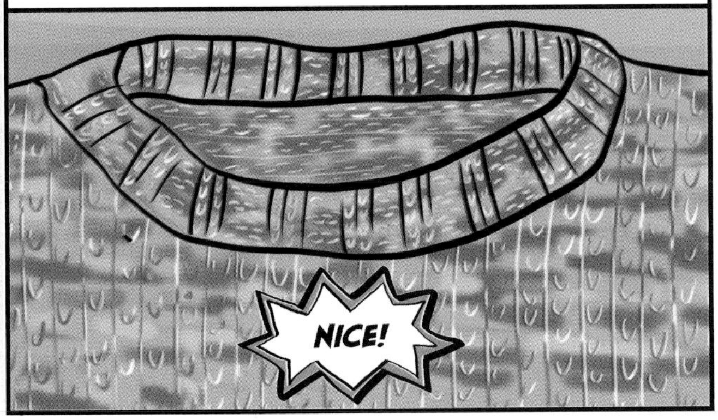
NICE!

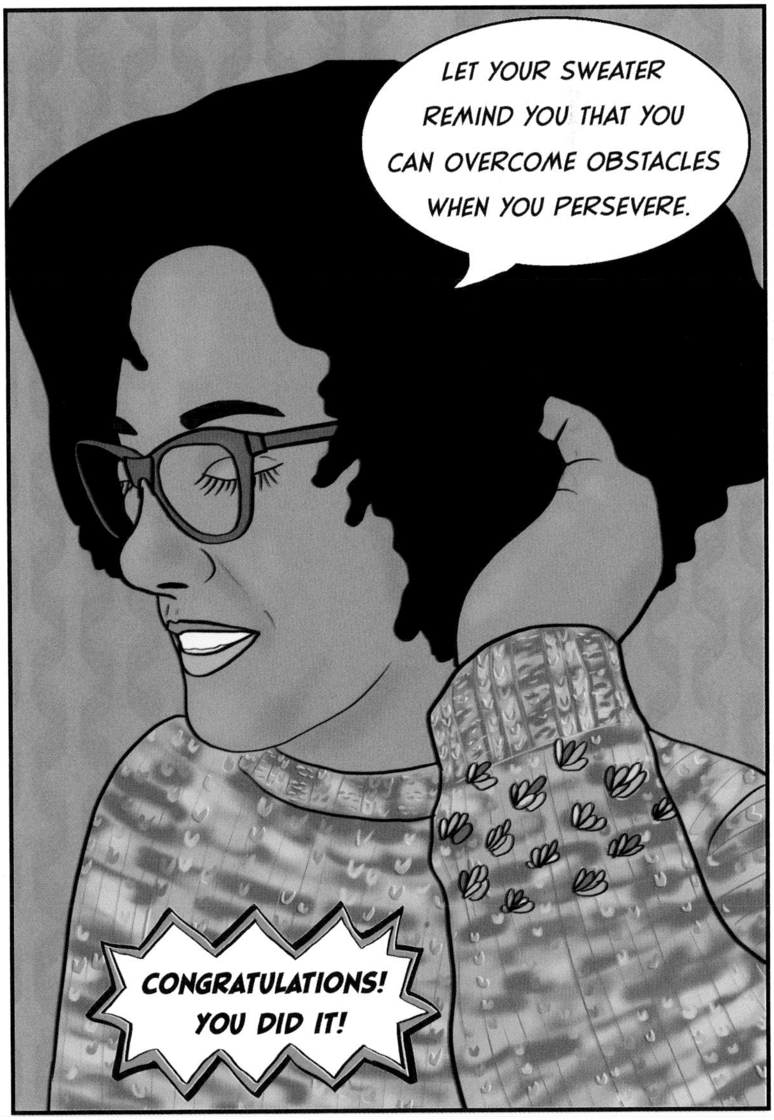
LET YOUR SWEATER REMIND YOU THAT YOU CAN OVERCOME OBSTACLES WHEN YOU PERSEVERE.
CONGRATULATIONS! YOU DID IT!

Instant Heirloom

BY NATALIE WARNER

THIS LOVELY LACE-PANEL SHAWL IS YOURS FOR THE KNITTING. PRESENT AND FUTURE GENERATIONS WILL MARVEL!

MATERIALS: Any fine or lace-weight yarn. A mohair/silk blend will give warmth and loft. Smoother yarn will give the lace more definition. Long circular knitting needles.

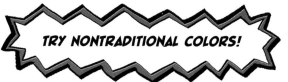

TRY NONTRADITIONAL COLORS!

GAUGE: Lacy. Work a gauge swatch in the triple leaf lace pattern. Make sure it is at least 2 reps wide and 3 reps long, and block the swatch! **TECHNIQUES:** Reading a lace chart, k3tog, sssk, M1pw.

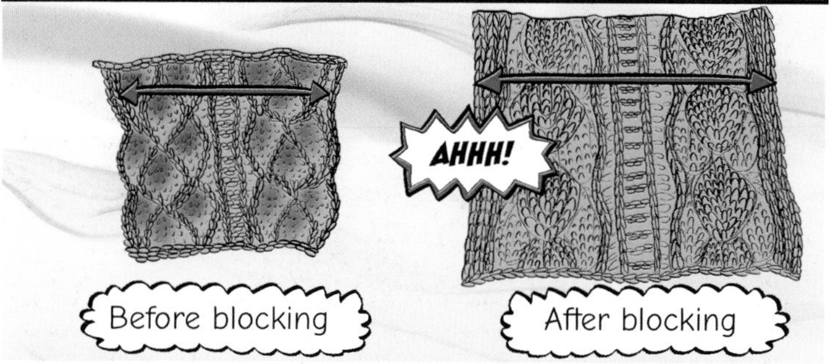
AHHH!
Before blocking
After blocking

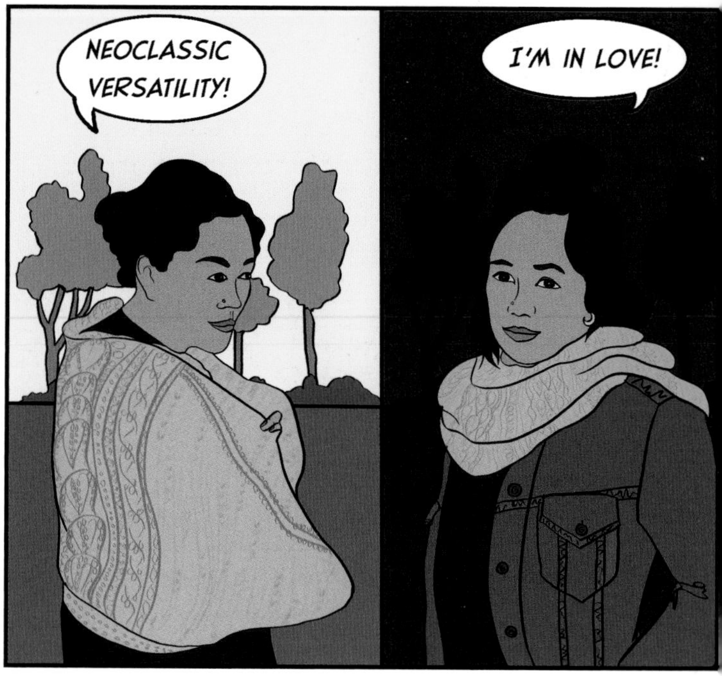
NEOCLASSIC VERSATILITY!
I'M IN LOVE!

SIZE: Measure the distance between the outer edges of the collarbone of the wearer, 3–4 in (7–10 cm) below the nape of their neck.

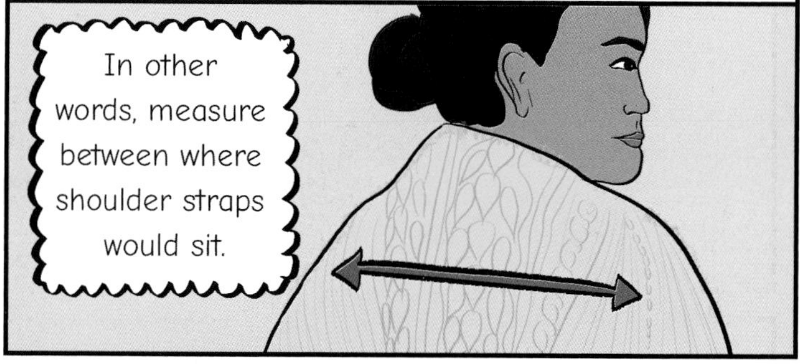
In other words, measure between where shoulder straps would sit.

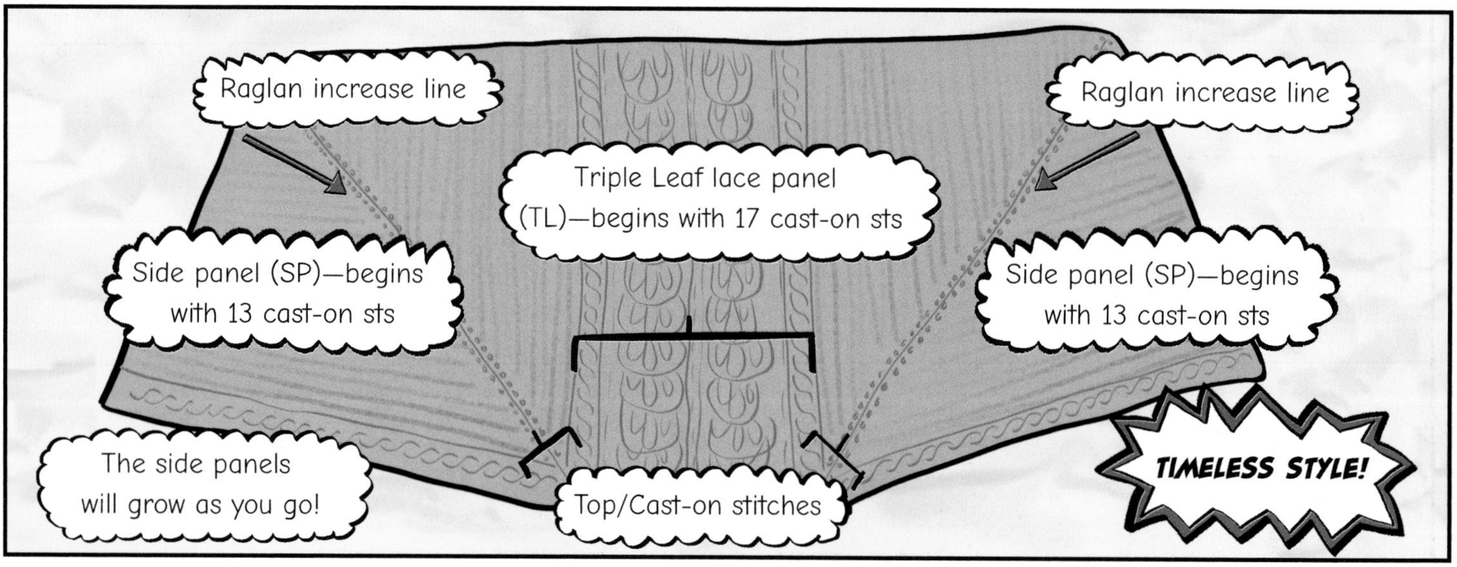
Raglan increase line
Raglan increase line
Triple Leaf lace panel (TL)—begins with 17 cast-on sts
Side panel (SP)—begins with 13 cast-on sts
Side panel (SP)—begins with 13 cast-on sts
The side panels will grow as you go!
Top/Cast-on stitches
TIMELESS STYLE!

TIME FOR MINI-DEMO!

K3tog is knit three together. It's like k2tog, but uses three stitches instead of two.

2 sts dec— right slant

Sssk is slip, slip, slip, knit. It's like ssk, but uses three stitches instead of two. Insert the left needle into the front of all three slipped stitches to knit.

2 sts dec— left slant

M1pw is make one purlwise. Start by scooping the bar between stitches from the front, onto your left needle.

Now with the working yarn in front, purl into the back of it. Your needles will almost be parallel, and pointing toward you. Here are front and side views.

YOWZA!

S1, k2tog, psso means to slip one, knit the next 2 together, then pass the slipped stitch over the completed k2tog.

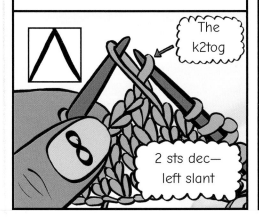

The k2tog

2 sts dec— left slant

Reading a lace chart: This pattern uses two charts that show both RS and WS rows. The odd-numbered rows are the RS rows. The even-numbered rows are the WS rows. On RS rows, read the chart right to left. On WS rows, read the chart left to right. Everything you need to do between casting on and the border is in these charts. Each box in the chart represents a stitch in your work. Keep in mind that your stitch count should match a given row after you knit it, but it may not match before you knit it, because you increase or decrease stitches in the row when you work it. The key shows symbols that tell what action to do for each box, or stitch.

CHART KEY

☐	RS: knit; WS: purl
⊡	RS: purl; WS: knit
▨	no stitch here
⊙	yo
◪	k2tog
◩	ssk
◪	k3tog
◩	sssk
◁	sl1, k2tog, psso
⊗	M1pw

Let's read lace charts! Side Panel: The side panel begins with 13 cast-on stitches. There are 15 boxes on the first row because you increase two when you work the first row.

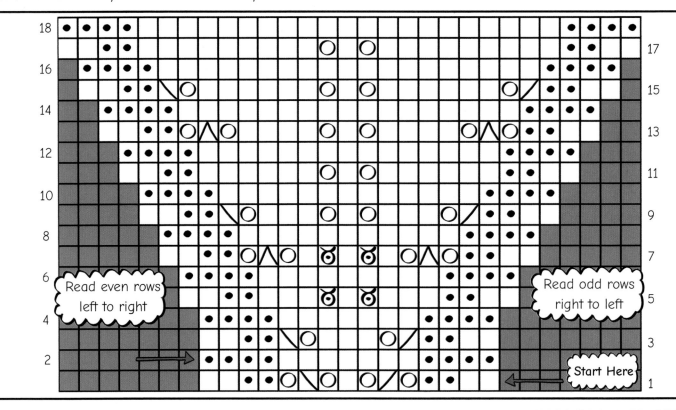

Read even rows left to right

Read odd rows right to left

Start Here

METHOD: The shawl is worked from the neckline down. Determine the width of a single triple leaf lace pattern from your swatch. Divide your cross-back measurement by this width to find the number of triple leaf pattern repeats you need to get your cross-back measurement. If you do not get a whole number, round up the number of repeats. The center panel stitches will be a multiple of 17. Add 13 stitches on each side of the center panel stitches for the two side panels to get your total stitches to cast on.

Triple Leaf: The Triple Leaf chart begins with 17 cast-on stitches. You increase 6 and decrease 6 on the first row, so there are 17 boxes on the first row. Note the columns of Garter stitch on each side of the chart.

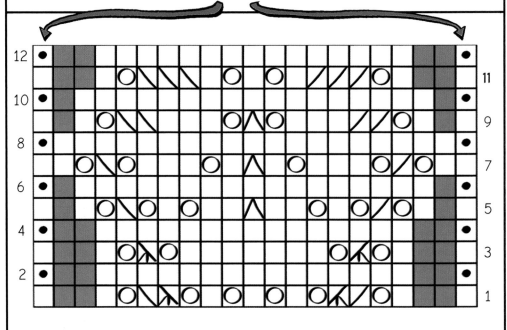

Long-tail cast on the total number of sts. Place markers on either side of the central lace panel stitches.

Side Panel (13 stitches)

Triple Leaf (multiple of 17 stitches)

Side Panel (13 stitches)

SO EXCITED TO START THIS!

ROW 1: Start at lower right corner of the Side Panel chart, and work across the row. Proceed to the Triple Leaf chart. Work Row 1 of that chart from right to left, as many times as you are repeating it. Come back to the lower right of Row 1 of the Side Panel chart and work it again for second side panel. Row 1 is done.
ROW 2: Turn and work, following the chart from left to right across the Side Panel, Triple Leaf chart multiple, and Side Panel charts. Row 2 is done.

YOU CAN RELAX ON THE EVEN ROWS!

Continue to work the charts. When you get to the top of the Triple Leaf chart, start from the bottom (Row 1) and work up it again. When you get to the top of the Side Panel chart, continue to work the pattern as established in the last 6 rows of the chart (Rows 13–18). Your Stockinette stitches will continue to increase on either side of your raglan line.

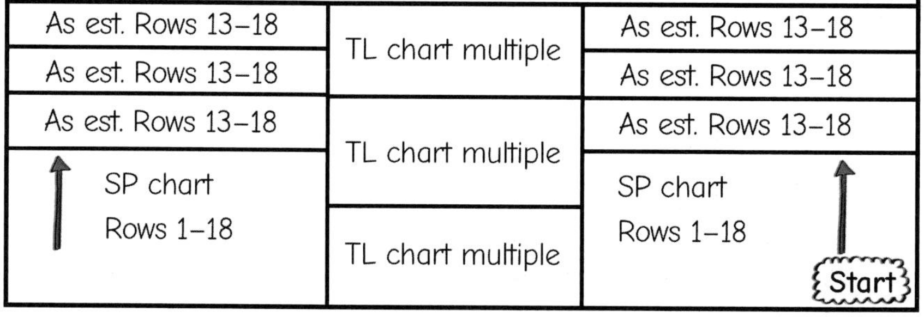

As est. Rows 13–18	TL chart multiple	As est. Rows 13–18
As est. Rows 13–18		As est. Rows 13–18
As est. Rows 13–18	TL chart multiple	As est. Rows 13–18
↑ SP chart Rows 1–18		SP chart Rows 1–18 ↑
	TL chart multiple	Start

Your Stockinette sts in the SP will increase on either side of the center raglan line as you go. Try it on! Work until you are about 1½ in (4 cm) from your desired depth. For a Garter stitch border, place a marker in the center raglan line stitch of each side panel. Knit across, and make 1 (M1) on either side of each marker on every RS row. Knit WS rows plain. Work this border for 1½ in (4 cm). Bind off loosely. Give it a good block to show off the details! Darn in ends, and bask in the glory of it.

WOW, MOM, THIS SHAWL IS SO PRETTY!

DID THIS BELONG TO GREAT-GRANDMA?

THANKS! I MADE IT!

CAN I HAVE IT?

GREAT JOB, MOM!

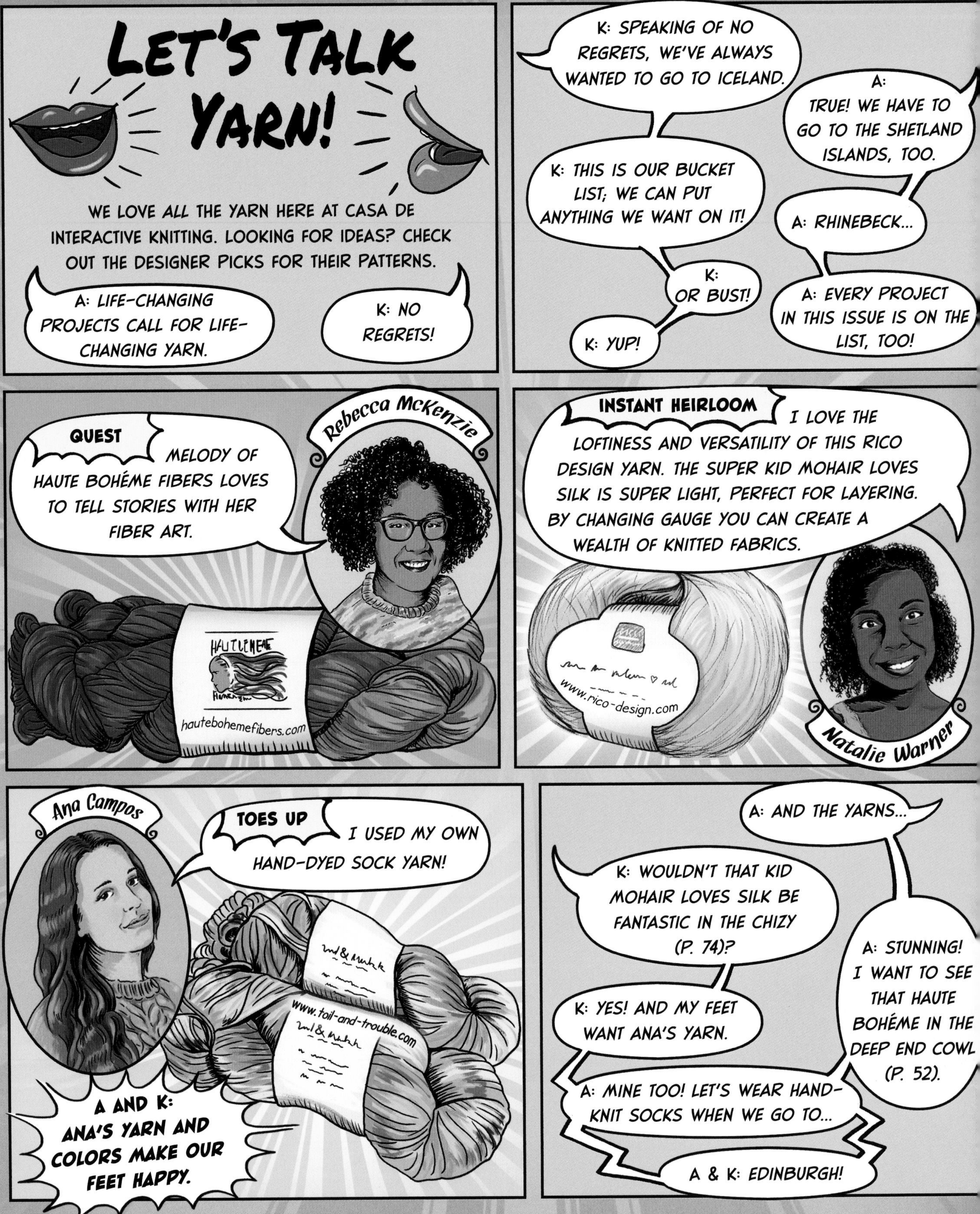
LET'S TALK YARN!
WE LOVE ALL THE YARN HERE AT CASA DE INTERACTIVE KNITTING. LOOKING FOR IDEAS? CHECK OUT THE DESIGNER PICKS FOR THEIR PATTERNS.
A: LIFE-CHANGING PROJECTS CALL FOR LIFE-CHANGING YARN.
K: NO REGRETS!
K: SPEAKING OF NO REGRETS, WE'VE ALWAYS WANTED TO GO TO ICELAND.
A: TRUE! WE HAVE TO GO TO THE SHETLAND ISLANDS, TOO.
K: THIS IS OUR BUCKET LIST; WE CAN PUT ANYTHING WE WANT ON IT!
A: RHINEBECK...
K: OR BUST!
A: EVERY PROJECT IN THIS ISSUE IS ON THE LIST, TOO!
K: YUP!
Rebecca McKenzie
QUEST
MELODY OF HAUTE BOHÉME FIBERS LOVES TO TELL STORIES WITH HER FIBER ART.
hautebohemefibers.com
INSTANT HEIRLOOM
I LOVE THE LOFTINESS AND VERSATILITY OF THIS RICO DESIGN YARN. THE SUPER KID MOHAIR LOVES SILK IS SUPER LIGHT, PERFECT FOR LAYERING. BY CHANGING GAUGE YOU CAN CREATE A WEALTH OF KNITTED FABRICS.
www.rico-design.com
Natalie Warner
Ana Campos
TOES UP
I USED MY OWN HAND-DYED SOCK YARN!
www.toil-and-trouble.com
A AND K: ANA'S YARN AND COLORS MAKE OUR FEET HAPPY.
A: AND THE YARNS...
K: WOULDN'T THAT KID MOHAIR LOVES SILK BE FANTASTIC IN THE CHIZY (P. 74)?
A: STUNNING! I WANT TO SEE THAT HAUTE BOHÉME IN THE DEEP END COWL (P. 52).
K: YES! AND MY FEET WANT ANA'S YARN.
A: MINE TOO! LET'S WEAR HAND-KNIT SOCKS WHEN WE GO TO...
A & K: EDINBURGH!

BONUS PATTERN!

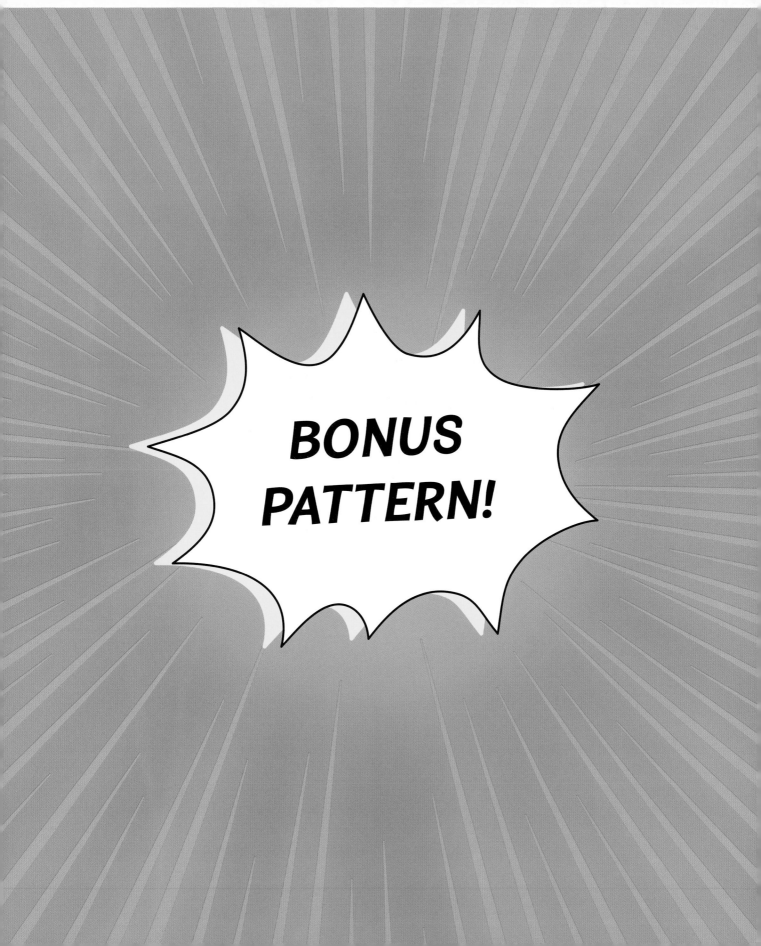

Welcome to Cables

BY NORAH GAUGHAN

CABLED SWEATERS ARE ONE OF THE MOST WIDELY RECOGNIZED AND ICONIC KNITTED GARMENTS. THIS DROP-SLEEVE CUSTOM CABLED SWEATER PATTERN INVITES YOU TO COMBINE CABLE ELEMENTS FOR A GARMENT LIKE NO OTHER. FEEL DAUNTED? START WITH A SMALL ONE, LIKE KAREN DID!

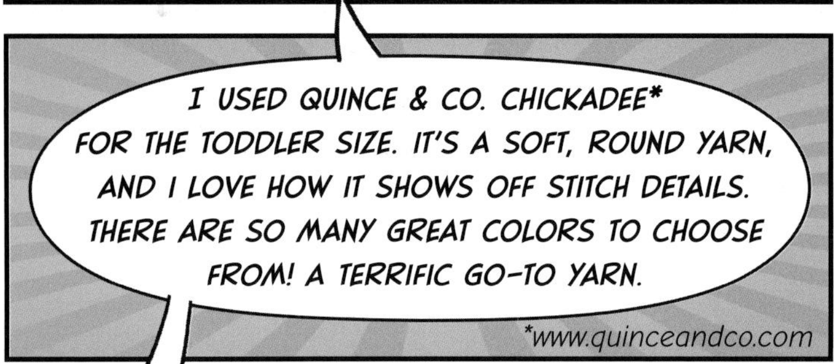
I USED QUINCE & CO. CHICKADEE* FOR THE TODDLER SIZE. IT'S A SOFT, ROUND YARN, AND I LOVE HOW IT SHOWS OFF STITCH DETAILS. THERE ARE SO MANY GREAT COLORS TO CHOOSE FROM! A TERRIFIC GO-TO YARN.
*www.quinceandco.com

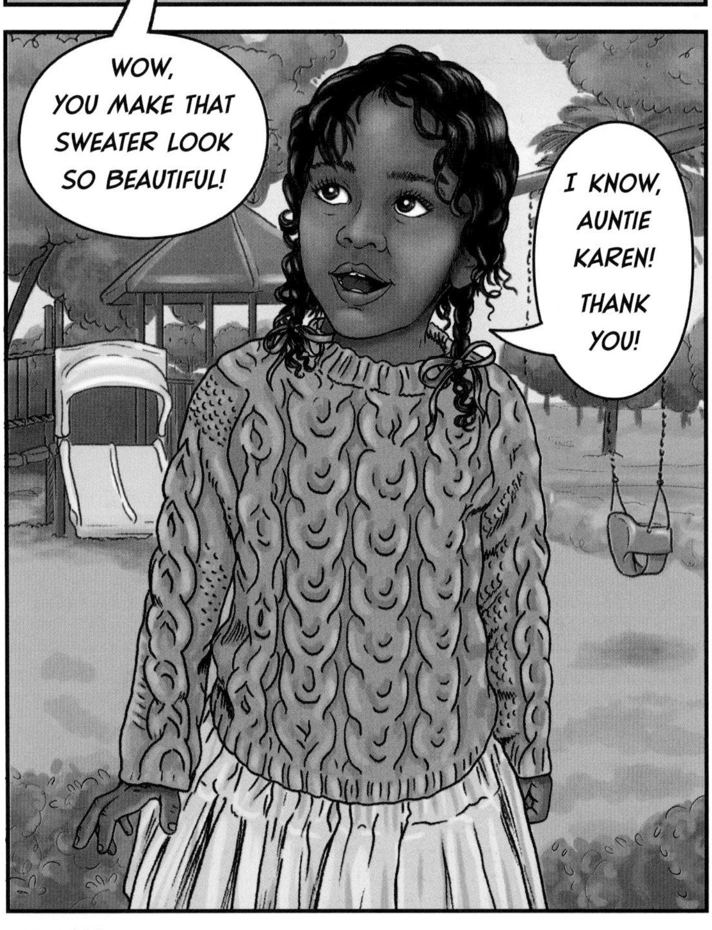
WOW, YOU MAKE THAT SWEATER LOOK SO BEAUTIFUL!
I KNOW, AUNTIE KAREN! THANK YOU!

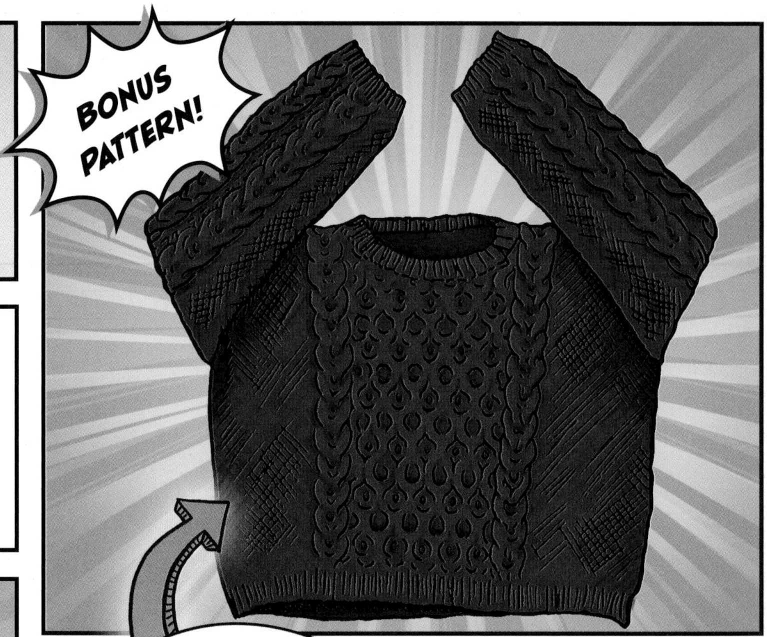
BONUS PATTERN!

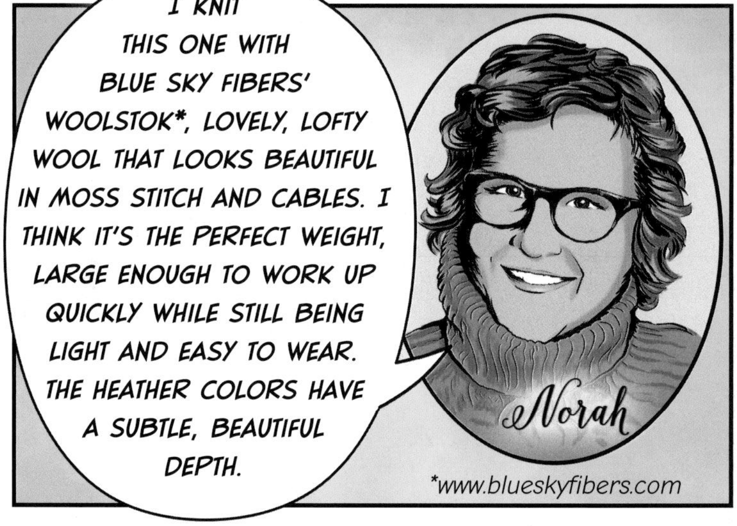
I KNIT THIS ONE WITH BLUE SKY FIBERS' WOOLSTOK*, LOVELY, LOFTY WOOL THAT LOOKS BEAUTIFUL IN MOSS STITCH AND CABLES. I THINK IT'S THE PERFECT WEIGHT, LARGE ENOUGH TO WORK UP QUICKLY WHILE STILL BEING LIGHT AND EASY TO WEAR. THE HEATHER COLORS HAVE A SUBTLE, BEAUTIFUL DEPTH.
Norah
*www.blueskyfibers.com

MATERIALS: Fingering to Aran-weight yarn, DPNs, and short and long circular needles for body and sleeves, needles two sizes smaller for ribbing, graph paper, optional cable needle (CN). **GAUGE:** Medium to Chewy will give your cables the most structure. Determine your blocked gauge in American/Irish Moss stitch and each of the cable elements you plan to use. Make sure you have two repeats (width and height) of the cables in your swatches. **TECHNIQUES:** American/Irish Moss stitch (st), Double Horseshoe cable, Double O cable, Honeycomb cable, Horizontal Stockinette (p. 76), tapering sleeves, Jeny's Surprisingly Stretchy Bind-Off (JSSBO, p. 98).

SIZE: Norah suggests measuring a drop-shoulder sweater (see p. 77) with a fit you like. Cables are bulky, so add more ease if the garment has thinner fabric. Lay the garment flat and measure the following:

NW	SL
ND	RIBBING
SW	RIBBING
ST	L
W	RIBBING

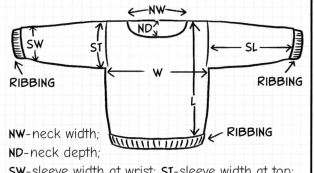

NW-neck width;
ND-neck depth;
SW-sleeve width at wrist; **ST**-sleeve width at top;
SL-sleeve length; **W**-body width at underarm;
L-body length from shoulder to top of ribbing

Don't have a sweater? Bring your tape measure into a clothing store, and measure any size you need!

METHOD: First, design your sweater using graph paper, your measurements, and the cable elements of your choice. Front and back are worked separately from the bottom up, then seamed at the shoulders. Sleeve stitches are picked up and worked top-down, flat. The neckline is picked up and finished, and side seams are sewn.

THERE ARE MANY CABLES AND STITCHES TO CHOOSE FROM! JUST ASK NORAH. HERE ARE SOME OF OUR FAVORITES.

AMERICAN/IRISH MOSS STITCH (M). This is worked over an even number of sts. **Rows 1 and 2**: (K1, p1), repeat to end. **Rows 3 and 4**: (P1, k1), repeat to end. Repeat Rows 1–4.

This is the chart key for the next three cables.

▨	Purl on RS, knit on WS
☐	Knit on RS, purl on WS
⧄	2/2 Left Cross (LC)
⧅	2/2 Right Cross (RC)
⧄	3/3 Left Cross (LC)
⧅	3/3 Right Cross (RC)

DOUBLE HORSESHOE (DH) WITH REVERSE ST ST (16 sts):

ROWS 1, 3, 7, 11: P2, k12, p2.

ALL WS ROWS AND ROW 12: K2, p12, k2.

ROW 5: P2, 3/3 RC, 3/3 LC, p2.

ROW 9: P2, k2, 2/2 RC, 2/2 LC, k2, p2.

Repeat Rows 1–12.

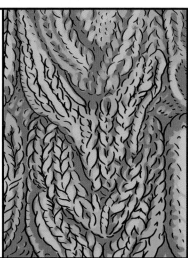

Cable chart for Double Horseshoe (DH) with reverse St st (16 sts)

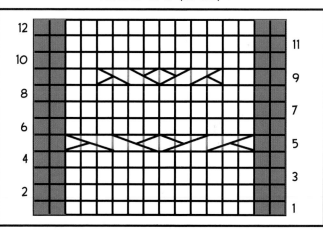

DOUBLE O (DO) (12 sts):

ROWS 1, 3, 7, 11, 15, 19, 21: K12.

ALL WS ROWS AND ROW 22: P12.

ROW 5: 3/3 RC, 3/3 LC.

ROW 9: K2, 2/2 RC, 2/2 LC, k2.

ROW 13: K2, 2/2 LC, 2/2 RC, k2.

ROW 17: 3/3 LC, 3/3 RC.

Repeat Rows 1–22.

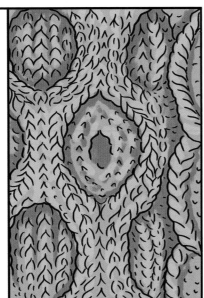

HONEYCOMB (8 sts):

ROW 1: Knit.

ALL WS ROWS AND ROW 8: Purl.

ROW 3: 2/2 RC, 2/2 LC.

ROW 5: Knit.

ROW 7: 2/2 LC, 2/2 RC.

Repeat Rows 1–8.

Cable chart for Double O (12 sts)

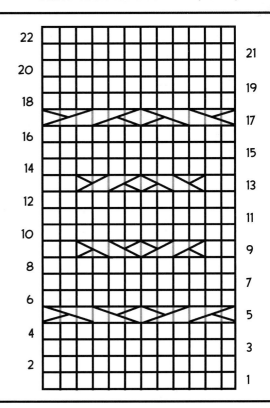

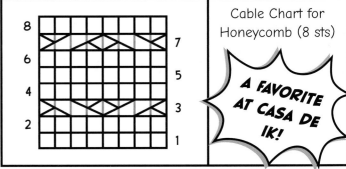

Cable Chart for Honeycomb (8 sts)

A FAVORITE AT CASA DE IK!

CABLES DEMYSTIFIED AND MINI-DEMOS! When cabling a group of stitches, sts from the left lean right, and sts from the right lean left, crossing each other. In a Right Cross (RC), the sts on the left travel on top and lean right. In a Left Cross (LC), the sts on the right travel on top and lean left. If you put the right sts to the back, the left will be on top, and you'll get a RC. If you put the right sts to the front, they'll be on top and you'll get an LC. Our demos show 2/2 cables, but the techniques are the same for different numbers of sts.

STS TO BACK = RC, STS TO FRONT = LC

Here are examples of Left and Right Crosses.

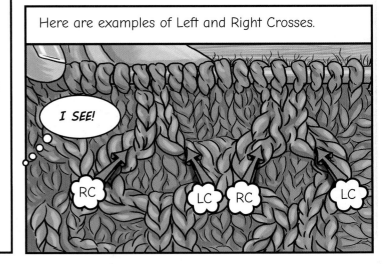

I SEE!

RC   LC   RC   LC

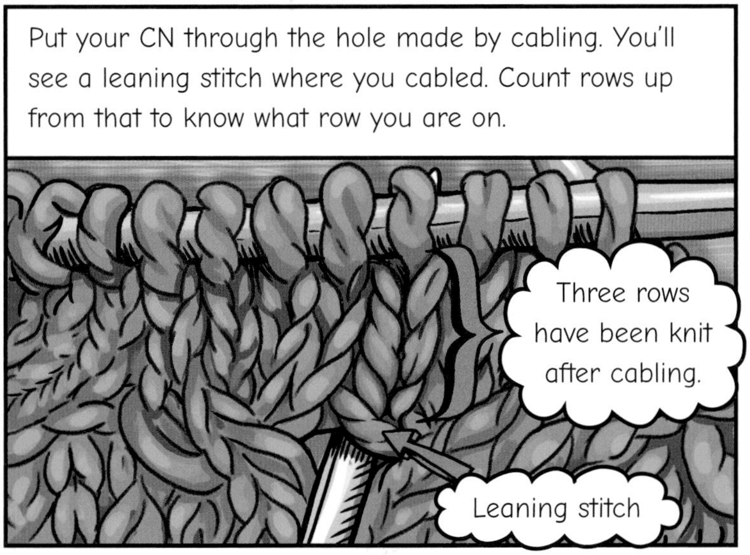
Put your CN through the hole made by cabling. You'll see a leaning stitch where you cabled. Count rows up from that to know what row you are on.
Three rows have been knit after cabling.
Leaning stitch

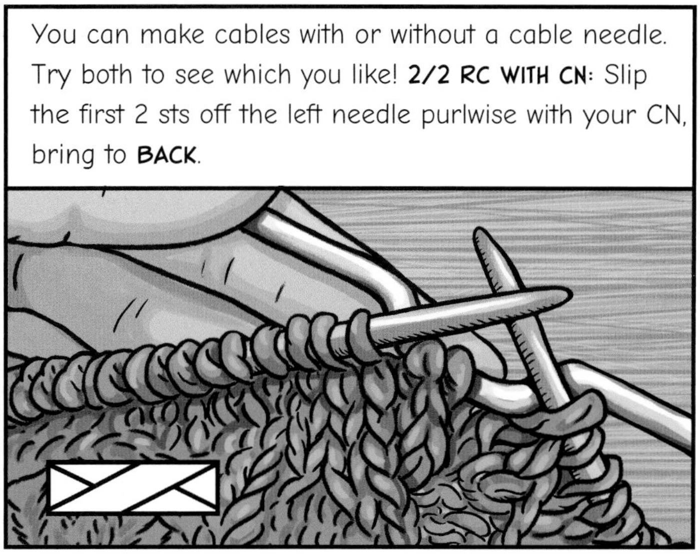
You can make cables with or without a cable needle. Try both to see which you like! **2/2 RC WITH CN:** Slip the first 2 sts off the left needle purlwise with your CN, bring to **BACK**.

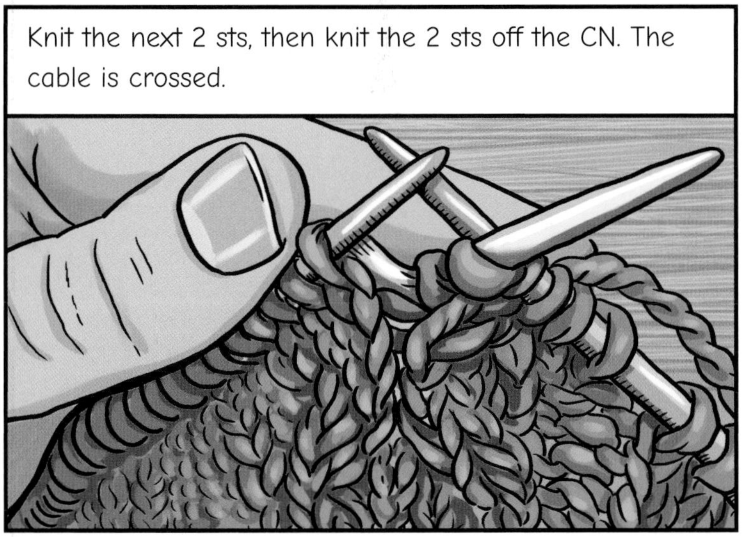
Knit the next 2 sts, then knit the 2 sts off the CN. The cable is crossed.

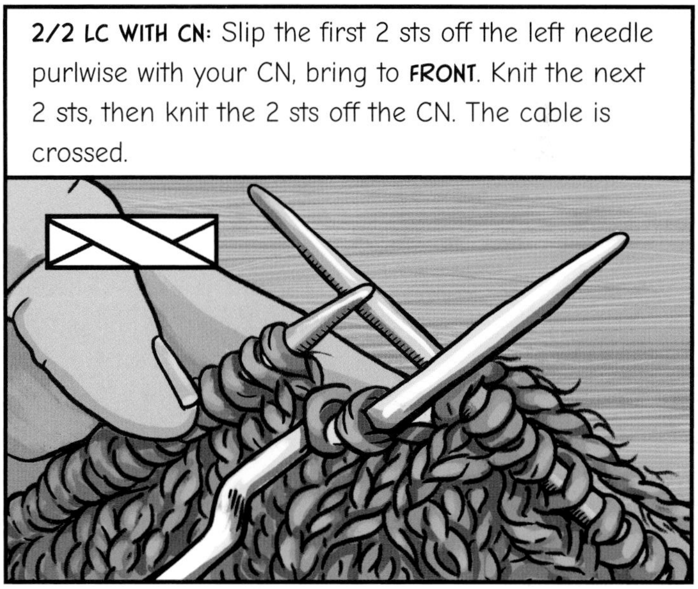
2/2 LC WITH CN: Slip the first 2 sts off the left needle purlwise with your CN, bring to **FRONT**. Knit the next 2 sts, then knit the 2 sts off the CN. The cable is crossed.

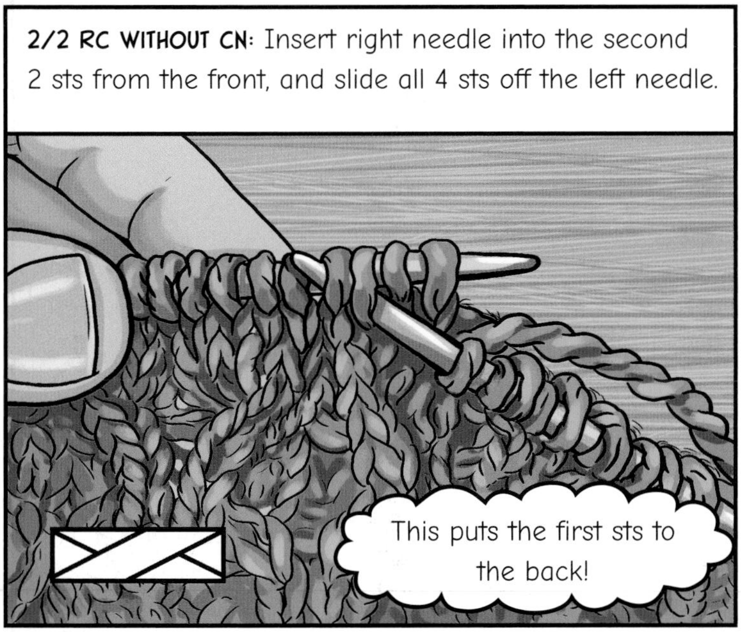
2/2 RC WITHOUT CN: Insert right needle into the second 2 sts from the front, and slide all 4 sts off the left needle.
This puts the first sts to the back!

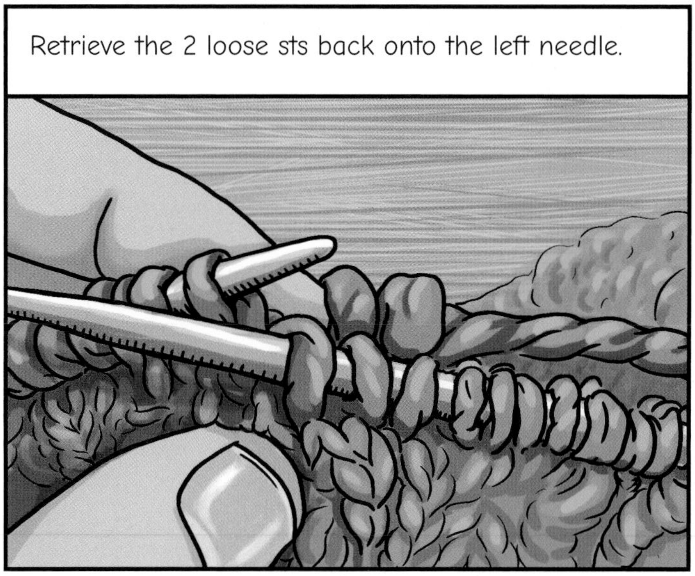
Retrieve the 2 loose sts back onto the left needle.

Put the two sts from the right needle back onto the left needle. The cable is crossed. Knit the 4 sts to complete the RC.

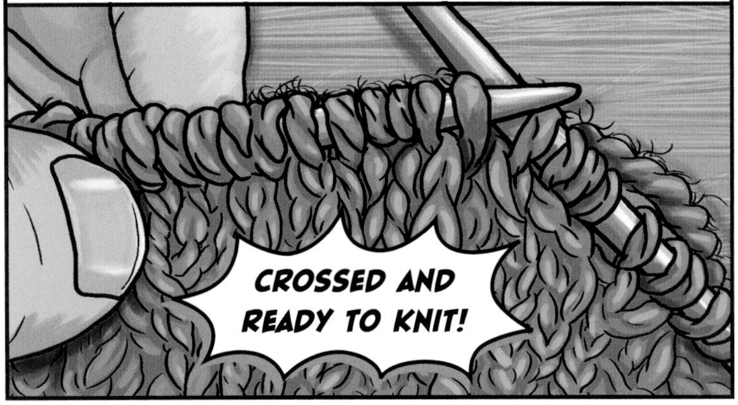
CROSSED AND READY TO KNIT!

2/2 LC WITHOUT CN: Insert right needle into the second 2 sts from the **BACK,** and slide all 4 sts off the left needle.

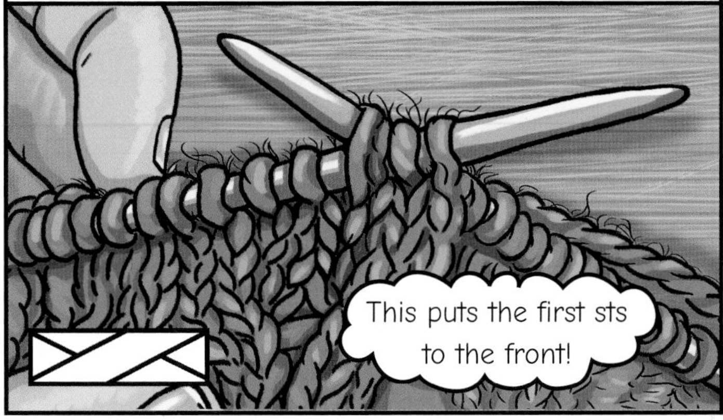
This puts the first sts to the front!

Retrieve the 2 loose sts back onto the left needle. Put the two sts from the right needle back onto the left needle. The cable is crossed. Knit the 4 sts to complete the LC.

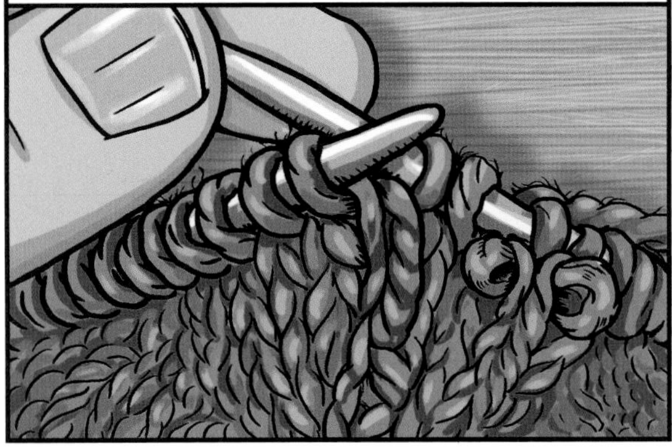

Armed with your measurements and your gauges, it's time to sketch your design. Draw a scale version of your sweater on graph paper.

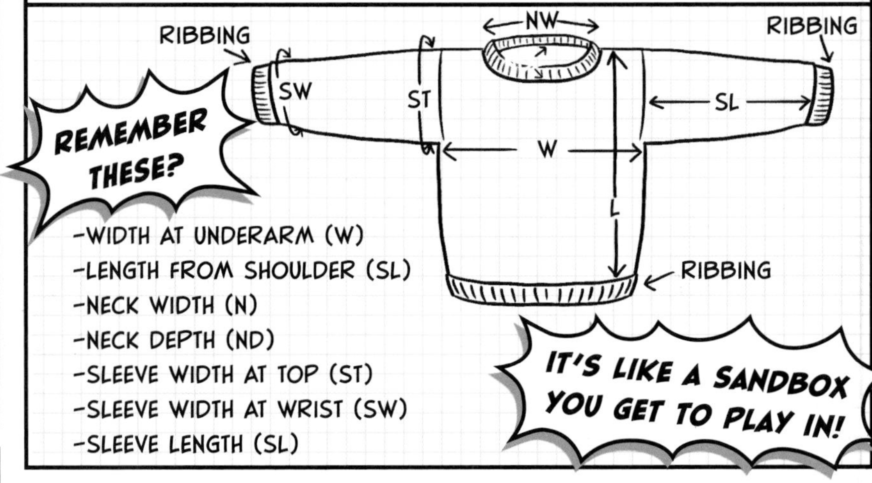
RIBBING
NW
RIBBING
SW
ST
SL
W
L
RIBBING
REMEMBER THESE?
-WIDTH AT UNDERARM (W)
-LENGTH FROM SHOULDER (SL)
-NECK WIDTH (N)
-NECK DEPTH (ND)
-SLEEVE WIDTH AT TOP (ST)
-SLEEVE WIDTH AT WRIST (SW)
-SLEEVE LENGTH (SL)
IT'S LIKE A SANDBOX YOU GET TO PLAY IN!

Have fun sketching different placement and numbers of cables. Draw your elements to scale. The width of all your elements should add up to the width of your sweater. Karen did 3 DHS in the center, 1 DO on either side, and filled the remaining space on the sides with Moss stitch. For the sleeves, she did one DHS down the middle with Moss st on the sides.

Use Moss st to "fill in" on the sides. Rev St st can also be used between elements.

Once you have your elements arranged, figure out how many sts are needed for each element. Add them up to get the total number of sts you use for the main body of the front and back (X).

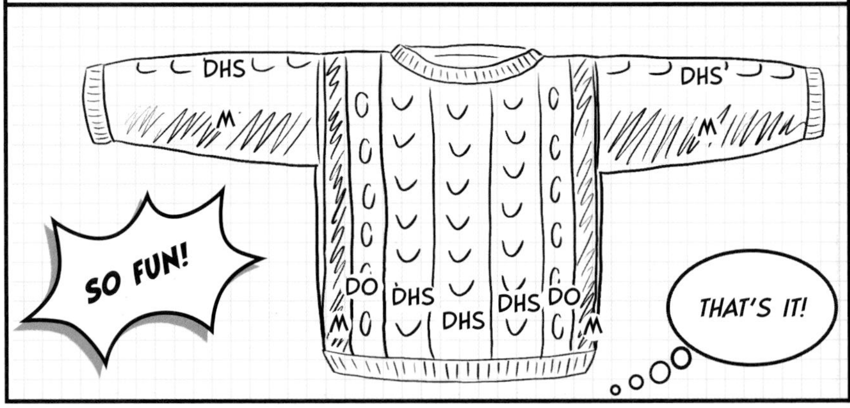
DHS
M
DHS'
M'
DO
DHS
DHS
DHS
DO
M
M
SO FUN!
THAT'S IT!

To calculate the number of sts to cast on for the ribbing, add: (the number of cable stitches) plus (the number of Moss sts x 1.1), and let the total be divisible by 4.

Karen's sweater had 68 cable sts and 16 Moss sts. So she had 68 plus 1.1 x 16 (18 sts), or a total of 86. She adjusted this to 84.

I CAN HANDLE 84 STITCHES.

Start with the back of the sweater. With needles 2 sizes smaller than the ones you'll use for the cables, cast on and work in K2P2 rib. When you finish ribbing, decrease down to your total body sts (X). Subtract the body sts from the ribbing sts; you will decrease with p2tog that many times, evenly spaced around (p. 59). You now have X sts. Start at the lower right of your drawing, and work from right to left across on the RS, and from left to right on the WS. When the back reaches L, bind off all sts.

KNITTY KNIT KNIT!

Plan the neckline for the front. Place a pin on the back ND down from the top. Move the pin up or down so the cable pattern ends nicely before the neck bind-off. Measure N and count the sts needed for the neck. Count the rows from the pin to the top.

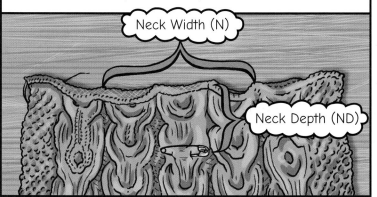

Neck Width (N)

Neck Depth (ND)

Work the front as you did the back until you reach the bottom of the neckline. Group your N sts into thirds: ⅓ on the left side for decrease, ⅓ of the center neck stitches will be bound off, and ⅓ on the right for decrease.

~⅓   ~⅓   ~⅓

To draw and work your custom front neckline, follow the instructions on p. 106. Your total neck stitches are N. Your row count will be ND x row gauge. For the center front, bind off ⅓ of the N stitches. Here is Karen's. Your stitch count could be different.

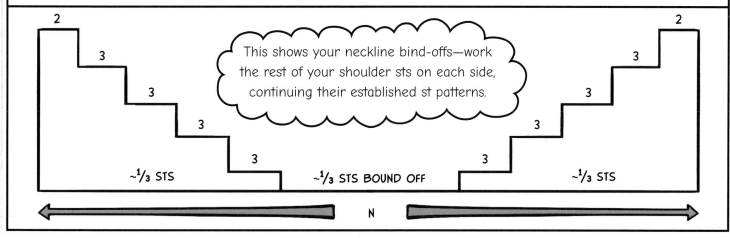

This shows your neckline bind-offs—work the rest of your shoulder sts on each side, continuing their established st patterns.

2   3   3   3   3   3   3   3   3   3   2

~⅓ STS   ~⅓ STS BOUND OFF   ~⅓ STS

N

Seam the shoulders: Lay out the front and back flat, RS up, shoulders aligned. Scoop one st from each shoulder edge back and forth with your darning needle, until you run out of front shoulder sts (see p. 76). Repeat on the other side. Fasten off securely.

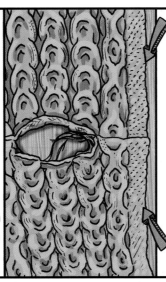

Sleeve time! Add ½ in (1.25 cm) to half of the sleeve width. Place a marker on front and back, each side, this far down from the shoulder seam. Add up the sts you need for your sleeve elements (Y).

That extra bit makes the sleeve lie nicely.

*With larger needles, on the RS, pick up Y sts for your sleeve between the markers.

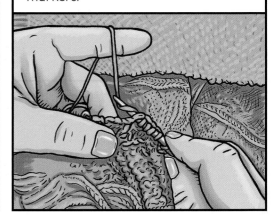

Purl one WS row. Start your charts on the next RS row. Here's how to **TAPER YOUR SLEEVE**: Multiply SW x gauge to calculate your target sts at the wrist. Subtract that from the ST sts on the needle. To get your number of decrease rows, divide that by 2, since you will be working a double decrease, one stitch on each side. Divide SL by your number of decrease rows to determine the length to leave between the decrease rows.

Karen started with ST = 10½ in (27 cm; 54 sts) and had to get down to SW = 8½ in (22 cm; 44 sts). She needed to decrease 10 sts over her SL of 10 in. She will double decrease every 2 in (5 cm), 5 times.

When you've reached SL, change to smaller needles and work 1 row in St st, decreasing as necessary to get a multiple of 4. Work K2P2 ribbing as desired and BO. Repeat from * for second sleeve.

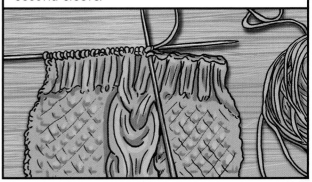

Use Gauge Translation (p. 67) to finish the neckline. Measure the neck opening, then multiply by your Moss st gauge.

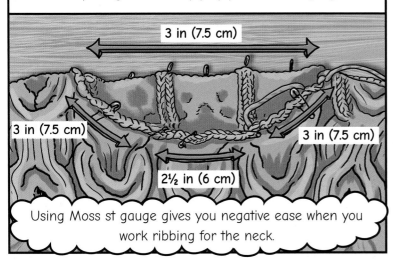

3 in (7.5 cm)

3 in (7.5 cm)

3 in (7.5 cm)

2½ in (6 cm)

Using Moss st gauge gives you negative ease when you work ribbing for the neck.

With smaller needles, pick up evenly spaced sts to a multiple of 4. Work in K2P2 rib to desired depth, then **JSSBO** (p. 98) in rib.

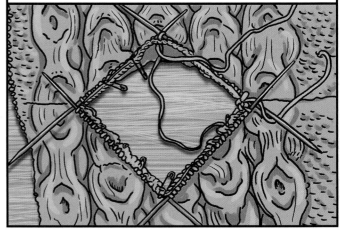

Almost done! Wet block and rest up. Pin your garment at the edges, then sew up the sides and sleeves.

Pin the cuffs, hem, and underarms first, then pin in between.

MINI-DEMO! Seaming Moss st: Insert the needle from back to front on the right at the cast-on edge. Repeat on the left. Insert the needle back into the first sts from the right. This matches up the bottom edges.

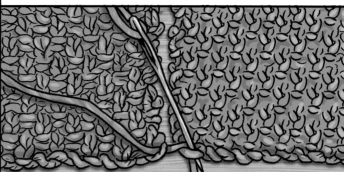

The side edges have two rows of St sts and two rows with reverse St (rev St) sts. For the St sts, pick up the bar between the two edge sts and pull the threaded needle through.

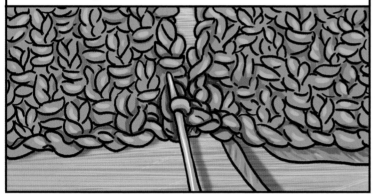

On the other side, pick up the bar between the two edge sts or, if it's rev St st, pick up the purl bump. Go back and forth from side to side. Sew loosely and tighten every few rows. When done, sew in ends and enjoy.

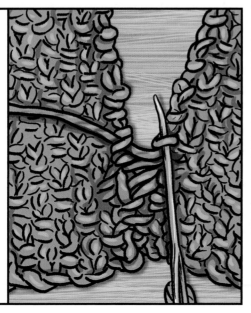

LET'S GO PLAY!

I'M GOING TO MAKE ONE FOR MYSELF...

Oh by the Way

We love wool at Casa de IK. Why? It's renewable, biodegradable, and flame resistant. It wicks water away from the body and can absorb 30% of its weight and still feel warm. Wool provides instant, gentle warmth when it comes to rest on the body.

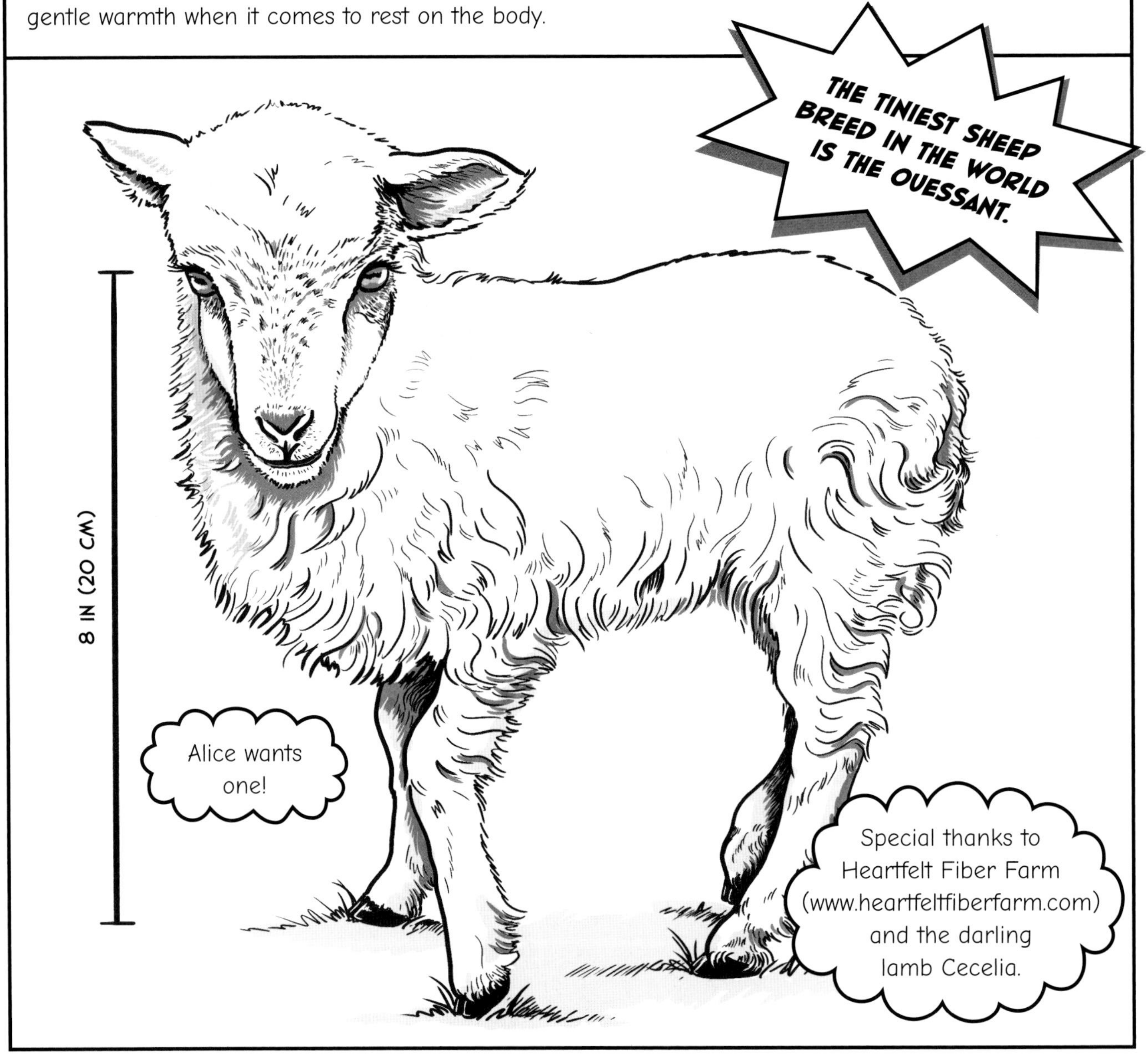

THE TINIEST SHEEP BREED IN THE WORLD IS THE OUESSANT.
8 IN (20 CM)
Alice wants one!
Special thanks to Heartfelt Fiber Farm (www.heartfeltfiberfarm.com) and the darling lamb Cecelia.

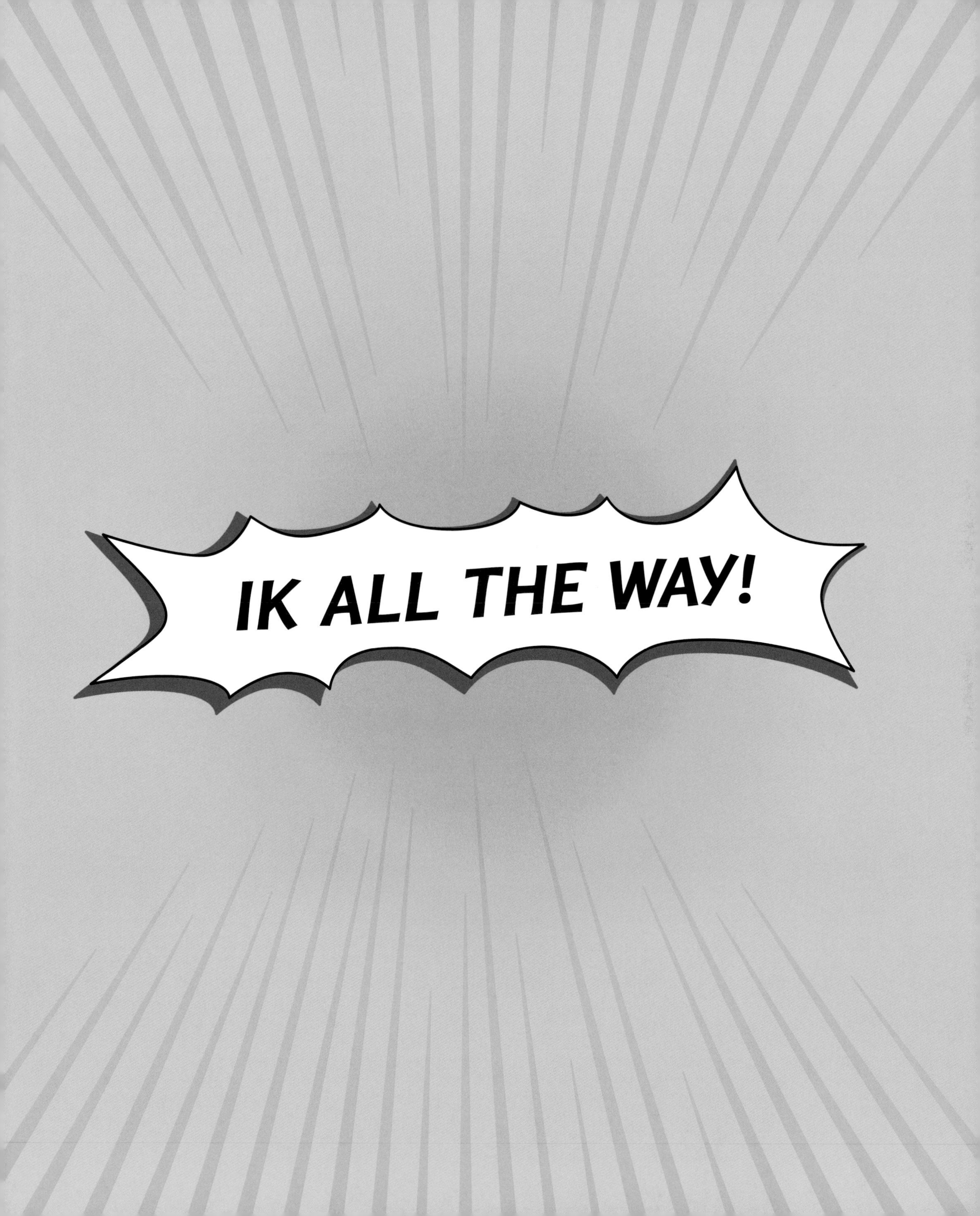
IK ALL THE WAY!

ABBREVIATIONS

2CB: two-color brioche

3NBO: Three-Needle Bind-Off

cm: centimeter(s)

dec: decrease

DK: double-knitting-weight yarn

DPNs: double-pointed needles

g: gram(s)

GT: Gauge Translate or Gauge Translation

GTBO: Garter Tab Bind-Off

GTCO: Garter Tab Cast-On

in: inch(es)

inc: increase

JMCO: Judy's Magic Cast-On

JSSBO: Jeny's Surprisingly Stretchy Bind-Off

k: knit

k2tog: knit two together

k3tog: knit three together

KFB: knit in the front and back of the stitch

KTBL: knit through the back loop

L: liter(s)

m: meter(s)

M1L: make one left

M1pw: make one purlwise

M1R: make one right

ml: milliliter(s)

OMJOM: One More, Just One More!

oz: ounce(s)

p: purl

pm: place marker

psso: pass slipped stitch over

rnd: round

RS: right side

sl1: slip one knitwise

S2KPsso: slip two knitwise together, knit the next stitch, pass the two slipped stitches over the knit stitch

ssk: slip, slip, knit two slipped stitches together through the back loop

sssk: slip, slip, slip, knit three slipped stitches together through the back loop

st(s): stitch(es)

St st: Stockinette stitch

STASH: Skeins That Are Special and Here

TSLTCO: two-stranded long-tail cast-on

WS: wrong side

y: yard(s)

yo: yarn over

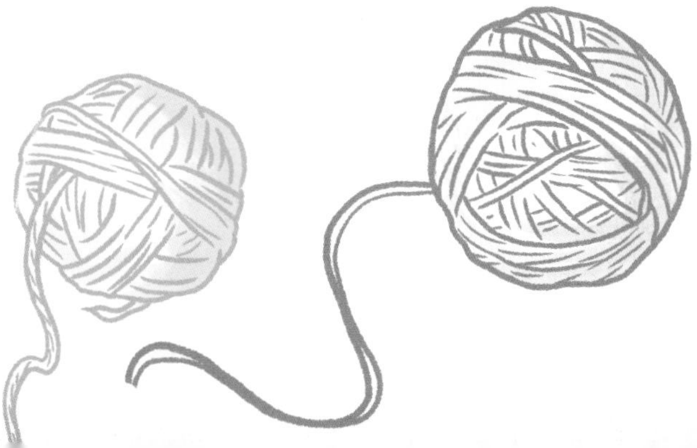

Oh BY THE Way

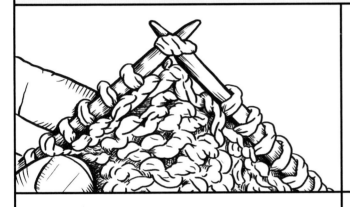

Ever have mysteriously tight stitches on your needles? Maybe you're working on the tips. If you work your stitches at the tips of your needles, it is like you are working on smaller needles. The stitches then feel tight when they slide along the full diameter of the needle.

Make sure your needles cross at their full diameters when working your stitches to avoid tight knitting and to get correctly sized stitches for the needles.

AHH—THAT'S BETTER! NOW THE STITCHES GLIDE ALONG THE NEEDLES WITHOUT HAVING TO STOP AND SCOOCH THEM.

TECHNIQUE INDEX

TECHNIQUE	TYPE	PATTERN	ISSUE	PAGE
Baking	Cookies	IK Cookies	STASH	86–87
Bind-Off	Garter tab	Double Feature	OMJOM	25
	Jeny's Surprisingly Stretchy Bind-Off (JSSBO)	Toes Up	BL	98
	Knit 5 below bind-off (K5BBO)	Nocoshoco	FP	51
	Standard	FBS	STASH	64
	Three-needle	Quest	BL	108
Blocking	Wet blocking	IK Gauge	Intro	7
Border & Trim	Fringe	FBS	STASH	64
	Garter	Team Blanket	STASH	69
	I-cord	Urhat	STASH	73
	Lettuce-leaf edge	Dashwood	FP	42
	Quick border	Log Cabin	OMJOM	35
Cables	Basics	WTC	Bonus	118–120
Cast-On	Garter tab	Double Feature	OMJOM	22
	Judy's Magic Cast-On	Toes Up	BL	94
	Provisional	Body Snatcher	OMJOM	17
	Two-stranded long-tail	Omnimitts	STASH	84
Colorwork	Extra-loose colorwork	Dashwood	FP	41
	Fair Isle	Urhat	STASH	72
	Garter intarsia	Double Feature	OMJOM	23
Darning	Basket	Darning, Darling	OMJOM	28–29
	Patch-and-Seed	Darning, Darling	OMJOM	30–31
Diagonal (aka Bias) Knitting	Basics	FBS	STASH	64
Gauge	Basics	IK Gauge	Intro	7
	Gauge Translation	Team Blanket	STASH	67
Grafting	Basics	Team Blanket	STASH	68
How to Read Knitstrips	Basics	All	All	2
Lace	Basics	Instant Heirloom	BL	111
Log Cabin	Basics	Log Cabin	OMJOM	33
Miter Squares	Center out	Team Blanket	STASH	66–69
Reading Charts	Cable charts	WTC	Bonus	117–118
	Fair Isle charts	Urhat	STASH	40, 72
	Lace charts	Instant Heirloom	BL	111–112
	Sequence knitting	Lucky Hat	FP	58

TECHNIQUE	TYPE	PATTERN	ISSUE	PAGE
Seaming	Garter stitch	Omnimitts	STASH	85
	Hemline	Body Snatcher	OMJOM	19
	Horizontal Stockinette	Chizy	STASH	75
	Moss stitch	WTC	Bonus	123
	Shoulders	WTC	Bonus	122
	Vertical Stockinette	TDE	FP	54
	Whipstitch	Darcy	OMJOM	27
Shaping	Bust	Quest	BL	105
	Neckline (front)	Nocoshoco	FP	49
	Neckline	Quest, WTC	BL, Bonus	106–107, 121
	Neckline (sideways)	Nocoshoco	FP	49
Short Rows	No wrapping	S3	STASH	81
	Wrapping	Toes Up	BL	93, 96–97
Sleeves	Drop sleeves	WTC	Bonus	122
	Ruching sleeves	Body Snatcher	OMJOM	20
	Tapered sleeves	Quest	BL	108–122
Stitch Decrease	Evenly spaced	Lucky Hat	FP	59
	Knit 3 together (k3tog)	Instant Heirloom	BL	111
	Slip, slip, slip, knit (sssk)	Instant Heirloom	BL	111
	Slip 1, knit 2 together, pass the slipped stitch over (S1, k2tog, psso)	Instant Heirloom	BL	111
	Slip 2, knit, pass two slipped sts over the knit stitch (S2KPsso)	Urhat	STASH	72
Stitch Increase	Evenly spaced	Lucky Hat	FP	59
	Knit front and back (KFB)	FBS	STASH	64
	M1R & M1L	Toes Up	BL	93
	Make 1 purlwise (M1pw)	Instant Heirloom	BL	111
Stitch Patterns	American/Irish Moss	WTC	Bonus	117
	Basket weave	Chizy	STASH	75
	Double Horseshoe cable	WTC	Bonus	117
	Double O cable	WTC	Bonus	118
	Honeycomb cable	WTC	Bonus	118
	Sequence knitting	Lucky Hat	FP	57–59
	Single knot	Quest	BL	105
	Two-color brioche	Wowl!	FP	45–47
Yarn Bombing	Basics	Yarn Bombing	BL	102

The Body Snatcher
Issue No. 1: OMJOM…15

The Chizy
Issue No. 3: STASH…74

The Darcy
Issue No. 1: OMJOM...26

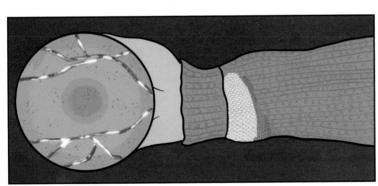

NOT SURE WHAT TO KNIT? TAKE A LOOK AT PAGE 10!

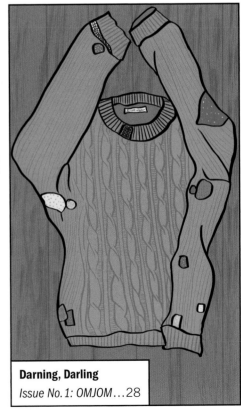

Darning, Darling
Issue No. 1: OMJOM...28

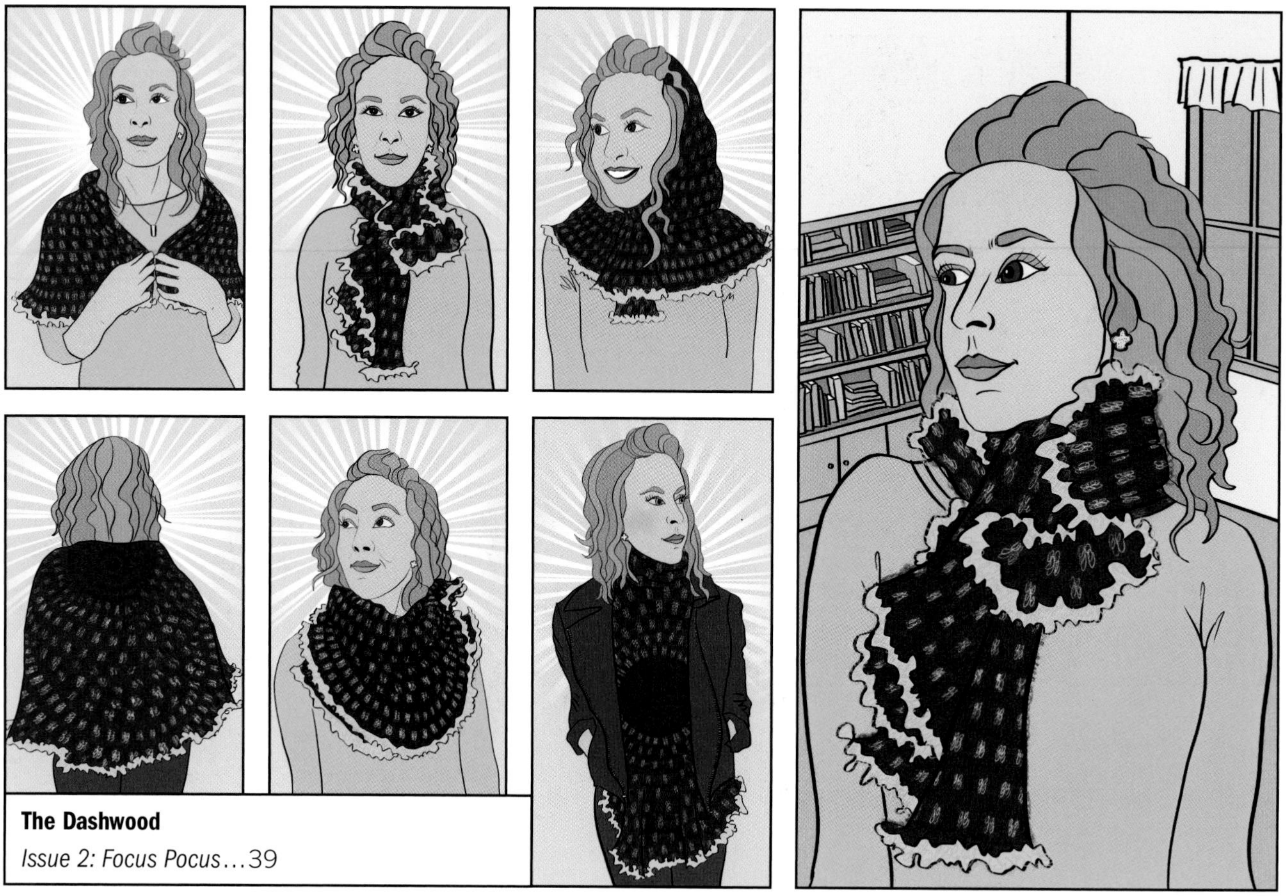

The Dashwood

Issue 2: Focus Pocus...39

WHETHER YOU'RE IN THE MOOD FOR MINDLESS KNITTING, OR KIND-OF INTENSE KNITTING, WE'VE GOT YOU COVERED.

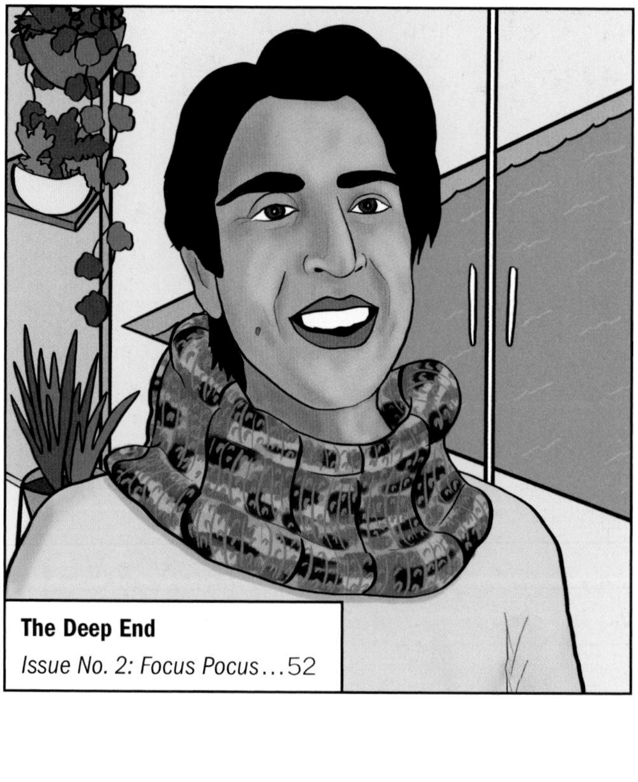

The Deep End

Issue No. 2: Focus Pocus...52

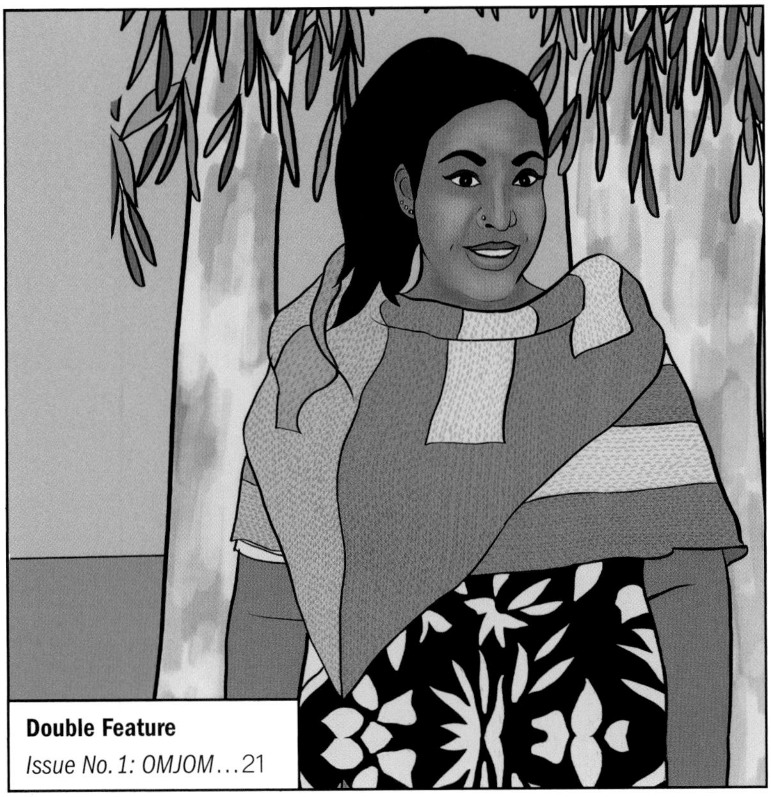
Double Feature
Issue No. 1: OMJOM...21

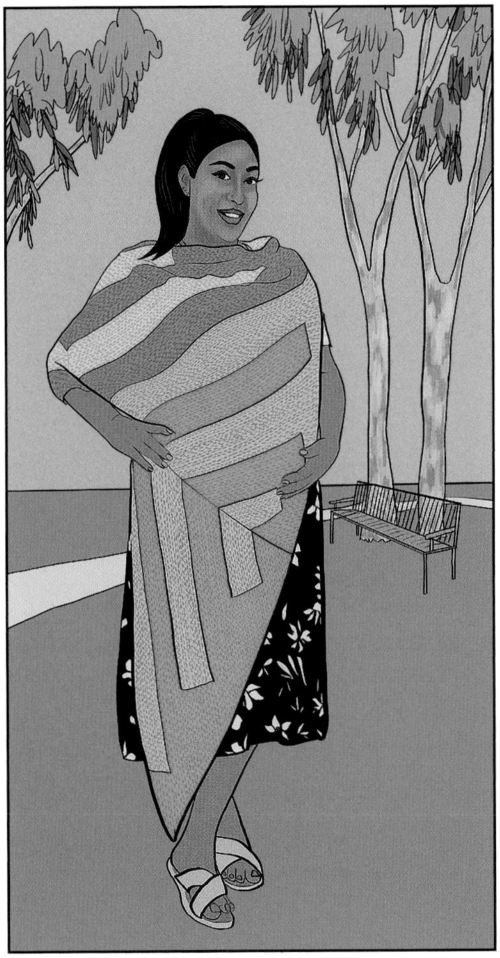

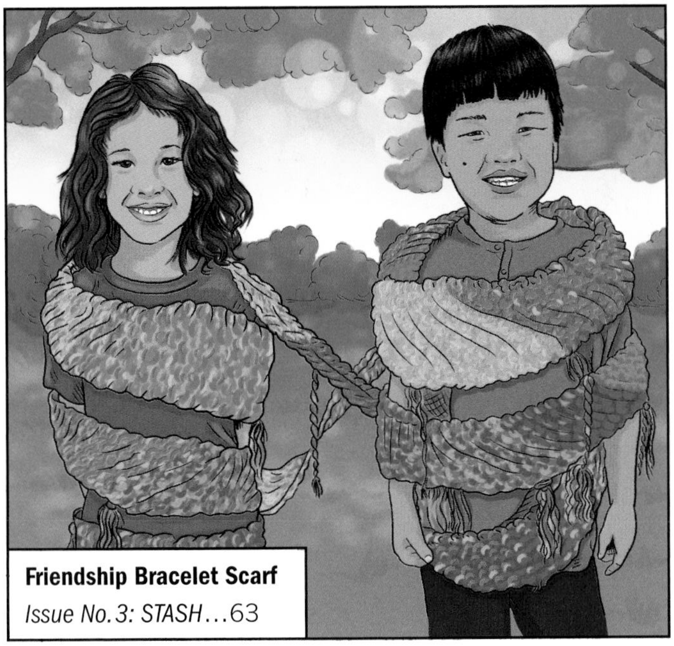
Friendship Bracelet Scarf
Issue No. 3: STASH...63

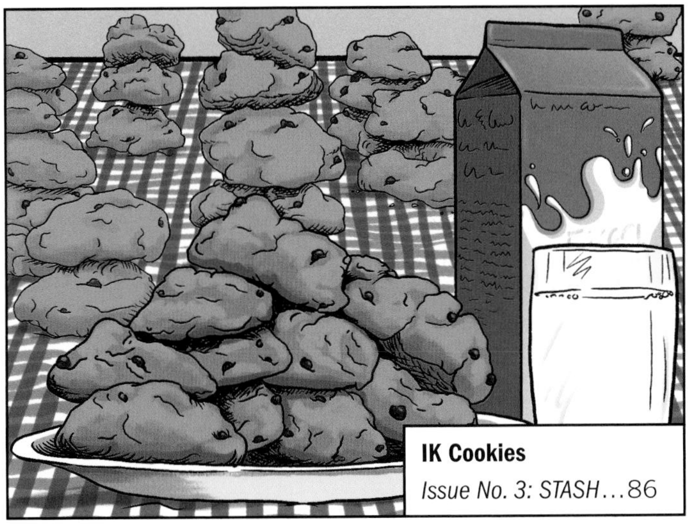
IK Cookies
Issue No. 3: STASH...86

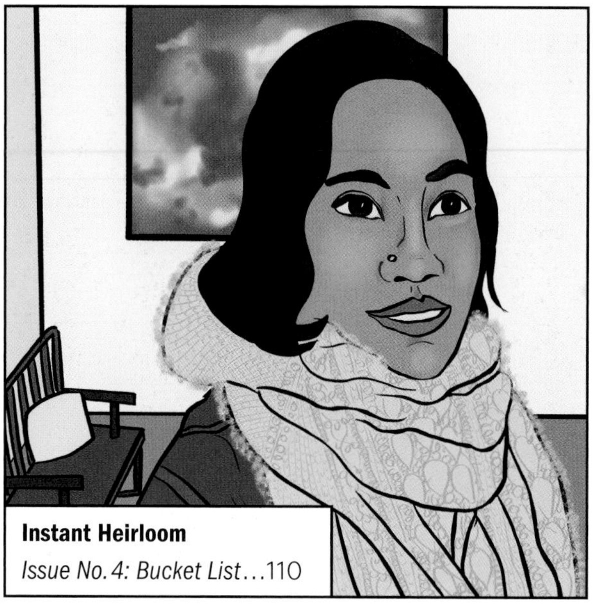

Instant Heirloom
Issue No. 4: Bucket List...110

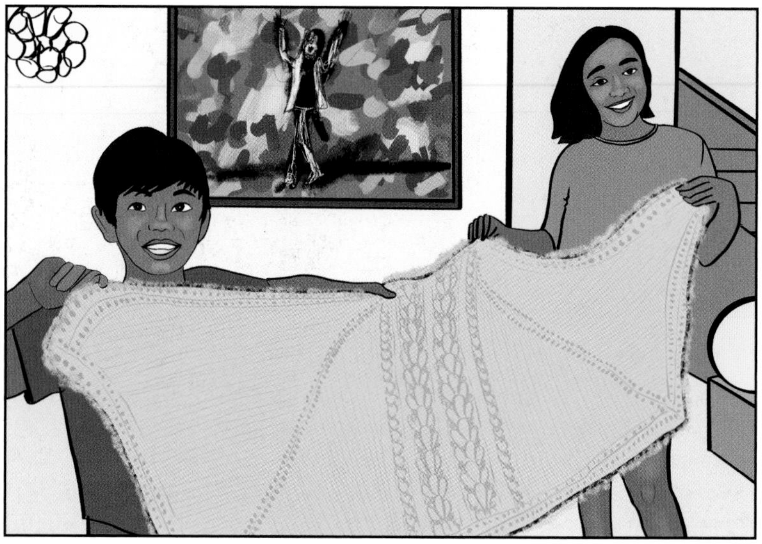

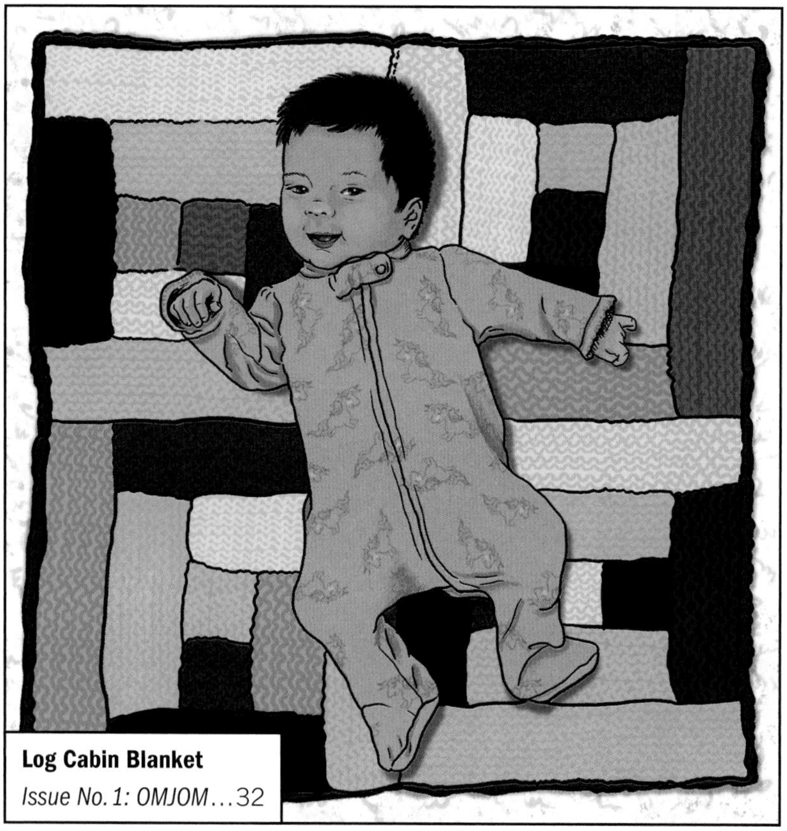

Log Cabin Blanket
Issue No. 1: OMJOM...32

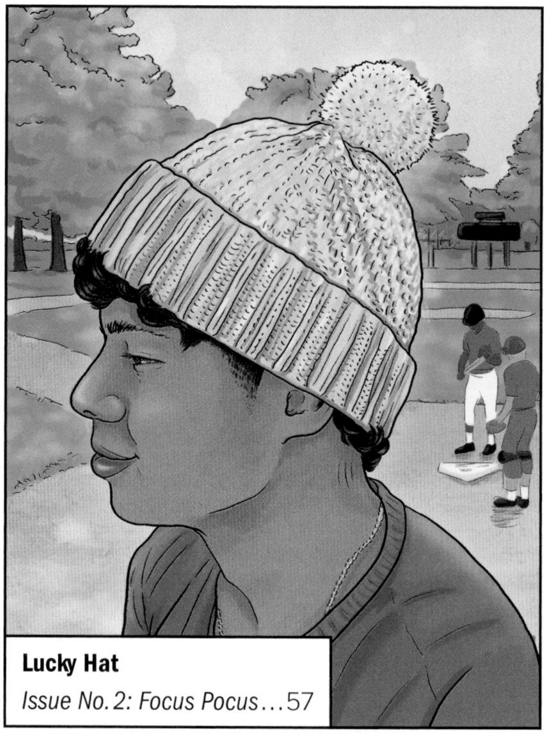

Lucky Hat
Issue No. 2: Focus Pocus...57

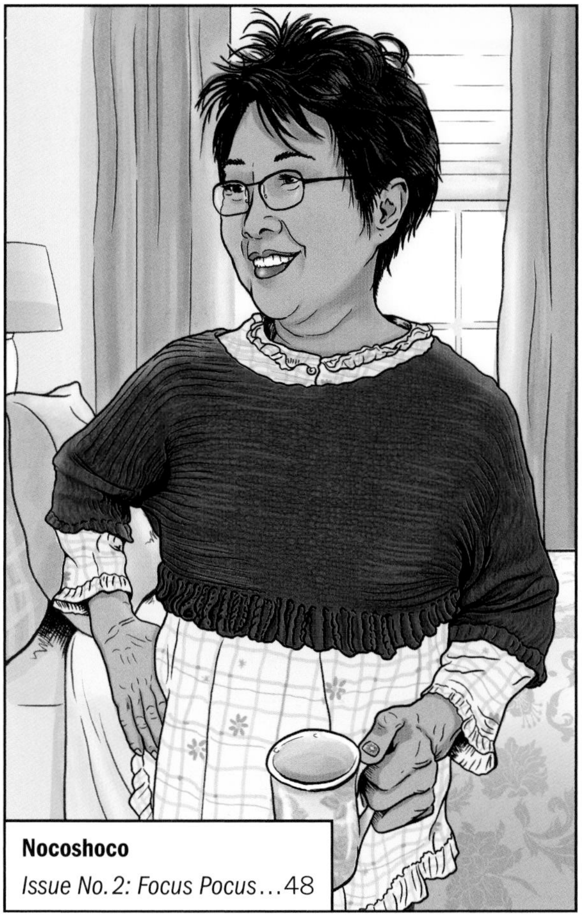

Nocoshoco
Issue No. 2: Focus Pocus...48

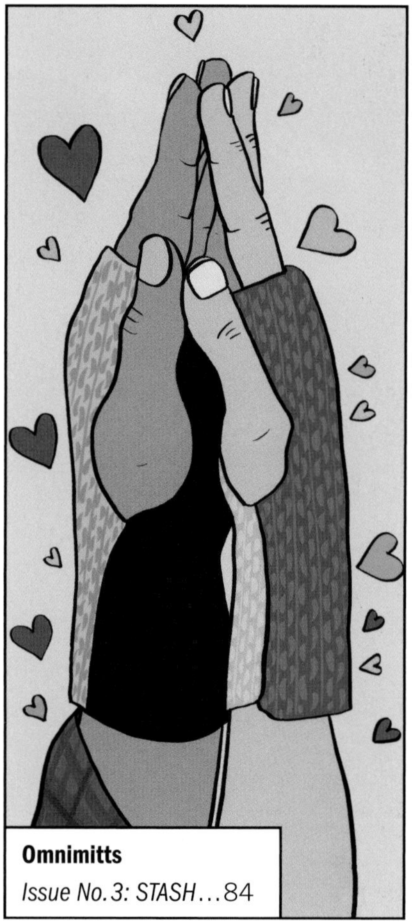

Omnimitts
Issue No. 3: STASH...84

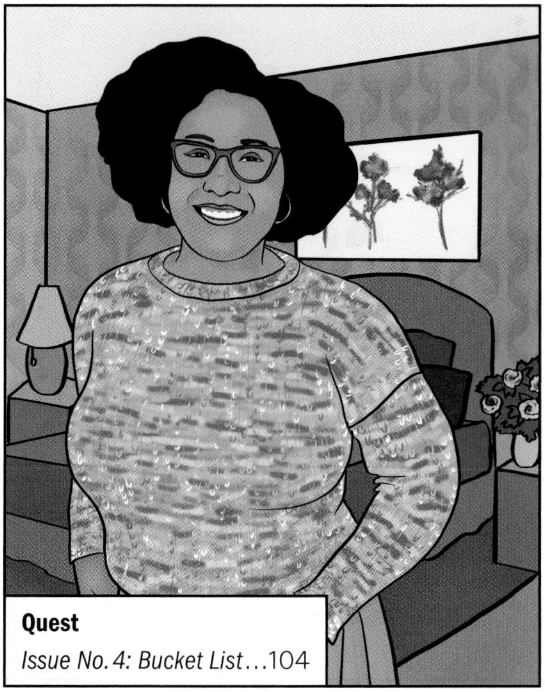

Quest
Issue No. 4: Bucket List...104

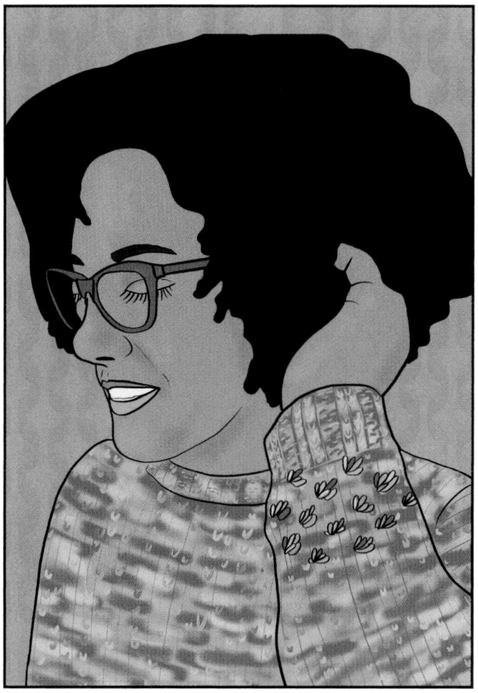

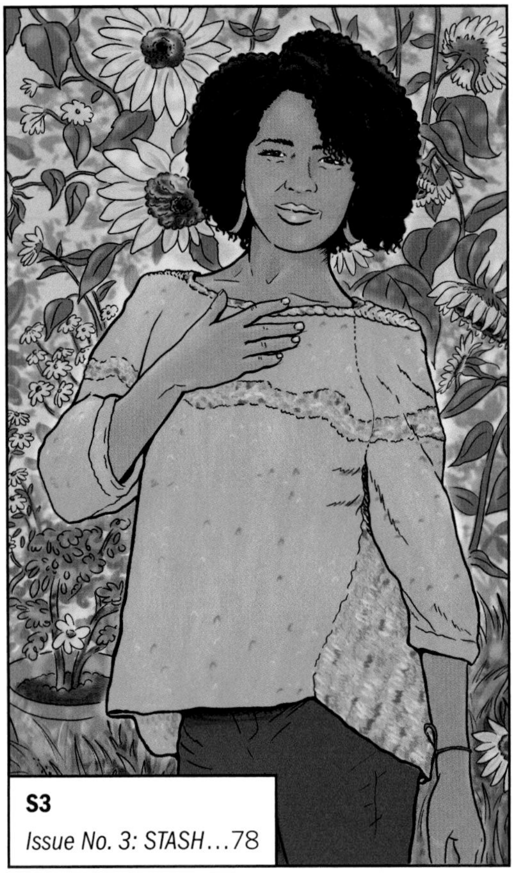

S3
Issue No. 3: STASH…78

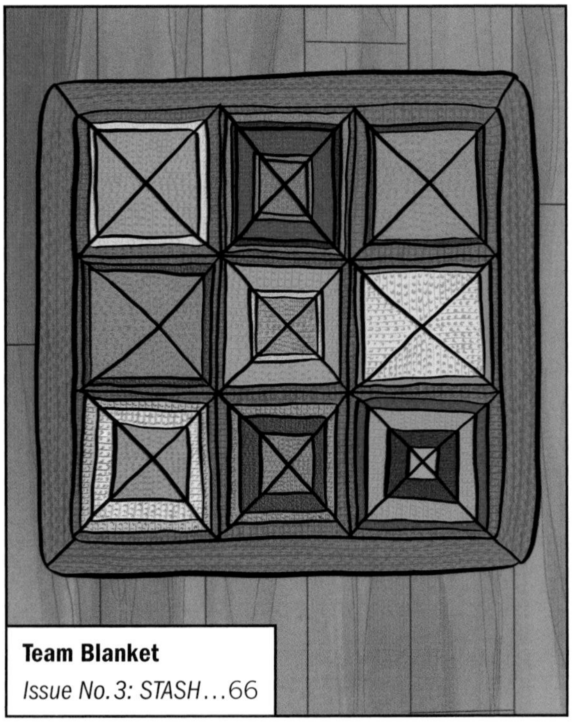

Team Blanket
Issue No. 3: STASH…66

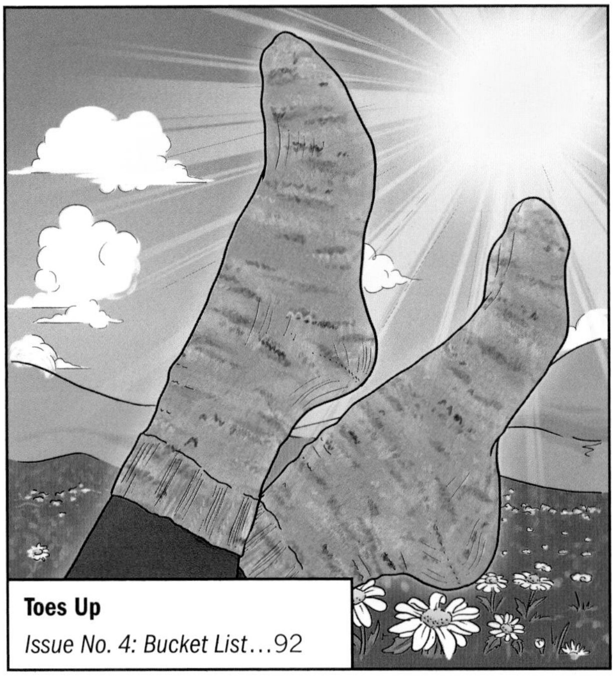

Toes Up
Issue No. 4: Bucket List…92

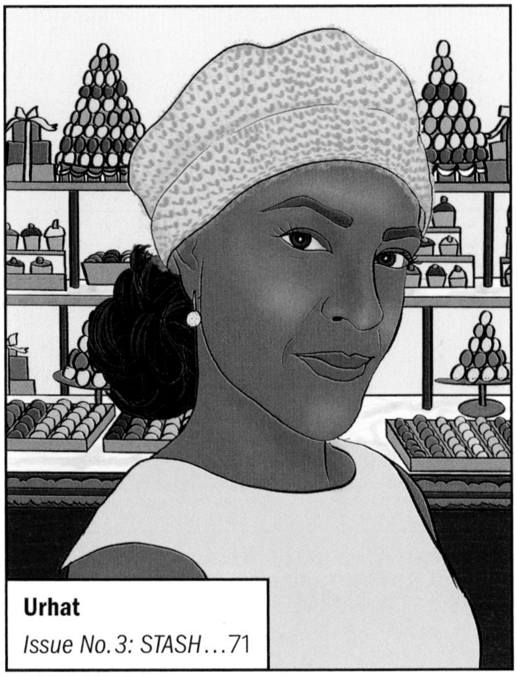

Urhat
Issue No. 3: STASH…71

Welcome to Cables
Bonus Pattern!...116

WOWL!
Issue No. 2: Focus Pocus...44

Yarn Bombing
Issue No. 4: Bucket List...100

ACKNOWLEDGMENTS

THIS PASSION PROJECT WAS MADE POSSIBLE THROUGH THE KINDNESS, GENEROSITY, AND SUPPORT OF MANY PEOPLE.

WE WOULD LIKE TO THANK: SHAWNA, OUR EDITOR, FOR ENVISIONING KNITSTRIPS AS A BOOK.

THE ABRAMS TEAM, SHAWN, HELENA, LISA, AND DEB, FOR THEIR EXPERTISE AND ATTENTION TO DETAIL.

JOY, OUR AGENT, FOR TAKING ON TWO NEWBIES AND SUPPORTING US IN A PROJECT THAT HAS MORE MOVING PARTS THAN THE PANAMA CANAL.

ANN AND KAY AT MODERN DAILY KNITTING, FOR GIVING KNITSTRIPS SPACE TO BE BORN.

OUR AMAZING ILLUSTRATORS, LAURA AND MICHELE, WHO MADE KNITSTRIPS ACTUALLY HAPPEN ON THE PAGE.

OUR TALENTED COLLABORATING DESIGNERS: ANA, CASEY, CECELIA, HIKARU, JEANETTE, JULIA, JULIE, LAUREN, NATALIE, NORAH, REBECCA, AND SHERY, FOR SHARING THEIR POINTS OF VIEW WITH US AND THE WORLD.

OUR WONDERFUL MODELS, FOR THEIR TIME AND FOR MAKING THE KNITTED PIECES EVEN MORE BEAUTIFUL:

CASEY, MARSHA, RENEE, REDMOND, BABY EMI, OSAHON, JANET, JOSÉ, JUSTIN, IMOGENE, LIONEL, TUESDAY, SO HEE, LAUREN, VINCE, WINIFRED, DESMOND, ANITA, LINH, MICHELLE, REBECCA, ANN, ARJUN, ASHA, AND JADA.

OUR AMAZING TECHNICAL EDITORS AND TEST KNITTERS, BARB, DEBBIE, NELL, AND SUSAN, FOR HELPING US BE BETTER.

OUR ON-CALL PHOTOGRAPHERS, CHLOE, DESMOND, LIONEL, REDMOND, VINCE, AND WINIFRED.

OUR BRILLIANT SUBJECT-MATTER EXPERTS, LIZ, MINAH, AND REDMOND, FOR KEEPING US OUT OF TROUBLE.

THE FABULOUS LOAN FOR ALWAYS INSPIRING AND ENABLING US.

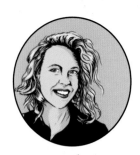

I AM PARTICULARLY GRATEFUL TO MY DAD FOR THE OUTINGS THAT ALWAYS ENDED WITH A FISTFUL OF NEW COMIC BOOKS,

AND MY MOM FOR PUTTING KNITTING NEEDLES IN MY HAND.

TO MY BIG SISTER, SUSAN, WHO ACTUALLY WORE THAT FIRST HAT I KNIT AND WAS INDISPENSABLE IN EDITING THE CONTENT OF THIS BOOK.

TO VINCENT, MY SPOUSE, WITHOUT WHOM I WOULD NOT BE WHOLE.

MY TWO DAUGHTERS, WINIFRED AND IMOGENE, WHOM I LOVE WITH ALL MY HEART.

KAREN, FOR MAKING THIS BOOK POSSIBLE, FOR SHOWING ME TRUE GRACE, AND FOR HER ENDURING FRIENDSHIP.

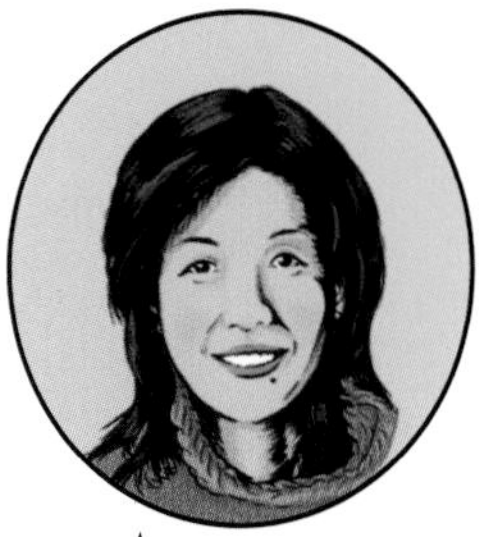

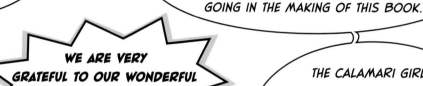

WE ARE VERY GRATEFUL TO OUR WONDERFUL YARN SPONSORS!

A Verb for Keeping Warm averbforkeepingwarm.com
Blue Sky Fibers blueskyfibers.com
Haute Bohéme Fibers hautebohemefibers.com
Hedgehog Fibres shop.hedgehogfibres.com
Ito Yarn ito-yarn.com
Jill Draper Makes Stuff jilldraper.com
La Bien Aimée labienaimee.com
Lion Brand Yarn Co. lionbrand.com
LolaBean Yarn Co. lolabeanyarnco.com
Noti Yarn notiyarn.com
Quince & Co. quinceandco.com
Rico Design rico-design.de
Shibui Knits shibuiknits.com
Third Vault Yarns thirdvaultyarns.com
Toil & Trouble Hand Dyed Yarns toil-and-trouble.com
WitchCraftyLady etsy.com/shop/WitchCraftyLady

I'M ALSO THANKFUL FOR REDMOND, DESMOND, AND LIONEL FOR COOKING ALL MY FAVORITE MEALS AND GIVING LOTS OF FAMILY-HUGS TO KEEP ME GOING IN THE MAKING OF THIS BOOK.

THE CALAMARI GIRLS: JUNG, RHONDA, SO HEE, AND SUSAN FOR GRACIOUSLY ACCEPTING MY NOT-SO-PERFECT HAND-KNITS AND LAUGHING AT MY JOKES.

THE EAT-N-STITCH HERMANAS: ANITA, HEATHER, LINH, MICHELLE, PATI, AND SEAN FOR BEING ON THE TRAIN.

MY EVER-HONEST SISTER, TINA, WHO THINKS THIS BOOK IS COOL.

MY PARENTS FOR THE AFTER-SCHOOL TRIPS TO THE WEST COVINA LIBRARY.

ALICE, FOR INVITING ME ON THIS PROJECT, FOR SHARING HER BRILLIANCE AND SPIRIT, AND FOR HER ENDURING FRIENDSHIP.

ABOUT THE GUEST DESIGNERS

ANA CAMPOS

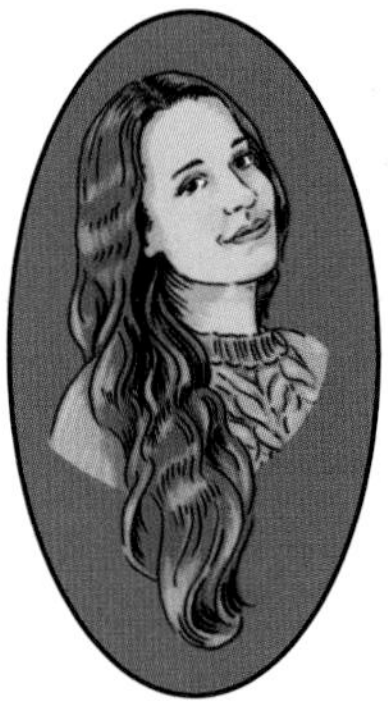

Ana Campos is a Brazilian knitting instructor, fiber witch, and designer with more than twenty years of knitting experience. She currently makes her home by the sea in Salem, Massachusetts, known as the Witch City. As a Latina and an immigrant, she values the opportunities for connection, community, and common ground that knitting creates. Ana's love for the knitting community led her to open Circle of Stitches, the witchiest yarn shop, in 2015. Her focus is on empowering knitters to grow their skills and technical knowledge, so everyone can make pieces they love. She is passionate about teaching students how to customize patterns for the perfect fit. She also loves teaching Portuguese knitting, which reminds her of her grandma Tina back home in Rio, and hosting her monthly tarot study group.

Ana is an inaugural member of the Vogue Knitting Diversity Advisory Council and a cocreator of Latines y Lana, an ongoing project to elevate and share the work of Latine fiber artists. Ana loves helping folks find inspiration and expand their skills, and her favorite projects are sweaters and socks.

When she is not at her shop, you can find her elbows-deep in her dye pots. Growing up in the tropics gave her a lifelong passion for bright colors and bold combinations, which she brings to her line of hand-dyed yarns, Toil & Trouble. She loves dyeing colorful sock yarns and hopes this book will help you fall in love with socks, too! Find Ana online at www.circleofstitches.com and on Instagram @circleofstitches, and visit her store in person at 66 Wharf Street in Salem, Massachusetts.

CASEY RICH

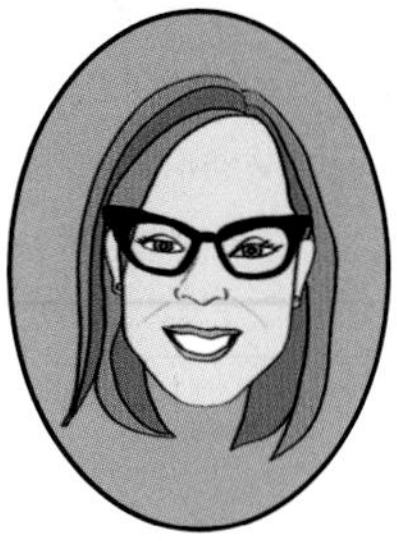

Casey Rich began knitting, sewing, and dreaming in fiber at a young age, realizing early on that clothing can be sculpture that the wearer brings to life. She followed this love of three-dimensional design to college, earning a bachelor's degree in fashion design and production, where she was encouraged by incredibly creative mentors who immersed her in fashion history, illustration, draping, and pattern drafting for sewn garments.

After some brief exposure to the commercial fashion industry, Casey knew that she'd be happier creating by her own rules. These days, she is most inspired by the freedom to improvise and loves to work with thrifted and repurposed fibers, taking direction from her materials to discover what they can become. She is thrilled to have this opportunity to encourage other makers to follow their own winding creative paths, flex their own design muscles, and create one-of-a-kind pieces.

Casey balances her creative work with a professional career in research administration, managing regulatory work for oncological clinical trials. On her nights and weekends, she creates alongside her husband and dog from their home in Gloucester, Massachusetts. She can be found on Instagram as @gingerpidge and on Ravelry as Caseyarich.

CECELIA CAMPOCHIARO

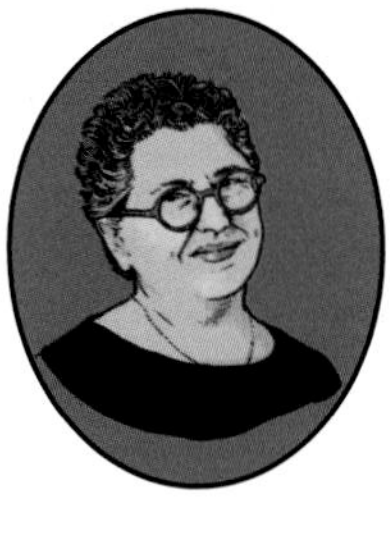

Cecelia Campochiaro appeared on the knitting scene in 2015 with her debut book, *Sequence Knitting*. Knitting was a hobby until she had an aha moment in 2010 and realized that interesting textured fabrics could be created by the simple repetition of a sequence of stitches. This idea evolved and led to her writing *Sequence Knitting*, a reference book about this mindful approach to knitting.

In the years since *Sequence Knitting* debuted, she has continued to develop new ideas in knitting. While *Sequence Knitting* is about texture, her second book, *Making Marls*, published in 2020, is about color. In *Making Marls*, she shows how the act of working multiple strands together as one can be used as an approach to colorwork in handknitting.

Cecelia lives in Silicon Valley, where for many years she developed specialized microscopes used in computer chip manufacturing. Textiles, photography, and the arts have been a lifelong passion running parallel with her technical life. In high school and college, even though her main studies were in the sciences, she studied drawing, printmaking, ceramics, and photography.

She is interested not only in the arts and knitting but also in books. Books have been the primary mechanism for knowledge transfer for more than a thousand years. One of Cecelia's missions is to honor that tradition and create books that are both informative and beautiful objects in and of themselves. Makers love beautiful things, and Cecelia feels strongly that books should be as lovely as our tools and yarns. Today she is fully dedicated to the fiber world and "unventing" new ways to make amazing knit fabrics.

You can find Cecelia through her website, www.ceceliacampochiaro.com, or at the Friends of Cecelia Campochiaro group on Ravelry.

HIKARU NOGUCHI

Hikaru Noguchi has been a leading knitted-fabric designer since the early 1990s, her work being influenced by traditional knit patterns and craft techniques. She works with small knit workshops where attention to detail and quality are still valued, seeking a look that is sophisticated and quirky, achieved through unusual juxtapositions of color and texture. In recent years she has added traditional darning and mending techniques to her work, aiming to promote sustainability in textiles and garments.

She can be found at www.hikarunoguchi.com, www.darning.net, and on Instagram @hikaru_noguchi_ design.

JEANETTE SLOAN

Jeanette Sloan is a British hand-knit designer, writer, tutor, and maker who lives in the seaside town of Hove, on the south coast of England. She inherited her crafting skills and a love of making from her Barbadian mother, Marjorie, who taught her to knit at age seven. After developing these skills into her teens, Jeanette went on to study for a degree in textile design, where she specialized in hand and machine knitting.

She has worked as a textile designer for nearly thirty years, during which time she embraced crochet, beading, and embroidery and has developed a color aesthetic that's become essential to both her process and her design identity.

As a self-confessed "accessories obsessive," Jeanette has designed hand-knit, machine-knit, and embroidered fabrics for ready-to-wear, produced patterns for the hand-knitting industry, and written for a number of publications, including *Knitting* magazine and *Laine*. She's also written or contributed to seven books on hand knitting, most recently *Warm Hands*, coedited with Kate Davies, and *Field Guide No. 15: Open* for Modern Daily Knitting.

In 2018 Jeanette became involved in online discussions about the lack of representation of BIPOC (Black, Indigenous, and People of Color) in the fiber community.

Exploring these conversations, she wrote two articles, "Black People Do Knit" and "A Colourful Debate," and later went on to create BIPOC in Fiber. Launched in the spring of 2020, www.bipocinfiber.com is a website that celebrates and highlights people of color working with fiber through its interactive directory of BIPOC fiber artists from across the globe and covering a broad range of craft disciplines.

As well as running BIPOC in Fiber, Jeanette continues to write, blog (albeit less often than she'd like), and self-publish her designs, which can be found on the Jeanette Sloan Design website (www.jeanettesloandesign.com), her Ravelry pattern store (Jeanette Sloan Design), and LoveCrafts (Jeanette Sloan). When not working, she can probably be found in the kitchen cooking up a storm or in her garden tending to her seedlings.

JULIA FARWELL-CLAY

There's a boundless curiosity in the way Julia Farwell-Clay explores knitting, pulling ideas from sources as diverse as science-fiction novels, a famous painting, and a length of handprinted fabric, all the while blending traditional and modern elements. As a writer, teacher, lecturer, designer, and catalyst in the knitting world, Julia has for the past twenty years dug herself ever deeper into the world of textile traditions and personal decoration. Julia has created more than eighty patterns and has been published in *Knitty*, *Interweave Knits*, *Pom Pom Quarterly*, *Twist Collective*, and *Vogue Knitting*, and created collections for Classic Elite Yarns and *Field Guide No. 7: Ease* for Modern Daily Knitting.

You can contact Julia at juliafarwellclay.com and on Instagram @farwellclay.

JULIE KORNBLUM

As a contemporary fiber artist, Julie Kornblum combines ancient arts with the immediacy of the plastic pollution crisis. She weaves, knits, crochets, and makes baskets from the stuff we all throw away: disposable packaging, abandoned plastic objects, and industrial surplus.

Julie loves the concept of combining some of the oldest hand-crafting processes with the surplus of some of the newest industrial by-products. Historically, these ancient arts were utterly essential throughout human society. Textiles and baskets were our containers and fasteners for tens of thousands of years. Now they are not so necessary, just like the heaps of (plastic) materials we have developed to replace things like baskets and textiles. This intersection of New-Yet-Disposable and Ancient-But-Not-Obsolete is at the core of her work.

Over the past fifteen years, Julie has exhibited widely, has been published in books and magazines, has curated art exhibitions, and has coordinated large public yarn-bombing projects. She speaks about the plastic pollution crisis that informs her artwork and teaches workshops.

Julie's love of fiber arts is rooted among her earliest memories of her mother at the sewing machine. Her grandmother knit and crocheted constantly and taught her to crochet during one of her family's summer visits from Arizona to their hometown in Pennsylvania. She learned to sew in junior high, and it was like she was born to do it. She also explored embroidery, crochet, macramé, and batik.

When Julie arrived in LA at the age of twenty, the only real skill she had was sewing. Sewing for income led to the fashion design program at Los Angeles Trade-Technical College and becoming a pattern maker in the garment industry. Marriage and children followed a few years later while teaching fashion design at Otis College of Art and Design and attending night classes to complete her AA degree. Julie taught at Otis for seven years and transferred to California State University at Northridge to complete her bachelor's degree in art. She can be found at www.JulieKornblum.com, on Instagram @JulieKornblumStudio, and on Facebook as JulieKornblumStudio. You can email her at julie@juliekornblum.com.

LAUREN McELROY

Lauren McElroy, owner and operator of Mother of Purl, is a multidisciplinary fiber artist who uses a variety of fiber-based mediums and methods in her work. Lauren designs knitting patterns, hand-dyes and hand blends fiber, creates handspun yarn, and teaches classes on knitting and spinning under the name "Mother of Purl." Her art is ever expanding. Lauren is a self-taught designer, spinner, and dyer. In addition to her love for the fiber arts, she also enjoys gardening and singing, often at the same time. Lauren incorporates sustainable practices into her art such as sourcing local fiber and natural dye materials in her designs. Her style is inspired by traditional crafts and contemporary styles. Lauren's aim is to use her art to effect positive social and environmental change.

Lauren can be found online at motherofpurl.net, on Instagram @motherofpurll1, and on TikTok @motherofpurll.

NATALIE WARNER

Natalie Warner comes from a family involved with tailoring and needlecrafts, started sewing and knitting as a child, and has been making clothes since her early teens. She now lives and works in London as a fashion and textiles lecturer and designs knitwear on a freelance basis. Her work has been published by *Knitting* magazine, the Fibre Co., and Arnall-Culliford Knitwear, and she has also taught classes at Vogue Knitting LIVE.

As a designer, Natalie is often drawn to early to mid-twentieth-century fashion details and aims to create a strong, feminine, and classic look that works with contemporary wardrobes and is flattering to wear and easy to style. The slow process of knitting and the relative lack of time modern people have available for knitting prompts her to design clothing and accessories that strike a balance for those who enjoy the process of making, like a bit of technique to keep themselves stimulated, but do not necessarily want to labor over a project for too long. Rhythmic patterning and resting rows that allow for breaks in concentration are typical of Natalie's designs, and part of what drew her to *Knitstrips* was the opportunity to create a different kind of dialogue between designer and knitter. That and seeing the illustrations come to life!

You can find Natalie on Instagram @natalieinstitches, and at https://natalieinstitches.com/.

NORAH GAUGHAN

Norah Gaughan was raised by artists in the Hudson Valley. Her father, Jack Gaughan, was a well-known science fiction illustrator in his day, while her mother, Phoebe Gaughan, illustrated how-to books and magazines in the home and crafts fields. While immersed in both art and the needle arts from an early age, she also maintained an intense curiosity about science and the natural world, going on to earn a degree in biology and art from Brown University. During the years that followed she concentrated on her greatest love, knitting, first as a freelancer for yarn companies and knitting magazines, then as the design director at JCA, followed by a nine-year stint as the design director at Berroco, where she headed up the design team and published sixteen eponymous booklets. Norah's upbringing, schooling, and experience coalesce in her three hardcover volumes *Knitting Nature*, *Norah Gaughan's Knitted Cable Sourcebook*, and *Norah Gaughan's Twisted Stitch Sourcebook*. As an independent designer working out of her studio in historic Harrisville, New Hampshire, her smaller ventures include designing as a team member with Brooklyn Tweed, designing collections for Quince & Co., the Fibre Co., and Wool Studio, as well as collaborations with the magazines *Making* and *Pom Pom Quarterly*. Now the editor in chief of *Vogue Knitting*, Norah continues to design and teach whenever and wherever she can. Follow Norah on Instagram @Norahgn and on her website, www.norahgaughan.com.

REBECCA MCKENZIE

Rebecca McKenzie is the creator and knitwear designer behind the Raging Purlwind brand. Raging Purlwind grew out of Rebecca's desire to empower people to be able to confidently make their own custom-fit wardrobe. She believes that creating your own custom clothes promotes self-love and self-care. Rebecca draws her inspiration from history, art, and stories to create whimsical, vintage-inspired designs that embrace color, texture, and lace. She loves designing knitwear pieces that can easily become staples in an everyday wardrobe.

Each Raging Purlwind design is created with a story in mind and with a focus on the knitting experience. Every stitch is carefully chosen to convey different elements of that story, and this translates into a crafting experience that is both relaxing and fun for those who choose to knit them.

Rebecca learned to knit at an early age from her grandmother, has taught numerous knitting classes, and enjoys sharing all she has learned as a knitter with others. She has collaborated and released designs with the Fibre Co., Darn Good Yarn, Yarn Crush, Lady Dye Yarns, Birch Hollow Fibers, and ThreadHead Knits Co. She has also taught virtual lace knitting classes with PeaceTree Fiber Adventures.

For more about Rebecca and her designs and patterns, visit Raging Purlwind on Ravelry, Etsy, and Lovecrafts.com. Also, follow her on Instagram as @ragingpurlwind, or join her email list here: https://mailchi.mp/6e1f789f4adb/ragingpurlwindemaillist. You can email Rebecca at aragingpurlwind@gmail.com.

SHERY COOK

Shery Cook is a self-taught knitter and dyer. She began dyeing yarn to fill her need for specific colorways that were not in the marketplace. Pulling inspiration from nature and her Asian heritage, she focuses on colors she likes to wear and that she feels are flattering for people of color. She loves bright and unexpected color pairings and has developed a line of variegated skeins with matching semisolids. Shery lives and dyes yarn in Copperas Cove, Texas. Find her at www.notiyarn.com, on Facebook as Notiyarn, and on Instagram @Notiyarns.

ABOUT THE ILLUSTRATORS

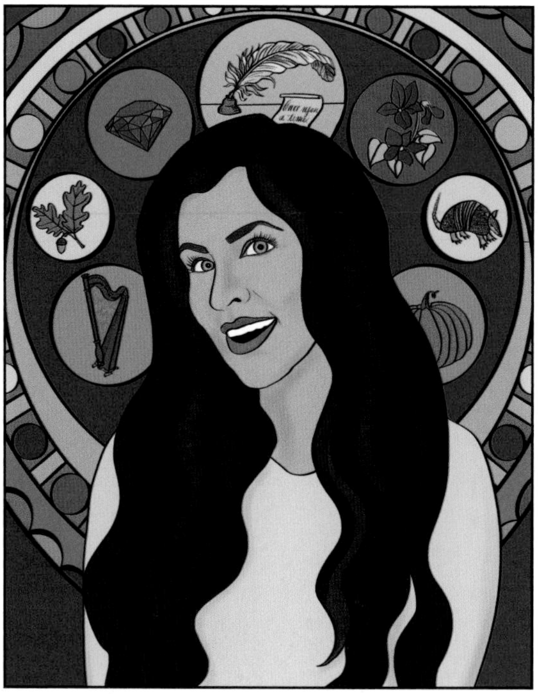

LAURA IRRGANG

Laura Irrgang has been making art for as long as she can remember. She splits her time between fine art, illustration, writing, music, and cartooning.

After receiving a degree in fine arts from Tarleton State University, she taught high school art and theater. Laura served as assistant director of F8 Fine Art Gallery in Austin, Texas. She was an instructor for the University of Texas Informal Course program, teaching painting and art history, and was the summer art program director for a children's museum. Laura continues to show art at galleries and gives public talks about her work.

Laura was the 2020 recipient of the Hunt County Public Art award for her "You Be You" mural in downtown Greenville, Texas. "I'm trying to spark an interest in nature and the conservation of our parks and wildlife. To be good stewards of our land and wild creatures, you first have to relate to those things on a personal level. Maybe this mural will be a starting point for some people. Conserving our wild spaces is extremely important to me," says Laura. "The theme of my mural is individuality. I want to encourage everyone, but particularly young people, to follow their own creative spirit. If you have a calling to do something, a pull to a profession or hobby, I say go for it! Most people want to conform and be like everyone else, but I think that can be detrimental to your life if you deny your inner calling. That interesting, unique talent you have inside you is your gift to the world."

Laura created the comic strip *Glitterville*, featuring Eunice the pathologically positive unicorn and Nadine the nasty narwhal. She also created the COVID-19-related comic strip *Gregg*. She is a member of the National Cartoonists Society's Texas Chapter, the Texas Cartoonists.

She sings and plays multiple instruments, but harp is her favorite. She enjoys writing and performing songs, particularly lullabies. Laura is a Girl Scout leader and loves working with kids. She teaches art courses online and volunteers with fine-arts-related events in her community.

Laura loves fairy tales, flea markets, cryptids, and the woods. Her weird-things-in-jars collection is always growing, and she also collects Mexican folk art. She adores Halloween and has an entire Halloween-themed room in her studio.

Laura lives in Lone Oak, Texas, with her husband, Adam, and daughters, Violet and Piper.

MICHELE PHILLIPS

Atlanta, Georgia–based award-winning illustrator and artist Michele Phillips has been telling stories with art since she was barely big enough to grasp a crayon. As a five-year-old entre-preneur, she even sold small drawings to her mom's friends and neighbors (she was saving up to buy a Corvette—and a horse).

Since then, she's honed her skills in many mediums: pencil, ink, watercolor, acrylic, digital and mixed media, encaustic wax, and skin. Childhood drawing sales aside, Michele's professional career began after graduating from Florida State University's fine arts program and moving to Phoenix, Arizona, for a tattoo arts apprenticeship under Jim Watson. It was her time as a tattoo artist that solidified her passion for great linework and hand lettering—a hallmark of her signature style.

Later work in design and illustration for commercial industries and publishing added more tools to her toolbox. Armed with those, Michele has created hundreds of illustrations and art pieces that have appeared in retail products, magazines, music and stage promotions, galleries, murals, people's homes (and bodies), and books for all ages—including illustration for a 2015 Nautilus Award Winner: Silver for Children's Illustrated Fiction. She is daunted by no surface and loves the challenge of bringing concepts and characters to life with art.

Much of Michele's work draws upon the natural world of flora and fauna—particularly her love of animals—and the mystical, magical, and fantasy realms (whenever she can, she'll absolutely add a unicorn). She is frequently sought out for her relentless obsession with detail and her razor-sharp clarity of visual communication.

Michele never did get that Corvette…but she did indeed get the horse.

You can see more of Michele's work at michelecreates.com, and follow her on Instagram (@MicheleCre8tes), where she shares more about her process and the occasional glimpse into her studio, family, and menagerie.

ABOUT THE AUTHORS

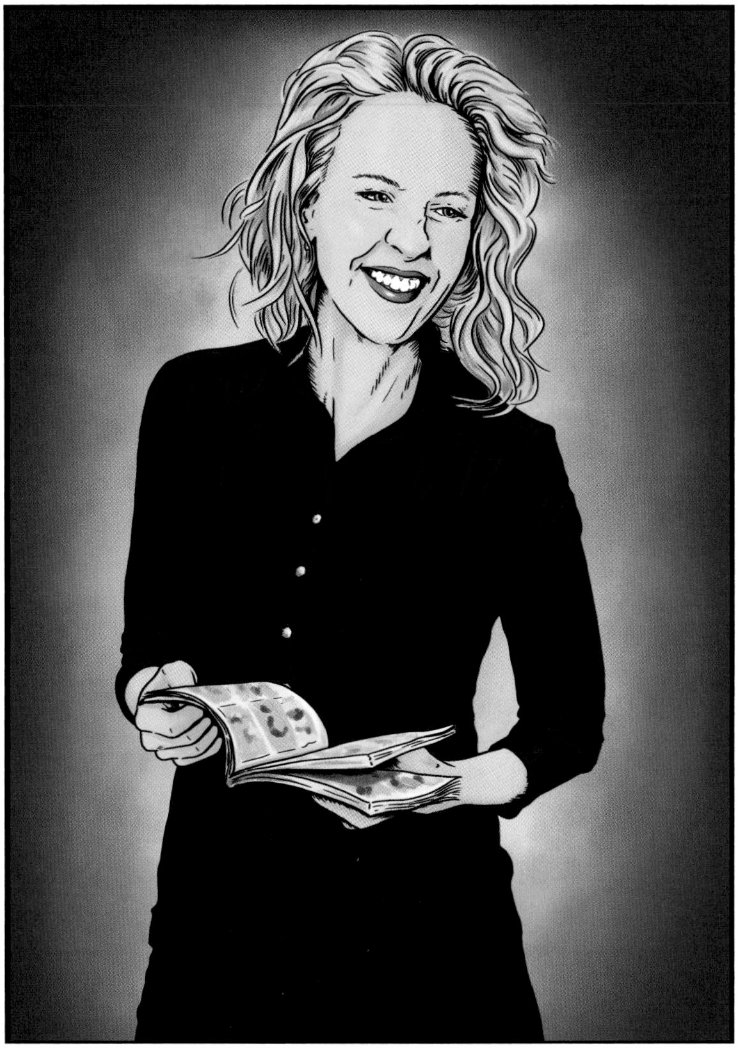

ALICE ORMSBEE BELTRAN

When she was a kid, Alice put down her comic books long enough to pick up knitting and a strong preference for open-ended patterns. She came upon Len Deighton's ***Action Cookstrip Cookbook***, which sparked the seed for Knitstrips. Interactive Knitting, and eventually this book, emerged in the course of her ongoing conversation with Karen. Alice lives in sunny Long Beach, California, with her spouse, two daughters, two lovebirds, yarn, and comic book collection. She can be reached at knitstrips@gmail.com.

KAREN KIM MAR

Karen taught herself how to knit from library books as a child and has been perpetually knitting ever since. Her unique point of view, easy disregard for norms and rules, and self-guided exploratory approach to knitting found resonance in her ongoing conversation with Alice. Before she knew it, they were writing a knitting book. Karen lives in the foothills of Southern California with her husband, two young sons, two poodles, parakeet, and school of fish. There is yarn in every room. She can be reached at knitstrips@gmail.com.

Oh by the Way

Did you ever notice that one tail gets used up faster in the long-tail cast-on, and wonder which one it is? Let's find out! We started with two equal lengths of yarn.

Left
Right
The right side swoop is the one that goes around your needle, and uses more yarn.
NOW YOU KNOW!

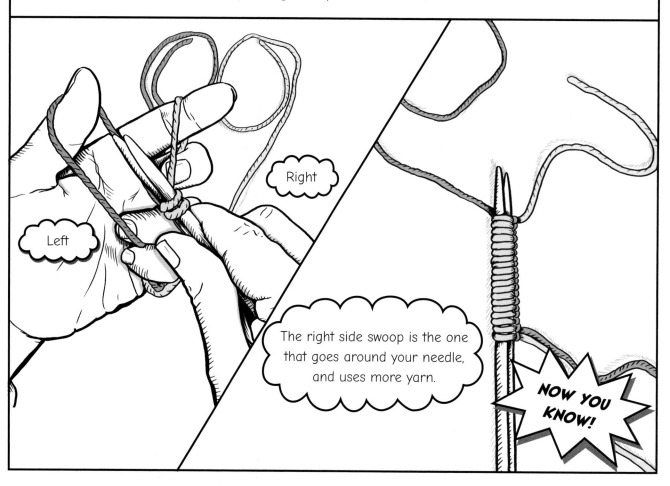

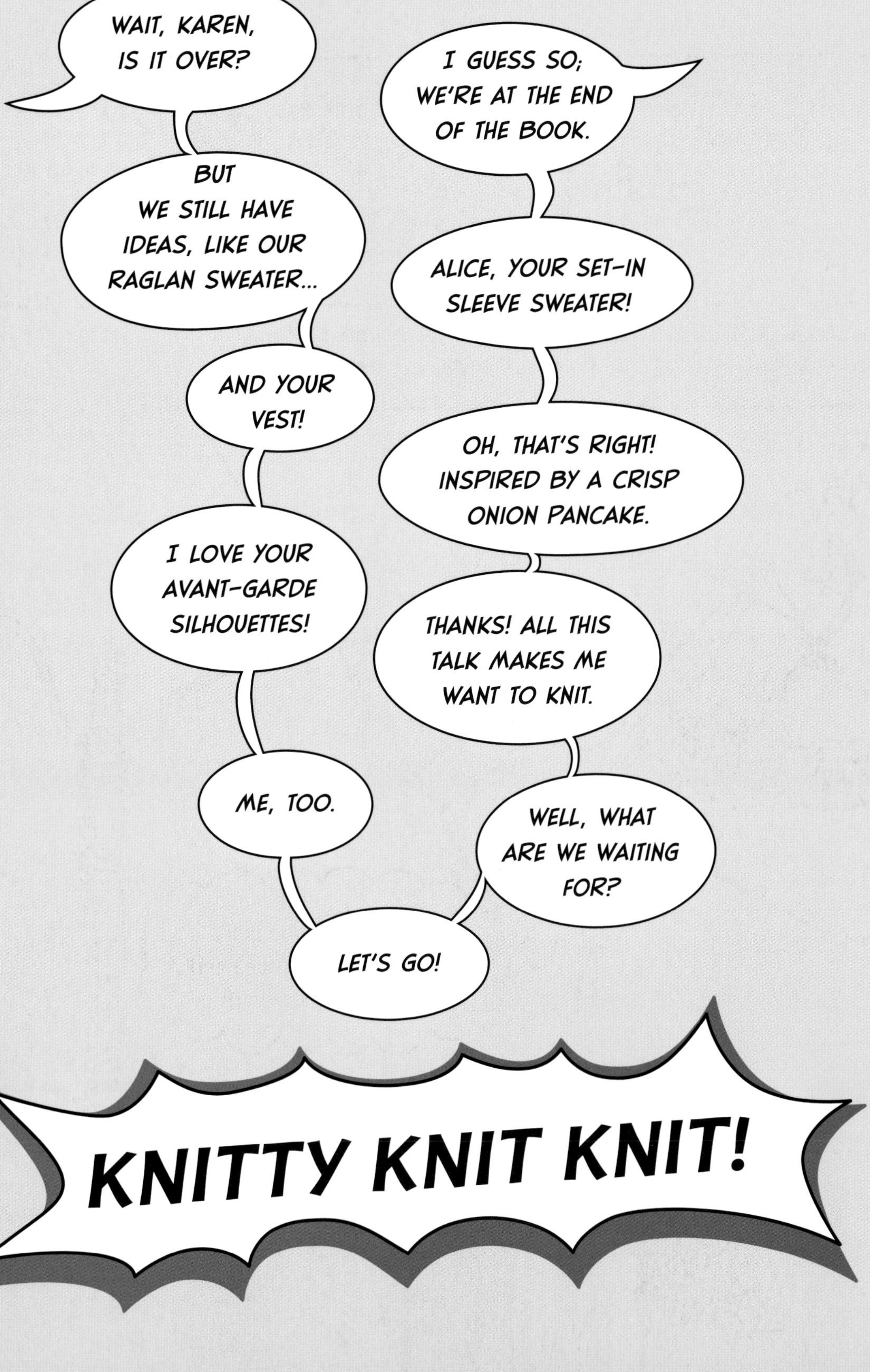
WAIT, KAREN, IS IT OVER?
I GUESS SO; WE'RE AT THE END OF THE BOOK.
BUT WE STILL HAVE IDEAS, LIKE OUR RAGLAN SWEATER...
ALICE, YOUR SET-IN SLEEVE SWEATER!
AND YOUR VEST!
OH, THAT'S RIGHT! INSPIRED BY A CRISP ONION PANCAKE.
I LOVE YOUR AVANT-GARDE SILHOUETTES!
THANKS! ALL THIS TALK MAKES ME WANT TO KNIT.
ME, TOO.
WELL, WHAT ARE WE WAITING FOR?
LET'S GO!
KNITTY KNIT KNIT!

IK

COMICS